The Legacy of
Apartheid

The Legacy of
Apartheid

Edited by **Joseph Harker**

Contributions by **Nelson Mandela, Desmond Tutu, Peter Preston**
Anton Harber, Donald Woods, Roger Omond, Stanley Uys, Paula McBride
David Beresford, Patrick Laurence, Nokwanda Sithole, Victoria Brittain
and forty six years of reporting from *The***Guardian**

Police with dogs raid Crossroads squatter camp,
Cape Town, 1978
Apartheid consigned millions to a life of squalor,
as those who could not survive in the homelands
were forced to squat near prosperous white
towns, hoping to obtain work. Their misery was
compounded by police raids as the government
tried to bulldoze these camps out of existence
MAYIBUYE CENTRE

The first edition of the Guardian, May 5 1821, contained two letters from British immigrants living at Algoa Bay, South Africa. The writers described the settlement as a "savage wilderness, surrounded by wild beasts" and as the "most barren and desolate [place] you can imagine"

The Manchester Guardian.

Manchester: Printed and Published by J. GARNETT, No. 29, Market-street.

First published in Great Britain in 1994
by Guardian Newspapers Limited
119 Farringdon Road
London
EC1R 3ER

British Library Cataloguing in Publication Data
A catalogue record for this book is available from the British Library

The right of Joseph Harker to be identified as the compiler of this work has been
asserted by him in accordance with the Copyright, Design and Patents Act 1988.

ISBN 0 - 85265 - 042 - 6

Produced by PD2, The Guardian
Designed by Neville Brody Studios
Art direction: Simon Staines
Cuttings and picture research: Roger Diski
Layout: John-Henry Barac, Joanna Kordina, Lance Bellers
Graphics: Finbarr Sheehy
Sub-editors: Michael Ticher, Fiachra Gibbons, Pat Devereaux,
Jim Davies, David Girling, Ron Buchanan, Margareta Simons, Dave Davis,
Veronica Horwell, Frances Peel Yates
Special thanks to: David Beresford, Roger Omond, Bessie Tugwana, Gary Phillips

Printed in Great Britain by
BPC Hazells Ltd, a member of the British Printing Company Ltd
Origination by Metropolis Ltd
Distributed by Central Books

Contents

Foreword / Nelson Mandela ——————————————— **15**

Foreword / Peter Preston ——————————————— **17**

Introduction / Joseph Harker ——————————————— **18**

Section 1

South Africa before apartheid / Roger Omond ————————— **24**

The economics of apartheid / Howard Preece——————————— **28**

Afrikaner thoughts / Piet Cillié ——————————————— **32**

The word on the street ——————————————————— **36**

The legacy of apartheid / David Welsh / Victoria Brittain ——————— **40**

Section 2

The pillars of apartheid / Michael Stent ——————————————— **53**

The homelands / Patrick Laurence ——————————————— **67**

Living under apartheid / Nokwanda Sithole ————————————— **77**

The freedom movement / Tom Lodge / Kaizer Nyatsumba ——————— **95**

The pulpit and politics / Charles Villa-Vicencio ————————— **117**

State repression / Paula McBride / Beathur Baker ——————————— **127**

Censorship / Anton Harber——————————————————— **147**

Sanctions / Joseph Hanlon ——————————————————— **161**

Township violence and the 'Third Force' / David Beresford — **175**

The end of apartheid / Stanley Uys ——————————————— **189**

Section 3

Endpiece / Desmond Tutu ——————————————————— **208**

Chronology / Roger Diski ——————————————————— **211**

Contributors

Beathur Baker
is a feature writer on the Johannesburg Star, where she has a human-interest column. She has worked for the Weekly Mail and contributes to several leading black magazines.

David Beresford
is former Guardian Northern Ireland correspondent and author of a best-selling book on the 1981 Irish hunger strike. He has twice been voted international journalist of the year at British press awards for his reports from South Africa.

Victoria Brittain
is the Guardian's Africa specialist and assistant foreign editor. She is the author of Hidden Lives, Hidden Deaths: South Africa's Crippling Of A Continent (Faber,1988).

P J Cillié
was editor of Die Burger, the leading Afrikaans daily newspaper, from 1954 to 1977, when he became chairman of the publishing house Nasionale Pers. He has written several collections of essays and speeches.

Roger Diski
researched the newspaper extracts and photographs for this book. He is co-recipient of the Martin Luther King Memorial Award for his book The Child Is Not Dead: Youth Resistance In South Africa, 1976 To 1986.

Dr Joseph Hanlon
is an academic and author who has written widely on Southern Africa. He is an acknowledged expert on Mozambique and on the impact of sanctions on South Africa.

Anton Harber
is a founder and co-editor of the Weekly Mail and Guardian of Johannesburg. He is a recipient of the Pringle Award for press freedom and an executive member of the Foundation of Freedom of Expression.

Patrick Laurence
was the Guardian's South Africa correspondent throughout the upheavals of the 1980s. He now writes for the Johannesburg Star.

Tom Lodge
is author of the definitive Black Politics In South Africa Since 1945 and lectures at the University of Witwatersrand.

Paula McBride
is a civil-rights activist with the Pretoria-based Lawyers for Human Rights group. She is best known for campaigning for the abolition of the death penalty and has written widely on the subject.

Kaizer Nyatsumba
is a political correspondent for the Johannesburg Star. He has written several essays on South African politics and is the author of a collection of poetry, When Darkness Falls, and of two collections of short stories, A Vision Of Paradise and In Love With A Stranger.

Roger Omond
works on the Guardian Foreign Desk and is the author of three books on South Africa: The Apartheid Handbook, The Sanctions Handbook (both published by Penguin) and Steve Biko And Apartheid (published by Hamish Hamilton).

Howard Preece
is deputy editor of Finance Week and was the finance editor of the Rand Daily Mail from 1974 until its closure in 1985.

Peter Preston
is editor of the Guardian.

Nokwanda Sithole
was editor of Tribute, a magazine for black professionals, from 1989 to 1992. She has contributed to international publications on South African issues and is now working for the Independent Media Commission.

Michael Stent
was editor of Drum magazine from 1980 to 81, and assistant editor of the Rand Daily Mail until its closure in 1985. He is now a freelance writer for the Guardian and Observer.

Stanley Uys
was political editor of the Johannesburg Sunday Times and South Africa correspondent for the Guardian and Observer from 1960 to 1976. He is a lecturer and broadcaster and has contributed to books on South Africa and Namibia.

Charles Villa-Vincencio
is Professor of Religion and Society at the University of Cape Town.

David Welsh
is Professor of Southern African Studies in the Political Studies department of the University of Cape Town.

Donald Woods
is a freelance journalist who was banned by the South African government in 1978 and moved to London. He is the author of six books including Biko: Asking For Trouble and South African Dispatches.

Many of the photographs in this book are from the Mayibuye Centre at the University of the Western Cape. The Centre is an archive/museum which houses over 70,000 photographs and over 1,000 film and video productions. Much of this collection was donated by the International Defence and Aid Fund for Southern Africa which closed in 1991.

'Democracy means more than just the vote. It must be measured by the quality of life of ordinary men and women, young and old, rural and urban. It means giving all South Africans the opportunity to share in the country's wealth'

Foreword: **Nelson Mandela**

AT LAST the day is arriving when all South Africans will be able to vote for a government of their choice.

In 1986, when I suggested from my prison cell to the government that the time had come for us to resolve South Africa's problems through negotiations, I was confident that my endeavour to bring peace and democracy through dialogue would finally bear fruit.

Today we are almost there. This is a tribute, above all, to the efforts and sacrifices of millions of South Africans. It is also a tribute to the support that the anti-apartheid struggle has received throughout the world. Sustained international pressure and economic sanctions played a very important role in ensuring that it became impossible to continue with apartheid.

The African National Congress's vision of a South Africa in which people live in peace and with equal opportunities is an ideal which sustained me during my 27 years in prison. I live in the hope that those years were not in vain. I am confident that over the coming years, the vast majority of South Africans will work together to build a united nation in a non-racial, non-sexist and democratic South Africa.

Democracy means more than just the vote. It must be measured by the quality of life of ordinary men and women, young and old, rural and urban. It means giving all South Africans the opportunity to share in the country's wealth, to contribute to its development and improve their own lives.

The children and grandchildren of South Africa should never again know the violence and suffering, the shame and pain, many of their parents endured. They should enjoy their childhood secure in family life, and grow up with equal opportunities to live life to the full.

To ensure this, South Africa needs a growing economy based on a new trade and industry policy, which will focus on the creation of job opportunities and the strengthening of our manufacturing and export capacity. Our economic programmes will take into account the need for sustainable development which does not destroy our natural resources.

To achieve these plans, we need large scale international investment. As the first truly democratic and legitimate administration, an ANC-led government of national unity and reconstruction will be able to create an environment of peace and stability, where investments will be secure.

I call on the international community to join us in building reconciliation, peace and a better life for all South Africans.

THE GUARDIAN

MANCHESTER, WEDNESDAY,

May 26, 1948

SOUTH AFRICA

South Africa — that is to say, the British and Dutch citizens who make up between them a minority of the population of the Union and a vast majority of its electors — votes to-day for a new Parliament.

A Nationalist victory to-day would be a disaster. Dr. Malan has chosen, for what seemed no doubt strong electoral reasons, to fight on the worst possible field — racialism — and to put forward the worst possible policy — "apartheid," or wholesale segregation of black from white. He and his friends wish to sweep away what little political advance the Bantu majority has made in the Union — the Native Representative Council, the three members elected to represent them in the House of Assembly; to stop any further movement of the Bantu into the towns; and to forbid them any scope for advancement anywhere but in the Reserves. This is not so much a policy as a neurotic fantasy: it could not be realised even if the Nationalists came into power. The Bantu cannot be confined to the Reserves, because these are neither big enough nor fertile enough to maintain them. They cannot be excluded from the towns, because they are needed there; South Africa's industry cannot grow without them. To put this wild stuff forward as "a solution once for all" of the problems of race relations in South Africa is merely irresponsible. The one inescapable fact which dominates the future of the African continent is the slow — often painfully slow — but ultimately irresistible movement of the African peoples towards the standards of European civilisation. This movement will not go by the same path, nor at the same speed, in all the African territories. It will create different problems in each and call for different solutions. The one outcome which is not conceivable is what Dr. Malan demands — to reverse the trend "once for all."

'The motorway to Pretoria has been lined by gleaming new factories and plants. But it lies only a brief drive from the fearsome shanty huddle of Alexandra township, where the Third World bangs ominously on the windscreens of passing cars'

Foreword: **Peter Preston**

WHEN YOU stand on the steps of the president's office, on the hill overlooking Pretoria, the sense of imperial permanency is overwhelming. Great lumps of stone tower over a city devoted to the business of ruling. Nothing, says the bulk of Pretoria, can ever change.

And yet it has and it will. This is change to turn the world head over heels; greater even in emotional dimension than the fall of the Berlin Wall — the troubled, bloodied but willed handing of power to the dispossessed.

This book is, thus, a celebration, an analysis and a raw history of profound upheaval. But to see the story of modern South Africa purely in terms of victors and vanquished, of the defeat of evil by good, is to spin a tale which has an ending. That is not the reality of South Africa, nor of this book.

The Republic has the most tumultuous of histories, as befits the most tumultuous and varied of lands. Nothing in such a truncation of events argues that the history is over. The motorway to Pretoria has been lined, these last few years, by a gleaming array of new factories and plants — as though London's Docklands were suddenly unravelled and stretched 20 miles along a strand of concrete. Here is the South Africa that the new leaders feel could be the economic motor of all southern Africa.

But it lies only a brief drive from the fearsome shanty huddle of Alexandra township, where the Third World bangs ominously on the windscreens of passing cars.

The legacy of apartheid — the well of bitterness — seems too deep and current to be obliterated by the mere embracing of partnership. The contrasts remain too stark. The thought that this adventure in humanity can be turned into success is often absurd. Yet that is the common resolve and the task.

The Guardian, through the years of oppression, did not let South Africa rest. It reported the facts, the details and the horrors. It saw that this was a universal story. They say foreign news does not sell papers. The issue the morning after Nelson Mandela's release sold more copies than any other front page of the year.

And now things move on. Now the outsiders prepare to move to the inside. Now we pause to reflect and to look forward. Can it, against all the odds, be made to work? Can reconciliation turn to something lasting and fruitful? Unless we remember, we shall never feel the crushing difficulty. But unless we look forward, to the fresh stories and the new amazements, we shall never grasp the opportunity either.

Introduction: Joseph Harker

SLAVERY, the holocaust, apartheid. All seemed convenient models at the time of their inception: provide labour for the sugar and cotton plantations; wipe out an annoying minority which is gaining too much economic strength; and order society into groups where each knows its place in the pecking order.

Now, like its evil companions, apartheid is dead. Its cost in human terms has been immense: millions killed through war, political violence, starvation and neglect; millions more forcibly removed from their homes; even more consigned to a life of poverty and humiliation.

The story of apartheid is of an ideology in which economics triumphed over humanity, and whose implementation required one hundred per cent commitment. It was apparent that, were any cracks to appear, the whole edifice would come crumbling down.

As the black population rejected its fourth-class status, the state responded with a chilling system of repression, which grew more extreme and sophisticated as the resistance continued.

A network of informers was set up. Activists, suspected activists, friends and family of activists, or those simply in the wrong place at the wrong time, were beaten, detained, put in solitary confinement, tortured or killed. They left jail to find that employers would not give jobs to "troublemakers". Death squads were introduced to quell protests by instilling more fear; and *agents provocateurs* were used to breed an atmosphere of chaos, and scupper moves towards democracy.

This was the price Africans had to pay in order to keep the wealth of the nation within a few greedy white hands.

Despite this, the people remained unbowed in their quest for freedom. By confronting the state incessantly, they revealed the brutal lengths the minority was prepared to resort to in order to cling to power.

Eventually, the regime's closest international friends realised that time was running out for apartheid. Without the support of overseas investors, the end soon followed.

Now, four years after negotiations formally began for its dismantling, apartheid is officially over. But the system will live on in the minds of the population for many years. Feelings of superiority, resentment and exclusion will be hard to overcome — systems of privilege cannot be broken down overnight.

Apartheid's legacy will be long and enduring, but an understanding is crucial in interpreting the progress the first democratic government will make and the pitfalls it faces.

The new government will have to walk a tightrope in trying to make progress towards equality without losing the education and professional skills which have so far been reserved for the white population. Mistakes will certainly be made, and more lives will be lost in the attempt to reconcile the mixed-up factions and ideologies within South Africa's 40 million population.

This book aims to provide an understanding of the current situation, mixing current commentary with historic reporting from the Guardian's archive.

The first section gives an overview of apartheid: its roots; its effect on citizens of all races; and the rebuilding work necessary to get the country back on its feet.

The second section examines the many aspects of the apartheid system in greater detail — its horrors and why its end was inevitable.

The following record contains stories both tragic and absurd, revealing obsessive thinking which we would consider insane. It looks at the depths of deprivation and heights of achievement that have moulded the new South Africa. More than anything, it is a tribute to the courage of those who overcame what once seemed impossible odds to gain their freedom.

In 1992, the white population voted by two to one to continue the process of reform which would ultimately end apartheid. Now, as that reality dawns, we dedicate this book to all South Africans who wish to see a fair and equal society.

'Feelings of superiority, resentment and exclusion will be hard to overcome. Apartheid's legacy will be long and enduring, but an understanding is crucial in interpreting the progress the first democratic government will make and the pitfalls it faces.'

The Voortrekker Monument was opened by prime minister Malan in 1949 in front of a crowd of 100,000, said to be the largest gathering assembled in South Africa up to that time. Although this massive granite monument celebrated Afrikaner history, it actually symbolised the Boer triumph over their main foe, the British

TOPHAM

Section 1

South Africa before apartheid/Roger Omond

SOUTH AFRICA, the land of apartheid, is struggling to wipe out that unhappy legacy. A massive debt has to be repaid. It is not merely a matter of removing legislation based on race from the statute book, or of introducing a colour-blind, one-person-one-vote franchise, or of installing Nelson Mandela as its first black head of state. It involves trying to create, for the first time in nearly 350 years, a society in which skin colour is an unremarked fact of life rather than a determinant of fate.

It was inevitable that white rule would crumble. The question was when? In the 1960s after the Sharpeville massacre, there seemed, in Mandela's words, no easy walk to freedom. In the mid-1970s, the Soweto uprising brought renewed hope that, although the struggle would be hard, the human spark had not been extinguished. In the 1980s, successive states of emergency again failed to crush black aspirations.

It was not only the armed struggle which eventually forced the white government to begin negotiations. Economic sanctions, imposed by an increasingly outraged world community, played a part. The long and lonely stand by white liberals and radicals against their own unjust society also contributed. World events — the collapse of Communism in Eastern Europe, for example — were important in President de Klerk's timing when he lifted the legal ban on the ANC on February 2 1990 and, nine days later, freed Mandela.

De Klerk's actions broke with his past. It is in that history of South Africa — white and black, English and Afrikaans-speaking — that the roots of white privilege and black deprivation lie. Just where and how the roots were planted is a matter of dispute. At its most simplistic, responsibility is placed in the hands of the National Party which defeated the United Party government in May 1948. On a different time-scale, but again rather simplistically, emphasis has been laid on the symbolic fact that the first whites to establish a base at the southern tip of Africa in 1652 soon planted a hedge of bitter almonds to separate white from black.[1]

The first white settlers were Dutch, sent not by a colonising power but by a commercial enterprise, the Dutch East India Company (VOC). It wanted a victualling station for ships en route between Europe and the East Indies. Over the years, central control weakened, a number of former company servants became "free burghers" allowed to sell their produce to the VOC. Some became *trekboers*, roving farmers, competing for natural resources with the native Khoisan — earlier known as Hottentots and Bushmen — and, much later, with other Africans.

When the free burghers were first granted land in 1657, the VOC created four distinctive legal status groups — company servants, free burghers, slaves, and Khoisan. Different groups had different rights and obligations of domicile, marriage, movement, taxation, militia service, and land ownership among others. Class, race and legal status coincided: there were no white slaves and few landowners were black.

The Dutch settlers appear to have brought with them a conviction that whites were superior to other races. This, it is said, was reinforced by their Calvinist religion which saw the world divided into two classes, the saved and the damned,[2] and their conviction that the Dutch were a chosen people.[3] But this interpretation, long favoured by liberal historians, has been challenged by critics who claim it has not been shown that Calvinism was influential at all before the 1830s; that religious fervour declined in 18th century Europe so that later immigrants (who in any case included non-Dutch) would have contributed to the decline of Calvinism; that the number of clerics diminished over the years; and that church control was weak. Newer research claims that "primitive Calvinism" was a later invention, "a mythical construct brought into being in the specific conditions of late-19th century Cape parochial politics."[4]

On the other hand, theological sophistication was unlikely to develop in a culture where the Bible was often the only literature available to the *trekboer* and where literacy tended to decrease with time and distance away from Cape Town.

For many years the white population lived on a changing frontier. It has been argued that under these conditions "the frontiersman regarded the non-white only as a servant or an enemy."[5] But this, too, is disputed. It is certainly not sufficient to "explain" later racism. The frontier bred people "suspicious of and hostile to the authority of government".[6] The

Apartheid did not happen overnight. Racism found an early expression in the laws of the new colony. Prohibition of sexual liaisons across the colour line came as early as 1685

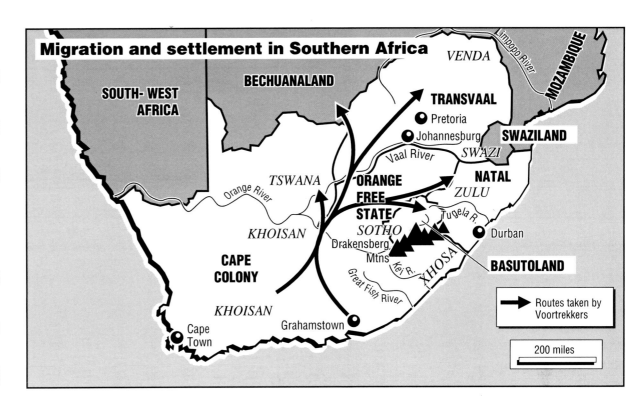

Migration and settlement in Southern Africa

Routes taken by Voortrekkers

200 miles

trekboers were "a ruggedly independent race of individuals"[7] — different from the reality, if not the self-image, of conformist Afrikaner Nationalists of the mid-20th century.

Cape society was based mainly on race, in part because the economy was simple, with few jobs that could not be filled by white labour (although a number of slaves or ex-slaves were artisans in Cape Town). The colony expanded with a tradition of social mobility which made it more difficult for free black and Khoisan people to break through their legal disabilities. All these factors encouraged whites to retain closer links with their fellow whites than with other groups they lived among.[8]

Early racism was soon to find expression in law. Regulations, precursors of the pass laws, controlling black people's movement were introduced. The first prohibition against sexual liaisons across the colour line came in 1685, forbidding marriage between white and full-blooded black people, although it was still permitted between the white and mixed-race population.[9] Other regulations aimed at discouraging miscegenation were also promulgated during the first years of VOC rule.[10]

The laws failed. Miscegenation did take place between whites (residents and visiting sailors), slaves from the East Indies and East Africa, Khoisan, and Africans. The children of such liaisons became known — and eventually legally categorised — as "coloured". At the height of apartheid, when every child born was classified by race, the government legislated to divide so-called "coloured" people into seven sub-groups.[11]

By the end of the 18th century, a number of the *trekboers* had established themselves in what is now the Eastern Cape. The eastward expansion of the colony was halted as whites encountered Africans. Into this situation came the British government, whose permanent occupation of the Cape began in 1806 as part of the Napoleonic wars.

The British were something of a threat to the "traditional" Dutch way of life. But there was no sudden arrival of a liberal, non-racial society. Khoisan, slaves and black people were still strictly controlled, although there was an assumption of equality before the law. The British also brought with them the "coherent assumption that Europeans were unique and special."[12] The white population they found there had a similar view, based on slightly different premises:

"European supremacy was not a product of frontier violence. Instead it was the result of an agricultural system characterised by abundant land, scarce capital, and scarce labour. This economy developed within a political system that enabled Europeans to monopolise land and access to capital and that made it difficult to coerce whites to work as labourers. This social system was most firmly established in the arable regions of the south-western Cape, and it was this region which developed the symbols of European identity and notions of superiority on which the colonists relied."[13]

The British government did intervene more in Cape society, which annoyed those in the Eastern Cape, long used to minimal controls. The British also imported 5,000 settlers on the eastern frontier.

The 1820 settlers brought with them a rather different world view. The combination of interventionism and more efficient administration led to Ordinance 50 of 1828, which repealed the "pass" laws and established the principle of equality between whites and "all persons of colour"[14]. Slavery was abolished in 1834, compounding labour problems. Local government was reorganised, abolishing Boer posts. English became the language of justice, the legislature, and administration. Education, too, placed more emphasis on English. Economically, it was a difficult time as the Cape became part of the world economy through the British and their empire. Missionaries from London cast what the Boers called "unjustifiable odium" on the treatment of black people. A new war with Africans on the eastern frontier broke out.

In response, many of the Boers moved on in a migration known and mythologised as the Great Trek. The disaffected Boers wanted both to escape the profoundly threatening impact of the British and to re-establish their own societies and values in the interior of the country. Coincidentally, they moved at a time when much of the interior was under-

'Urban labour was stratified by race. No community of interest developed between the black and white working class. Controls over black labour were tightened, while white workers were keen to protect their own position'

populated by Africans. The Boers had a relatively easy time in establishing their new states, first in Natal (which they left after wars with the powerful Zulus and when the British annexed the territory) and then in the Orange Free State and Transvaal.

By that stage the Trekkers — numbering about 16,000 by 1845 — had the strength to maintain themselves, but not to establish undisputed political control.[15]

Their societies were small, often divided and fragmented, with rudimentary institutions, and lacking in education, religion, or trade. They became progressively poorer and more isolated. They wrote into their constitutions the principle of "no equality in church or state" and maintained their racial exclusivity. They survived yet another attempt by the British to extend control and in 1852 and 1854 the two independent republics were given formal recognition.

It was not to last long. In 1867 diamonds were discovered at Kimberley and in 1886 gold on the Witwatersrand. The two events were to change the sub-continent profoundly. The industrial extraction of the minerals meant a huge demand for a cheap, controlled labour force.[16] This changed rural black society, much of which until then had not been greatly touched by the arrival of whites.

By the turn of the century, the compound system had been developed, whereby migrant African male mineworkers, first in Kimberley and then on the Witwatersrand, were housed in segregated camps.

They were usually underpaid, justified by the theory that subsistence farming in the black areas subsidised the family's living costs. And although racism was not invented on the diamond fields of Kimberley, their development did usher in massive urbanisation and more systematic discrimination.

Urban labour was stratified by race. No community of interest developed between the black and white working class. Controls over black labour were tightened, while white workers were keen to protect their own position. This spread from the mines to the burgeoning industrial sector. In later years, "job reservation" came to be applied even to lift attendants and traffic policemen.

The uneven development of a large urbanised African workforce came about as the twin interests of the British Empire and capitalism coincided in their desire for control of the Transvaal state and the gold mines. This led to the Anglo-Boer War of 1899-1902 and the defeat of the Boers. Its generals, however, emerged triumphant when the Union of South Africa was established from the four colonies — Cape, Transvaal, Free State and Natal — in 1910. Three of the Boer commanders (Botha, Hertzog and Smuts) were to rule as prime ministers until the "purified" National Party's unexpected 1948 election victory.

These three northern leaders managed to impose many of their racial attitudes on the entire country. Before Union, franchise policies had differed among the separate states. In the Cape a non-racial franchise

was introduced in 1853 in an effort to incorporate the Dutch and the "coloureds" and then Africans into the state. The Cape Attorney-General spelled out the reasoning: "I would rather meet the Hottentot at the hustings voting for his representative than meet the Hottentot in the wilds with his gun upon his shoulder."[17]

It was aimed, too, at creating a peasant class of Africans who would both supply raw materials for merchants and provide a consumer market for their goods. By 1910 about 15 per cent of the Cape electorate was black, with two "coloureds" for every African. This non-racial tradition provided ideological succour and inspiration for generations of black people in the years after Union as their rights were progressively stripped away.

The other English colony, Natal, practised non-racial tokenism, with only a few black people on the voters' roll. In the Free State and Transvaal the franchise was confined to whites.

When it came to Union, the Boer leaders insisted there could be no extension of the Cape franchise system throughout South Africa. An uneasy compromise was reached, whereby each of the four colonies (or provinces as they became in 1910) would continue as before. But no black representatives could sit in the new House of Assembly or Senate.

The pattern of discrimination and segregation was to be consolidated by a legislature overwhelmingly controlled by white people. The 1913 Natives Land Act forced hundreds of thousands of Africans off

Boer commander . . . General Jan Smuts was one of the three generals to triumph when the Union of South Africa was established. He went on to become one of the three prime ministers who ruled until the Purified National Party's unexpected 1948 election victory

farms which they had bought or were squatting on in the Transvaal and Free State. As supposed compensation, the African "reserves" were to be set aside for Africans only. A later Land Act (1936) pledged that, in return for Cape Africans being removed from the common voters' roll, the reserves would be extended.

More immediately, Africans on their separate roll were allowed to elect three white MPs and four Senators, although even that was abolished in the late 1950s.

In opposition to the pattern of discrimination, the African National Congress was formed shortly after Union. Membership was small, its leadership Christian black middle-class gradualists seeking greater equality of opportunity rather than a revolutionary new society. Separate organisations also existed for "coloured" and Indian people, but in time the ANC became home to most who believed in non-racialism. The rise of African political consciousness mobilised in the ANC coincided with the growth of the National Party as the vehicle of Afrikaner nationalism.

This nationalism is generally recognised to have its origins as a conscious movement in the 1870s and first half of the 1880s.[18] It was then that the notion of "primitive Calvinism" of the Boers as a *volk* and a chosen people, and of Christian Nationalism took root. Historical incidents were mythologised and folk heroes created.[19]

Afrikaans was fostered as a living, nationalist language. Most of this first took place in the Western Cape. From the establishment of the secret Afrikaner organisation, the Broederbond,[20] in 1918, Afrikaner nationalism was combined with the urgent desire to uplift the white *volk* from poverty. The same process of urbanisation and industrialisation that had affected the Africans with the discovery of gold and diamonds also had its impact on Afrikaners. Nationalists wanted to "rescue" their compatriots from falling to the level of black people and to enlist them in the cause of the *volk*. According to an analysis of right-wing Afrikaners, the vast majority are from the poorer strata of white society — ones who fear they have the most to lose in the event of a black government.[21] The threat of a black takeover was one of the planks in the National Party's 1948 election campaign, but the policy of apartheid itself arrived late on the agenda. It was not until 1944 that serious party attention was given to "native policy".[22] What emerged was not an ideological blueprint but disparate and sometimes conflicting views.[23] At one end of the spectrum was simple, naked white domination; at the other, what some idealists thought was a just and moral separation of the races.

The experiment in social engineering, whether a new theory or an adaptation of old practices, failed, at huge cost. The task now facing South Africa is to overcome its past. The alternative, as BJ Vorster said in 1974, "is too ghastly to contemplate".

Roger Omond is a Guardian journalist and author

Footnotes

1. Allister Sparks, The Mind Of South Africa, Mandarin, 1990, pxv-xvi & 38.
2. Martin Legassick, The Frontier Tradition In South African Historiography, Shula Marks and Anthony Atmore, Economy And Society In Pre-Industrial South Africa, Longman, 1980, p53-54.
3. Andre du Toit & Hermann Giliomee, Afrikaner Political Thought: Analysis And Documents, Vol. One 1780-1850, David Philip, 1983, p528-9.
4. Elphick & Giliomee op cit, p527-528; Shula Marks and Stanley Trapido, The Politics Of Race, Class And Nationalism In 20th-Century South Africa, Longman, 1987, p14; Andre du Toit, No Chosen People: The Myth Of The Calivinist Origins Of Afrikaner Nationalism And Racial Ideology, American Historical Review, 88, 1983, p920-952.
5. Legassick op cit, p45.
6. Ibid.
7. Andre Brink, Mapmakers, Faber & Faber, 1983, p15.
8. Elphick & Giliomee op cit, p543.
9. Eric Walker, A History Of Southern Africa, Longmans, 1962, p24-25.
10. Richard Elphick & Robert Snell, Intergroup Relations: Khoikhoi, Settlers, Slaves And Free Blacks 1652-1695, in Elphick & Giliomee op cit, p194-195.
11. Roger Omond, The Apartheid Handbook, Penguin, 1986, p24-25.
12. Elphick & Giliomee op cit, p549.
13. Elphick & Giliomee op cit, p552.
14. T Davenport, South Africa: A Modern History, Macmillan, 1981, p35.
15. Du Toit & Giliomee op cit, p16-20.
16. Shula Marks & Richard Rathbone, Industrialisation And Social Change In South Africa: African Class Formation, Culture And Consciousness 1870-1930, Longman, 1982, p3.
17. Quoted in Marks and Trapido op cit, p5.
18. Hermann Giliomee, Western Cape Farmers And The Beginnings Of Afrikaner Nationalism 1870-1915, Journal Of Southern African Studies Vol. 14 No. 1, October 1987, p38; Marks and Trapido op cit, p10-15; Du Toit & Giliomee op cit pxiv.
19. See LM Thomson, The Political Mythology Of Apartheid, Yale University Press, 1985.
20. Ivor Wilkins & Hans Strydom, The Broederbond, Jonathan Ball/Paddington Press, 1978.
21. See for example Robert Taylor, Between Apartheid And Democracy: The South African Election of 1989, in South African Review 5, Ravan Press 1989, p56 and Craig Charney, Restructuring White Politics: The Transformation Of The National Party, South African Review One, Ravan Press, 1983.
22. Marks and Trapido op cit, p19.
23. See Deborah Posel, The Meaning Of Apartheid Before 1948, Journal Of Southern African Studies, Vol 14 No 1, October 1987.

The economics of apartheid/Howard Preece

SOUTH AFRICA has gone backwards since the late 1960s in terms of average real living standards. The population as a whole is worse off than it was in 1970. There has, of course, been positive economic growth overall since then. But it has fallen marginally short of the 2.4 per cent rate of increase in the population.

This would seem, at first sight, to be overwhelming proof that apartheid proved not only morally indefensible but also disastrously inefficient economically.

The long-term position is, however, much more complex. For example, the economy grew at an average annual rate of 5 per cent between 1920 and 1970, even with the depression years of the early 1930s. That put South Africa in the premier division of the world growth league, albeit at the lower end.

However, the average rise each year in real gross domestic product (GDP) in the 1970s was down to under 3.3 per cent. For the 1980s it was below 2.2 per cent — 1.5 per cent if the spectacular gold boom years of 1980–81 are excluded. Add in the longest recession in the country's history, from late 1989 to the end of 1992, which saw an absolute decline of 3 per cent in GDP, and the result is that per capita living standards are no higher today than they were in 1966.

The contrast between the general and sustained surge in the economy for the 50 years before the 1970s and its generally dismal performance since, suggests an alternative interpretation of the impact of apartheid: that apartheid was for decades a help to economic growth. This came about essentially through the provision of plentiful cheap migrant labour (for the mining industry in particular) and through the suppression of almost all forms of trade union activity by black workers.

But, following this interpretation, apartheid ultimately caused great damage to the economy. It did this not directly, but by gradually creating international hostility which led to trade bans, sanctions and foreign disinvestment. These dated back in some cases to the world outcry over the Sharpeville massacre in 1960, or even earlier — certainly way before 1985, when sanctions are believed by many analysts to have effectively started.

There was, for example, large British disinvestment from South Africa in the early 1980s — Associated British Foods, Metal Box, Barclays Bank, Standard & Chartered, British Steel and Courtaulds all substantially or totally withdrew their direct presence from South Africa. Furthermore, this was at a time when UK companies were under less pressure from their own government — under prime minister Margaret Thatcher — to pull out of South Africa or to hold back on investment than almost any of their foreign counterparts.

However, even the claim that apartheid was initially conducive to economic efficiency, or at least neutral in its effects, is open to two main challenges. First, although the economy performed well by overall international standards in the earlier period, it still did nowhere near as well as it could and should have done, because of the self-inflicted limitations imposed by apartheid.

Second, the real growth that took place and the resulting increases in national wealth accrued almost entirely to the white minority. In other words, the economy did nothing for the great mass of the people even when it was prospering strongly at the macro level.

This view has now become dominant, crucially, within the African National Congress (ANC) and its allies in the so-called "triple alliance", the Congress of South African Trade Unions (Cosatu) and the SA Communist Party.

A 1991 ANC policy statement unequivocally asserted: "Our country's economy is in need of fundamental restructuring. For decades various forces within the white minority have used their exclusive access to political and economic power to promote their own sectional interests at the expense of black people. The black people have been systematically excluded and disadvantaged economically, with the result that South Africa now has one of the most unequal patterns of distribution of income and wealth in the world."

Consider first, however, the argument that, although the South African economy appeared to flourish under apartheid, it still failed to achieve anywhere near the growth levels potentially attainable. This is certainly true. What's more, it was not only conceded by the National Party but, at least

Although the South African economy appeared to flourish under apartheid, it still failed to achieve anywhere near its growth potential. Even its architect, Hendrik Verwoerd, accepted it was not compatible with a modern economy

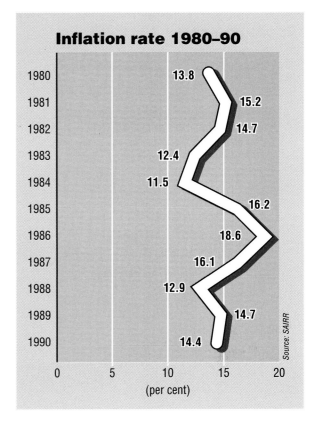

until the late sixties, actually welcomed. Hendrik Verwoerd, in particular, made it absolutely clear that maximum economic growth was not an objective of apartheid. Rather, it was accepted that apartheid was not compatible with optimum growth. For Verwoerd, apartheid took priority.

Naturally this absolutist view was not fully shared by a great many National Party supporters, especially those in the emerging Afrikaner business class. But there was no apparent need in the 1950s and 1960s for political confrontation on this issue within the National Party. An average economic growth rate of over 5 per cent still worked out at close to 3 per cent a year in per capita terms. So long as average white real incomes could advance at roughly that rate, then white living standards would continue to keep pace with Western Europe, the US and the old "white Commonwealth".

Even the English-speaking business community, with a few exceptions, made little serious protest about apartheid. Conditions generally were good — and the government was a dangerous enemy to challenge.

By the late 1960s, however, the restricting effects of apartheid on economic growth, and thus on business, were beginning to be felt. The claim, from a moderately liberal business standpoint, that apartheid was not helpful either to business or to the broader economy, was put by the then chairman of Anglo-American Corporation, Harry Oppenheimer, in 1971.

Oppenheimer argued:

"We are approaching the stage where the full potential of the economy, as it is at present organised, will have been realised, so that if structural changes are not made we will have to content ourselves with a much lower rate of growth ... Prospects for economic growth will not be attained so long as a large majority of the population is prevented by lack of formal education and technical training or by positive prohibition from playing the full part of which it is capable in the national development."

To many business analysts, Oppenheimer's words are now seen as a prescient warning of the economic decline facing South Africa and as confirmation that apartheid was inimical to macro-economic performance and in conflict with the fundamental nature of capitalism. Today, business leaders, particularly market-oriented economists, insist apartheid is the antithesis of free-market economics, that institutionalised racism must by definition be as interventionist in its economic workings as any other form of statistical social engineering.

The theoretical case in support of this approach can muster some apparently impressive evidence. Under apartheid the South African economy developed behind a strongly protectionist framework. Companies were legally restricted from expanding operations in whatever part of South

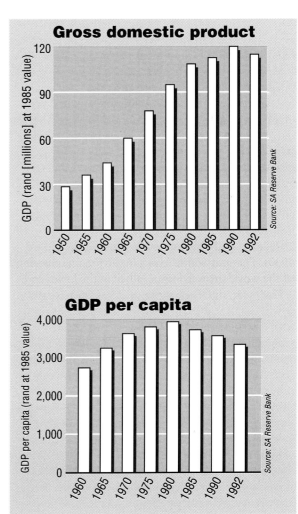

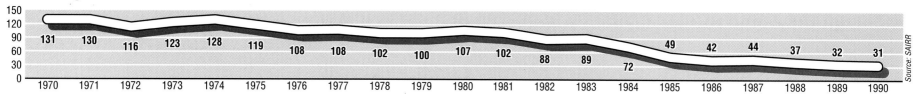

Exchange rates 1970–90

131 130 116 123 128 119 108 108 102 100 107 102 88 89 72 49 42 44 37 32 31

1970 1971 1972 1973 1974 1975 1976 1977 1978 1979 1980 1981 1982 1983 1984 1985 1986 1987 1988 1989 1990

Weighted average exchange rate of rand against six major currencies. 1979 =100

Source: SAIRR

Africa they might have wished under such legislation as the Physical Planning Act, which also limited their freedom to offer employment where they liked.

Moreover, there was, and still is, a heavy degree of public ownership in railways, airlines, electricity, gas, water, steel, post and telecommunications and even in the key areas of forestry and road haulage. Even in the 1970s, interest rates, including mortgages, were strictly controlled and foreign exchange controls extensively applied. As the International Monetary Fund has stressed, tax levels on business and on middle and upper-income individuals are now very much in line with those for major industrial nations. Bodies such as the South African Chamber of Business (Sacob), the main employer body, claims that it is nonsensical to say that apartheid was ever the friend of capitalism.

Well, yes, but! The crucial problem for business now is that it is perceived by the majority of the South African population to have been a vital accomplice of apartheid and to have profited handsomely from it. The mining industry paid large dividends to shareholders for generations from the rewards of a cheap and endless pool of migrant labour, a direct consequence of apartheid. Business in general is seen to have colluded with the government in seeking to suppress any black-dominated trade unions, even into the late 1970s.

Although statutory job reservation was confined almost solely to the mines, black people were in practice denied equal opportunities in almost every

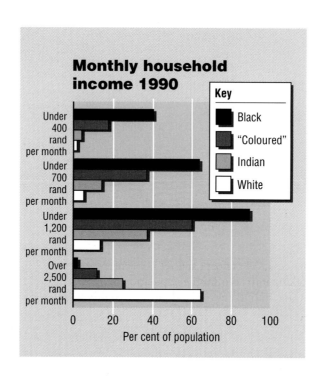

Monthly household income 1990

Key
- Black
- "Coloured"
- Indian
- White

Under 400 rand per month

Under 700 rand per month

Under 1,200 rand per month

Over 2,500 rand per month

0   20   40   60   80   100

Per cent of population

sector of the economy for decades. In any case, the monstrously unequal education systems dictated by apartheid made it extremely difficult, sometimes impossible, for black workers to be able to compete equally with their white counterparts.

That was in part the point that Oppenheimer and others in business were making over 20 years ago. But what many were effectively asking for, although they never saw it that way, was apartheid with a

human face — the scrapping or easing of enforced racial segregation where it adversely affected the workplace — but not the abolition, except in some far-off and undefined future, of white rule.

On the other hand, the claim of the ANC and others that the great mass of the black population enjoyed little or no benefit from South Africa's economic growth is also open to question. It is true that statistical evidence (which is itself disputed) on black real incomes indicates that they hardly improved between 1920 and 1970.

However, liberal economists such as Witwatersrand University's Charles Simkins, banned for alleged subversive activities for a period in the 1970s, and Natal University's Julian Hofmeyr, have found that black people overall did gain significantly from the long period of solid growth. The gains were mainly reflected in new employment creation rather than in appreciably higher real wages for those already employed — another consequence of higher black population growth.

Hofmeyr notes that only after this extended period of absorption of labour into the economy could there be much room for real income increases. Between 1970 and 1984, the economy suffered severe skills shortages, while de facto and then de jure urban black unionisation increased rapidly. During this period average black real wages doubled, against a 9 per cent average rise for white workers. The black share of the national wage bill increased over that period from 20 per cent to nearly 30 per cent.

'Apartheid locked intrinsic economic weaknesses into the economic system, especially chronic shortages of skilled and semi-skilled labour, a huge bureaucracy, and the creation of costly multi-layered infrastructures'

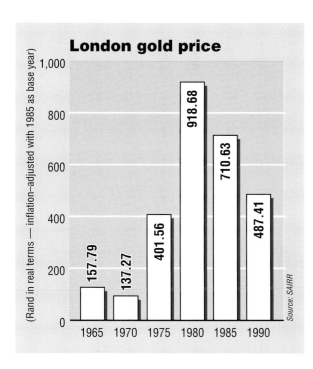

London gold price

(Rand in real terms — inflation-adjusted with 1985 as base year)

Year	Price
1965	157.79
1970	137.27
1975	401.56
1980	918.68
1985	710.63
1990	487.41

Source: SAIRR

Simkins finds that the extreme degree of income inequality in South Africa also eased over the 1960s and 1970s.

Overall, there can be no doubt that apartheid retarded economic growth in South Africa — in part by deliberate intent — from the 1920s through to the 1980s. Apartheid locked intrinsic economic weaknesses into the economic system, especially chronic shortages of skilled and semi-skilled labour,

a hugely wasteful apartheid-related bureaucracy, the creation of costly multi-layered infrastructures, and decentralisation policies related almost solely to political rather than economic factors.

In addition, the economy suffered progressively severe constraints caused by foreign trade and financial sanctions and the resulting huge expenditure on efforts to reduce South Africa's dependence on imports of oil, military equipment and other actual or perceived needs.

In theory at least, the South African economy without apartheid would be in immensely better shape today than is now the case. In 1990, 1991 and 1992, South Africa's aggregate real GDP fell by 0.5 per cent, 0.4 per cent and 2.1 per cent respectively. Taking into account the population increase, this meant a GDP per capita slump of roughly 9 per cent over those three years.

The economic crisis facing the first ANC-dominated government can essentially be seen in these figures.

But it does not follow that the economy would in practice be much better off if majority rule had come 20, 30 or 40 years ago. Since the ANC was wholly committed throughout almost that whole period to Eastern-European-style socialism, it is possible that the economic catastrophe undergone by the Soviet Union and its satellites could have been replicated in South Africa and might even have been more damaging than apartheid.

Of course if South Africa had embraced the

majority rule route decades back and if this had been accompanied by the kind of social market economics that the ANC now espouses that would have been massively different and colossally beneficial.

But such ideal, counter-historical scenarios, while they may be interesting to economists, are of little practical use to South Africans who now face an economic future which is, at best, uncertain.

Howard Preece is deputy editor of Finance Week

A leading Afrikaner nationalist explains how his people came to terms with the need for change and for a new South Africa

Afrikaner thoughts/Piet Cillié

AS AN Afrikaner myself, and a Nationalist, I have often, when reading attempts at in-depth analysis of this mysterious species of anthropoid, felt like D H Lawrence when another writer depicted him in a novel: "Well damn my eyes! I said to myself. Well damn my little eyes! If this is what Archibald thinks I am he sure thinks a lot of lies!"

A generalised and simplified image of the Afrikaner has been that of a stubborn colonialist in an anti-colonialist age, an irremediable drop-out from Western civilisation, and an oppressor and slave-driver of black people for three-and-a-half centuries. (In fact, the first massive contact of white and black in Southern Africa occurred in the Eastern Cape during the early half of the 19th century.) Now, all of a sudden, like Saint Paul on his way to Damascus, the Afrikaner has seen the great light of democracy. He has extended a monopolistic white vote to a vast majority of the black population, and is prepared to share governmental power with erstwhile enemies.

I shall try to supplant such obvious myth-making with some real history. For a moment we have to go back in time.

At least some Afrikaners have been in the vanguard of anti-colonialism in southern Africa ever since they became conscious of being a *volk* (people or nation) apart from their imperial Dutch masters and took the adopted name of Afrikaner to confirm it. In their perception of history, their "finest hours", to adapt Churchill's phrase, were mostly anti-colonialist ones.

Early in the 18th century, an amateurish and short-lived revolt of angry farmers was suppressed by a corrupt Dutch governor at the Cape. Near the end of the century, two equally amateurish and short-lived Afrikaner republics, inspired partly by the French Revolution, were established in the interior of the Cape colony in defiance of the Dutch authorities.

The British occupied the Cape during the Napoleonic era to prevent a French invasion — and, typically, stayed on. So the Afrikaners' next and supreme anti-colonial efforts were staged against British imperialism: number one, the Great Trek away from British rule during the 1830s, leading to the creation of the two Boer republics of the Orange Free State and Transvaal; and, number two, their extinction by the British during the drawn-out Anglo-Boer War at the dawn of the 20th century. It awoke world-wide attention and sympathy for the Boers although it gained them no worthwhile help. But it did signal the coming decline of British imperialism and Western European colonialism in general.

These two events created a deep and persistent wariness and suspicion in the collective Afrikaner consciousness of black numerical power and British economic and cultural power. The latter was seen to be exercised by the elite South African minority of British descent after direct British rule had been terminated. The dominant political ideal of the National Party gradually came to be not simply a place in the sun for the Afrikaners, but an impregnable ruling power to safeguard the existence of a nation that had experienced utter defeat.

What was not so obvious was the persistence, at the same time, of the anti-colonialist tradition in Afrikaner history. While celebrating their heroes of the Great Trek and the *Tweede Vryheidsoorlog* (Second Freedom War), they were also affirming, albeit subconsciously, the anti-colonialist principle: that domination of one people by another is morally wrong and therefore untenable in the shorter or longer run.

In religious mood, they often insisted that God had planted them in Africa for the divine purpose of spreading the light of his word and the virtues of civilisation. They were thus prepared to grant the indigenous Africans what they themselves enjoyed. Large-scale missionary work has been a feature of Afrikaner as well as English church activity.

The Afrikaners found themselves in a similar position to that of the American people in the 19th century. They had fought their war of independence for national liberty and the proposition that all men are created equal, but had defaulted by tolerating slavery for the best part of a century afterwards. They had mounted a tiger of principle that turned on them with a vengeance in the shape of a ghastly civil war. A hundred years later the tiger was still gnawing at America by way of the civil rights movement.

I have often pondered the depth and modern

Picture: MAYIBUYE CENTRE

relevance of the opening sentences of Abraham Lincoln's Gettysburg Address: "Fourscore and seven years ago, our fathers brought forth upon this continent a new nation, conceived in liberty and dedicated to the proposition that all men are created equal. Now we are engaged in a great civil war, testing whether that nation — or any nation, so conceived and so dedicated — can long endure."

In other words, are the democratic ideals of liberty, equal rights and opportunities for all, even realisable in a collection of humans regarding themselves as a nation but made up of diverse ethnic, religious and cultural components?

The whites' position up to now can be regarded, more or less accurately, as that of an imperial power with its "colonial peoples" all mixed up within its borders. Just imagine the British people having arisen as a nation, not in their "sceptered isle", but on the Indian subcontinent, eventually emerging as rulers. How do you "liberate" a huge colonial population composed of diverse and often mutually hostile groups in such a situation without the minority nation being swamped? As early as 1950, at a prestigious conference of Afrikaner intellectuals and churchmen, only two years after the assumption of power by the apartheid government, the Afrikaners' anti-colonialist commitment was reaffirmed by a conference overwhelmingly sympathetic to the ruling party.

It concluded that the future of the black population posed two clear alternatives: as their attainment of freedom was in essence irresistible and therefore inevitable, they had to achieve it either in parts of South Africa or within the same political structures as the whites in a unified country.

The latter was rejected, as it raised the spectre of black domination, even more abhorrent than the previous British domination. *Gebiedskeiding* (territorial separation or partition) for the black peoples was accepted as the only policy worth living and working for. It should be noted that this declaration of principle by Afrikaners for Afrikaners preceded the wave of *uhuru* (freedom) that swept through Africa during the fifties and sixties.

Obviously the practicability of this vision of black self-government depended on the economic viability of the area to be assigned to the black population. This seminal conference was followed in the mid-1950s by the publication of the so-called Tomlinson Report, named after the Afrikaner economist who led the government team that produced it. Without discussing the political future of the black population, it outlined the economic state and

potential of the existing "native reserves" — tribal areas reserved for exclusive black occupation. These were so retarded in economic development that large numbers of their male population had already flocked to the "white" industrial centres. A similar process of migration and urbanisation was causing headaches all over Africa, and in fact all over the Third World.

Not only the economic, but also the political implications of the Tomlinson Report were formidable. It sketched the sort of dynamic development that had to be tackled in the reserves to render them viable and stem the human tide to the white cities and towns.

In the event, the implementation of the report's recommendations, not all of which were accepted by the government, was less than half-hearted. I then discovered that "too little, too late" was worse than a reproach — it appeared to be an inexorable law of politics.

In the meantime, the propaganda for political *gebiedskeiding* went on unabated. It received behind-the-scenes encouragement from the then prime minister, Johannes Strijdom. He urged its advocates to prepare the way for the politicians, as partitioning South Africa to create independent black nation states was clearly a radical prospect.

In 1958 Strijdom died, and was followed by Hendrik Verwoerd. Soon after his accession, he proclaimed increasing autonomy for the "Bantu homelands" to be government policy. Asked what

would happen if these homelands (soon nicknamed "bantustans") were to demand independence, he answered: "Who is going to stop them?" At the same time, Verwoerd abolished a residual representation of the Cape black population by three whites in the House of Assembly (our House of Commons). It was an obvious attempt to divert black aspirations from the white centres of power towards their burgeoning homeland institutions.

From the beginning, the economics of the homelands operation lagged behind its politics, so that as early as the mid-sixties, faith in the policy of "grand apartheid" as a viable solution was faltering among government supporters.

However, the alternative, of being "swamped" by black migration was still too ghastly to contemplate — even by the white opposition in parliament, who had consistently prophesied the failure of bantustans. Their exercises in alternative policies were hesitant, to say the least. It was evident — to adapt a conclusion of Gunnar Myrdal about the post-war US — that the "non-white problem" in South Africa was a problem in the heart of the white South Africans, English people as well as Afrikaners.

The adoption of the bantustan policy had relieved the conscience of government supporters, stirred in 1960 by the so-called Sharpeville riots. Its central feature was an unplanned police shooting at an unarmed mob, giving rise to worldwide condemnation of apartheid (literally "separateness"). The Afrikaner newspaper which I edited, *Die*

> **'The stark alternatives became clear: ruthless suppression of all protest, of which the security forces were still quite capable; or moving towards a full implementation of "government of the people, by the people, for the people"'**

Burger, staunchly Nationalist at the time, wrote that the word, originally substituted as a more positive term for the traditional "segregation", had lost any useful purpose and had become a term of universal opprobrium for the worst kind of racial oppression. In spite of never being embodied in South African law, it hung about South Africa's neck and was kept there for three decades. Sharpeville was our Amritsar, apartheid our stinking albatross.

As *Die Burger* prophesied, we were thrust into the role of the world's polecat. In 1963 my newspaper was telling its mainly Afrikaner readership that we, once in the forefront of anti-colonialist crusades, had allowed our good name, "the immediate jewel of our souls", to be filched from us. We had to return to our faith in freedom as a political principle, however difficult the problems it raised. For practically the next two decades, we held on to our belief in autonomous national states for the various black peoples as a partial way out of our dilemma. So did the government. With prodding from Pretoria, four homelands were declared independent states without being recognised as such by the international community. The death knell for our line of thinking was sounded in 1982 when a thorough study of black urbanisation was published by two Afrikaner intellectuals of impeccable repute: the present principal of Pretoria University, Professor P Smit, and the vice-chancellor, JJ Booysen.

In handing them an annual award as authors of the best work of non-fiction produced by a company with which I was associated, I summed up their message: "Urbanisation in Third World societies was a cataclysm of our times, unstoppable and irreversible like an earthquake or a volcano of which the consequences can be mitigated, but cannot be unmade or turned back. The authors show us to be irrevocably on the road to growing economic integration as well as intimate residential and social coexistence. In other words, they are pointing the way to an integrated, non-racial society.

"We have been hoping too long, against overwhelming evidence, that the homeland policy would accomplish more, would succeed better to recreate South Africa as a plausible nation-state with its people more or less happy and free in its own promised land. Now we are forced by the facts, the imperative facts marshalled in this book, to rethink our situation — a process bound to be profound and far-reaching. The recent split in the National Party is only the beginning of our anguish."

This was a reference to the establishment, by a large group of Nationalist MPs, of a Conservative Party, mainly in protest against the creation of a three-chamber parliament in which white, "coloured" and Indian people were allotted separate elected houses. Ultimate power, however, was still vested in the white chamber.

This quite radical experiment in extended democracy came to grief within a few years, as did the setting up of local councils for urbanised black people in the townships. Establishment Afrikaners knew what these events, accompanied by increasingly violent mass demonstrations and the detention of more and more "subversives", were costing their country economically and morally. The tentative liberalisations during the regimes of premiers Vorster and Botha were not working.

The stark alternatives became clear: either the ruthless suppression of all extra-parliamentary protest, of which the security forces were still quite capable, but which no longer held any promise of creating confidence; or liberating the pent-up forces and moving towards a full implementation of "government of the people, by the people, for the people".

Never before, to my knowledge, has such a sudden extension of the franchise to a huge "colonial" majority by a ruling Western nation been attempted. Indian and Nigerian independence offer no parallels, because the imperial rulers withdrew to their distant land; but even so the sequel included a horrible bloodbath in both cases.

President FW de Klerk, sharing the Nobel Peace Prize with Nelson Mandela, could well be considered for the title of most courageous political leader in recent times.

So here we are, in Lincoln's words, to test whether a nation, conceived in liberty and committed to the proposition that all men are created equal, can long endure. Wish us well!

Piet Cillié was formerly editor of Die Burger

The word on the street

South Africans of all races were interviewed in

Johannesburg by Weekly Mail & Guardian journalists

and asked their views on the ending of apartheid

THELMA (would not give her last name) (43), a black receptionist from Soweto:

"The worst thing about apartheid was the pass laws. We couldn't even have visitors overnight if they did not have permits to be in the area. The police would just come and arrest them. I hate apartheid. I hate it, hate it, hate it!

"The ANC has always fought for the liberation of our people and I'm sure

they will carry on fighting for us. I fear that the far-right AWB will carry on warfare behind our backs, but all in all I think this country will come right."

BENEDICT MPEKE (27), a black police officer from Soweto:

"I remember in 1972, we were tear-gassed inside the classroom. When we

ran out, we were heavily *sjambokked* (whipped).

"Later on, in 1983, there was a general boycott of classes. I was held without trial for six weeks and we embarked on a hunger strike for the last three weeks of our detention.

"Now I am hoping that our colour differences and ethnic groupings will blend into one united nation of South Africa. I have no fear."

PAULINE SEKETE (44), a black tea lady from Palm Springs, West Rand:

"Small incidents used to happen every day. Like when I was sent to the bank by my boss. A white boy of about 11 was helped before me. I felt bad. But after the elections I will get my dignity back. People will start treating me as a human being."

JULIA GREY (25), a white teacher from Yeoville, Johannesburg:

"One day, when I was six, my friends and I walked past an old black man sitting under the tree on the pavement. As we went by, we all said 'kaffir' (derogatory term for Africans). I remember it gave me a horrible feeling after saying it.

"I think we will all gain from escaping the oppression of apartheid.

"On the day Nelson Mandela was released, I went with my two white friends to see the celebrations because we were excited. But our car was stopped and surrounded by a group of people who rocked it, and my friend in the back seat was punched. I realised that if I wanted to celebrate, I'd have to stay home.

"I just want to find a place for myself inside the new society. I hope people will learn to see difference as something that enriches all of us."

SANDRA SMIT (22), an Afrikaner student from Johannesburg:

"As youngsters, apartheid influenced our way of thinking about black people. We were taught to believe they were sub-human. That led to communication breakdowns, because we never had a chance to know who they really were.

"I wish that crime would come down and that our economy would improve. I would like to walk around freely without fear. I'm very optimistic that things will turn out well for us all. But who knows?"

RICHARD SINGO (42), a black petrol station cashier from Meadowlands, Soweto:

"Surely things will soon be better. We will all get equal treatment and payment with our white counterparts; same skills, same job opportunities.

"I was once arrested for not having a pass book (identity document to be carried by all those who were not white) with me — I had mistakenly left it at work. Two days later, I appeared in court.

"I remember one day reading in an article that both black and white train commuters would be allowed to use first class compartments, if they had the tickets.

"I bought a ticket but a white policeman grabbed me. He showed me a 'Whites Only' sign and said he was enforcing the

law written on the sign, not what was written in the article."

DENISE (would not give her last name) (22), a white social worker from Florida, Witwatersrand:

"As a social worker, I have seen how apartheid has separated families. This is still a reality for black people. My biggest hope is that families will be united. I don't feel that I will personally lose out from the end of apartheid: I do feel that we can lose out as a country. The new government might be as repressive as the last one."

THEO OOSTHUIZEN (24), a "coloured" manager of a car dealership from Bosmont, Johannesburg:

"Apartheid made us better people because of the struggle. We became more than conquerors. We fought for equal rights from the

'I hope that South Africa will become united and that the health and education of our people will improve. What scares me is that people might not negotiate and that this could lead to a civil war'

Ashley Padaychee

system. "Police would come and chase us with batons and some would lose their lives. One of my friends jumped out of a classroom window and fell to his death.

"There are still many people who are afraid of the idea of having a democratic country. But I am sure things will come right, I'll gain my freedom as a human being and no longer be judged according to the colour of my skin."

WILLIE (would not give surname) (17), white sales representative from Johannesburg:

"People were happy under apartheid. There was no violence. People could walk outside late at night and leave their houses open. No one was afraid, but the worst was that I couldn't be friends with black people.

"My hope for the future is that we will all be equal and share in the country, but I am afraid that we will have to leave because Inkatha and the ANC don't want any white people in the country. I think it will be a good future, though."

ASHLEY PADAYCHEE (22), an Indian medical student from Pietermaritzburg, Natal:

"Apartheid did not really have a negative effect on me. Where I lived, we had a good education and a good life.

"I hope that South Africa will become united and that the health and education of our people will improve. I think this country will be a great place to practise medicine. What scares me is that people might not negotiate and that this could lead to a civil war."

ABE MOLOI (28), a black sales consultant from Soweto:

"I was detained without trial for a year during the apartheid era and placed in solitary confinement. After my release, it was hard to mix with people and I had a nervous breakdown.

"Now I hope to see people getting equal treatment. But I fear the ANC being the only party in power because I personally know of some guys within the organisation who are corrupt. But there's nothing to lose from the end of apartheid. Instead we black people will regain our dignity."

REVEREND VICTOR MALEFETSE, a black priest in his mid-30s from Tlhabane, Western Transvaal:

"My memories of apartheid are unemployment, inferior education, maltreatment of my black elders by whites. Now I fear the disunity of the black people and hope that the parties will ultimately realise the futility of violence. I am pessimistic because all parties are not involved in the changes. But I think, after elections, I will get back my respect, equal opportunities and my own land."

MYNA KHUMALO (40), a black florist from Orange Farm squatter camp, Johannesburg:

"I'm hoping for a job with a living wage for me and my children. I'm afraid that white people will emigrate if there's a black government, and we won't be able to get jobs. Then we will suffer much more than we do now.

"I had to get a pass document to live here. I ended up marrying somebody I did not love out of desperation. Right now I'm divorced and a single parent struggling to raise my kids alone.

"After elections, I will live more freely. Right now I can't go everywhere I want as I fear I will be killed."

UNA KOSTER (54), an Afrikaner from Rustenburg, Western Transvaal:

"I fear that the far right will soon blindly start a war in which the lives of every citizen will be at risk. This will also damage the economy and the infrastructure.

"But there is hope, because so many of our people are talented and intelligent, and have managed to create a good life for their families against all odds.

"I hope that they will be determined to build on the foundation of the negotiation process and not allow their dreams to be stolen away from them."

INNOCENT NDLOVU (23), a black newspaper vendor from the Witwatersrand:

"I hope for an increase in salaries. The government did not pay our parents enough money, so they could not send me to school. I am now selling newspapers and getting little pay. I am definitely not going to lose anything after the election, but I don't know yet what I will gain."

MOSES DLAMINI (30), a black petrol station attendant from Soweto:

"When I was at school, I used to work for white people during the holidays. They used to treat me like rubbish and they did not pay well at all. I suppose that happened to all black

Racial harmony: will the good feeling evident in this Johannesburg peace demonstration hold together the new South Africa?

> '**After apartheid is over, things will get better for me — I want a job and housing. The ANC told us, on television, that companies will come into the country after the elections and will offer us jobs**'
>
> Dumisana Galela

people though. One thing I remember from those days is not funny but we still laugh about it. My friend jumped out of a third-floor flat to avoid a policeman because he did not have a pass. To this day, he has a limp.

"I'm looking forward to having a vote. I know that there will be many problems, and I know that there is a lack of money. I'm sure it will work out though. I am looking forward to the day I have a decent job and make enough money to feed my family and my children."

ERIC VISSER (50), an Afrikaner copywriter from Johannesburg:

"I hope for political stability and an economic recovery. It is terribly important that people have houses and education. I am also hoping for the accommodation of diverse ethnicity, but people should still maintain their roots and identities.

"I fear that we will have extreme elements from either side of the

political spectrum disrupting the process of the 'new' South Africa. But I am still very optimistic."

CAROL KOFFMAN (25), a "coloured" psychologist from Johannesburg:

"In 1983, I was at a mixed private school and, on an outing, they asked us to take the bus to town. When we got there the driver said that I could not get into the bus — it was for whites only. I had to get off, but none of my friends got off with me. I felt really humiliated and lost faith in my school and my friends. I'm scared that being coloured will not be considered black enough, and that if affirmative action is applied incorrectly, I may personally lose out."

K H DONGES (49), a self-employed German South African from Johannesburg:

"I am half optimistic and half pessimistic. I don't want the old

restrictions replaced by new ones in different shapes. I don't believe in socialism."

NATANYA NAGAN (18), an Indian student from Johannesburg:

"Violence is my biggest fear for the future. Also, I think there might be reverse apartheid. But I am still optimistic about the future. I will be more free to communicate with people of other races. I will go anywhere I want and that will mean a lot to me."

PELO SIHLAHLA (32), a black hairdresser from Diepkloof:

"During my early high-school years, I was unlucky. I was picked up by the police, taken to prison, beaten and later released without explanation. I had not even been taking part in the boycotts, but I associated with some activists.

I still have serious backache from the beatings.

"I look on the bright side. The country does not have to go to the dogs if everyone is determined to make it work. I feel the country can be manageable."

DUMISANI GALELA (19), a black unemployed man from Johannesburg:

"My worst memory of apartheid is Bantu education in school. We wanted to go to university, but our English was too poor and they would not accept us. I finished matric (equivalent of O-levels) in 1992 and have not been able to find a job since. After apartheid is over, things will get better for me — I want a job and housing. The ANC told us, on television, that companies will come into the country after the elections and will offer us jobs."

Interviews by **Mapula Sibanda, Annie Mapoma, Sibusiso Bubesi, Africa Boso, Chantil Thomas, Hlengiwe Tenza, Nombuyiselo Maloyi, Mathlodi Malope, Sibusiso Nxumalo, Phylicia Oppelt.** *Photographs by* **Clinton Asary and Mark Izerow.**

The legacy of apartheid/David Welsh

IN THE four decades after 1948, apartheid divided people, regimented them, tied them up in bureaucratic and legal constraints, destroyed communities, and centralised political control in a massive leviathan of a state. Apartheid's challengers were put down with ferocity in a process that saw the destruction of the rule of law and civil liberties.

The "new" South Africa has had a traumatic birth and it will bear the scars of this painful genesis for a long time. For the purpose of analytical convenience the legacy of apartheid may be divided into two sections: the material legacy of inequality, which can to some extent be quantified; and the attitudinal legacy, which deals with the question of how South Africa's diverse people will relate to one another after the alienating, indeed brutalising experience of apartheid. It must be stressed, though, that the material and attitudinal dimensions of apartheid's legacy are anything but discrete, for in many respects they both cause and reinforce each other in a reciprocal relationship. The impoverished African squatter looks upon the affluence of middle-class white (or, for that matter, "coloured" or Indian) suburbs with an ill-disguised envy; conversely, the bourgeoisie's nightmare is that of being overrun by an undisciplined and covetous African proletariat, intent upon seizing their property. The nightmare may be unlikely to come true, and squatters may be more realistic about their life-changes than is commonly supposed. Nevertheless, it is clear that a powerful sense of past injustice rankles in the minds of apartheid's victims, while the "haves" fear for the security of their property.

The following sections of this chapter show the inequality.

Education

The most damning aspect of apartheid's legacy in this field is the politicisation of all levels of education. In a notorious speech in 1954, Hendrick Verwoerd (then minister of native affairs and subsequently prime minister from 1958 to 1966) spelled out precisely how African schools were to be yoked to the aims of apartheid. In the new dispensation, African education would be tightly controlled by the central government and the previous strong missionary element would be eliminated; syllabuses would be adapted to ensure that education should have its roots in the "native areas", said Verwoerd. In the same speech Verwoerd expressed views that have been flung back at education authorities by successive generations of pupils who accuse them of offering "gutter education":

"The Bantu must be guided to service his community in all respects. There is no place for him in the European community above the level of certain forms of labour. Within his own community, however, all doors are open. For that reason it is of no avail to him to receive a training which has as its aim absorption in the European community while he cannot and will not be absorbed there. Up till now he has been subjected to a school system which drew him away from his own community and partially misled him by showing him the green pastures of the European but still did not allow him to graze there."

African opposition to the new policy was ignored, and implementation proceeded remorselessly. From now on pupils were expected to be taught in vernacular languages until standard four (their sixth year of schooling), whereas both English and Afrikaans were taught from the earliest years as "foreign" languages. A consequence of this emphasis on instruction in the mother tongue was a steady decline of Africans' ability to read and write English.

Tertiary education was similarly subjected to apartheid. In 1959 the euphemistically titled Extension of University Education Act deprived white universities of the right to admit students of all races, except by permit, which would be granted only in certain circumstances (usually when a student who was not white wished to study courses not offered at an institution catering for his/her racial or ethnic group). Additional legislation created two university colleges for Africans (both situated in remote "homeland" areas) and one each for the Indian and "coloured" communities. In addition, Fort Hare University college was deprived of its autonomy and placed under the control of the central government as an institution catering for Xhosa-speakers. Fort Hare had been established in 1916

The 'new' South Africa has had a traumatic birth and it will bear the scars of this painful genesis for a long time. The traces of apartheid run deep on all sides in many different ways

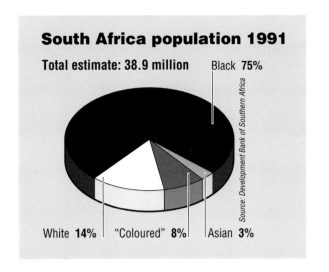

South Africa population 1991

Total estimate: 38.9 million

Black 75%

White 14% "Coloured" 8% Asian 3%

Source: Development Bank of Southern Africa

under missionary auspices and it had played a significant role in producing a new African elite, not only for South Africa but for several other African colonies as well.

The major effect of the new educational system was to emphasise differentiation and shut African, "coloured" and Indian students out of the mainstream of education into channels that offered a distinctly inferior type. It produced also bitter resentment which, in time, would transform many schools and universities into "sites of the struggle". The Black Consciousness Movement (associated principally with the name of Steve Biko) was essentially a product of this stultifyingly system of education. In the turbulent 1980s, the angry youth were at the forefront of the mass uprising.

Quantitatively, however, African education expanded rapidly, especially at the primary level, on the eve of the new system's introduction. In 1953, 41 per cent of Africans of school age were at school, by 1975 this figure had nearly doubled and would continue to grow. Today's exact figure is not known, but research by an independent organisation in 1992 estimated that 1.7 million black youngsters (including Africans, "coloureds" and Indians) between the ages of six and 17 were not at school. High drop-out rates, rapid population growth and accelerated urbanisation aggravate the difficulties. Official figures released in March 1993 showed that approximately 320,000 children enter schools every year (or one million every three years), requiring

annually an additional 320 schools. Notwithstanding the high percentage of GDP spent by the South African government on education (5.4 per cent), which compares favourably with the average percentages spent in both developing and developed countries, delivery remains poor and education for whites and Africans remains unequal. An indicator of this inequality is the per capita expenditure on education: in 1969–1970 the ratio was 16.62 to 1, in favour of whites; by 1991–1992 the ratio had been reduced to 3.5 to 1.

Part of the continuing disparity is explained by the substantial difference in the qualifications of white and African teachers, respectively. Salaries account for approximately 75 per cent of the overall expenditure on education. In 1993 it was estimated that only 25 per cent of African teachers possessed the minimum required qualification for teachers, which is Matriculation (equivalent to O-levels) plus a three-year qualification, while the corresponding figure for white teachers was 100 per cent.

Pupil/teacher ratios are another important indicator of inequality. In 1992, the ratio in African schools was approximately double that in white schools, meaning that in the majority of African schools teachers have to cope with classes that are often larger than 50 and are, moreover, frequently unamenable to discipline in times of political tension. It is not surprising that many African teachers suffer from stress, or that morale in the profession tends to be low.

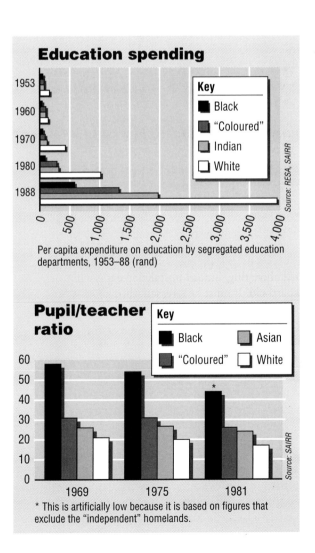

Education spending

Key
- ■ Black
- ■ "Coloured"
- ■ Indian
- □ White

1953
1960
1970
1980
1988

0 500 1,000 1,500 2,000 2,500 3,000 3,500 4,000

Per capita expenditure on education by segregated education departments, 1953–88 (rand)

Source: RESA, SAIRR

Pupil/teacher ratio

Key
- ■ Black   ■ Asian
- ■ "Coloured" □ White

60
50
40
30
20
10
0

1969   1975   1981

* This is artificially low because it is based on figures that exclude the "independent" homelands.

Source: SAIRR

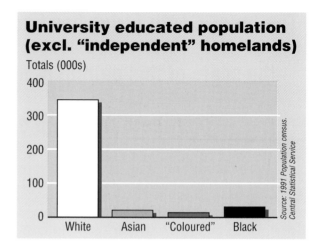

University educated population (excl. "independent" homelands)

Totals (000s)

Source: 1991 Population census. Central Statistical Service

In the 1980s, the call of the youth was for "No education before liberation". Like its companion, the call to "Make the townships ungovernable", it succeeded all too well. The challenge that faces the post-apartheid government is to restore what is called "a culture of learning" in the schools. Another challenge will be to improve the holding power of schools: it has been estimated that more than half of African pupils drop out of school before completing Standard 5 (seven years of schooling); and only 16 per cent of those who enter the school system reach Matriculation, the figure for whites being 85 per cent. Matriculation results in African schools, where disruption has been frequent, are abysmal: for the past three years the average matriculation pass rate in African schools in the so-called "white" areas has been little more than 40 per cent.

Another fact has been the persistent bias in African schools against science, mathematics and other vocationally-oriented subjects. A survey of all African schools in 1988 showed that only 30.2 per cent of pupils were taking mathematics and 17.1 per cent physical science as Matriculation subjects. Pitifully low percentages succeed in passing these subjects.

The serious recession in the South African economy and the lingering effect of sanctions have exacerbated the problems of school-leavers among all groups, but no group is worse affected than African school drop-outs. Nearly 400,000 people enter the labour market annually, but between 1983 and 1993

fewer than 10 out of every 100 were able to find employment in the formal sector (recognised business). As the economy has contracted, so formal sector jobs have declined — by 2 per cent in 1992, according to the ministry of finance. Official figures give an unemployment figure of 46 per cent, but this is partly mitigated by the expansion of the informal sector which, according to estimates, provided employment for over two million people (or 14.4 per cent of the economically active population) by the early 1990s. Most jobs in the informal sector, however, provide only low incomes.

Minimal or negative growth rates (minus 2 per cent in 1992) have been accompanied by a population growth of 2.4 per cent per annum. The Ministry of Finance suggests that an annual economic growth rate of 3.5 per cent each year is needed to prevent unemployment rising and that to reduce the absolute numbers of unemployed a sustainable growth rate of 7.5 per cent will be necessary. It is hard to see this being attained in the foreseeable future.

Housing

Apartheid's legacy in this field was the grotesque skewing of provision for affordable housing in the towns and cities.

The Group Areas Act, which provided for racial zoning, was responsible for the removal of 745,000 people from their homes. Overwhelmingly these were "coloured" and Indian people, although a few whites were also affected. African freehold rights in

the white areas were largely extinguished. Urban freehold communities and black schools (properties owned and farmed by African smallholders) were with marginal exceptions, eliminated – since it was a core principle of apartheid that freehold rights in white areas were incompatible with Africans' status as members of the various homelands. Some 3.4 million people were forcibly moved as a consequence of these policies.

Apartheid's planners sought vigorously to reinstate the old principle that urban Africans were "temporary sojourners", whose presence was required only to satisfy labour needs. The pass laws (influx control) were greatly tightened and extended to women in an effort to erect barricades against urbanisation. Verwoerd sought to freeze the number of "detribalised" African townspeople and, as far as possible, to require employers to use male African migrants whose labour contracts could not exceed one year. In emulation of the compounds used by the mining industry, barrack-like hostels were to accommodate them.

In furtherance of this policy, calculated measures were adopted to make urban circumstances as unattractive as possible for Africans. A major component of this aspect of policy was the discontinuation of the provision of sub-economic housing (i.e. with subsidised rentals) for urban Africans. As Verwoerd put it with characteristic candour in 1952, every additional house for a non-European means an additional burden to the

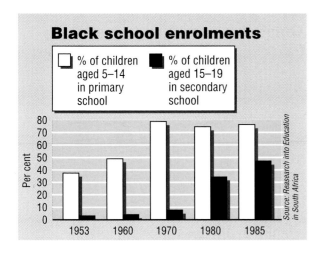

Black school enrolments

- ☐ % of children aged 5–14 in primary school
- ■ % of children aged 15–19 in secondary school

Per cent (y-axis: 0, 10, 20, 30, 40, 50, 60, 70, 80)
Years: 1953, 1960, 1970, 1980, 1985

Source: Reasearch into Education in South Africa

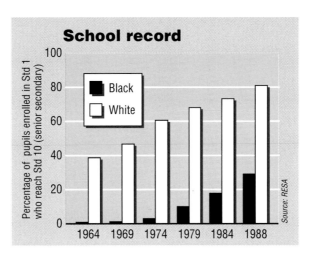

School record

- ■ Black
- ☐ White

Percentage of pupils enrolled in Std 1 who reach Std 10 (senior secondary) (y-axis: 0, 20, 40, 60, 80, 100)
Years: 1964, 1969, 1974, 1979, 1984, 1988

Source: RESA

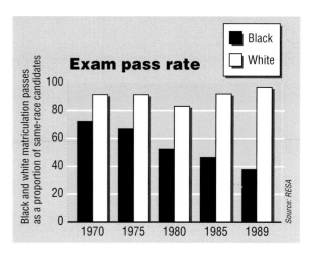

Exam pass rate

- ■ Black
- ☐ White

Black and white matriculation passes as a proportion of same-race candidates (y-axis: 0, 20, 40, 60, 80, 100)
Years: 1970, 1975, 1980, 1985, 1989

Source: RESA

European community. Over the longer term, the consequences were catastrophic. In effect, the provision of houses fell far below the needs. Between 1970 and 1980, only 5,000 were provided for urban Africans, with the result that overcrowding became endemic and informal/squatter settlements arose on the peripheries of all the major cities and towns.

By 1989, at least seven million people were living in such circumstances and, with the abolition of influx control in 1986, the dam walls that checked (but by no means stopped) the flow of rural people into urban areas were breached. Between 1985 and 1991 the population of the metropolitan areas increased by 2.8 million. Projections by the Urban Foundation indicated that between 1990 and the year 2000, 300,000 people each year would move to the urban areas. The magnitude of this shift, combined with population increase, has obvious and daunting implications for the provision of housing, schooling and welfare facilities.

Apartheid's central thrust, to abort the urbanisation of Africans, was a calamitous and costly failure. The legacy has many aspects, but the most pressing of all is housing. According to the minister of national housing, in 1993 there was a backlog of approximately 1.4 million housing units for lower income groups. According to the ANC-sponsored Macro-Economic Research Group's Reconstruction and Development Programme, if rural housing needs and the elimination of the 240 hostels that accommodate over 600,000 people are included, the backlog increases to approximately three million. There is substantial consensus that between 300,000 and 330,000 units will have to be built annually. A coherent programme of housing could also have important multiplier effects in job-creation. There are no legal obstacles to Africans owning houses in freehold, but widespread poverty and high interest rates limit the extent to which they can do so. Approximately one-third of the housing loans granted to Africans by lending agencies are in arrears, involving an amount of R3 billion. Not unreasonably, many financial institutions are wary of the African housing market.

Closely related to the housing shortage are ancillary problems: 23 million people do not have access to electricity; 21 million do not enjoy adequate sanitation; and 12 million do not have easy access to water. Fuel shortages are severe in many areas, with the consequence that many surviving indigenous forests are threatened by the quest for wood.

Health

As one might expect, health standards among white people resemble those in developed countries, whereas those among Africans resemble those in developing countries. Life expectancy for whites is 73 years; for Africans it is 63 (which is a significant improvement on the figure of 45 recorded for 1950). Another critical indicator is infant mortality. According to the minister of national health, in 1992 the infant mortality rate per 1000 live births was 52.8 for Africans and 7.3 for whites.

Preventable diseases associated with poverty remain rife, especially in the rural areas where poverty is direst and medical facilities are most thinly spread. Tuberculosis is the major killer, and there have been reports that up to 35 people die from it each day. There are, however, signs that Acquired Immune Deficiency Syndrome (Aids) will eclipse it. Although fewer than 3,000 Aids cases had been reported by December 1993, the National HIV surveys carried out each year on all women attending antenatal clinics have shown a steep rise since 1990.

In its appalling way, Aids may serve to bring down, if only slightly, a birth-rate that is too high. Among white, "coloured" and Indian people, the birth rate has declined radically; among Africans, however, it remains high — 2.8 per cent per annum for 1991-2. This figure conceals the large difference in fertility rates between rural and urban areas. That urban women produce fewer children is a virtually universal phenomenon. Access to better housing, better health care and lowered infant mortality rates are conducive to reducing the birth rate. Family planning programmes in South Africa were, as a result of foolish appeals by white politicians for white women to produce more babies, seriously compromised by being politicised. It is to be hoped that the new government will use its legitimacy to publicise the need for smaller families.

Present projections show the estimated doubling-time for South Africa's population is a mere 30 years.

The truth is that the country will not have the resources to cope with a population of that size.

No discussion of apartheid's legacy in the field of health can omit reference to the psychological scars left by nearly two decades of intermittent conflict. Combatants on both sides were brutalised. Township children grew up in environments in which violence was "normal". Violent clashes with the security forces were common enough, but endemic criminal violence and family violence (most commonly abuse of women by men) have taken their toll as well. Much has been said of the approximately three million "marginalised youth" (sometimes referred to as the "lost generation"). Many are school drop-outs, unemployed and living hand-to-mouth. They have been "socialised into a political culture of defiance in which all forms of authority have been eroded," says the writer, Steve Mokwena.

One of apartheid's most insidious legacies has been how it deprived individuals of their self-esteem and reduced their capacity to act as self-steering individuals. This was the diagnosis advanced in the 1960s by exponents of Black Consciousness, and it contains much truth. Strategies for dealing with these problems must include the re-establishment of legitimate authority structures, attracting drop-outs back into training systems that will equip them for jobs, and a determined campaign against all forms of violence.

As with so many items on South Africa's want list, a crucial determinant will be whether jobs can be generated. Large-scale efforts at socio-economic improvement are required, not only in accordance with principles of justice and fair play, but also in the interests of social stability. The danger of this approach, however, is that the continued stress on "victim status" and the development of what the African-American author, Shelby Steele, calls "a culture of entitlement" will be wholly inimical to the development of those qualities of self-reliance and self-esteem that are vital to the emotional growth of both individuals and communities. Development that entrenches a dependency complex is worse than useless.

The attitudinal legacy

High levels of race consciousness are certain to endure for many generations. In asserting this, one is not thereby singling out South Africans, and especially white South Africans, as having a unique propensity for racist thinking. Racism, alas, appears to be a universal phenomenon, displayed by Chinese, Japanese, Russians, Europeans and Americans alike. Particular circumstances, like economic recessions, often exacerbate racist sentiment, as has been the case in Germany in recent years. Racism may also vary in its virulence. Of critical importance is the state's ability to prohibit or curb the translation of racist thoughts into racist actions, like violence against minorities, discriminatory hiring practices, and the utterance of racial slurs.

South Africa's principal parties have committed themselves to "non-racialism", and the interim constitution rests squarely on non-racial principles. The issue is whether these admirable goals will resonate with real attitudes within the society. "Non-racialism" may be construed in two ways (that are not mutually exclusive). It may refer to what has been mentioned above, the maintenance of non-discriminatory norms, at least in the public sphere. It may also refer to the attitudinal sphere, implying the extent to which the irrelevance of colour penetrates the consciousness of members of society. How far, in other words, does non-racialism become an attitudinal predisposition that becomes part of the very fabric of society?

Apartheid was notorious for the obscene lengths it went to in deliberately maintaining and heightening race consciousness among whites. Given the long history of racial domination, it was never difficult for Nationalist politicians to whip up racist sentiment — or, for that matter, Afrikaner ethnic sentiment directed against "the English". *Swart gevaar* (black peril) electioneering has a long and disreputable tradition. Apartheid sought also to encourage ethnicity among Africans by emphasising vernacular languages, insisting on "ethnic grouping" in townships, and by creating "homelands" along ethnic lines. On balance these transparent attempts at divide-and-rule are more likely to have caused a backlash against ethnicity than succeeded in raising ethnic consciousness. No homeland leader, with the exception of chief Mangosuthu Buthelezi of

Township children have been brutalised. Clashes with the security forces were common enough, but endemic criminal and family violence have taken their toll as well

KwaZulu, was able to create a mass following, and, again with the exception of Buthelezi's Inkatha Freedom Party (which has claimed not to be an ethnic party), mobilisation along ethnic lines has not occurred. Unlike Zimbabwe, Namibia and other African states, no single African ethnic group commands a majority, a demographic fact that tends to militate against ethnic mobilisation.

The decision by state president FW de Klerk and Nelson Mandela to initiate a negotiating process, whose first stage has culminated in the Interim Constitution, reflected their mutual recognition that the conflict was deadlocked. Perpetuating the conflict could mean only intensified violence and further economic decline. The ANC and the NP government approach each other with profound suspicions that have by no means been allayed. Both, however, accepted that a degree of co-operation was necessary to carry the process forward, and both acknowledge that South Africa is too volatile and complex a society to be governed by a single party, especially in view of the heavy domination of the upper echelons of the bureaucracy, army and police by whites and the dependence of the private sector on white skills and capital.

South Africa, in other words, is likely to be held together by a strong sense of interracial interdependence, even mutual deterrence, more than by a flowering of attitudinal non-racialism. The ANC's strong commitment to non-racialism, however, deserves note. The severity of racial conflict

might have caused it to embrace a form of counter-racism, which runs deep in its rival, the Pan Africanist Congress.

At the elite level, South Africa has come surprisingly far in developing what is widely termed a "culture of negotiation". This phenomenon owes something to the pioneering efforts in the 1970s of business and the trade unions to regulate a potentially confrontational style of industrial relations. Politicians, too, have been on a steep learning curve during the arduous negotiating process. Even greater skills will be required to keep the multi-party Government of National Unity on an even keel by avoiding paralysis and providing effective government.

A high degree of racial polarisation in party preferences will still be prevalent. This means that very few whites (2 per cent perhaps) support the ANC, and, conversely, very few Africans support the NP or the largely white Democratic Party. A much wider spread of opinions occurs among the intermediate "coloured" and Indian categories. Many "coloured" and Indian people find themselves in the classic bind of vulnerable minorities, fearing the power of the African majority, but hesitant about supporting the NP whose Group Areas Act destroyed so many of their communities.

Few, if any, multi-racial or multi-ethnic societies have been able to generate that overarching sense of political community that creates the nation state, in its true sense. South Africa is likely to remain a

deeply divided society whose integrity will have to be ensured by the real, if fragile, bonds of interdependence and a sense of shared fate. The leaders of the new government, especially those of the ANC, which will be the biggest component, will have to display political skills of the highest order in simultaneously diffusing hope, as well as visible gains, to an impatient constituency, while refraining from riding roughshod over minority interests.

The axiom that "a rising tide lifts all ships" is appropriate. Poverty sharpens the cutting edge of conflict. Steady economic growth, more widely diffused prosperity, and the elimination of the brutalising and alienating conditions in the townships must be South Africa's priorities. Legitimate government is a necessary, though not sufficient, condition for tackling these challenges with some hope of success. The stakes are high, and South Africa's political leaders know it.

Dr Welsh is professor of South African history at the University of Cape Town

David Welsh expresses grateful thanks to Virginia van der Vliet. Acknowledgement is made to the following sources of data: SA Institute of Race Relations: Race Relations Survey, 1991–2 and 1992–3. South African Communication Service: Policy Review RSA (1992 and 1993 issues). Ministry of Finance: The Key Issues in the Normative Economic Model (March 1993). David Everatt and Elinor Sisulu (eds.) Black Youth in Crisis (Johannesburg: Ravan Press, 1992). Dept. of National Health and Population Development, Epidemiological Comments Vol. 20, No. 11, November 1993.

South Africa's policy of destabilisating neighbouring countries which did not agree with it cost the region $100 billion, nearly a third of that was in military expenditure. Millions of lives were also lost

The regional legacy/Victoria Brittain

THE LAST two decades of apartheid saw the nine neighbouring countries of Southern Africa at war with the apartheid state as Pretoria tried to use them in defence of the status quo. With its formidable propaganda apparatus, and the aid of its Western allies, the South African government was able to wage its semi-secret war of destabilisation largely ignored outside the region.

In the 1980s Pretoria invaded three capitals (Lesotho, Botswana, Mozambique) and four other countries (Angola, Swaziland, Zimbabwe, and Zambia); tried to assassinate two prime ministers (Lesotho and Zimbabwe); backed rebel groups in two countries (Angola and Mozambique) and disorder on a smaller scale to two others (Zimbabwe and Lesotho); disrupted the oil supplies of six countries (Angola, Botswana, Lesotho, Malawi, Mozambique and Zimbabwe); and attacked the railways providing the import and export routes of seven countries (Angola, Botswana, Malawi, Mozambique, Swaziland, Zambia, Zimbabwe). Twelve years of this destabilisation cost the region $100 billion, according to official estimates. Nearly a third of that was in additional military expenditure. The rest was the cost of direct war damage, on dams, bridges, factories etc, plus the losses from diamonds; semi-precious stones; timber; ivory from 10,000 or more elephants smuggled out through South Africa; the bill for hundreds of thousands of refugees; and loss of production and development as the countries' energies were diverted into defence and vast areas of

farming land were rendered unusable by the laying of tens of thousands of mines. The people of the region have paid an incalculable price for ending apartheid – the price of the first post-independence generation's lost hopes of development. The highest price of all was paid in Angola and Mozambique. These were the key targets for political assassination and South African-sponsored, and often South African-led, terror attacks on civilian centres by what began as proxy armies for South Africa — Unita in Angola and Renamo in Mozambique. In the 1980s a million people died in Mozambique and 500,000 in Angola, according to UN figures.

The legacy in those two countries today is a virtually collapsed state; slender prospects of rebuilding a strong and coherent government in the aftermath of an unfinished electoral process, where the proxy armies have been made equal political partners; the imposed reversal of the populations' political choices made before independence 20 years ago; and, in the case of Angola, half a million more deaths in the last 18 months, courtesy of Jonas Savimbi, South Africa's trump card during its 20 years of destructive policies.

The roots of this disaster sprang from 1975, when Angola and Mozambique became independent from Portugal. For white South Africa, a close ally of Portugal, that moment was a traumatic end to the safety of its white-ruled security cordon. This had kept South Africa, and illegally occupied Namibia, apart from black Africa, which was dominated from

the 1960s by nationalist and socialist ideals. Encouraged by the United States, South Africa made an initial attempt to hold on to its influence in Angola. It launched a full-scale invasion of the country in 1975 to seize the capital, Luanda, and pre-empt the declaration of independence by the Popular Movement for the Independence of Angola (MPLA). Stopped by Cuban troops brought halfway across the world to defend the MPLA in Luanda, the South Africans retreated into Namibia, and began the transformation of the CIA's client movement, Savimbi's Unita.

Henry Kissinger, in a meeting at the State Department in December 1975, put the Cold War case for a policy in Angola which dovetailed with South Africa's own preoccupations. "I don't care about the oil or the base, but I do care about the African reaction when they see the Soviets pull it off and we don't do anything. If the Europeans then say to themselves, 'If they can't hold Luanda, how can they defend Europe?' The Chinese will say we're a country that was run out of Indochina for 50,000 men and is now being run out of Angola for less than $50 million," he said.

The liberation movements' wars against Portugal, itself supported by the West, had been helped with training and arms from the Soviet Union as well as by radical states like Algeria and Cuba.

In reaction to the Portuguese collapse, and before the new states could consolidate themselves, South Africa's politicians and generals in the late 1970s

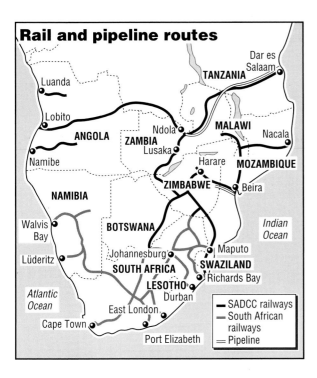

Rail and pipeline routes

Luanda · Lobito · **ANGOLA** · Namibe · **NAMIBIA** · Walvis Bay · Lüderitz · *Atlantic Ocean* · Cape Town · Port Elizabeth · East London · **SOUTH AFRICA** · Johannesburg · **BOTSWANA** · **LESOTHO** · Durban · Richards Bay · Maputo · **SWAZILAND** · **ZIMBABWE** · Harare · Beira · **MOZAMBIQUE** · Nacala · **MALAWI** · Ndola · Lusaka · **ZAMBIA** · Dar es Salaam · **TANZANIA** · *Indian Ocean*

— SADCC railways
— South African railways
= Pipeline

devised a "total strategy" to deal with what they labelled a Soviet-inspired plot to overthrow white rule. Total Strategy was a mix of diplomatic, military and economic actions, targeted differently on each of the nine countries of the region. P W Botha, the former defence minister who became prime minister in 1978, spelt out the imperative as he saw it. "The ultimate aim of the Soviet Union and its allies is to overthrow the present body politic in South Africa and to replace it with a Marxist-oriented form of government to further the objectives of the USSR."

The South African government saw all Southern Africa as a key strategic target for the Soviet Union and believed that – following Russia's success in backing independence movements in Angola and Mozambique – its influence was spreading to Zimbabwe, Botswana and Lesotho and into South Africa itself through support for the African National Congress and the South African Communist Party.

In fact the influence of the Soviet Union was not great in any of these countries, though its supplies of arms for defence against South Africa, and generous aid in education and training, filled a vacuum created by the myopic world view represented by Kissinger and embraced by the South Africans. Foreign minister Pik Botha, for instance, warned that "like creeping lava and suffocating gas … the menacing hegemony of Russia is spreading over this planet".

Although only the US administrations openly responded in taking sides in this undeclared corner of the Cold War, most of Western Europe effectively accepted the logic of the South African position and ignored its devastating war against the front-line states.

In fact it was the nationalist victories themselves, in Angola and Mozambique in 1975, and in Zimbabwe in 1980, which had immense impact in South Africa. They gave both a psychological boost to the anti-apartheid movement inside South Africa, and opened new possibilities for armed resistance from bases outside the country by the thousands of young activists who fled the apartheid regime.

Angola, for one, gave bases for training, as did Tanzania, and later Uganda. Military activity took place across the region from Mozambique, Zimbabwe, Swaziland and Lesotho. The Zambian capital, Lusaka, was home to the ANC's headquarters. One key goal of destabilisation was to deter the newly independent states from allowing the ANC to operate from their territories.

A second goal for Pretoria was to undermine the possibility of the frontline states establishing an alternative grid of regional economic activity, through the newly set up Southern Africa Development Co-ordinating Conference, which could challenge South Africa's historical dominance.

The third goal behind the covert policy of aggression was to ensure failure of the multi-racial, socialist leadership in Angola and Mozambique as an ideological lesson to South Africans of the dire consequences of a similar political path. The Reagan administration introduced two diplomatic concepts which were key to the success of South Africa's strategy. The first was "constructive engagement", which reversed Jimmy Carter's line of isolating South Africa and instead sought to encourage change in the apartheid system from within the regime itself. The second was "linkage" which tied the UN's demand for an end to Pretoria's illegal occupation of Namibia to the entirely separate issue of the Cuban forces defending Angola from South Africa's repeated incursions. South Africa's generals saw constructive engagement as a kind of licence to attack its neighbours after their first cross-border attack, on the Mozambique capital of Maputo 10 days after Reagan took office, went uncensured by the US. As for linkage, initially rejected outright by most countries, the US finally forced its acceptance by the international community and even a reluctant Angola, thus succeeding in getting both the Cubans and the ANC military camps out of Angola. The scene was set for the new balance of forces in the country in which South Africa's ally, Unita, had unprecedented military and political leverage.

Destabilisation of the region was a highly effective policy for the apartheid regime in South Africa. It changed the regional political context so that by the time majority rule was inevitable the democratic movement was prepared to cede a transition on terms which were considerably more favourable to the former rulers than anyone would have forecast a decade earlier.

Victoria Brittain is the Guardian's Africa Editor

Soweto hostel dweller Isaac Zondo takes leave of his wife after spending the weekend at home in KwaZulu. Families had to seperate to survive under apartheid which aimed to turn the black workforce into migrant labourers

GIDEON MENDEL/MAGNUM

Section 2

Apartheid was not simply a more severe form of racism. The ideological necessity to determine status according to race was pursued to its grotesque, but logical, conclusion. The crucial pieces of legislation which cemented the apartheid system into South African society were passed within just two years of the National Party's victory in the 1948 election

The pillars of apartheid/Michael Stent

THEY CAME straggling off the farms: families defeated by drought, primitive agricultural methods and limited markets; young men and women for whom there was no space on the family farm and no work in the villages; others lured by gold, diamonds and dreams of wealth. They came to the towns, first Kimberley and later those on the Witwatersrand, in search of work in the mines and the young industries growing up around them. They found they had neither the education nor the skills to cope in urban society. These migrant Afrikaners found disillusionment, poverty and despair. So began the process which would result in apartheid.

The brief period after diamonds were discovered in South Africa in 1866, and gold about 20 years later, was the defining era of modern Afrikaner nationalism. The symbols and mythology would come from different events — the Great Trek, the time spent trying to carve a living in the interior of a hostile continent, the Boer wars. But the political and economic dynamics that shaped South Africa in the second half of the 20th century derived from this early clash between a pastoral society and the discovery of great mineral wealth.

It became a three-cornered struggle. Economic power was held by English-speakers, mine owners such as Cecil Rhodes, who were fiercely loyal to the Empire. They struggled with the Boer republics and ultimately overcame them. After Union in 1910, the Empire and the mining houses were joined by some of the Boer leaders. Pre-eminent among these was Jan Smuts, who served in the British war cabinets in both world wars and was a founder of both the League of Nations and the United Nations.

Many Afrikaners, though, were excluded from this arrangement. They were the "poor whites", a traumatised and uprooted working class who found themselves competing with black workers and losing. It mattered not that they were God's chosen people nor even that they were white. The realities of urban life pitted them against the burgeoning black proletariat, and they felt the political and economic elite did little to protect them in this struggle.

While Afrikaners were facing new and difficult realities, black South Africans, the third side of the triangle, were being forced off the land. The imposition of

taxes, for example, compelled subsistence farmers with no access to cash markets to go to white farms and towns to earn wages. The urban confrontation peaked with the Rand revolt in the early 1920s, when white workers and the state clashed violently over the issue of Chinese and black mineworkers. It was a short, but brutal, conflict and the state and mine owners won. But the employment colour bar was further entrenched as the price of peace. Nevertheless, the Afrikaners' twin fears of being assimilated by the English and swamped by the black masses persisted. All the elements that would distinguish apartheid were in place before the second world war, but they were within the kind of state segregation which applied throughout the Empire and, indeed, persisted in the southern United States of America well into the 1960s. The principal debate within Afrikanerdom was how much to compromise with the English and the Empire.

There was an implicit belief that black people were inferior beings and did not enter the political equation except at its very margins. They were to be controlled and used as cheap labour. "Native" policy, such as it was, was geared to those ends.

A new political generation was stirring, however — intellectuals who looked to the Netherlands and Germany for theological, philosophical and political inspiration. Unlike the old elite, which intended to hold black people in an inferior position within a common society, they aspired to an exclusively white society. One of their leaders was Nico Diederichs, later to become finance minister and state president. Like many of his generation, he studied in Germany in the 1930s.

The Third Reich inspired these young Afrikaner leaders and its philosophy gave voice to their instincts about nation, race and destiny. On his return to South Africa in 1935, Diederichs wrote a pamphlet called Nationalism As A Philosophy Of Life And Its Relation To Internationalism, which is quoted in Allister Sparks's outstanding book, The Mind Of South Africa. In it, he praised the concept of nation: "God willed that . . . at the human level, there should be a multiplicity and diversity of nations, languages and cultures . . . and just as it would be a violation of God's natural law to try to reduce all colours to one colour and all sounds to one sound, everything in nature to one dull monotony, so it is just as much of a

The apartheid laws

Passed		Repealed

1949 — **Prohibition of Mixed Marriages Act** — **1986**
Imposed a ban on marriages between white and other races, and nullified mixed marriages entered into by South Africans abroad.

1950 — **The Immorality Amendment Act** — **1986**
Extended the 1927 Immorality Act, to make all sexual relations between white and other races illegal.

1950 — **Population Registration Act** — **1991**
Entered the entire population on a central register and classified it as either White, Native or Coloured. Coloured people were subdivided into ethnic groups including Indian, Griqua, Cape Malay and Chinese.

1950 — **Suppression of Communism Act** — **1990**
Practically any person or organisation hostile to government policy could be defined as Communist and banned by the government. There was no right of appeal.

1950 — **The Group Areas Act** — **1991**
Gave the government powers to segregate the entire country by allocating separate areas to the different population groups. To implement this policy, the Act provided for forced removal and resettlement.

1952 — **Natives (Abolition of Passes and Co-ordination of Documents) Act** — **1986**
All black people over the age of 16 were required to carry a passbook and present it to police on demand. Apart from personal details, the book contained information on employment, poll tax and influx control.

1953 — **Separate Amenities Act** — **1990**
Provided for separate amenities for white and non-white races in all public places and vehicles. It also stipulated that separate amenities need not be of equal quality.

1953 — **Bantu Education Act** — **1991**
Set down rules governing the curriculum for black education — a limited curriculum for black students. The Minister for Native Affairs could close black schools not adhering to this curriculum.

1959 — **Extension of University Education Act** — **1988**
Excluded all other races from white universites and established five "ethnic" universities.

1959 — **Promotion of Bantu Self-Government Act** — **1994**
Established the plan to transform the black reserves into self-governing homelands.

1970 — **Bantu Homelands Citizenship Act** — **1994**
All black South Africans were to become citizens of the tribal homelands, irrespective of whether they had ever lived there. They would then be regarded as aliens in South Africa.

Picture: JÜRGEN SCHADEBERG

desecration of His law to want to destroy the multiplicity of nations in the world for the sake of a monochromatic, monotonous and monolithic humanity."

This was a prelude to a much darker agenda. Among this multiplicity of nations, there was a hierarchy, and in South Africa, Afrikaners should, and would, occupy the highest place. The ad hoc racism and pragmatic segregation of the Smuts generation would not do. The new Afrikaner nationalists demanded a complete separation under Afrikaner domination. Beneath all the philosophical flummery, a simple and brutal four-pronged policy lay in wait: define them; separate them; put them in their stratified place; and keep them there.

The new generation had several years and a war to endure before they had the opportunity to put their plans into practice. For the "pure" Afrikaner nationalists, led by D F Malan, the war represented a breathtaking opportunity. They were in little doubt that Germany would win, the Empire and Commonwealth would disintegrate, and they would reach an amicable agreement with the triumphant Reich. But, as happened frequently throughout Afrikaner history, entropy set in.

Ranged to the right of Malan's National Party were several organisations, more or less overtly fascist and committed to German victory. The most powerful of these was the *Ossewa-Brandwag* (loosely, Ox-Wagon Sentinels), a paramilitary organisation which attracted people such as the future prime minister, B J Vorster, and indulged in sabotage. Thus a divided Afrikanerdom saw out the war, jockeying for position and seeking to be in the right place when Germany's inevitable victory came. Pre-eminent among these political street-fighters was Malan, and by the time Britain and its allies finally prevailed against the inevitable, he was the undisputed leader of the nationalist movement.

Despite its inherent suspicion of "British-Jewish democracy", the National Party prepared with vigour for the 1948 election and a new word entered the political lexicon — apartheid.

Against all expectations, the National Party won enough seats in 1948 to form a coalition government with the now mightily-shrunken Afrikaner Party, which had split with Smuts at the outset of the war. Malan became prime minister and launched his policy on a largely unsuspecting country and world. Many people

Victims of forced removals under the Group Areas Act
Sophiatown, Johannesburg, 1955

Fined for going into restaurant

From our Correspondent
Johannesburg

JOSEPH Mosoeu, a 27-year-old African, was today found guilty of contravening the Group Areas Act and fined £30. The case arose out of an attempt by a mixed party to break the colour bar by entering a restaurant in the city centre and asking for service.

29.3.61

Jewish MPs are jeered

From our Correspondent, Cape Town

A JEWISH Opposition MP, Mr Alec Gorshel, told jeering Nationalist members to "go to hell" as baiting of Jewish MPs reached a new intensity in the House of Assembly here today.

Amid derisive laughter from the Nationalist ranks, Mr Gorshel, a former Mayor of Johannesburg, had been strongly protesting against the references to his "race" and to the dragging in of arguments about Israel in dealing with Opposition Jewish members' objections to the drastic Bantu Laws Amendment Bill. When two other Jewish members, Mr Hymie Miller (United Party) and Mrs Helen Suzman (Progressive Party) rose together to catch the Speaker's eye, the Nationalist members called out again, "Look how the Jews are getting up."

19.3.64

Casualty of apartheid

A WHITE man critically injured in a car accident lay on the road for an hour and a half last night because an ambulance which arrived on the scene was for non-whites only and went away empty.

He was eventually taken in an ambulance for whites.

2.8.67

Only blacked out

From STANLEY UYS

THE WORD "Only" is to be removed from "White Persons Only" notice boards in South Africa. This change will give apartheid a kindlier appearance, it is thought.

"We are not just going to paint out the word 'Only'," said a spokesman of the Department of Public Works. "Our department does not approve of shoddy workmanship of this kind. We will rather make new boards in the course of time, as the existing boards become old and ugly." The decision to change the apartheid notice boards was taken by the Cabinet, according to a pro-Government newspaper. "The new boards will give less offence to non-whites," it says. "The world 'Only' indicated exclusivity, and this was grist to the mill of the Government's critics. It was exploited particularly in photographs sent overseas."

23.1.69

Baby without a name or a race

Johannesburg

WELFARE authorities at Vereeniging are caring for a baby that not only has no name and no known parents or home but does not even belong with certainty to any particular racial group — an important factor in this racially segregated country.

A few days ago the baby, a boy, was left, wrapped up in what looked like just a bundle, by an African woman in a rural shop near Vereeniging, 36 miles from Johannesburg. He was taken to hospital, where doctors tried to determine his race. After checking his gum and tooth structure, eye colour, and hair texture, they decided that, provisionally at least, he was white.

There have already been inquiries from local white families who would like to adopt him. But there is another, and unmentioned, aspect of the case which would make this difficult; time may show that he is not white but a half-caste.

25.2.67

Chinese puzzle at S. Africa racecourse

CHINESE race-goers have been barred from entering the members' enclosure at the exclusive Turffontein race course here, after years of being admitted without question.

This is the latest controversial decision affecting Johannesburg's Chinese community of about two thousand which lives a puzzling "half-white, half-nonwhite" existence under South Africa's racial laws.

The restriction on Chinese entering the member's enclosure at Turffontein was imposed last month when the Turf Club decided that it must obey the Government's proclamation of February 11 restricting racially mixed audiences.

A leading member of the Chinese community said: "It is increasingly difficult for us Chinese in South Africa to know just where we stand. How much better it would be, in a way, if we were Japanese."

The few Japanese in Johannesburg, mostly non-resident business men, are classified to all intents and purposes as "honorary whites." Chinese, even if born in South Africa, are not classified as South Africans or even nonwhites on the population register but as "Chinese."

Under the Electoral Act, they are treated as nonwhites and therefore have no vote.

Under the country's Immorality Act, which prohibits sexual intercourse between people from different race-groups, they are officially classified as nonwhites.

But they are classed as whites on public transport and are given beds in white hospitals.

14.9.65

Picture: facing page ROGER OMOND

'Each of these pieces of legislation might have been comic had it not been for the enormous suffering, disruption and degradation they also brought'

thought apartheid was merely an electioneering slogan, an evocation of the *swart gevaar* (black peril) to gain votes, and that normal pragmatic business would then resume.

Not so. Although hampered by dependence on their coalition partner, Malan and his team began to lay the foundations. The first target was to secure a more compliant electorate. Indians, who had been granted a limited franchise in Natal in 1946 (although they had not been able to exercise it in the 1948 election), were removed from the voters' roll. Stricter conditions were imposed on "coloured" voters in the Cape, so that the 50,000 who voted in 1948 became 20,000 in 1958 (when they lost the vote altogether).

In 1949, marriages between people of different races were banned and the regulations governing the movement of Africans to the cities were strengthened. The following year the main pillars of apartheid started to go up. The first was the Population Register. Everyone was obliged to be classified according to race; how they were defined would then affect every aspect of their lives.

Once classified, they were then separated. The Group Areas Act formalised the existence of separate areas for each racial group and started the process that would uproot and move hundreds of thousands of people from their homes to ideologically-determined areas. After the ban on mixed marriages came the prohibition of sex across the colour line, the Immorality Act.

Each of these pieces of legislation might have been comic had it not been for the enormous suffering, disruption and degradation they also brought. Squads of officials checked the structure of peoples' hair, their nose shapes or the colour of their fingernails to reach a decision that would determine where they could live, how they would be educated, what medical care they would receive, what jobs they could do, who they could sleep with, who they could marry, even where they could be buried. Families were shattered when these pseudo-scientists decided a child was "coloured" and her parents white; a husband this, his wife that. Police raided rooms and pounced upon cars in lonely backwoods to prevent and punish racially-incorrect copulation.

One pillar remained unbuilt and it, too, went up in 1950. The Suppression of

Facing page top: **During the Defiance Campaign of the late 1950s, black activists protested against the pass laws by burning their passes. Among them was Nelson Mandela (top centre)**

White man's justice

by Mary Benson

According to the latest available figures, in South Africa during the twelve months ending June 30, 1966, 479,114 Africans were prosecuted for offences against the pass laws. Nine years ago this week, members of the Pan-Africanist Congress protested at Sharpeville against the pass laws, by attempting to hand in their passes to the police station. The police shot into the crowd. Sixty-nine people were killed, and 180 people were wounded. This article is from a forthcoming book by a South African

AFTER A hot afternoon in down-town Johannesburg we were driving home. With sunset the air had cooled and we began to breathe again. Ahead of us appeared a looming huddle of men . . . four black men handcuffed together and, with them, two policemen. I glimpsed one face in close-up, raw-boned, desperate, then a policeman grabbed him and shook him like a bundle.

"Charlie!" shouted Jake, "Ma, they've got Charlie!"

There was a moment's pandemonium among the children with us before Shulamuth stopped the car, told us to wait, got out and slammed the door. The kids were peering from the windows as she hurried, half-stumbling, towards the group. A pick-up van was pulling up, she was remonstrating, a policeman's voice rose: "No use, lady, he's under arrest . . ." And her low voice sounded: "But he told you, his pass is in his room, we're just outside the gate." "Lady, there's nothing I can do . . . normal procedure . . ." The men were being jostled into the van, locked in, driven away.

Then Shulamuth came back to us and told the children it was nothing serious, that Charlie had left his pass again and she would have to bail him out. There was nothing to worry about . . . While I wondered: those huddled men, the raw-boned face, was there ever a time when it had not happened? — policemen accosting, interrogating, demanding passes, handcuffing, hustling off — there must have been a time surely. . . No, I could not recall . . .

Next morning Shulamuth and I sat on the public bench in the dingy courtroom. We could see the cage outside crowded with Africans; there was a conspicuous lack of laughter.

A white-haired, bland man entered the court: the Bantu Commissioner. For whom we rose. A black interpreter lounged against the dock. Two or three petty officials sat about. No one appeared to notice us, yet we had the sense of being observed.

Shulamuth's purple velvet toque was calculated to intimidate the toughest official, so she had said before we set out, when I had gazed transfixed. Then when my eyes met hers, we had collapsed in helpless giggles. Now the sight of it left me dull.

An order was given and from the cage came a tall unshaven man . . . Number One, accused of altering a date in his "reference" book. The Commissioner asks: "Guilty or not guilty?" The man says earnestly that when he was discharged from his job his master wrote the wrong date in his pass book; he therefore corrected it.

"A serious matter" says the Commissioner, looking bored. "Two rand or seven days." Thump of a rubber stamp.

Number Two is in the dock. Thin, raggedly dressed, sullen, holding an obstreperous orange hat. He says he has lost his book. "Sixteen rand or eight weeks." Thump. An aggressive-looking man; behind his defiance, apprehension. Numbers Four, Five, Six. How long for each trial? One minute? Two? . . .

When I was a child in Pretoria, when the rest of the family were out or too busy, from the time I could write well enough Amos and Cornelius would come to me: "Can I have a night-pass, please nonnie?" Then I would spell out on a piece of paper "Please pass native Amos," adding the curfew time, our address, the date. And would sign my name.

Number 13 is in the dock, a boy, very frightened. He says something timidly, is told to speak up. "I was working in the school holidays." He bows humbly. He is under 16. He goes free.

A booklet — scraps of paper — what is your name? Who is your boss? Have you paid your taxes? A word, a figure out of place? It is not in your pocket? Ten rand or five weeks. Sixteen rand, eight weeks. In gaol, a criminal, striped vest and shorts, head shaven, barefoot. Humiliate. Degrade. Emasculate. Thump of rubber stamp. Women as well — "Two rand, seven days." The children? That's their look-out. Their mothers shouldn't be so careless.

"Kaffermaid, waar's jeu pas?" God almighty! And we a part of it, sitting here, witnessing, pitying, feeling brave for having come. Patronise. Emasculate. Never had I felt so white; so middle-class, so "privileged," so guilty. Sharpeville, this is what they protested about, those men, those women, those children.

Number 25: very young, shabby. "Guilty or not guilty?" He fumbles in his pocket, brings out the booklet. The police had not asked for it. "Case withdrawn."

Number 30. Charlie! He does not see Shulamuth, being wholly intent on the process. A good-looking young man, usually cocky. Now uneasy. Shulamuth is smiling brightly, I find I am, too. Cheer up, Charlie, your madam and her chum have come to rescue you!

Forgot his pass in his room, went a few hundred yards to the shops, was rounded up on his way back, he told the police but they would not . . . "Ten rand or five weeks."

As he turns to leave the dock he sees us, Shulamuth nods hard, we go at once to the office to pay the ten rand.

Outside again we did not speak, only cast off our respectable headgear.

24.3.69

Communism Act, apart from banning its obvious target, the South African Communist Party, defined the offence of Communism so widely that virtually all dissent could fall within its reach. It provided for detention without trial; "listing" people as Communists; and banning, which confined people to particular areas and restricted their activities. It was the first weapon in an arsenal that would expand over the years, and the government was not loath to use it.

Thus, within only two years of being elected, and despite the restraining influence of the Afrikaner Party, Malan had instituted the key elements of a policy his loyalists had been dreaming about for years.

In 1951, the National Party lost its dependence on the Afrikaner Party and its programme gathered speed. The advisory Native Representative Council was abolished, although it had already ceased to function because of a boycott by its ANC majority. Local councils, nominated by the government, took its place. In these was the germ of the "homelands" policy, as the black population began to be defined not as a homogenous mass, but in far smaller, more malleable groups. "Coloured" people were also removed from the common voters' roll, although the Appeal Court vetoed this. This heralded a long and bitter fight in which the judiciary sought to maintain its independence. Parliament struck back the following year by asserting its right to overrule the Appeal Court.

In 1952, the party's chief ideologue and Native Affairs Minister, Hendrik Verwoerd, introduced the Native Laws Amendment Act, which severely limited the right of black people to live in urban areas. Permanent urban residence was restricted to those who had been born there, lived there continuously for 15 years, or who had worked for one employer for 10 years. The others, and of course there were hundreds of thousands, were expected to return to their putative homelands, from whence they could offer themselves as migrant labourers on a fixed contract. Marriage was no protection and the provisions applied equally to men and women. All these details had to be entered in a "pass book" which all black people had to carry at all times.

Of course the "homelands" were home to very few of the victims of this policy. They were small, over-populated, poverty-stricken, barren bits of land that could

Mr de Wet, the magistrate in the Blacking case
(see cutting left), peering through a bedroom window
of the professor's house to check evidence of whether he
was having sex with Dr Desai

Anguish as daughter declared 'Coloured'

A DISTRAUGHT white South African couple whose 11-year-old daughter has been classified as Coloured and been forced to leave a boarding school for whites are to appeal to the Government against the decision.

The girl, Sandra Laing, is a genetical throwback. She is clearly Coloured in appearance, with her African traits overwhelming her white ones. "What do I have to do to keep our daughter? Will we have to register her as a servant to keep her with us?" her father, asked reporters.

13.12.66

Couple's 'guilt'

A WHITE university professor and an Indian woman doctor each received suspended sentences of four months' imprisonment in the Johannesburg magistrates' court today for "conspiring to commit intercourse."

Professor John Anthony Randall Blacking (40), professor of social anthropology at the University of the Witwatersrand, and Dr Zureena Desai (24), were convicted under the Immorality Act which prohibits sexual relations between whites and non-whites. The magistrate said that suspended sentences were appropriate. The evidence against Blacking and Desai was mainly circumstantial.

Four policemen had testified to peering through windows of Blacking's house and seeing the couple "caressing and kissing." Later, said the magistrate, they were seen getting into bed.

The magistrate said that taking into account that Blacking's wife and children were away in Natal on holiday, he could come to no other conclusion than that there was a concurrence of purpose between them. At a previous hearing police had said that they found Blacking and Desai in night attire when they entered Blacking's house. The couple were taken for a medical examination but tests were negative, a medical witness had said.

At their previous appearance Blacking had declared: "We have been made to look like criminals for what is not a crime in another country.

"I cannot avoid the conclusion that we are in the dock because our relationship has contradicted certain theories on race and culture by showing that a beautiful relationship can exist between people of different colours, raised in different cultural environments."

There was nothing surreptitious or sordid about his relationship with Desai. A relationship between a man and a woman concerned them alone and perhaps those close to them, he added.

10.4.69

The blacks and the bees

The other South Africa – JONATHAN STEELE reports

TEN O'CLOCK in the evening. We are sitting in the front room of a house in Brakpan, a smallish, mainly Afrikaans town on the East Rand, a few miles from Johannesburg. Suddenly the stillness is shattered by the ugly wail of a wartime air-raid siren. "Oh, it's just the curfew," I'm told. "All non-whites must be off the street by 10 pm."

What happens in Brakpan happens in many other towns as well. They sometimes tell you apartheid is invisible. You'll soon get used to it. You won't notice after a time.

It's true that one "Whites only" sign looks much like another. And since you expect to see them in South Africa, there's no real feeling of shock. But what is extraordinary is the way the signs pop up in the most absurd places, the way apartheid and apartheid attitudes are all-pervasive.

Can you really overlook apartheid when you pick up a newspaper and read of a man who was stung so "black" by a swarm of bees that he was taken to a hospital for non-whites? Embarrassed doctors discovered the mistake and had him hurriedly transferred.

Apartheid signs are going up in places where they never were before. In a Post Office in Queenstown in the Eastern Cape I saw two shelves by a wall, where one might write one's envelopes, or stick on stamps. They were not more than three feet apart, but one was marked "White," the other "non-White." At Cape Town railway station, they've put up a new sign above a hatch which reads incredibly, "Forwarded baggage for whites tendered by non-whites."

There are apartheid signs on some of the beaches now. In Cape Town the Coloureds are allowed to swim off the rocks. The buses in Cape Town have now, since December, come into line with the rest of the country. The old system whereby whites and non-whites sat in the same bus but on a different set of seats has been "rationalised." There are now separate buses.

Probably the last integrated public transport facility in the whole of South Africa is the cable car that takes you up Table Mountain. Perhaps I shouldn't mention that. Foreign journalists are sometimes told not to report things like that in case the Government decides to close them down. But with the cable car there would, to put it mildly, be considerable engineering difficulties in providing a separate non-white cable. In any case the company needs the non-white market.

What you can't help noticing are the people. People working in other people's houses for a pittance of a wage. People living in outhouses in the garden, or in a string of little servants' boxrooms on top of a large block of luxury flats (what they call "locations in the sky"). People on foot on a hot road in the country walking from nowhere to nowhere, a suitcase on their head. Tired people. Unpeople.

They can take down every apartheid sign in the country, instead of putting more and more of them up, as they are doing now. But it will not end white supremacy.

Barring a sprinkling of lone voices, the white electorate, Afrikaans- and English-speaking, is more united in favour of white supremacy than ever before. That's another thing you can't help noticing.

4.3.70

not support anything like the population which was meant to live in them. Black people inevitably sought to stay in the urban areas where they could find work, schools, doctors and homes. And, equally obviously, yet more squads of officials were deployed to ensure these "illegals" were rooted out. The pass laws thus touched every black family and, within a few years, more than half-a-million people a year were being arrested for "pass" offences.

Verwoerd's second coup was the introduction in 1953 of a black education policy to replace the previous ad hoc approach. Black people, said Verwoerd, had a predetermined station in life, and the education system should reflect this: "Racial relations cannot improve if the wrong type of education is given to natives . . . if the result of native education is the creation of frustrated people who . . . have expectations in life which circumstances in South Africa do not allow to be fulfilled immediately." It was, in short, a policy to train people for positions of inferiority.

Malan, having laid the foundations of apartheid, retired and was succeeded by Johannes Strijdom, the "Lion of the North". Fierce he might have been, cunning he certainly was not. His fours years as prime minister were distinguished by the bludgeoning of the courts into submission over the issue of "coloured" voters. He expanded the Appeal Court with his nominees and enlarged the Senate to guarantee the National Party a two-thirds majority in both houses.

The ideologues wanted more, and Verwoerd, their champion, took over in 1958. Henceforth, the logic of apartheid would prevail. The "homelands" policy was gathering pace, and legislation the following year provided for limited self-government in the reserves. The grossly misnamed Extension of Universities Act was also passed in 1959, barring black students from "white" universities. The feebleness of the white opposition encouraged Verwoerd to pursue another cherished dream of nationalism: the creation of a republic.

The British prime minister Harold Macmillan had identified the wind of change blowing through Africa, a wind which Britain had little inclination to resist. What he seemed to have overlooked, however, was that the same spirit of anti-imperialism was thriving in white South Africa. Macmillan's famous address to parliament in Cape Town on February 3 1960 sounded like an appeal to fellow

A 'vicious' Act

From STANLEY UYS in Cape Town

Last year 511 people were convicted under South Africa's Immorality Act which prohibits sex relations between whites and non-whites. This is 100 more than in 1966.

"Thus sentences under the Immorality Act are in no way proving a deterrent," comments Dr van Niekerk, senior lecturer in law at the University of the Witwatersrand, Johannesburg. He believes that the "vicious" Act should be abolished or drastically amended, because it is helping to bring the whole administration of justice into disrepute.

The Act was introduced by the Nationalist Government in 1951 to halt miscegenation and to emphasise the boundary between whites and non-whites. The Act is frequently being broken, however, sometimes by leading whites, including business men, clergymen, and policemen.

One of the most disturbing aspects of South Africa's race laws, according to Dr van Niekerk, is the differentiation between the races. "A white man can be acquitted and yet his 'immoral' non-white partner convicted. This sort of thing can only bring the law into disrepute and encourage the opinion held generally outside South Africa that there is one law for the whites and one for the blacks in South Africa."

The penalty for a first offence under the Act usually is imprisonment for three months to six months without the option of a fine. The maximum penalty is seven years' imprisonment.

2.12.68

Church minister 'under tension' sent to prison

A Dutch Reformed Church minister was sent to prison for six months today after admitting he 9intended having sexual intercourse with an African girl of 16.

Matteus Gerhardus Fiourie (28), married with two children, pleaded guilty to infringing South Africa's Immorality Act which forbids sexual relations between whites and non-whites.

Fouruie, who said he was under great tension, at the time, told the court "the worst did not happen". The girl, who initially a[ppeared with Fourie, pleasdewd not guilty and was remanded on bail until early next year.

2.12.66

'Blood apartheid' death

From our Correspondent
Cape Town

"BLOOD APARTHEID" may have caused the death of an African, Phillip Shakwane, who was injured in a level crossing accident in Nelspruit, in the Eastern Transvaal.

Dr J.P. van der Merwe said at the trial of the train driver today that he amputated Shakwane's left leg below the knee and gave instructions for him to receive a blood transfusion. Two hours later, when he returned, Shakwane was in a serious condition. He had not been given a transfusion.

When he asked why, he was told the hospital had run out of "African blood." Two pints of "white blood" were then sent for Shakwane, said the doctor, but he died soon afterwards.

14.3.73

How apartheid destroyed two families

From STANLEY UYS in Capetown

THE SUICIDE of a coloured boy aged 20 here has brought to light an apartheid tragedy almost unparalleled in South Africa's history.

The boy threw himself under a train at a suburban station when he learnt that his white girl friend was pregnant. He could not marry her, because the Mixed Marriages Act prohibits marriages across the colour line. He left his girl friend all the money he had — £30 — to help her buy clothes for the baby. He asked her in a suicide note to name the baby after him if it was a boy. The girl's father took the money and used it to pay for an abortion — a legal abortion could be obtained because the boy was Coloured.

The girl then tried to commit suicide by cutting her wrists, but failed. She was unaware that her boyfriend was classified as Coloured. She learnt of his death when he failed to arrive to take her to a cinema.

2.9.74

Whites turn shirty

From STANLEY UYS in Cape Town

THE BANNING by the South African censors of a T-shirt bearing the head of a woman and the words "Black is Beautiful" was described in the Supreme Court, Cape Town, today as "a complete and gratuitous insult to every person of colour in south Africa."

Counsel for the company which printed the shirt said the ban implied either that only white was beautiful or that black was not beautiful.

However a part-time member of the Publications Control Board, professor J P Jansen, Head of the Department of African study at the University of Stellenbosch, told the court.

"The black power movement in the United States has already taken hold in south Africa and 'Black is Beautiful' is a slogan of this movement. The publication of this slogan on shirts contributes to the instigation of antipathy against whites and the propagation of a bloody revolution."

17.9.74

Picture: ELLEN ELMENDORP

colonisers to do the decent thing. In fact, it eloquently expressed the position of Afrikaner nationalism and propelled it to its next decisive stage: the severing of the final tenuous links with Britain and the international community which Smuts had so assiduously courted. South Africa's acrimonious referendum on becoming a republic was staged the same year.

The majority of English speakers and a minority of Afrikaners wished to cling to the European umbilical cord. But the result was never in doubt — demography and demagoguery assured the victory of the National Party and the republic. The following year South Africa left the Commonwealth. Whatever slight restraints the links with Britain and the Commonwealth might have entailed fell away. Now the government would concentrate on the fourth pillar of apartheid policy, the repression of black opposition. Just as Verwoerd had codified racism while stalking power from the "native" affairs ministry, so his successor was vigorously making a name for himself from the pinnacle of the security apparatus.

Balthazar Johannes Vorster had been interned during the war for his role as a leader of the Ossewa-Brandwag, but this had done him no lasting political damage among the hard men of Afrikaner nationalism. After the Sharpeville and Langa massacres a state of emergency was declared and Vorster oversaw the banning of the African National Congress and Pan Africanist Congress.

Black leaders were arrested or banned under the Suppression of Communism Act, and dissent ruthlessly suppressed. Over the coming years, the provisions for detention without trial would progressively be raised from 12 days to the indefinite terms allowed for under the Terrorism Act of 1967.

In 1963, the homelands policy began with the passage of the Transkei Constitution Act. But neither the 1963 law nor "independence" in 1976 was greeted with much enthusiasm by the Xhosas they were supposed to liberate. Black people of different tribal provenance were equally unenthusiastic. In the cities, in particular, they regarded themselves as black, rather than Zulu, Xhosa, Tswana, Sotho or whatever. If anything, apartheid and its emphasis on tribal heritage served to hasten detribalisation among the majority of black South Africans.

Vorster's successor, P W Botha, was from the supposedly more enlightened

'Everyone was obliged to be classified according to race; how they were defined would then affect every aspect of their lives. Once classified, they were then separated'

White mother faces 'blackout'

RITA HOEFLING, a white hospital worker, is going through what in race-conscious South Africa is a nightmare: her skin is gradually turning darker.

"I can scream," Mrs Hoefling said last night. "I'm finding out what apartheid is like at its very worst."

She has been ordered off whites-only buses and door-to-door salesmen who come to her flat in Sea Point, Cape Town, ask her to "call the madam." Her son and husband have left her and her 16-year-old daughter "who is as white as snow" was kicked off a whites-only bus last week because the driver has seen her together with her dark-skinned mother. Pictures of Mrs Hoefling taken 10 years ago show her light-skinned. She said her colour began changing in 1974 when doctors discovered she had a brain tumour and she developed related skin conditions.

Because she had an adrenal gland operation five years before and also underwent cobalt treatment, doctors believed it too risky to operate.

The local bus company has given her a card which states that she is white and can travel on whites-only buses.

But this week when she was on her way home from Groote Schuur Hospital, where she is a voluntary worker, "a bus driver told me to get off his bus. He wasn't interested in my card," she said.

21.1.78

Skin operation for 'white' girl

Johannesburg

A WHITE South African schoolgirl whose skin turned dark after an operation may go for treatment in London to save her from being thought "non-white."

The girl is Jane-Anne Pepler, aged 17, whose skin changed from fair to very dark after an operation to counteract a sudden increase in weight.

The girl's mother, Mrs Anna Snyman, said: "It is heartbreaking to see Jane-Anne being spurned by people who think she is Coloured. It is particularly embarrassing for us because we are a purely Afrikaans family and strong Nationalists. We believe in white supremacy."

19.6.72

A drive against apartheid

A WHITE South African women cab-driver is campaigning for an end to "taxi apartheid" after mistaking a tanned French tourist for a Coloured girl.

Mrs Susanna Meyer, aged 56, who works as an independent cab-driver based at a Johannesburg hotel, says she is tired of being called a racist. The law forbids "whites-only" cabs from carrying South African blacks, although foreign blacks are exempted.

Mrs Meyer said: "I have not got light-meters in my eyes so I cannot always tell whether a person is white or not. Last week, two white men and an attractive young woman who looked Coloured wanted me to take them to a restaurant. Because I didn't want to risk breaking the law, I was placed in the very embarrassing position of having to ask the woman for her passport."

23.8.77

Apartheid victim

A SOUTH African traffic policeman barred three black nurses from treating a white man injured in a car crash, who later died, the Johannesburg Star newspaper said yesterday.

The nurses passed the scene of the crash in an ambulance and volunteered to give emergency treatment to the badly injured motorist, but a traffic officer told them he had already called an ambulance and refused them access.

20.11.87

Abandoned baby was 'Coloured' say police

Johannesburg

POLICE SAID yesterday that they have determined that a month-old baby girl found in a field is Coloured, but the Government has not yet formally classified the child's race.

The debate about the girl's race has focused attention on South Africa's race classification system. The race assigned to the girl, given the name Lisa Venter by Pretoria West hospital staff, will determine which schools she attends, and where she can live.

Maj-Gen. Lothar Neethling said: "For investigation purposes, the South African police scientifically determined that the child was of mixed race." He said the decision was made based on a strand of the girl's hair.

Newspapers reported that police believe the baby had been abandoned because her parents feared prosecution under the Immorality Act, which forbids sexual relations across the colour line. General Neethling would not comment on such "speculation."

26.7.83

Cape wing of the National Party. His power base was the military, which he assiduously courted as minister of defence and which he sent to invade Angola in 1976. By the time he took over from Vorster after a bloody bout of internecine brawling, there was little that could be done with the policy of apartheid.

The great gestures had been made, the definitive pieces of legislation were in place, the power to enforce it was as sleek and muscular as it would ever be. Some more "homelands" would follow Transkei to "independence" — Venda, Ciskei and, most ludicrous of all, Bophuthatswana. Under Botha the enthusiastic unity of Afrikaner nationalism waned and finally died. He recognised the need for change, but failed to understand quite how deep it would have to go. He fiddled with constitutional arrangements and some of the seemingly less fundamental aspects of apartheid — those which liberal critics had wrongly called petty apartheid.

The right-wing of his party broke away to form the Conservative Party, for they knew that apartheid was indivisible. Every aspect of the policy tied in with every other. That was the nature of the beast: it was a logical system, appalling in all respects, but logical none the less. Apartheid was over long before FW de Klerk assumed power. His remarkable achievement was to recognise this, and act decisively to try to make something out of the dreadful mess he had helped to create.

It was remarkable that Afrikaner unity lasted as long as it did. The Great Trek itself, much-loved in Afrikaner nationalist mythology as a nation journeying into an untamed continent in search of self and God, was marked by schism as much as anything else. No sooner had Cape Town's Table Mountain disappeared over the horizon than the voortrekkers began long and bitter squabbles.

The ideal of apartheid, like the ideal of freedom from government of the voortrekkers who inspired it, was bound to fail for every conceivable reason.

A house of straw, built on wild and violent dreams, had to fall. But just as apartheid grew out of the world which preceded it, so it will leave its mark on the democratic country which is struggling to emerge.

Michael Stent writes for the Guardian and the Observer

Rita Hoefling (left), with her daughter. Mrs Hoefling claimed she had been discriminated against after her skin turned darker due to a skin condition

'Families were shattered when pseudo-scientists decided a child was "coloured" and her parents white . . . squads of officials checked people's hair, their nose shapes, the colour of their fingernails'

The drive to establish 'homelands' for South Africa's black population was the logical conclusion of apartheid ideology. The abject failure of the policy sounded the death-knell for Verwoerd's grandiose dreams — but not before it had uprooted millions of people and dumped them in the most inhospitable regions of the country, leaving a legacy of bitterness and violence

The homelands/Patrick Laurence

THE MOST durable of South Africa's notorious apartheid laws were those providing for the establishment of black quasi-states, known as "homelands" or "bantustans". Their abolition coincides with the birth of a united and non-racial South Africa on April 26 to 28 1994.

The convergence of these events is no accident. It underlines the importance of these policies as an integral part of the apartheid system and thus as an obstacle to the new order. Under these laws, 10 tribally based statelets were established on less than 14 per cent of the area of South Africa. Stretched along a horseshoe-shaped area of territory on the periphery of South Africa, they were described as "homelands", a term which implied that the black population belonged there and that therefore they were mere sojourners in the remainder of South Africa.

These territories were not, as apartheid apologists often argued, the original heartlands of the indigenous black population, but rather the scattered remnants of their ancestral lands after the invasion and conquest of South Africa by white settlers and their descendants.

The "homeland" system was designed to fulfil three central purposes:
- to provide a moral justification for white domination in the rest of South Africa, the rationale being that black hegemony in the homelands was a trade-off for white rule over most of the country;
- to deflect black political aspirations from the centre to the periphery by focusing black attention on subordinate legislatures in the "homelands" instead of South Africa's white-dominated parliament in Cape Town;
- to reduce the black population in white-designated South Africa and thus to reduce the immediate threat to the white minority.

South Africa's raw population statistics posed an immediate problem. White people made up less than 15 per cent of the population but controlled over 86 per cent of the land. It was a challenge to the ingenuity of apartheid's supporters. One argument which they came up with was that some of the "homelands" were located in the higher rainfall area of the country and as a result the territories contained 25 per cent of South Africa's arable land.

The attempt to redirect black political initiatives illustrated the direct relationship between the black nationalist challenge to the white government and laws aimed at accelerating political development of the tribal territories.

Thus the Sharpeville massacre of March 1960, sparked off by the anti-pass law campaign of the militant Pan-Africanist Congress, came immediately after the Promotion of Black Self-Government Act of 1959 and led to the Transkei Self-Government Act of 1963. Similarly, the 1976–77 black student revolt provided the impetus for the Transkei and Bophuthatswana State Acts which conferred nominal independence on Transkei in 1976 and Bophuthatswana in 1977.

The sharper the challenge, the quicker the political evolution of the "homelands"; the faster their development, the stronger the black response.

Nor was the hope that "separate development" would neutralise international hostility to South Africa realised. One reason was that it was devised by a white government in the interests of white people. Another — a corollary of the first — was the manifestly unfair nature of the system, starkly displayed in the inequitable division of land and resources. The lion's share of the land, including all the major cities and all the functioning ports, remained in white hands.

Moreover, the bantustans were vehemently opposed by the major black nationalist organisations: the ANC, its PAC off-shoot and, in the 1970s and early 1980s, the Black Consciousness Movement founded by Steve Biko. Even tribal leaders who co-operated in its implementation did so only on a qualified basis, arguing either for a greater allocation of land and resources to their allotted "homeland" (Kaiser Matanzima of Transkei) or for adapting the system into a form of federalism (Mangosuthu Buthelezi of KwaZulu).

Not even the granting of putative independence to four of these quasi-states — Transkei (1976), Bophuthatswana (1977), Venda (1979) and Ciskei (1981) — persuaded the international community to reappraise its stance. They failed to secure recognition from a single country and so existed in a condition of political incest, interacting only with each other and with South Africa.

The only leader who could have given any credibility to "independence" was Buthelezi, the officially recognised leader of the Zulus, the largest of the black tribes. But he steadfastly refused to countenance it. The logical end of grand

Lucas Mangope, president of Bophuthatswana (left), with Transkei's president Botha Sigcau in 1978. Behind them is Transkei prime minister Chief Kaiser Matanzima

Facing page: **Weena resettlement camp, Natal**

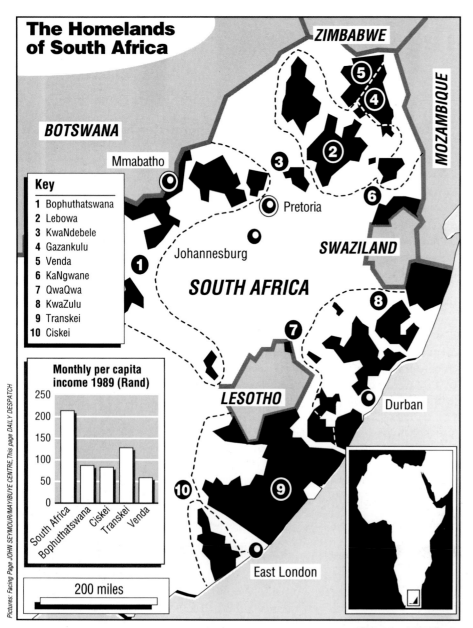

The Homelands of South Africa

ZIMBABWE

BOTSWANA

MOZAMBIQUE

Mmabatho

Key

1 Bophuthatswana
2 Lebowa
3 KwaNdebele
4 Gazankulu
5 Venda
6 KaNgwane
7 QwaQwa
8 KwaZulu
9 Transkei
10 Ciskei

Pretoria

SWAZILAND

Johannesburg

SOUTH AFRICA

LESOTHO

Durban

Monthly per capita income 1989 (Rand)

250
200
150
100
50
0

South Africa
Bophuthatswana
Ciskei
Transkei
Venda

East London

200 miles

Pictures: Facing Page JOHN SEYMOUR/MAYIBUYE CENTRE; This page DAILY DESPATCH

apartheid was the creation of 10 independent tribal states. It should not be forgotten that it was Buthelezi, later severely at odds with the ANC and its allies, who thwarted the realisation of that objective. He refused to sacrifice the rights of black people to full South African citizenship in return for bogus independence.

A major turning point came in the mid-1980s when an attempt by the chief minister of KwaNdebele to accept independence was defeated. A resolution by the KwaNdebele Legislative Assembly calling for independence was withdrawn after a revolt by black youths in the territory. It was a clear sign to even the most dedicated apartheid devotee that the game was up.

Perhaps the most telling evidence of the failure of the bantustan system came in the run-up to the 1994 election. The system was devised as a bulwark against black nationalism. The leaders of the different homelands were seen as men who, when the chips were down, would side with the white government against black radicals. As the beneficiaries of grand apartheid and champions of tribalism or ethno-nationalism, they were expected to oppose the ANC and the PAC.

These expectations were heightened by extravagant promises from Matanzima and Patrick Mphephu, who led Venda to independence, to resist ANC guerrillas to the "last drop of blood". But once the ANC was unbanned in February 1990, Nelson Mandela was able to win most of these leaders to his side and to use them to gain the ascendancy both at the negotiating table and in the election contest.

Five of the 10 bantustan leaders were members of the ANC-led Patriotic Front. They included Bantu Holomisa, the audacious military ruler of Transkei, who came to power in a bloodless coup in December 1987 which ended the corrupt regime of the Matanzima brothers, Kaiser and George. Holomisa used his power base in the Transkei to defy the South African government, even to the extent — according to an inquiry by Judge Richard Goldstone — of allowing fighters of the PAC's guerrilla army, APLA, to operate in and from the Transkei.

Of the remaining five "homeland" leaders, two were neutral and three linked to the Freedom Alliance, the umbrella grouping of Inkatha and the white far-right. The neutral leaders were Kenneth Mopeli of Qwaqwa and the late Hudson Ntsanwisi of Gazankulu. Freedom Alliance members included Buthelezi of

While Dr Vorster has been in Europe defending South Africa's internal policies, Pretoria has this week taken the first step to create a new separate reservation for Zulus.
Here JONATHAN STEELE reports on an extraordinary book causing a row in the Prime Minister's own backyard.

The Baedeker of the Bantustans

FOR AN Englishman to take out South African citizenship so that he can criticise South Africa and be immune from deportation sounds just a little foolhardy. There are plenty of things worse than deportation that South Africa reserves for its citizens. But Father Cosmas Desmond wanted to say what he thought and be able to stay to face the consequences. As a Franciscan priest he does have respectable friends in high places. No divisions perhaps, but the moral authority of the Catholic Church. Let us hope it is enough to protect him.

Father Desmond has written a book which tears off, strip by bureaucratic strip, the verbiage, the posturings, the apologies in which South Africa wraps its policy of "separate development." As a priest, Desmond found he had one great advantage in his calling. The clergy can go into the hidden and not-so-hidden reserves and "homelands" unchallenged. They are about the only white men, apart from government officials or farmers coming to load up a batch of cheap African labourers, to be allowed to do so.

So Desmond came and saw and noted it all down. His book is a kind of Baedeker of the Bantustans, a detailed, dry, unemotional journey through virtually every rural homeland and resettlement area in South Africa. These are the places for Africans who need to be removed from "white" areas, for women and children sent out of the cities, for the old, the "non-productive labour units," the "superfluous appendages," as the Deputy Minister of Justice — yes, Justice — has called them.

Village by village, Desmond describes it all, places with names that so often have their own sick appropriateness — Morsgat (messhole), Weenen (a place of weeping), Stinkwater. (Morsgat has now been renamed Modikwe after the Minister of Bantu Administration found the original name, though not the place it described, "unfortunate.") To all but a few Liberals and Progressives, to the editors and reporters of the "Rand Daily Mail" who have carried the occasional story, to some missionaries, a doctor here and there, the names mean little on the verandas, lawns,

and golf courses of white South Africa. One day, when the sigh eventually goes up, "But we never knew this was going on," they may in their lesser way be the Dachaus, the Treblinkas, and Buchenwalds of apartheid.

Desmond gives these places flesh and blood. No, flesh and blood is not the right word. For it is a story of malnutrition, disease, and starvation. Kwashiorkor is a word that first hit most people in Europe when reading about war-torn Biafra. It is there in South Africa, too, in the richest country on the continent, in peacetime.

Writing of the African reserve near the white village of Herschel in the Eastern Cape he says: "All forms of malnutrition are obviously a problem throughout the reserve. The doctor at the Anglican mission runs a kwashiorkor home, where malnourished children are admitted and their parents stay with them."

Or take this from last year's annual report of the St Michael's Mission Hospital Batlharos in the Northern Cape: "During the winter of 1968 the number of in-patients rose to 400 and the widespread starvation and very real suffering witnessed then in and around the hospital can only be described as a disgrace to the country . . . The children's ward, originally built for 40 cases, housed last winter over 160 at one time, all of whom were seriously ill and would certainly have died if they had not been admitted."

Desmond spent a year travelling round these settlement villages and towns, on dirt roads in the reserves. The pattern everywhere was similar. Contact the local clergy, mission station or hospital, if there was one and usually there was not. Get information from them if they would give it and sometimes they did not. Then go into the villages and talk to the people. Sometimes they thought he was a government official. Once or twice they begged money (though this was very rare). Usually they just told him what had happened.

Typically, it went something like this. Forced out of one area by bureaucratic decree, the people had to leave their homes without compensation. They are taken by lorry to a new place, without sanitation, often

without houses, with poor water supply. Rent is charged for the land. There is no work. Bus fare to the nearest white town, and work, is expensive. Emergency rations may be provided by the Government, or they may not be. Tents may be provided, or they may not be. Medical facilities are miserable.

For the flavour of it all, take Mogogokela, 50 miles from South Africa's capital, Pretoria. Mogogokela is fairly typical of settlements in the area and one of the biggest. It is a Trust farm with about 1,000 families.

The people were transported by government lorry and brought the building materials from their old houses; with these they built temporary shacks to live in while they were building their houses, since they were not provided with tents . . . Having recovered from the actual move, they are now concerned mainly about work and water.

"There is, of course, no work available in the vicinity. There is nothing in the vicinity except bush. For the whole settlement there is one bore-hole operated by a windpump. When this runs dry, as it often does, water is brought in by lorries from the Apies River and sold. There is one primary school for the building of which each family was asked to contribute £11; but many did not do so. There is no clinic or visiting doctor. A nurse visits once a week. She charges two shillings a visit. The nearest hospital is the Jubilee Mission Hospital at Hammanskraal, 15 miles away.

"Local missionaries say that there was a tremendous number of deaths from malnutrition and cold in 1966/7 when the people were still in temporary shacks. There are still obvious signs of malnutrition everywhere.

And so it goes on. "Separate development" or apartheid means that so far as possible in every sphere of the white economy Africans should be migrants. Women, and children, and the old, and the unemployed get out to their "homelands." But, as Dr J.H. Grobler of the Highveld Research Institute has said, the homelands barely provide subsistence level living even for half their present population of five millions.

19.6.70

KwaZulu, Lucas Mangope of Bophuthatswana and Oupa Gqozo, of Ciskei. Mangope and Gqozo were both forced out of office before the election.

Not a single bantustan leader was aligned with de Klerk's National Party, whose predecessors established and financed the homeland system in the belief they were cultivating black auxiliaries to fight on their side in future battles. The ANC even included its allies from the pro-ANC quasi-states in its election lists.

Their usefulness to the ANC varied. The popular Holomisa was undoubtedly a major asset. Nelson Ramodike, of Lebowa, and James Mahlangu, of KwaNdebele, were of more questionable value, but by co-opting them the ANC ensured that the leaders could not be coaxed into joining an anti-ANC coalition, whether under de Klerk or the Freedom Alliance.

The third objective of the bantustan system — to reduce the number of black people living in white-designated South Africa — failed as miserably as the first two. A combination of incentives (development of the territories) and coercion (deportations and forced removals of black people from white-designated land) was used in a bid to concentrate the black population in its allotted "homelands".

Hendrik Verwoerd, the high priest of apartheid, believed with almost mystical fervour that the establishment of the "homelands" would see a reverse in the flow of black people to the towns and cities of white-designated South Africa. He even set a date when the human tide would start to turn, 1978. Verwoerd's assassination in 1966 saved him from seeing his prediction confounded by the sustained influx of black people to the designated white areas.

South Africa's apartheid governments simply did not devote enough resources and money to develop the "homelands". Thus, instead of attracting black people, they exported migrant labourers to white-designated areas. The white authorities did, however, make a determined bid to reduce the black population in white areas by forced removals of entire communities to the "homelands". Their prime targets included "black spots", enclaves of black-owned land in areas set aside for white occupation, and black tenants of white-owned farms.

In the 1970s more than 300,000 black people were sent back to their allotted "homelands". During the same period the same number of tenants were uprooted

Main Picture: JOHN SEYMOUR/MAYIBUYE CENTRE; Top right: ORDE ELIASON/LINK

Although a small ruling elite grew rich, for the vast majority life in the homelands offered slow starvation

Main picture: Corrugated iron toilets await inhabitants at Welcome Valley resettlement camp in Transkei, 1968

Right: African women collect the laundry at Sun City in Bophuthatswana, the holiday complex which attracts thousands of wealthy South Africans

Black shanty homes demolished

Cape Town

THOUSANDS of black squatters stood by in helpless, angry silence yesterday as bulldozers and tractors demolished their shantytown homes here.

The clearance by local white authorities looked like causing not only heartache and suffering for the displaced blacks, but a major row with the Government of Transkei, the black homeland which South Africa proclaimed independent last October. Most of the blacks involved are Xhosas, who belong to the Transkei and should go back there, according to Pretoria.

"The justification for continued diplomatic ties is becoming more and more questionable," Transkei's Foreign Minister, Digby Koyana, said. "The basis for friendship as neighbours with South Africa is diminishing fast." He said Transkei rejected the idea that South Africa could dump its "unwanted people" on his country.

About 140 shacks in the Modderdam squatter camp had been razed by noon, leaving 1,059 more to be destroyed as well as 2,409 at two adjoining shantytowns, Unibel and Werkgenot, according to official counts. Together, they house up to 26,000 blacks, well over half of them illegal "immigrants" in terms of South Africa's race laws.

"I have nowhere else to go," said a bewildered mother of three whose makeshift home was demolished yesterday. "I will just have to leave my stuff on the pavement and wait."

Mrs Parslena Nyathe, from Transkei, also watched her shack being demolished. "A man told us through a loudspeaker to take our things out of our homes," she said. "My husband had already gone to work. I don't know what he will think we must do." She added that she was not legally permitted to be in South Africa, but her husband was because he had a job as a domestic worker in Cape Town.

Mrs Patricia Sopete lives with her mother in the Modderdam camp. Her husband lives in the single-men's hostel in nearby Langa township. Their house was demolished while they were at work. Yesterday they joined the crowds of bewildered squatters who watched the demolition and at one stage came face to face with armed police and their Alsatians who converged on the scene after a bulldozer had broken down.

A spokesman for the local Bantu (African) Affairs Administration Board, administrative director F. J. van Eeden, said the squatters had to be moved because there was no running water, sanitation, or refuse facilities at the camps. He said camp-dwellers with no right to be in South Africa had been offered free rail tickets to the Transkei or the Ciskei but had not taken up the offer.

10.8.77

Two dead in SA raids

TWO MEN were shot dead, a woman was wounded in the arm, and a baby trampled to death yesterday during police raids on the emergency squatter camp of Crossroads, near Cape Town.

The first man, Mr Sindile Ndela, was shot during a police raid before dawn yesterday. The second, Mr Fanele Manyisana, was fatally wounded in the chest in a second raid after sunrise.

The baby died in a stampede to escape a teargas attack during the second raid. The infant died on its mother's back, and has not been identified.

The State-owned radio described the raids as an anti-crime exercise. Sources close to the squatters, however, described the raids as pass raids.

Hundreds of black squatters were arrested, among them the chairman of the Crossroads committee, Mr Ngkobo Ngwane. Several whites were arrested as well, among them a priest, father Des Curran, of the Roman Catholic Church, community workers, and members of the Women's Movement For Peace.

The Divisional commissioner of Police in the Western Cape, Brigadier J F Rossouw, said yesterday after the raids: "The police were attacked with sticks and stones. A man was shot in the process." The raid was a routine crime prevention manoeuvre, he said.

The raids followed a similar raid last week. Most of the people arrested in that raid were charged as illegal immigrants or as harbouring illegal immigrants.

According to Mr R N Robb, of the Black Sash, not a single person was charged with being in possession of a dangerous weapon, Mr Robb said of yesterday's arrests: "We have already received 75 requests for legal assistance from the families of arrested people."

Sister Benigna, of the Roman Catholic Church, told yesterday of how the squatters had anticipated the pre-dawn raid and sat around camp fires awaiting the arrival of the police. Brigadier Rossouw had earlier described the camp as "wide awake" when police arrived at 1.30am. Sister Benigna said: "The squatters had posted sentries and scouts since the recent police raid on the camp. They were certain the police would come."

The squatters refused to allow the police into the camp, Sister Benigna added. During last week's raid doors to the shanties were allegedly kicked in. Police were accused of behaving in an aggressive manner towards the squatters during the raid.

Mr Ndela was shot dead at about 3.40pm, Sister Benigna said. She added: "Someone said: 'There he lies, all for the sake of a pass. A life for a piece of paper' Then the raid was over."

The police came back after sunrise and their arrival triggered stone-throwing, Sister Benigna said. Tear-gas was fired as police moved in to pull squatters from their shacks and arrest them.

Crossroads residents declared yesterday a day of mourning. The 20,000 strong community is the last of the black squatter camps left in the environs of Cape Town.

Condemning the police raids yesterday, Mrs Helen Suzman, the veteran white Opposition MP, said: "The only sin that these people have committed is in trying to maintain family life in the teeth of the inhuman pass laws and the ludicrous policy of excluding blacks from the West province."

Dr Francis Wilson of the University of Cape Town, said yesterday: "The tragedy of Crossroads is symbolic. South Africa is at the crossroads. It must decide whether to accept the consequences of urbanisation or whether to aggravate its dislocating impact."

15.9.78

'White people paid the price for their silence after the abolition of influx control laws in the mid-1980s, when black squatter communities sprang up around the opulent white cities like avenging armies of the poor'

from white-owned farms and sent to the bantustans, often at gunpoint.

In total, an estimated 3.5 million people were forcibly removed under various apartheid laws between 1960 and 1985, according to a study by the Surplus People's Project. The human cost was enormous. White people paid the price for their silence or connivance during these forced removals when, after the abolition of influx control laws in the mid-1980s, black squatter communities sprang up around the putatively white cities and towns. They bivouacked around the relatively opulent cities like avenging armies of the poor.

Faced with the realisation that black people would not move voluntarily to their "homelands" in large numbers and that even forced removals could not eliminate the black presence, the proponents of apartheid tried a last desperate ploy — the concept of extra-territorial citizenship.

All black people were deemed to be citizens of one or another of the "homelands" for internal purposes, including the exercise of political rights. They retained South African nationality for international purposes. But if any of the "homelands" accepted independence, their designated citizens were deprived of South African nationality, irrespective of whether they lived in the "homeland" or not. In this way an estimated nine million black people were deprived of South African nationality and citizenship.

This was the closest the "homelands" policy ever came to its ultimate objective which was, in the chilling words of former cabinet minister Connie Mulder, a South Africa without black citizens.

But the attempt to deprive the black population of South African citizenship provoked an even greater determination by them to defend their right to it. Their ultimate victory came with passage of the 1993 Electoral Act. It extended the vote to the people of nominally independent "homelands" for the 1994 election. Far from realising the dream of apartheid's architects of a South Africa for whites only, the "homelands" proved by their very failure to be a crucial and symbolic factor in the demise of apartheid itself.

Patrick Laurence was formerly the Guardian's South Africa correspondent

A resident of the Unibel squatter camp, near Cape Town, flees as the bulldozers move in, 1978

South Africa 'frees' second homeland

From PATRICK LAURENCE in Mafeking

AT MIDNIGHT last night South Africa surrendered formal sovereignty over an area the size of Switzerland and deprived 2.1 million people of South African citizenship. With that act the independent homeland of Bophuthatswana was born. In official South African eyes, and those of the followers of the Tswana leader, Chief Lucas Mangope, Bophuthatswana was heralded as the 51st independent state in Africa. But to the Organisation of African Unity and most of the world it remains a bantustan satellite of Pretoria.

The independent homeland consists of six separate territories scattered across South Africa like bits of a jigsaw puzzle. Most of its citizens — two-thirds according to the 1970 census — lived in white-designated South Africa and not within their new "country."

Chief Mangope, the 54-year-old President-elect of the new state, once sought to eliminate these anomalies as a precondition to accepting independence. Bophuthatswana is situated on the 14 per cent or less of South African land set aside for blacks by the 1936 Land Act.

In January 1974, Chief Mangope rejected the Act as a basis for independence, saying: "In no way did the law . . . provide additional area for future independent sovereign states." But less than two years later, although the South African Prime Minister, Mr Vorster, had repeatedly rejected appeals to scrap the Act and agree to a new land dispensation, he won a mandate from his legislative assembly to negotiate for independence.

Chief Mangope did try to resist South Africa's insistence that all Tswana-speaking South African Africans forfeit South African citizenship on independence and automatically become citizens of Bophuthatswana. In May, in an open letter read in Parliament, he threatened to break off independence negotiations unless Tswanas were given the right to renounce Bophuthatswana citizenship and to regain South African citizenship automatically.

His demand was not met, but he agreed to independence. He explained: "We have never been citizens of South Africa in any meaningful sense, and the South African Government is now adamant that blacks, whether opting for independence or not, will never be citizens of South Africa. But I can see signs that make it reasonable to expect there could be change at some stage in the future, so we made provision that our people are not left out as and when (blacks) become citizens of South Africa."

He denied that opting for independence was an endorsement of apartheid, adding: "In the meantime I felt I could not retard the development of my people in the physical, mental and spiritual sense any longer merely because of what amounts in the present circumstances to a technicality.

"I see this independence we are embarking on now as merely a stepping stone to a federal system encompassing all of South Africa."

The debate inevitably leads to the question of whether Bophuthatswana will be a "Trojan horse" within the former boundaries of South Africa or whether it will be a captive bantustan providing a protective buffer for the white industrial core.

Those who believe in the Trojan horse theory point out that Bophuthatswana, like its sister independent homeland, the Transkei, has adopted a non-racial policy and that it will repeal inherited racial laws. According to these theorists, Bophuthatswana's influence will radiate inwards.

Bophuthatswana has attracted as much industrial investment as the rest of the homelands combined, and is rich in minerals, particularly platinum. But it is still dependent on South Africa for money, and for work for its population. In 1975-76, 80 per cent of its budget came from South Africa. Chief Mangope already has come under pressure from militants. His legislative assembly and several schools have been burnt down. This is certain to make him more dependent on South Africa.

6.12.77

Ciskei leadership smothers opposition to 'independence'

MORE THAN 320 people have been detained without trial this year in the Ciskei, which achieves "independence" from South Africa today according to the authoritative International Defence and Aid Fund for Southern Africa.

Last year, 157 people were detained. The increase is partly attributable to opposition within the bantustan to independence, which will deprive two million of South African citizenship.

Opposition to independence has been focused on the South African Allied Workers Union — 205 of whose members were detained in September — and the Border Civic Organisation. Political parties in the Ciskei, apart from the ruling Ciskei National Independence Party, have been reduced to impotence by among other measures, a bill denying registration to parties with fewer than 10,000 members.

The Ciskei Leader, Chief Lennox Sebe, and his brother, Major-General Charles Sebe, who is head of the security services, maintain tight control over dissent; several former Cabinet ministers have been detained in recent years. The Sebe brothers, like the Matanzima brothers in Transkei, have ensured mute acquiescence for independence among most of their voters, even though 90 per cent of the electorate, according to a survey conducted by an independent commission, favoured universal adult suffrage in a non-racial South Africa.

The official vote — in favour of Ciskei independence — was influenced by a combination of fear, "including a veiled threat of possible imprisonment" for anybody opposing independence or boycotting the polls, according to Professor L Schlemmer of the University of Natal.

Chief Sebe has good reason to fear dissent: the Eastern Cape, where the Ciskei is situated, has produced much of the leadership of the banned African National Congress, Pan-Africanist Congress, and Black Consciousness Movement which all oppose the fragmentation of South Africa into "independent" homelands.

Chief Sebe, under some pressure from Pretoria, has moved from opposition to independence to enthusiastic acceptance of running his own government, cushioned by many security laws inherited from South Africa.

Pretoria's original idea was for Transkei and Ciskei to form one "Xhosa National Unit", but rivalry between the leadership of the two territories made this impossible. Most observers expect the Ciskei to follow Transkei's path towards authoritarian rule marked by extreme poverty, with sporadic, and possibly violent, outbreaks of opposition to "independence".

4.12.81

Ill-starred start

THE FLAGPOLE collapsed twice and broke in two as Ciskei's flag was raised for the first time at midnight on Thursday. South African soldiers righted the broken pole and the flag was raised, but some Ciskeians believed it was a bad omen for the new "independent" state.

5.12.81

Stamping out

STAMP collectors are doubtless queuing up to obtain copies of a new set of stamps. These stamps come from Bophuthatswana, which became South Africa's second "independent" homeland at the end of last year.

The theme of the stamps is "Down with high blood pressure." This message is accompanied by little slogans and pictures. The 15 cent stamp, moreover, carries a picture of a knife, fork and spoon and a grim skull plus the slogan, "Overeating is dangerous."

It is also almost impossible in Bophuthatswana. Dr Donald Mackenzie, the medical superintendent of a hospital in the area, has written of "the appalling number of malnutrition cases. Many suffering from starvation died."

26.4.78

Mercy aid barred to stricken squatters

From John Kane-Berman in Johannesburg

THE SOUTH AFRICAN Government yesterday barred outsiders — including white women with food supplies — from access to black squatters in Cape Town whose shelters were destroyed by order of the Minister of Cooperation and Development, Dr Piet Koornhof, on a bitterly cold winter day.

One white woman was arrested while trying to take food to the squatters and charged with being in a black administrative area without a permit.

One of the last outsiders allowed in to see the families huddled together among the ruins of their hideaways, Mrs Helen Suzman, the veteran Opposition MP, yesterday accused the Government of trying to "starve or freeze them out" in its attempts to remove "illegal" blacks from the city. Mrs Suzman said: "It is my considered opinion that the Government has gone mad."

American congressmen who visited the squatter families wept at what they saw. Mr Howard Wolpe, chairman of the Africa sub-committee of the House Committee on Foreign Affairs, said: "We saw the degradation of humans in the exercise of police power that was beyond belief."

Newspapers have been barred from the area where the squatters have sought refuge, a piece of ground lying between the Nyanga township outside the city and the old squatter area known as Crossroads. Only clergymen are being allowed in.

Welfare workers said yesterday that the latest news they had heard from the squatter area was that Government officials had seized and burnt firewood donated to the families after their shelters had been demolished. The South African Press Association reported that Tuesday saw one of the severest daylight storms this winter, with hail and gale-force winds lashing Cape Town.

Mr Richard Ottinger, a congressmen from New York, said he and his wife had stood in hail and rain at Nyanga, which they could take for only 30 minutes, among women and children who had to spend the night there.

It is reported that two babies have been referred to the nearby Red Cross children's hospital with suspected pneumonia. A hospital official expressed amazement that some of the babies had not died, adding that they would not survive if white women, who have been taking them into their homes for hot baths, are no longer allowed to do so.

Mr Brian Bishop, chairman of the Civil Rights League in Cape Town, said yesterday that the situation of the women and babies in the squatter enclave, where more than 400 spent last night in the open, was "akin to the genocide of Nazi Germany."

Dr Koornhof said in Parliament last week it was his duty to ensure that, as far as possible, blacks living in white South Africa retained their bonds with their "national states."

Referring to the demolition of the squatters' shelters, Congressmen Ottinger said: "The people have two choices: they can go back to the homelands and starve to death or stay where they are and freeze to death."

13.8.81

PATRICK LAURENCE outlines the lifestyle which defies the homelands

A squat black living

THE PLIGHT of squatters in South Africa is manifest in their arrest and the destruction of their shelters in Nyanga, near Cape Town, but the roots of the problem line in the "Black Homelands" or reserves, which are unable to provide blacks with a living and force them to move in defiance of influx control laws to the white-controlled cities.

A study by Dr Jan Lange, an Afrikaans economist, provides a stark statistical backdrop to the conflict of wills between squatters determined to establish themselves in "prescribed urban areas" and bureaucrats striving to keep them out.

By leaving the homelands and unlawfully obtaining work in Cape Town, blacks improve their financial position by an average of more than 230 per cent, Dr Lange found. For blacks from Ciskei it is more than 760 per cent.

A black from the Ciskei will find it beneficial to work unlawfully in the Natal town of Pietermaritzburg, even if he has to spend nine months of the year in gaol, Dr Lange calculated. His findings point to an improvement of more than 230 per cent with only three months' work.

These figures explain the determination of the squatters. Their willingness to defy authority by building their shelters almost as soon as they are pulled down and by offering themselves for arrest. Blacks often see arrest as preferable to life in the homelands.

Except for a small elite, there are distinct disadvantages in living in the homelands.

Oriel Monongoaha, a squatters' leader in Pimville during the 1940s, said: "The government sends its policemen to chase us away and we move off and occupy another spot . . . we shall see who gets tired first."

21.8.81

Picture: ERNEST COLE/MAYIBUYE CENTRE

A family uprooted to Mondhlo resettlement camp, Kwazulu

Apartheid attempted to demoralise and humiliate black South Africans as well as physically repress them. Their response had to be both brave and imaginative. White people, on the other hand, only gradually acknowledged the true cost of maintaining their standard of living

Living under apartheid/Nokwanda Sithole

"WE NEVER killed people," says the "New" National Party, in its campaign to woo millions of black South African voters. "I never believed in forced removals," says Piet Koornhof, whose Nationalist government was responsible for the forced removal of 3.5 million black South Africans during its reign. Koornhof was the minister directly responsible for the relocation of most of those people. Twenty years ago he claimed that many had "written to me to thank me for being relocated".

Many white South Africans, in newspaper articles and radio talk shows, display a belief in the lie that the NP was never that bad, and that it was the acumen of NP leader FW de Klerk which made the liberation of the country's majority possible. This enduring belief is a sign of the tremendous challenges for any reconciliation programmes which will make South Africans understand their respective pasts and strengthen the possibility of building a common future.

The black majority does not have the same access to the mainstream media. Instead its repulsion for this rewriting of history is expressed in intimidation of the new NP campaigners in the townships, and the counter-democratic attempts to stop De Klerk's campaigns in black areas by force.

The ease with which NP supporters declare their innocence of the fundamental evils of the system is breathtaking. While occasionally acknowledging that "apartheid was wrong," at the same time they disregard or deny the reality of those millions who were beaten, maimed, criminalised or tortured under apartheid. For them the evil of the system — a doctrine to perpetuate the social, economic and political exploitation of black South Africans by the white minority — cannot be denied.

Under apartheid, educational and cultural systems were set up specifically to brainwash black South Africans into accepting the unequal social relations of capitalism and apartheid.

"When I have control of native education," said native affairs minister Hendrik Verwoerd shortly after the Nationals came into power in 1948, "I will reform it so that the natives will be taught from childhood to realise that equality with the Europeans is not for them." So it was that school syllabuses told a distorted South

African history, emphasising the defeat of blacks in the "Kaffir Wars" and stripping them of any historical dignity and intellect.

A systematic programme of control took away the land ownership and political rights of black South Africans and attempted to funnel their aspirations into ineffective state-initiated consultative bodies such as the Urban Bantu Councils. These powerless management structures, run by state-appointed black managers, were primarily repressive, but also had an ideological function — to frustrate the development of a common consciousness.

In conjunction with the eradication of freehold rights for black people, the government facilitated the construction of the reservoirs of labour — the townships — on a large scale.

The hated pass laws were the instrument employed to lock the black population away in the rural homelands, where subsistence was barely possible. Between 1951 and 1962 alone, four million black people were convicted — and criminalised — for pass offences. Millions had their citizenship taken away in homeland "independence" deals which sentenced people to live in impoverished, underdeveloped reserves.

Apartheid planted the roots of ethnic and class conflict, dividing the black majority into ethnic enclaves in townships and homelands and deliberately creating a small, paralysed black bourgeoisie which was supposed to buffer the state against the masses. Ironically, it was this class which would produce the leaders of the revolution.

Yet, in its own way, the black middle class was just as much a victim. As Verwoerd said: "There is no place for [the native] in the European community above certain forms of labour. Until now he has been subjected to a school system which drew him away from his community and misled him, by showing him the green pastures of European society in which he was not allowed to graze." The aspirations of the black population were frustrated in favour of satisfying those of the Afrikaners: by the Group Areas Act which limited black trading rights; by the prohibition of black students from white universities; and by job reservation.

With the exception of the pass laws, housing was perhaps the most hated

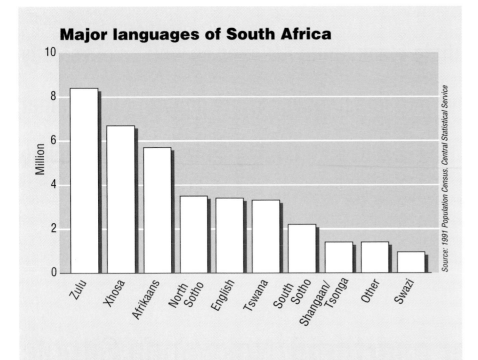

Major languages of South Africa

Million

Zulu, Xhosa, Afrikaans, North Sotho, English, Tswana, South Sotho, Shangaan/Tsonga, Other, Swazi

Source: 1991 Population Census. Central Statistical Service

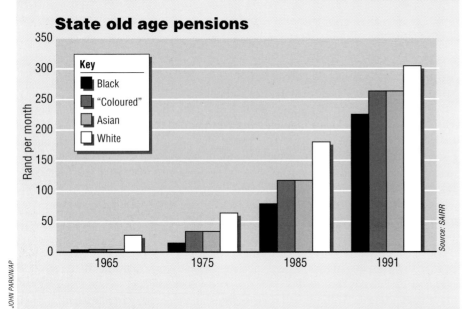

State old age pensions

Rand per month

Key
- Black
- "Coloured"
- Asian
- White

1965   1975   1985   1991

Source: SAIRR

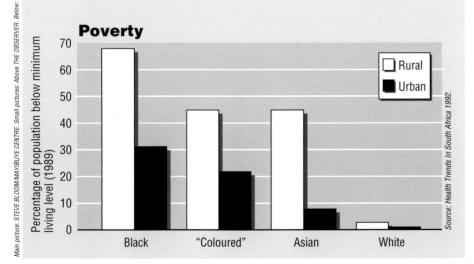

Poverty

Percentage of population below minimum living level (1989)

- Rural
- Urban

Black   "Coloured"   Asian   White

Source: Health Trends in South Africa 1992.

Main picture: STEVE BLOOM/MAYIBUYE CENTRE. Small pictures: Above: THE OBSERVER. Below: JOHN PARKIN/AP

instrument of social engineering. A number of black townships were literally built on municipal sewage deposit sites, with no facilities, frightening mortality rates, and ridiculously high rents and transport costs.

Movement to the cities continued despite the pass laws — more proof, if any were needed, of the squalor in the homelands. The local authorities were powerless to do anything about the housing backlog and huge squatter areas grew up alongside the townships. In some cases as many as 12 families lived on sites no larger than 50ft by 50ft.

Disease was rife and there were insufficient health facilities. But more insidious were the ideological tools employed to humiliate black South Africans and maintain white hegemony. Black parents were slapped by the police in front of their children, black youngsters were made to strip naked "to determine if they were of pass-bearing age", as were political prisoners during interrogation.

Nevertheless, resistance refused to die. As it persisted, the totalitarian methods of repression grew. Looksmart Ngudle became the first political detainee to die in prison, followed by over a hundred others. As the years passed, the official causes of death in detention became ever more ridiculous — detainees who had been "searched thoroughly" suddenly produced tools with which they killed themselves. Under Vorster in particular, the regime increasingly resorted to fabricating criminal charges against political activists to cushion the international political blows which followed the deaths of detainees.

The survival and the triumph which followed resistance and the limitations of a negotiated settlement are a celebration of the majority, who against great odds removed the mantle of apartheid from their daily lives.

Aside from the political culture, there existed in the townships an almost escapist buzz of laughter, song and dance — contradicting the squalor of the living conditions. There are incessant debates, between returned exiles, political convicts and "those who stayed behind", about who showed more commitment.

It is true that for the majority who stayed behind, organised political turbulence was something they only read about. However, the elements of struggle — whether and what the children will eat tonight, whether they will go to school

Below and main picture: **Life in the Crossroads squatter camp, near Cape Town**
Bottom: **Soweto children play football in the street**

Given the boot

Durban

AN AFRICAN servant whose employer often carries him in the closed boot of his car is considering changing his job after complaints by neighbours about the method of transport. He earns £4 12s a month.

The employer, Mr Frank Thompson, a Canadian immigrant, said: "I always take him in the boot – that's his place." Pointing to his American car, he added: "Goodness knows the boot's big enough. It's big enough for two."

31.3.69

White students protest against mixed parties

ABOUT 5,000 students from the University of Pretoria staged a demonstration here today. They marched eight abreast carrying placards which read: "English Ambassador, stop your mixed parties." and "US Embassy, celebrate your Independence Day in Washington in your own way."

Both the British and United States Embassies hold multiracial receptions on national days. Other slogans on the placards included "Mix your drinks but not your parties," "Mixed parties—mixed population," and "We shall maintain white civilisation."

9.4.65

No room for privacy

STANLEY UYS visits a Government hostel for black women

THE ADVERTISEMENT invited applications for the post of superintendent of what must be the biggest women's hostel in the Western world, with 2,800 occupants. It has huge iron gates to keep out unwelcome male visitors, latticed steel doors, operated from a master panel, to ensure crowd control, and facilities to dispense the pill. The superintendent is white, the occupants black.

The hostel is in Alexandra township, a black slum on Johannesburg's outskirts. The hostel, massive and forbidding, towers over the shacks awaiting demolition. By next month, it should be full. A stone's throw away is an identical hostel – for black men. It is already full. The Vorster Government plans to build 20 hostels of this kind in Johannesburg, housing some 60,000 black men and women.

The hostels are "horrifying" and an example of the "madness of Government ideology," say Opposition whites who have inspected them. The former manager of Johannesburg's Non-European Affairs Department, Mr Will Carr, describes them bluntly as "barracks." Dr Selma Browde, a Progressive Party city councillor, says they are "dehumanising."

In a statement, they declared: "The (Women's) hostel is built on bleak and austere lines. The dormitories are built entirely of concrete, and are cold and impersonal in the extreme. The place is completely deficient in all one normally associates with home life. There is no opportunity for living a family life."

The occupants of all the hostels will be "single" men and women. Many are, in fact, married, but are separated forcibly from their families by the apartheid system.

The system defines a "single" black man – apart from the true bachelor – as one who, because of Government restrictions, does not qualify to live in a particular area as a married man with his family, not even in urban black areas. Production of his marriage certificate is an irrelevancy.

A "single" black woman – other than one who is not married – is one who is married to a "single" black man as outlined above. This is the case, for example, with domestic servants, such as the ones who are being moved into the hostels. The system decrees that Africans can live in "white" areas only as "single" people.

Alexandra township, once a teeming, colourful place, with all the vice that goes with slums, is in a white area: hence Government agitation to break up black families living there; hence, too, the erection of hostels there for "single" black men and women.

The occupants of the two existing hostels come from flats north of Johannesburg's Houghton Ridge, where they work as domestic servants, cleaners, janitors. Each flat-block is being allowed a quota of sleeping-in workers of this kind: the rest have to go. They are not forced to move into the hostel, but the housing shortage is so acute in the black areas that they have no choice.

The iniquities of the system, where domestic servants are at the white employer's beck and call from early in the morning until late at night, are not denied. But at least the servants have the privacy of their own rooms where they can entertain guests, they are spared long bus rides in the morning and evening, and they usually get their meals free from their employers.

In the hostels, a lucky few have single bedrooms; the rest share two-bed and four-bed rooms (the men have up to eight-bed rooms). They are thrown in with complete strangers and there is the constant fear that their possessions will be stolen. Each occupant of a room is given an iron bedstead, a mattress, a narrow clothes locker, and a nail in the wall on which to hang a picture or a calendar — and that's all.

As we walked into one of these cheerless rooms, with the occupant's crockery stacked on a tray on the floor and a plastic curtain with a floral design hanging in front of the tiny window, my guide remarked, "Feminine, isn't it?"

"No chairs?" I inquired. "No," he replied. "Can you imagine 2,800 rioting black women, each armed with the leg of a chair? We hope to give them benches, though." He did not indicate where a bench could possibly be squeezed in.

Each room has one central light in the ceiling, and no way of reconciling the conflict if one occupant wants it on and the other wants it off. There are no electric plugs either to boil a kettle, although heating has been promised before next winter; and no shelves, except in the locker.

All other facilities are communally shared, such as washing and ironing. But to prevent thefts, the women have to sit and watch their washing dry – the guides admit this frankly. Each bath is shared by 20 women, each shower by 35, each gas burner by five.

Each woman is also given a small food locker in the communal kitchen. This is a small privately-operated shop selling foodstuffs and prepared meals. The "common room" is a beer hall seating 300 women – the pivot of their social life.

When a newspaper reporter asked Mr Coenraad Kotze, whose department is responsible for the hostel, what its occupants were expected to do for sex, he seemed nonplussed. "Sex?" he repeated. "The tone of his voice," said the reporter, "made it quite clear that the world's greatest life force was never top of the agenda at any of the discussions on the Alexandra hostels scheme."

22.9.72

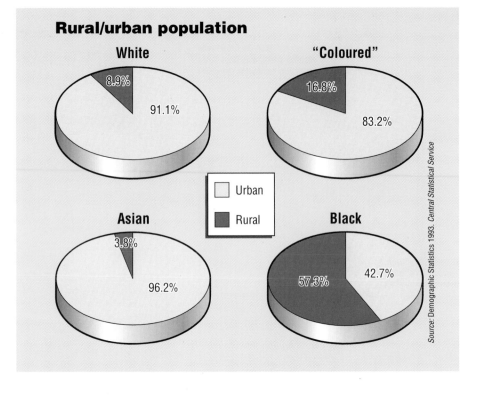

Rural/urban population

White: Urban 91.1%, Rural 8.9%
"Coloured": Urban 83.2%, Rural 16.8%
Asian: Urban 96.2%, Rural 3.8%
Black: Urban 42.7%, Rural 57.3%

Urban
Rural

Source: Demographic Statistics 1993. *Central Statistical Service*

next year, sometimes whether they will even survive — did not escape any who had been targeted for subjugation by the system. Their survival skills ranged from "legitimate" victories against impossible odds, to beating the system at its own game "by whatever means necessary" — even if those means were sometimes wrong in conventional moral terms.

Black South Africa produced inexplicable millionaires from the sixties onwards — men like Soweto's Ephraim Tshabalala — who had been denied an education but nevertheless succeeded in building business empires. Although trade was restricted by the Group Areas Act to their own areas, they made the most of it. Some of the businesses later collapsed because of lack of expertise, but their existence remains a symbol of the individual struggles to build and maintain esteem where there was supposed to be none.

If black history was denied by the official education system, it was kept alive in the names given to children — Bhambatha, Dingane, Biko, Nomzamo were common, while the family dogs were named Vorster, Verwoerd and Botha. If officials were around, you simply didn't call the dog.

The influx control laws were the NP's trump card in attempting to implement their 1948 election manifesto commitment: "The number of detribalised natives in the towns must be frozen . . . The native in the white urban areas should be regarded as a visitor who has come to offer his services to his own advantage and that of the white man." The pass books contained a "character column" aimed at maintaining a servile workforce. It was not uncommon, once the "native" had qualified for a pass and permission to work in urban areas, for an unscrupulous boss to endorse the employee's pass with "bad boy" for minor offences such as breaking a glass. Once labelled as such, the "bad boy" could never work again.

Forced into a life in the impoverished reserves, the bad boys went underground, at times buying passes from corrupt white officials in return for selling illegal liquor in the townships on their behalf .

The pass system forced many into a permanent life of criminality. Within the black community, tolerance, and even reverence, grew for the well-dressed, police-evading thugs who stole from white people and protected their own.

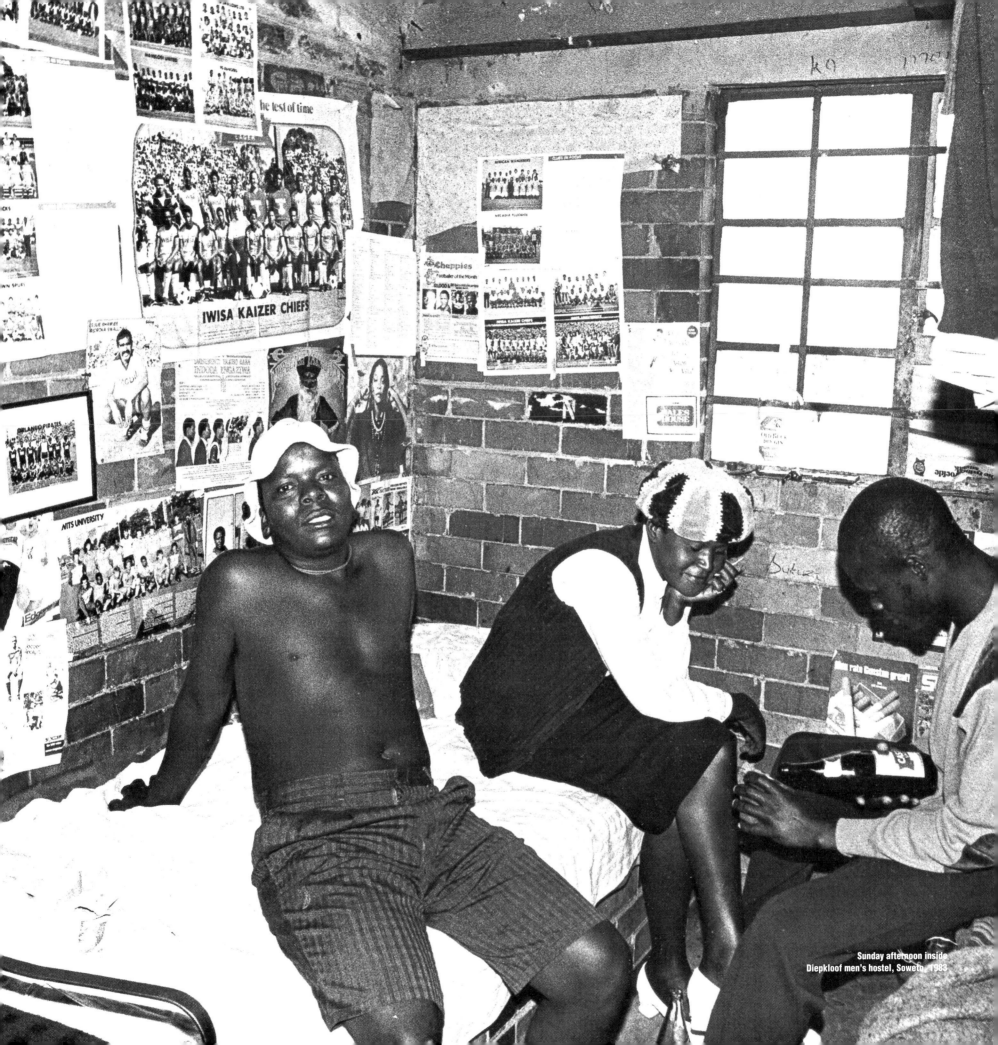

Sunday afternoon inside
Diepkloof men's hostel, Soweto, 1983

'Danger' of black nannies

A CHURCH marriage guidance counsellor in Johannesburg has urged white parents not to rely too much on black nursemaids because their children might grow up fond of blacks and break South Africa's law barring sex between races.

"I have nothing against black people," said Mr P. S. Oelrich, a counsellor for the Dutch Reformed Church for 30 years. "But my experience has shown that a black nursemaid who feeds, cleans, and clothes a white child becomes a replacement for the mother figure."

14.10.75

The scent of colour consciousness

From STANLEY UYS
Cape Town

MRS BETSIE VERWOERD, widow of Dr Hendrik Verwoerd, the South African Prime Minister assassinated in 1966 has run into a storm of criticism for suggesting that if white children are brought up by black nannies their colour consciousness will be blunted. They will develop a natural attachment for their black "mother."

"Even the characteristic smell, which is normally repulsive to a white person, will become associated in the child's mind with whom he spends most of his time," Mrs Verwoerd writes in the journal of the Afrikaans Language and Cultural Association. "Can this later repel him when he is grown up?"

21.11.73

Whites queue for dogs that killed black maid

Johannesburg:
SECURITY-MINDED whites have been trying to buy two watchdogs that mauled a black woman to death, the manager of an animal home said yesterday.

"I told them they were bloody mad," said Mrs Billie Greyvenstein, manager of the Florida branch of the South African Society for the Prevention of Cruelty to Animals, where police placed the dogs after the attack on Tuesday.

She said that on Wednesday, when the story appeared in the press, white callers started telephoning to express interest in the dogs, especially as guards.

"One security firm called. Others wanted to use them to keep the terrorists and the burglars away from the farms and factories," Mrs Greyvenstein said.

Large dogs are a common defence against assaults and burglaries in this country where whites are outnumbered by five to one.

Police blame the dogs, both mixed-breeds involving bull terrier lines, for savaging the black servant, believed to be about 21 and known only as Gladys.

Parts of her body were discovered around the yard, and part on the front porch, just a yard from the door. "The woman had put up a desperate, last attempt against the animal, as the male dog's one eye was swollen," said a police spokesman.

Police were summoned to the area after neighbours reported hearing frantic screams. The screaming, presumably from the maid, had stopped by the time the police arrived, so they left.

The victim's employer, who was boarding the dogs for a friend, discovered the body that night when he returned from work.

Unhappily for the would-be buyers, the dogs were destroyed on Wednesday.

16.9.83

Such "informal trading" came in many forms. Black prostitutes mocked the Immorality Act — which prevented sex across the colour line — when they were discovered in white areas in the middle of the night selling sex to white Calvinists.

It stretched to the townships, where women brewed illegal African beer for working men who had no other entertainment facilities. The women also became efficient at burying the evidence in the event of a police raid.

These were the beginnings of a shebeen (unlicensed tavern) culture which marked the development of innovative entertainment centres in the townships. An alternative consciousness thrived. The townships experienced an ideological unity which questioned submissiveness and "Christian" teachings which tolerated poverty on earth in exchange for riches in the hereafter. Black journalists, restricted by media ownership and law, did their utmost to mirror black experience. When they were prohibited from exposing army and police atrocities, they used apartheid's own separation doctrines and wrote about "Afrikaans-speaking men" who were killing people in dawn raids. Their readers knew exactly who would be speaking Afrikaans in the townships, at dawn.

From the squalor of slum areas, domestic and office labourers — mainly women — found other forms of revenge, such as dressing better than their white "madams". Sales on the black market, coupled with the marketing strategies of department stores which gave flexible repayment packages to a growing black market, made such flamboyance possible. The black market was not only confined to fashions but also encompassed household appliances, car parts and other consumer goods. The black middle class coined phrases such as "affirmative shopping" and "active redistribution of wealth" to explain the trend.

Astonishing achievements in closed-off academic and sporting areas spat in the face of the regime which had declared them non-persons. They boldly affirmed their contribution to the country despite white South Africa. And the story of the end of apartheid is unequivocally theirs — despite the claims by the new Nationalists that it was they who made it possible by releasing Nelson Mandela.

Nokwanda Sithole is a former editor of Tribute magazine

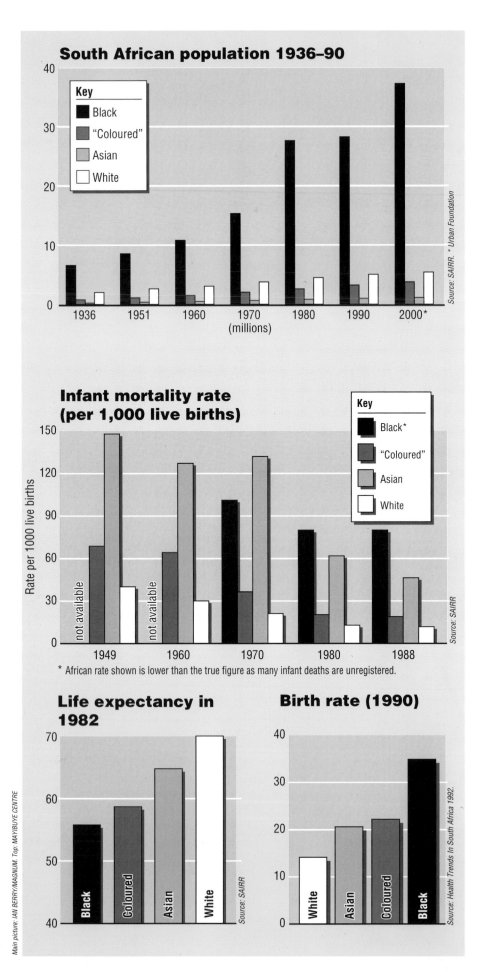

South African population 1936–90

Key
- Black
- "Coloured"
- Asian
- White

1936 1951 1960 1970 1980 1990 2000*
(millions)

Source: SAIRR. * Urban Foundation

Infant mortality rate (per 1,000 live births)

Rate per 1000 live births

Key
- Black*
- "Coloured"
- Asian
- White

not available · not available

1949 1960 1970 1980 1988

* African rate shown is lower than the true figure as many infant deaths are unregistered.

Source: SAIRR

Life expectancy in 1982

Black · Coloured · Asian · White

Source: SAIRR

Birth rate (1990)

White · Asian · Coloured · Black

Source: Health Trends In South Africa 1992.

Main picture: IAN BERRY/MAGNUM. Top: MAYIBUYE CENTRE

White people were immune to the hardship of apartheid and it took years before they perceived its folly

Donald Woods

TO WHITE people it was barely noticeable at first. You still got served before black customers in shops; you were still spoken to in a different tone of voice; you still had the best of what was going in the South Africa of 1948. Apartheid, after all, was not a change of direction but an intensification. It gave statutory teeth to many things that had been racial "customs", and it created new spheres and levels of discrimination in a complex code that eventually extended to no fewer than 317 laws.

It took me, as a teenager, nearly a year to notice any physical changes as a result of this much-used word "apartheid", and even then it was evident in apparently small things. Park benches that had been reserved for white people by custom or usage were now reserved by statute, with notices in both official languages saying "Whites Only". The Afrikaner Nationalist government of Dr DF Malan was obviously proud of its policy, and there was a clear implication of: "You ain't seen nuthin' yet . . ."

We sure hadn't.

The next manifestations of apartheid, for us, were elaborate extensions of the park bench notices. New public buildings had to have two entrances and extra elevators were installed in existing ones. Generally speaking the "non-white lift" and the "non-white entrance", not to mention the "non-white toilet", were the least conveniently located, as were the "non-white" seating areas at rugby grounds (usually behind the posts and never near the centre).

At first each bus was segregated, with the "black seats" at the back in single-decker buses, and always upstairs in double-decker buses. Then came total bus segregation. In all the main cities, the "white buses" were inevitably more frequent.

The better public transport for whites soon extended to better seats for whites in cinemas, then to all-white cinemas and progressed to better education in all-white schools and better facilities in all-white suburbs, all-white universities and better all-white jobs.

Along with the upsurge in apartheid statutes came a huge reallocation of national resources by the state, for this was now an Afrikaner government

Donkey races

BARRY NORMAN

I EXPECT you noticed the huge advance in racial integration that took place in South Africa yesterday when, for the first time, black children were allowed to ride donkeys in Johannesburg Zoo.

Can you not imagine the joyous cheering and shouting that went up in the African townships when the news was made known, the broken cries of "God bless you, baasie," that must have greeted the head of the zoo, the philosophical observation that this was "a small step for a donkey but a giant step for black mankind."

How it all came about is in itself significant. Mr Monty Sklaar, a Johannesburg city councillor, happened to notice that black children gazed enviously at white children as they trotted by on their donkeys. Now in the old days a black child found guilty of gazing enviously at a white child would naturally have been thrashed several times with a sjambok for his effrontery.

But Mr Sklaar, and those who run the zoo, are humane men and so it came about that yesterday black child and white child rode along side by side. Well, not quite side by side perhaps. Black children, obviously, had to ride their donkeys in the decent seclusion of a separate compound, so as not to give affront to those white visitors who still believe a donkey to stand fractionally higher in the evolutionary scale than a black child.

No matter. The donkeys bearing black riders may not have been exactly the same ones that bore white riders but they were so similar as to be almost indistinguishable, though I doubt whether there were any white donkeys in the black compound. You can't rush these things, you know, and after all a black person riding a white animal is against the laws of nature and an offence in the sight of God.

Now, of course, all South Africa holds its breath and awaits the next great development when black children may be allowed to ride the elephants, as well. Never mind that the animals will naturally have to be sorted out, some being designated as white elephants and others as non-white elephants, and that the non-whites will have to live in a separate paddock and carry passes. At least, when it happens it will be the perfect answer to those mischief maker who pretend that black people aren't always treated very nicely in South Africa.

9.10.72

Non-violence in South Africa

Leader coment

Eleven African miners were killed by the police in an outburst of violence at the Western Deep Levels mine in South Africa on September 11 last year. The incident was large enough and tragic enough to provoke international protests, although at the inquest the magistrate attached no blame to the police.

It now appears, however, that this was only the most publicised of many shooting incidents. Dr Muller, the Minister responsible for the police, announced on Tuesday that the police had shot dead 117 people and wounded 352 "in the execution of their duties" last year. Of the dead two were white and most of the rest were African.

More that twice as many Africans have been killed by Rhodesian forces since the guerrilla war started on the north-eastern frontier more than a year ago. But Rhodesia has a military conflict. South Africa is supposed to be at peace. Even South Africa must find it a terrible indictment that so many lives can be taken without civil unrest to justify the acts.

28.2.74

Maid killed

A SOUTH African woman who shot dead her black maid was yesterday given a three-year suspended prison sentence for culpable homicide by a judge who said she had an unnatural attachment to her pistol. Mrs Lillian Gordon, aged 30, was acquitted of murder but was said to have acted negligently in the use of her pistol. .

2.11.79

Turning the tables

CHIEF KAISER Matanzima, ruler of the Transkei – the first black homeland to be proclaimed independent – has fallen foul of South Africa's restaurant colour-bar laws. He was refused service with his three black bodyguards in a whites-only restaurant in King Williams Town.

Chief Matanzima said that, as a member of a foreign government, he could be served anywhere in South Africa, and eventually was allowed to eat his meal, watched by a large crowd.

23.7.77

Killer to die

A WHITE man who said he hated all blacks and shot three dead on a railway train was sentenced to death in Pietersburg, South Africa, yesterday. Pieter Willem de Beer, aged 21, and his brother Zacharius, aged 19, had been jointly charged with three counts of murder. The younger brother was sentenced to 12 years in gaol. The brothers said they hated all blacks because their mother had sexual intercourse with one many years ago.

12.11.83

Out of step

BLACKS ARE being allowed into 68 "whites only" sports clubs in South Africa, as long as they don't dance when whites are present. The clubs have been granted international status, allowing them to serve drinks and food to all races.

4.4.79

primarily serving Afrikaner interests, and before our eyes we saw the virtual eradication of the class of people known as "poor whites".

To English-speaking white schoolchildren, many young Afrikaners had seemed like beings from another planet — certainly beings from another income scale. When we played rugby against them, many of their junior teams played barefoot, and their heads were closely cropped. If they won, they got a 2lb packet of brown sugar to take home. Many came from families of tenant farmers, and the most they could aspire to when moving to the cities were low-paid jobs in the railways or the police force.

From the moment their government attained power, their situation improved. Afrikaner business boomed, thanks to lucrative state contracts. Afrikaner banks were founded and grew, receiving government loans and custom. Afrikaner printers were given the fattest contracts, such as the printing of telephone directories, official gazettes and state pamphlets; and Afrikaner insurance houses and mining companies began to prosper, thanks to official patronage.

Within one generation, young Afrikaners were able to look forward to a more varied and lucrative range of careers. A vast programme of building schools and expanding the university system provided a better-educated population to take advantage of the growing state largesse. Afrikaners were given the pick of state posts not only over black South Africans but over the English-speaking white population as well.

English-speaking officers in the armed forces were regularly passed over in favour of Afrikaners until all the key official posts in the country, both civilian and military, were securely in Afrikaner hands.

Naturally this made the new apartheid state even more precious to most Afrikaners. As for the English-speaking white people, they were generally economically better off to start with, since they had had their own run of affirmative action initiated by Lord Milner and other British colonial administrators up to the turn of the century.

The English-speakers were mostly interested in commerce and industry,

BFD558B

Near the Swaziland border, white children travel to school in Caspir armed vehicles to protect them from landmines. Black children...

Smile, please—you're a whiteman's char

Denis Herbstein visits his char at home in Soweto — two rooms for herself, her husband, and seven children

"SUCH HAPPY people, always smiling, punctual, and so honest there's no need to lock up a thing. Wish I had one of them in Hampstead. I've got this Irish char, well …"

We were going down the lift in a plush Johannesburg hotel, me and the lady from London who votes Labour when the candidate isn't a Socialist, here for a few weeks with her husband, an executive in a British company. She'd visited a school friend now comfortably settled in South Africa, been entertained by the wives of her husband's company at their swimming-pooled, tennis-courted homes, been down a mine, seen an African musical in a white theatre, and done the Soweto tour. "I know all about the horrors of apartheid," she said as the lift reached ground, "but you must admit 'they' (the whites) are doing a helluva lot for 'them' (the blacks)."

Back on the thirteenth floor Agnes, the smiling African maid, was preparing to clean out our rooms. At home, she is Mrs Agnes Ngwyena, a 41-year-old housewife living with her husband and seven children in two rooms of a friend's house in Zola, a suburb of Soweto, Johannesburg's dormitory city of a million blacks.

Agnes left Natal for Egoli (the City of Gold) at the age of 15 to seek work, and has been in domestic or hotel service ever since. She had no formal schooling, and can only write her name. She married in the Salvation Army Church, had six children and then divorced her husband for desertion. Though the innocent party, Agnes had to leave her home. The Bantu divorce court made no order for maintenance, even though the husband was working. She did get the children, however, but had to farm them out at a price so they could have a roof over their heads. Agnes married her second husband, Josiah, in 1973, since when her last (she hopes) child, Veli, has been born.

Now a sympathetic friend living alone in a three-roomed house has taken the family in and they are together again. But Agnes doesn't see much of them. She gets up at 4.30 in the morning, lights the coal stove in the kitchen, takes a cheroot taxi to the station, catches a train which is a hybrid of a football special and the Northern line at its tightest, stands for the 45-minute journey, and checks into the hotel by 7 am. An eight-hour day of cleaning, polishing, making beds and she leaves at 4 pm. Once on pay day tsotsis (black thieves) stole her month's wages in the crowded coach. By 6.30 she is home, makes supper for the family, does the washing and ironing, talks tiredly to her husband in the dining room decorated by three calendars, watches daughter Cynthia do her homework by candlelight, and retires to her bed by 9.30. The seven children, the eldest now lives in Natal, slide the table against the wall of the 12ft by 9ft room, arrange the blankets on the floor and catch some sleep. It's a bit like a scout tent, without the prospect of a comfortable bed at home when the camp is over.

Agnes works a six-day week, but only gets one Sunday off a month. Then she goes to church and sees her children by daylight.

For all this she earns £30 a month, her husband brings in another £50, while the daughter Ivy makes about £18 as a freelance washerwoman. Out of just under £100 the three breadwinners pay £7.50 each for transport, to work in the white man's city, and another fiver goes to the neighbour who minds little Veli while his mother is working. Then there are the medical bills, which at 30p a visit to the clinic mount up to several pounds in winter.

Mr and Mrs Ngwyena must feed, clothe, educate, and entertain their children and themselves on the £70 left over. No chance of television, for there is no electricity, but it's academic anyway because they can't even afford a radio.

It is hard to keep a child at school. Cynthia, a conscientious pupil in standard seven (about the first form) must pay school fees of £7 a year, and also find the money for most of her textbooks. Africans, unlike whites, do not get these free from the State and five pupils share the same textbook. There are 57 girls in her class, but she is determined to matriculate so she can become a nurse. Statistics are against her — of those African kids who do get to school only one in 400 advances to matriculation.

Four other children are at school paying smaller fees and less for books, but still a massive burden on the limited resources of the family. African schoolchildren, inheriting the outdated customs of the Anglo-Saxon education system, are pressurised by their headmasters to wear full uniform. They grow quickly, and dresses and jackets must be replaced every year.

But worst of all is the spiralling cost of food. Agnes says her children are going hungry these days. South Africa is in the grip of inflation as bad as anywhere in Europe, but the problems are compounded by the fact that supermarkets are few and far between in Soweto.

The wealthy white housewives of Houghton pay less for food and household necessities in their supermarkets than do Mrs Ngwyena and her friends in the black-owned corner shop in Soweto.

In spite of that ever-present smile, Agnes is a tired woman when she goes to bed at night and when she gets up in the morning. Her husband, Josiah, a solemn man, himself without formal education, is looking for another job. "I'm not afraid of hard work, and I'll do anything to pay for food for these children."

Their black landlord refuses to accept rent. Their name is down for a house, but with a priority waiting list of 8,000 in Soweto and less than 1,000 houses built last year, their prospects are gloomy. Even if they were lucky, the rent of £6 or more might be difficult to find. And then there's the furniture.

A million black people live in Soweto, yet the nearest the average visitor comes to it is in a luxury bus tour organised by the Department of Bantu Administration. The guide tells you how many clinics, with doctors, millionaires (five, he says), tennis courts, free library books, there are in this sprawling landscape of drab houses and eucalyptus-lined streets, smiling old ladies and waving piccaninnies with cuddly bellies. You never actually get to talking to a black person. Yet it is not illegal to enter an African township. All you need is a permit (a white man's "pass") from the local administration office and you can visit your chambermaid chez elle. It is more authentic than all the propaganda leaflets and guided tours.

Just up the road from Agnes's house is a bill-board sponsored by the all-white Collective Campaign Against Inflation. "Do something, it does help," is the admonition. Agnes smiles. "I'd like to help," she says, "but then the children will be very hungry."

28.5.76

'Even in the late seventies there were demonstrations by students in favour of imprisonment without trial, banning, and the forced removal of entire black communities'

generally enjoyed the sport and leisure made affordable by their high standard of living, and tended to leave politics to the Afrikaners . This was partly because, as a 38 per cent minority of the white population, they were effectively excluded from significant political influence. But most members of both the white language groups supported the policy to varying degrees.

There was, however, one significant difference. Whereas most individual English-speakers tended to be as conservative, as racist and as pro-apartheid as most Afrikaners, this was not true of the institutions of both language groups. The English-speaking churches, universities and newspapers tended to oppose apartheid excesses and infringements of civil liberty, whereas their Afrikaans-speaking counterparts enthusiastically supported them.

Even in the late seventies there were demonstrations on some Afrikaans university campuses by students in favour of imprisonment without trial, banning, and the forced removal of entire black communities in accordance with apartheid policy.

This attitude began to change towards the end of that decade. A growing movement among younger clerics in the Dutch Reformed Church questioned the Christian justification of apartheid that their church had maintained since 1948. Afrikaans newspapers and university campuses increasingly followed this trend during the eighties, and businessmen who lagged behind the new liberalism started catching up as the threat of economic sanctions began to build internationally.

It was this threat, coupled with the growing tide of black anger inside the country, which finally put paid to apartheid. White perceptions changed. Where they had once seen the system as their protector with both security and economic well-being, by the late eighties it had become increasingly apparent that apartheid threatened their very existence. The white population contemplated the increasing black birth-rate and the growing ranks of the unemployed and began at last to perceive the full folly of apartheid.

In certain manifestations that folly spilled over into madness, the sort of madness that required every new factory to provide a separate toilet for every unit

Below: **The cost of education: Uniforms, books and school fees place a massive burden on the average black family**

Right: **Those lucky enough to work queue up at crowded taxi routes in the early light of day for the journey into the city**

Barnard's new transplant trauma

PROFESSOR Christiaan Barnard's heart team is in the thick of a row today for transplanting a 28-year-old African's heart and lungs into the body of a 49-year-old coloured dental mechanic without obtaining the permission of the African's wife. The wife has since said that she would never have given her permission if she had been approached.

Yesterday's operation, performed at Groote Schuur Hospital, was Professor Barnard's first heart-lung transplant. This is the fourth such transplant to be performed in the world. In the three previous cases, the patients all died within hours.

Today's newspapers showed photographs of Barnard emerging from the operating theatre yesterday morning wearing a poloneck jersey, bellbottom trousers and a wide leather belt. The donor's wife, Mrs Rosalie Gunya, was shown lying slumped and shattered on a sofa in a friend's house in the township where she lived with her husband, Jackson.

27.7.71

'Deathtrap' claim as SA mine toll reaches 50

From David Beresford in Johannesburg

A BODY was yesterday spotted at the bottom of the St Helena mine shaft in South Africa's goldfields, making it almost certain that 42 miners trapped in a lift had died in a 400 metre plunge after their cable had been severed in an explosion.

Mine management were conceding that an underground explosion caused Monday's disaster, in which another eight deaths have so far been confirmed, bringing the likely death toll to 50. A spokesman for the St Helena company in the Orange Free State said that a methane explosion was one "likely" cause.

Previously, management had tended to discount an explosion, because of an absence of chemical traces.

In the mining industry there is a presumption of negligence where a methane explosion occurs, because safety precautions should obviate them. The St Helena mine confirmed on Monday that there had been traces of methane when the the disaster-struck number 10 shaft was sunk a few years ago.

The National Union of Mineworkers has bitterly criticised the Gencor group — owners of St Helena — over the disaster, describing their mines as "deathtraps". Gencor mines have suffered two other major disasters during the last year, including last September's Kinross tragedy, in which 177 miners were killed, and a methane gas explosion at the Ermelo mine in April which claimed 34 lives.

A spokesman for St Helena said yesterday that the NUM, together with other "employee organisations", was being fully briefed on what was happening at the mine. But yesterday afternoon the union's national safety officer, Mr Hazzy Sibanyoni, was to be found standing outside the gates to the number 10 shaft, complaining that he had been refused access three times. Journalists have been given repeated access over the last 48 hours.

Five survivors of the disaster were rescued overnight yesterday by a mine captain, Mr Nico Venter, from an intermediate pump station 695 metres down the shaft. Mr Venter — who had won an award for bravery last year after helping rescue a miner in another St Helena shaft — was lowered to the pump station in a makeshift bosun's chair suspended from an auxiliary cage (lift).

The condition of two of the survivors was described as serious, one of them being in a particularly critical state. Eight bodies were also discovered, at the pump station.

2.9.87

Pretoria's mass murderer smiled at his black victims

Judged sane, Strydom reflects insane system

David Beresford in Johannesburg

There was a young insurance salesman among the members of the public milling around in Pretoria's Palace of Justice this week.

Gerhard Van Wyk, aged 21, had taken time off work to show his support for a man he did not know very well, but whom he considered a friend. He was casually dressed – in a bomber jacket, khaki shirt and jeans he looked like any other white South African.

The friend that Mr Van Wyk had gone to support was Barend Hendrik Strydom, the mass murderer who trotted through the streets of Pretoria in November, smiling with apparent happiness as he shot 22 black people, killing seven of them.

'He did what many people in the country would do,' said Mr Van Wyk, during a break in the proceedings. 'I have much respect for him. He had guts. I wouldn't do the same, but I approve of what he did.'

The court has already found, on psychiatric evidence, that Strydom was not insane. The supportive presence of Mr Van Wyk and the backing of two rows of fellow rightwing extremists in the public gallery at the Palace of Justice suggests he is not alone. All of which raises the question: if Strydom is not insane, is he not at least a product of an insane society?

Strydom's background is not untypical in white South Africa. He is to some extent a creation of 'Christian national education', a school system designed to inculcate the values of Afrikaner supremacy.

'Each black person threatens the continued existence of whites, even an 88-year-old woman,' he said, referring to an elderly hawker who was among his victims. 'It is often the innocent black who causes the most problems,' he added. 'Scientists have shown that the oxygen is decreasing.

This is the fault of blacks, They are threatening the life of the entire planet.'

19.5.89

---

of 15 workers in no fewer than eight different categories — the male and female divisions of the four official racial classifications of white, black, "coloured" and Indian.

Those in search of signs of madness needed to look no further than the official definition of a white person in the Population Registration Amendment Act of 1967: "A white person is a person who in appearance obviously is a white person and who is not generally accepted as a coloured person, or is generally accepted as a white person and is not in appearance obviously not a white person."

By 1990, most white South Africans had realised that apartheid madness was threatening to destroy them as well as itself. When President FW de Klerk first articulated this, he was finding the courage for which two of his predecessors had groped in vain. BJ Vorster proclaimed that "the alternative to an accommodation with blacks is too ghastly to contemplate"; PW Botha admitted that "we must adapt or die."

De Klerk, at least, carried these concepts through to their logical conclusion. But he also carried into the consequent negotiations with Nelson Mandela a profound ignorance of his black compatriots.

During all the apartheid years, only a small handful of white South Africans had broken out of the laager of ignorance to acquaint themselves with that black generosity of spirit known as *ubuntu*.

Some were liberals like Alan Paton, Patrick Duncan and Randolph Vigne; others communists like Bram Fischer and Joe Slovo. Some, like Ruth First, Jenny Schoon and Neil Aggett, paid for it with their lives, and others were banned or imprisoned without trial.

That is the supreme irony of apartheid — that it was founded on the claim that a white future in South Africa could only be assured in strict isolation from black people — yet it became clear that the reverse was true. That the future would depend crucially upon black statesmanship.

Donald Woods is an author and former editor of the Daily Despatch newspaper

For gold and diamonds, black miners have to work hundreds of metres below the surface. Often, their working conditions led to tragedy.

Ten thousand people gathered to hear Chief Albert Luthuli address this ANC meeting in Sophiatown, Johannesburg, 1954. Walter Sisulu had to read Luthuli's speech as the Chief was served with a banning order on his way to the meeting. In the 1950s, those who opposed apartheid still believed that the government would listen to the voice of reason

ELI WEINBERG/MAYIBUYE CENTRE

The African National Congress looks set to become the driving force in South African politics. But it has been a long and bloody road to legitimacy, and the switch from liberation movement to political party has not been easy

The freedom movement/Tom Lodge

SINCE ITS foundation in 1912, the African National Congress has been the main force within South Africa's liberation politics, although it has had to tread a careful path between rival organisations and was, for the first 30 years, more a pressure group than a political party.

It was formed by members of a tiny professional elite, mostly graduates of Cape mission schools, following the abolition of African political rights in the Act of Union and the looming threat of the Natives' Land Bill. An assembly was held in Bloemfontein where doctors, ministers, teachers, clerks, journalists and landowners established the South African National Native Congress as a vehicle for agitation through "peaceful propaganda".

Various delegations to Cape Town and London between 1914 and 1919 received courteous hearings but failed to halt the passage of segregationist laws. Throughout the 1920s and 1930s, the ANC (which changed its name in 1923) remained an organisation of no more than 4,000 members grouped in a few dozen branches. Campaigning was sedate: the deputation, the memorandum and the petition were the tactics of choice. On the whole, the ANC left mass mobilisation to the Industrial and Commercial Workers' Union and the Communist Party.

Despite some overlapping membership, the ANC's relationship with the Communist Party was usually uneasy and sometimes tense. Between 1927 and 1930, an uncharacteristically adventurous ANC president, Josiah Gumede, attempted to persuade his executive to support the party's anti-pass protests. For his pains, Gumede was voted out of office and in the Western Cape the ANC split, with a Communist-influenced "Independent ANC" building up a militant following among farm workers.

In the 1940s, the transformation of the ANC into a mass organisation began. Its president, AB Xuma, devised a constitution which laid the foundations of a grass-roots structure, allowing branches to retain a portion of subscriptions and paying from his own pocket for full-time officials.

A young group of Fort Hare graduates established the Congress Youth League in 1944. The CYL aimed to redirect the ANC towards militant nationalism, emphasising African racial pride and cultural autonomy, and to persuade their elders to endorse a militant mass-based strategy. Youth Leaguers were inspired by the emergence of African labour organisations as well as by direct action taken by the urban poor in bus boycotts and squatter movements. Youth Leaguers won commanding positions in the 1949 ANC executive elections and gained the organisation's support for their programme of action.

The League's methods were implemented in the decade that followed, beginning with a well-supported strike to protest against the banning of the Communist Party. Former League principals Nelson Mandela, Oliver Tambo and Walter Sisulu, by now dominant ANC figures, revised their advocacy of African exclusiveness and their antipathy towards collaboration with Communists.

The ANC co-ordinated its activities with the Natal and Indian Congresses and sister organisations with white and "coloured" followers. Communists moved the organisation towards the multi-racial social democracy embodied in the Freedom Charter, adopted by the ANC in 1956.

Although efforts such as the Defiance Campaign of 1952 — in which 8,000 volunteers served prison sentences for civil disobedience — caught the public imagination, the ANC still did not represent a serious threat to the authorities. From 1955, it disrupted implementation of women's pass regulations, but this was exceptional — most of its attempts to resist apartheid laws were short-lived.

In April 1960, shortly after police fired into a crowd of anti-pass protesters mobilised by the ANC's combative rival, the Pan-Africanist Congress, the government proscribed both organisations. After the suppression of a three-day strike in May 1961 to challenge the transition to a republic, Nelson Mandela and other younger ANC leaders, in conjunction with the Communist Party, formed an insurgent wing, Umkhonto we Sizwe.

In December 1961, Umkhonto exploded the first home-made bombs in a two-year sabotage campaign. Intended as a last resort to "bring the government to its senses", the bombs were aimed at property, not lives. Meanwhile the ANC's external mission, headed by Oliver Tambo, began to train guerrilla recruits and build international backing for a trade embargo.

But, by 1964, Umkhonto's internal organisation was all but destroyed and most

11 AFRICANS DIE IN RIOTS

Assembly Ban Defied

POLICE FIRED on stone-throwing "Freedom Day" demonstrators in several townships throughout the Witwatersrand to-night, killing at least 11 and seriously wounding at least 20 others, according to the first official figures. Unofficial figures give 13 killed.

The disturbances broke out as darkness fell, after a May Day almost without incident except for unofficial walkouts of about 100,000 African workers from plants in Johannesburg and along the Witwatersrand for 50 miles on each side of the city.

All public meetings in the Witwatersrand and Transvaal areas had been banned by the Government from April 29 to May 2 because of Communist-led calls for African protest demonstrations for freedom of speech, movement, and assembly.

Police mobilised to enforce the ban were stoned in various Johannesburg suburbs, and were obliged to open fire at Sophiatown,

Alexandra, 15 miles north of the city, at Orlando, and at Benoni. Police escorting non-demonstrating Africans from their jobs to their homes in Moroka township, nine miles west of Johannesburg, opened fire in the dark under a hail of stones.

At Wynberg, Transvaal, demonstrators set fire to shops. Fire engines were also rushed to Sophiatown and adjoining Newtown.

At Benoni three Africans were shot dead and two wounded when a small force of police was attacked by about 500 Africans, holding a meeting in defiance of the Government ban. Charges failed to disperse the mob which surrounded the police and attacked them with sticks and stones. The police then opened fire.

Thirty-five miles from Johannesburg, at Brakpan, about one thousand Africans broke out of a compound and stormed towards the town. The police broke them up after a charge.

2.5.50

DEFYING DR MALAN

Campaign of Passive Resistance Begins

ACCORDING TO the latest reports, more than 130 Africans and Indians were arrested today on the first day of the non-Europeans' passive resistance campaign against the "unjust racial laws" of the South African Premier, Dr Malan. A white former Member of Parliament, Mr Kahn, was also arrested in Capetown; he was allowed bail. Mr Sita, the president of the Transvaal Indian Congress, was one of 47 Indians and Africans arrested at the Indian and Native location (township) at Boksburg, about 20 miles from here, after 50 volunteers had marched on the town with the intention of entering the location without permits.

Fifty Africans were arrested in Johannesburg tonight for defying the curfew law which requires Africans to be off the streets after 11pm.

In Capetown Mr Kahn, who was recently deprived of his seat in the House of Assembly under the Suppression of Communism Act, was arrested in the precincts of the City Hall after defying the Minister of Justice's order to stay away from City Council meetings. Mr Kahn later appeared at a magistrates' court and was charged under the Suppression of Communism Act. No evidence was offered and he was allowed bail.

26.6.52

Progressives crash colour bar

Aims of new S. African party

From our Correspondent

THE NEW Progressive party formed by 11 members of Parliament who broke away from the United Party three months ago was formally constituted yesterday at an inaugural congress of delegates from all parts of the Union.

In terms of South African politics the party has boldly crashed the colour barrier. It stands for a common voters' roll, with educational and property qualifications, and is to have a multi-racial membership. Planks in its policy include the abolition of the pass laws and influx control for Africans, discouragement of migratory labour, restoration of the freedom of trade unions, and extension to Africans of the right to form trade unions under the Industrial Conciliation Act.

The Sunday Times today hails the event as significant in view of the fact that this is the first time in South African history that a parliamentary group of more than 10 has advocated the vote for Africans, no colour bar in Parliament, and a multi-racial party membership. But the paper doubts whether the party will appeal to the South African electorate, which has always shown itself to be predominantly conservative.

16.11.59

BANTU EDUCATION PROTEST

African Campaign

THE AFRICAN National Congress to-day appealed to its branches to intensify their campaign against what it called "Bantu education." It also called on all African parents to withdraw their children from schools on April 23 in areas in which they have not already done so.

The ANC was protesting against the new Bantu Education Act, which transfers control of Bantu schools from the province to the Native Affairs Department of the Government, and which Africans have alleged will create a new type of inferior "Bantu education."

There was considerable improvement today in the attendance rate at African schools on the Witwatersrand, many of which have been almost empty since the protest against the Bantu Education Act began.

A gang of about 200 Africans, most of them youths, armed with knives, sticks, and other weapons demonstrated in the Germiston location (township) last night.

A further removal of African families from Sophiatown to a new township farther out of Johannesburg started this morning without incident.

21.4.50

'An exodus after the Soweto uprising supplied a fresh cohort of recruits for training camps recently established in Angola. Throughout the 1960s, guerrilla "armed propaganda" and foreign diplomacy enhanced the ANC's prestige, especially among young people'

significant ANC leaders were in jail or exile. Umkhonto's commanders, including Mandela, were imprisoned for life. Until the resumption of guerrilla operations inside South Africa in 1977, the ANC's activities were chiefly conducted in exile. During this period it drew closer to the Communist Party and developed an external bureaucracy in London, Dar es Salaam and Lusaka.

An exodus after the 1976 Soweto uprising supplied a fresh cohort of recruits for training camps recently established in Angola. Through the 1960s, guerrilla "armed propaganda" and foreign diplomacy enhanced the ANC's prestige inside South Africa, especially among young people. Although the ANC had only a skeletal internal organisation and could field no more than a few hundred armed combatants, it acquired immense influence, especially within the vast federation of voluntary associations formed in 1983, the United Democratic Front.

It also enjoyed increasing success in persuading Western governments to enforce economic sanctions against South Africa. By the end of the 1980s, economic recession and political stalemate prompted the government to legalise the ANC, release its leaders and initiate negotiations towards racial power-sharing. In 1990, the ANC's exile leadership returned home to begin building the largest and most sophisticated political organisation in South Africa.

In 1994, the ANC has a membership of more than half a million and a bureaucracy employing hundreds. The change from liberation movement to political party has not been easy. In the past three years, it has had to define coherent policies which can meet the expectations of its popular following and reassure foreign investors and the local managerial class, on whom the ANC will depend when it leads the post-apartheid governing coalition.

The ANC's present commitments to power-sharing for five years and economic moderation do not please all of its followers, nor its allies in the trade union movement. Last year, NUMSA, the miners' powerful affiliate of the ANC-aligned Congress of South African Trade Unions (Cosatu), voted to establish an independent workers' party — an ominous portent of the opposition the ANC may encounter when in power.

Of course, even today the ANC has no monopoly of black political support.

SLEGS BLANKES
EUROPEANS ONLY

Slow train to democracy: Members of the passive resistance movement lock themselves into a first-class compartment on the train to Cape Town, 1959

ARMED POLICE END MEETING

S. African Congress

ARMED POLICE broke up a nation-wide meeting of the "Congress of the People" at Kliptown Native area, just outside Johannesburg, today. About 3,000 delegates were gathered in the open air when they were surrounded by 200 policemen. The chairman of the meeting was told that the police were investigating a charge of high treason and that they were looking for subversive and inflammatory documents. A number of papers were seized, and police proceeded to take the names of those present, putting an effective stop to the proceedings.

The Congress of the People is composed of all races. Before the meeting opened, the secretary of the Transvaal Indian Congress stated that the police were stopping delegates in various parts of the country on their way to the congress. It was also alleged that lorry-loads of non-Europeans, who were on their way to Johannesburg, were stopped under the Road Motor Transport Act.

The object of the Congress was to adopt a "Freedom Charter" guaranteeing rights to all people irrespective of colour. The draft of the Charter was based on resolutions sent in by large and small meetings of Africans, "coloureds", and Indians all over South Africa where delegates were also elected to attend the Congress.

The congress was mainly propagandist. Having adopted the charter it is difficult to see what practical steps can be taken to carry it out.

26.6.55

Truncheon charge on African women

USING TRUNCHEONS, police charged 200 African women who stoned them today, and made one arrest. The women gathered from outlying districts, then marched along the main road to Camperdown, 35 miles from here, hoping to put their grievances to the Native Affairs Commissioner. Police told them the Commissioner refused to see them all and disapproved of their conduct. They should disperse and send a small deputation. While being questioned, the women started throwing stones.

25.8.59

African women in march: troops sent to mission

ABOUT 1,500 Native women marched today to St Faith's Mission, about 20 miles inland from the Natal coast, waving sticks and shouting in protest against a poll tax. They refused to give a magistrate a hearing, but quietened down when armoured troop carriers, filled with police reinforcements from Pietermaritzburg, arrived and they finally dispersed.

Trouble continued in other parts of Natal after the weekend of unrest. Police reinforcements left Port Shepstone for the Peak Trading Store near Ifafa on the coast, where 126 women were arrested during the weekend. And at Umtawaluni, in Southern Natal, 114 women have been arrested for creating a disturbance after stopping seven buses.

Open-air classes were organised for children at Sobantu, where rioters had burned down three schools on Saturday. Durban Corporation officials who went to the native township outside the city, to restore health services, had to withdraw because of the attitude of the Africans.

18.8.59

3,000 Africans riot in protest against banishment

AT LEAST 10 people were injured tonight when about 3,000 rioting non-Whites, mainly Africans, stoned and set fire to cars and attacked their occupants at Paarl, 36 miles from Cape Town. Five non-European casualties had been hit by bullets.

The rioters were screaming "kill Verwoerd" (the South African Prime Minister), and "kill the police."

The rioters gathered near the house of President of the African Food and Canning Workers' Union, Elizabeth Mafekeng, who has been ordered to leave the town by midnight to-night because her continued presence would be "injurious for the peace, order and good administration of Africa."

Mrs Mafekeng, mother of 11 children, has been banished to the remote Vryburg area, 700 miles away. She is allowed to take her children but must leave her husband and aged father-in-law behind.

10.11.59

The African politician whites queued to hear

By Myrna Blumberg

EVERYONE in South Africa who knows Albert Luthuli and many thousands who do not, black, white, or brown, call him simply "The Chief." I know of no other politician in South Africa who is looked up to in this way by all races, with so much straightforward love and faith.

There may be one or two politicians who are more brilliant, and some who are more important; but none more Christian, tolerant, forgiving. "I do not hold whites responsible (for apartheid) as individuals," he once said. "I do not hate the white man. You see his position of domination has placed him in a position of moral weakness. We must sympathise with him." To Luthuli, his politics are his practical interpretation of the Gospel. He is passionately Christian, and a Socialist, he would say, of the "Attlee variety." In addition, his unfaltering faith in passive resistance holds, like Ghandi's, a belief in the "purifying" force of non-violence.

Albert John Luthuli is now an elderly 62, suffering from high blood pressure and the effects of sleeping on the concrete floors of South Africa's prisons. He was born in Rhodesia, of Zulu Christian missionary parents, and educated at Adam's College, an American missionary school in Durban where he later taught for 15 years the subjects of teachers' training, music, geography, history, and Zulu.

He was always known among whites as a moderate. One day however he remarked: "Who will deny that 30 years of my life have been spent knocking in vain, patiently, moderately, and modestly at a closed and barred door? What have been the fruits of moderation? The past 30 years have seen the greatest number of laws restricting our rights and progress until today we have reached a stage where we have almost no rights at all."

24.10.61

Two other significant former exile organisations are contesting the election, while the Black Consciousness Movement has chosen to abstain. Each may represent a future challenge to the mildly reformist administration following the elections.

The first of these organisations is the South African Communist Party (SACP), founded in 1921 as a force in white labour politics but more or less predisposed to a black "national democratic" revolution from 1928. The party had a troubled history until the second world war, with ideological schisms reducing membership to a few hundred diehards. But its fortunes revived in the war when it helped to build a strong black trade union federation and a following among white servicemen after its decision in 1941 to support the war effort.

New white and black recruits were decisive in persuading the party leadership to work towards a "two-stage" revolution: national liberation first, socialism later. This was the line which predominated in the 1950s after the party was prohibited. Party activists played leading roles in the ANC and undoubtedly helped to radicalise the Congress Alliance. In exile after 1960, the SACP served as a conduit for Eastern-Bloc aid to the ANC.

Liberal critics of the ANC attacked its disproportionate Communist influence. But in many respects the Communists strengthened the ANC's commitment to social moderation — for example, by eschewing terrorism (for the most part) and in adhering to non-racialism. Joe Slovo, the party's senior ideologue, is the architect of the ANC's present power-sharing strategy. Communists are not contesting the election separately — they are well represented on the ANC's electoral lists and may hold a significant proportion of cabinet posts in the new government.

The party has grown since it was legalised in 1990. It now boasts 50,000 members, mostly concentrated in the trade union movement. Although the leadership may be sincerely committed to the kinds of compromises which public office will bring, its working-class following may feel differently.

Communist influence within the Congress Alliance in the 1950s was a factor in prompting the secession of the Pan-Africanist Congress in 1959. The PAC was critical of ANC "multi-racialism" and its disregard for the imperatives of African

'Biko argued that black people had to overcome their internalised sense of social inferiority. To this end, they should build and lead their own organisations, repudiating political connections with white people'

POLICE FIRE KILLS 63 AFRICANS

Armoured cars and sten guns used against crowd

PROTEST AT PASS LAW

European women injured, buildings ablaze

Fifty-six Africans, including women and children, were killed and 162 wounded when South African police opened fire on a crowd yesterday. At least seven others were shot dead in another incident and 50 injured, including four European women.

The Pan-Africanist Congress, an extremist break-away group of the African National Congress, had called on their members in the Union to come out without their passes and surrender themselves for arrest at the nearest police station.

In the first incident, at Sharpeville near Vereeniging, 20,000 Africans surrounded the police station, shouting. One African was shot dead and four injured after the police had been stoned. The Africans retaliated and then the police opened fire. The second incident took place at Langa, an African township of Capetown, where violence broke out after police had ordered a meeting to break up.

22.3.60

Photograph: Ian berry

Dr Verwoerd on risks of timidity

SOUTH AFRICAN Nationalist MP Dr Carel de Wet, said in the House of Assembly before it was known how many people died in today's pass riots: "It is very disturbing to me that when there are riots of this kind, whether it is rioting by whites or non-whites, that only one should be shot."

Whites' rights

He was speaking before it was known that more than one person had died, but he came under heavy criticism for his remark, which was taken by one opposition United Party member as meaning the police should use more violence than necessary to restore the situation, and that the shedding of blood should not be limited.

Dr De Wet rose after this and other criticism, and repeated his earlier statement, adding: "I say that because whites in this country also have the right to protection. If there had ever been a government which knew how to maintain law and order without sacrificing lives, it was the present South African government, but in recent times there had been certain cases of violence in which lives of whites had been lost."

The circumstances of today's incident at Sharpeville had been that between 4,000 and 5,000 Africans had marched on a police station. On the way they marched right through a white area, he said, adding that there was the possibility that they could have killed certain whites.

When it became necessary to use force it must be used in such a manner as to make it clear to everyone in the country that there was no place for murder in South Africa.

21.3.60

"They must learn the hard way."
Police officer's comments on the riots.

"I DON'T know how many we shot," said Colonel J. Piernaar, the local area police commander at Sharpeville. "It all started when hordes of natives surrounded the police station. My car was struck by a stone. If they do these things they must learn their lesson the hard way."

An official at Vereeniging Hospital put the casualties at 7pm to-night at 36 dead and 162 injured. Forty-four people, seriously injured, are in this hospital and the other 118 injured have been transferred to Baragwanath hospital near Johannesburg.

More violence broke out to-night, this time at Langa, where the injured included four European women whose car was stoned. Shops and an administration block were set on fire.

Shortly after 5pm about 6,000 men and women gathered in a square singing the African national anthem. Saracen and police vans approached.

A great roar echoed across the square as 60 police, carrying sten guns, riot sticks and revolvers, left the vehicles and faced the crowd. Supporting them were African police carrying riot sticks.

As the police moved forward, the crowd surged back.

Suddenly, the Africans turned about screaming and ran from the police, who waded into them, striking out with their sticks. As the police advanced, a barrage of stones, sticks and bottles rained on them and the crowd from surrounding buildings. The police returned to their vehicles and were followed slowly by the crowd.

A fresh barrage of stones struck the policemen, some of whom picked them up and hurled them at the crowd. Africans yelled at the police, "Cowards" and "Kill the white men." At this stage firing broke out and, after the square cleared, a number of bodies were seen on the ground.

Streets leading to the square were thick with yelling Africans. Some fired at the police from behind corners and out of windows. Above the rear of the crowd, sten gun bursts and the heavier thud of revolver shots were heard. The police later returned to Langa police station where they were joined by reinforcements.

Mr Owen Hodges, a commercial traveller who drove through the Vereeniging area today, said African men egged on by women pelted cars with stones and fruit. Sharpeville police station was "literally besieged" by thousands of African men and women, and police could only make contact with it by forcing their way through with Saracen armoured cars. Aircraft which dived over the area in an attempt to disperse the crowd only seemed to anger the Africans.

Like ninepins

The first African was shot dead and four Africans and several policemen were injured after the police had been stoned. The Africans retaliated, causing casualties among the police.

The police then opened fire with sub-machine guns, sten guns and rifles, and eye-witnesses said that the front ranks of the crowd fell like ninepins. The crowd then retaliated, leaving their dead and the wounded in the street.

Mangled bodies of men, women and children lay sprawled on the roadway in the square. One policeman described the scene as "like a world war battlefield."

A Johannesburg news photographer, whose own car was riddled with bullets, said, "I took pictures of more bloodshed than I have ever before seen in South Africa." The South African Press Associ-ation said one police officer instructed an African to collect pieces of a mangled body in a hat with a shovel and then spread sand over pools of blood in Sharpeville Road.

The police seemed to be rather shocked themselves at the scene. Traffic policemen and motor cyclist police patrols led ambulances and fire appliances and police trucks to and from the African hospital at Vereeniging and the police station at Sharpeville.

An African minister of religion took a piece of iron and scraped sand over the pools of blood.

The scene of shooting, after it was all over, was relatively quiet. But in the background the wailing and screaming of women could be heard.

Hospital wards were crammed with casualties. Some of the wounded were lying covered with blankets on verandahs of buildings near the casualty wards. Authorities of the Vereeniging hospital's non-European section issued an urgent SOS tonight for blood for the wounded.

The Pan-Africanist Congress President, Mr Robert Sobukwe, and the general secretary, Mr Potlako Leballo, who had expected 500 "resisters," led a party of 60 people to the Orlando police station, near Johannesburg, this morning. Mr Sobukwe, Mr Leballo and six other people were then held for questioning by the special (security) branch.

Dr Verwoerd, the South African Prime Minister, told the House of Assembly before the worst incident this afternoon that the Sharpeville trouble started last night, mainly at the neighbouring towns of Vanderbijlpark and Vereeniging, where Africans stayed away from work and marched on a police station.

March of 2,000

About two thousand marched through the third township involved in the trouble, Sharpeville, kicking open the doors of peace-loving people's homes, he said, intimidating them, and taking them on their march. The demonstrators also wrecked a number of telephone kiosks and took away their equipment.

At the beginning of today's trouble, he said, about five thousand Africans assembled at the police station. Their idea was to have themselves arrested for not carrying passcards or identity passes.

The crowd grew to 20,000, telephone wires were cut, and there were disturbances. The police then opened fire and about 25 people were killed and 50 wounded. The position there was now under control, he said.

Later he made a further statement that 43 Africans were killed and 156 wounded.

22.3.60

The horrific aftermath of Sharpeville

Mandela planned sabotage in struggle for emancipation

TWO AFRICAN leaders, Nelson Mandela and Walter Sisulu, told the court trying them today that their aim was emancipation from white domination, and they had come to regard violence as inevitable. Mandela, one of nine people charged with sabotage and plotting revolution, said: "We had either to accept inferiority or fight against it using violence. We chose the latter." Both strongly denied they were Communists.

The charges against Mandela, former leader of the banned African National Congress, and the other accused include sabotage involving nearly 200 incidents.

The eight others are former general secretary of the ANC, Sisulu, a former member of the banned Congress of Democrats, Dennis Goldberg, and a Johannesburg architect, Lionel Bernstein, both whites; former secretary of the Transvaal Indian Congress, Ahmed Kathrada; Govan Mbeki; Raymond Mahlaba; Elias Matsoaledi; and Andrew Mlangeni.

The case is known as the "Rivonia trial," named after the area north of Johannesburg where several of the accused were arrested in July.

The State has said the house was the headquarters of the "national high command" of Umkhonto we Sizwe (Spear of the Nation), a militant arm formed by the underground ANC to achieve the overthrow of the government. All but Matsoaledi and Mlangeni are alleged by the state to have been members of the "national high command".

Mandela spoke for nearly five hours. He said: "I do not deny that I planned sabotage. I did not do this in a spirit of recklessness. I planned it as a result of a calm and sober assessment of the situation after many years of oppression and tyranny of my people by the whites." He said he had practised as a lawyer.

"I admit immediately that I was one of the persons who helped to form Umkhonto we Sizwe, and that I played a prominent role in its affairs until my arrest."

Experiences

"We believed that as a result of government policy, violence by the African people had become inevitable and that unless a responsible leadership was given to control the feelings of our people there would be an outbreak of terrorism which would cause bitterness between the various races of the country.

"We felt that without sabotage there would be no way open to the African people to succeed in their struggle against the principle of white supremacy. All other means of opposing this principle were closed by legislation."

He said the ANC, formed in 1912, had adhered strictly to a non-violent policy until 1954. Then it launched a defiance campaign based on passive resistance. In the four-year treason trial which ended in 1961, in which he was one of the accused, "the court found that the ANC did not have a policy of violence."

In the 1959 referendum which decided that South Africa should become a republic, Africans were not entitled to vote, so it was decided to stage a "stay-at-home strike — a peaceful demonstration. "The government answered by mobilising its forces, sending Saracens into the townships to intimidate the people. This showed that the government had intended to rule by force alone. This was a milestone in the formation of Umkhonto."

Inevitable

He concluded that violence was inevitable and that it would be unrealistic for African leaders to continue a non-violent policy when the government "met our demands with violence." He said: "This decision was not easily made."

He said he had dedicated his life to end white domination — "It is an idea I hope to live and see realised, but it is an idea for which I am prepared to die."

21.4.64

NELSON MANDELA and his seven fellow defendants at Pretoria have all been sentenced to imprisonment for life. They have not been, as they could have been, sentenced to death. For that grain of mercy, they owe no thanks to the South African government. Mr Justice de Wet has shown before now that he is not Dr Verwoerd's office boy. He makes up his own mind. Yet, for all the noble plea for clemency put before the court by Alan Paton, he has passed the harshest sentence which could be passed, short of death, on the accused. And his unworthy suggestion that personal ambition was the driving force behind their activities is flatly at variance with Mr Paton's intimate knowledge of their personalities.

Within the terms of the Afrikaner state, the verdict and the sentence alike are proper. Mandela and the rest set themselves to weaken and in the end to destroy the regime, well knowing the penalties awaiting them if they were caught. They admit what they did. At liberty, they would do it again. Their defence is that what they did, and would do again, was just and necessary; that the Afrikaner state, rooted in the cardinal doctrine of apartheid, is itself so gravely and so irreparably wrong that there is no way to better it but by destroying it. In this they are right. These men are not scoundrels and eccentrics. Some at least of them are men who would be among the pillars of a just society. It is of the evil essence of the Afrikaner state that there is no place for them under its regime but in its prisons.

But it would be wrong despairingly to let things take their course. Isolated and fitful gestures of revulsion and rejection will achieve very little. Long-term measures of economic pressure may serve, if all the nations which express their indignation will act together, to give them concrete form.

Meanwhile we in this country must surely, in all honesty, end the concessions we still make, for reciprocal advantage, to the convenience of the Nationalist regime. The supply of arms is the most obvious of them. Such steps alone will not turn the scale. What is needed is to organise a great and growing pressure from many directions and along many lines — and under such prudent management that it does not reinforce the resistance which it seeks to overcome. That will not be achieved by public debate and demonstrations; yet without the force of popular opinion, it may not be attempted at all.

13.6.64

"nation building". Pan-Africanists also believed the ANC was too cautious and, to demonstrate their own militant credentials, they launched a mass civil disobedience campaign against the pass laws on March 21 1960. This was intended to be the first of a succession of campaigns which would culminate in an uprising to secure "independence by 1963".

Unfortunately for the PAC, it neglected to organise systematically. Its leadership was scornful of patient organisation-building for it believed people were ready to respond to a suitably phrased call to arms. "Show the light, and the masses will find the way," PAC president Robert Sobukwe was fond of saying. Response to the pass campaign was sporadic, although large crowds assembled outside police stations in several townships around Cape Town and Vereeniging. Police fired into a crowd at one of these, Sharpeville, killing 69.

After the PAC was banned, its leadership established itself in Maseru, Lesotho, and continued to plan for an insurrection in 1963. In the Western Cape, PAC slogans helped generate a following among migrant workers from the Transkei who began building a network of underground cells which they called *Poqo*, the Xhosa word for "pure". *Poqo* carried out attacks on chiefs in the Transkei as well as killing a white roadworker's family at Bashee Bridge.

Other PAC cells in the Transvaal, mainly recruited from schoolchildren, began preparing for a more co-ordinated general insurrection. Police intercepted messages from Maseru which included long lists of members and arrested several thousand suspects, hundreds of whom were imprisoned. From 1964, PAC activities within South Africa declined to a few isolated and sporadic conspiracies. In exile, based in Tanzania, the PAC never obtained aid on a scale to match the ANC and morale plummeted in its guerrilla-training camps.

A revival of its fortunes came in the late 1980s, however, partly thanks to more vigorous leadership from released Robben Island prisoners and help from Libya and other Islamic countries. Cadres of the PAC's armed wing, the Azanian People's Liberation Army, began military operations inside South Africa in 1985 and continued until the beginning of 1994, concentrating their attacks on township-based policemen and white farms. APLA operations have helped to

Right: **Nelson Mandela at the Algeria Military Headquarters in 1962, where he trained during a secret visit**

Above: **Walter Sisulu, one of Mandela's co-defendants at the Rivonia trial, addressing a human rights demonstration at the Alexandra township, 1952**

Durban liberals go out with dignity

From DEREK INGRAM in Durban

THE SOUTH African Liberal Party died in a side-street here at 9.30 the other night. There were no tears, no cries of anger; just a marvellous dignity.

After they had met in a small hall, Europeans, Africans, Asians, and "coloureds" stood round their president, Alan Paton, in the street outside and sang — haltingly, because not everyone knew the words — "For He's a Jolly Good Fellow!" "Nkosi Sikelele Afrika" (God Save Africa), and "We Shall Overcome." Mostly they were young, the Europeans in open neck shirts, their sweaters tied round their necks, the Asians and Africans neater in suits and ties.

Paton stood unobtrusively among the crowd, a sad and embarrassed figure. "I am by nature a private not a public person," he had just told the meeting. When the singing finished no one cheered or shouted. Paton just said, "Thank you," and turned away to his car. The crowd dissolved into the night. The rest is silence.

It had been an extraordinary and moving evening. We had been packed inside the Caxton Hall for the party's last meeting in Durban. Only one or two more meetings are being held in South Africa. Then, when the Government's Prohibition of Political Interference Bill becomes law, the party will cease to exist.

The Bill prevents people of more than one race belonging to any political party, and because this is a total denial of all the Liberal Party stands for, the party has decided it has no alternative but to disband.

16.5.68

Adam Raphael reports from Pretoria on a new, black-only party which could revivify the South African political scene

A still, small, black voice

BLACK POWER is the newest cry in the attempt to break South Africa's political stalemate. Thirteen years after Sharpeville, the structure of apartheid continues virtually unchallenged and apparently impregnable, in spite of minor tactical economic shifts, but there are at least signs of movement in the black political arena.

While anxious South Africa watches uneasily, uncertain how to react, the first stirring of a new black militancy has begun. A blacks-only political party, the Black People's Convention, held its first national congress this week at Hammanskraal, 30 miles from here.

Compared to the heated rhetoric of American black militants, whose clenched fist black power salute they copied, it was a mild affair. But for the first time in a decade the majority of the population of South Africa has been given the opportunity for an organised political voice. The speeches at the convention were moderate — they had to be if their authors were not to risk prosecution — and the constitution adopted was restrained. But no observer could mistake the hatred and contempt for white South Africa shared by the delegates.

Unlike its ill-fated predecessors, the new party refuses to have any dealings with white institutions or individuals, and claims to represent not just Africans but also Indians and "coloureds".

The constitution declares its aim to be nothing less than the liberation of all black people in South Africa and their emancipation from "psychological and physical oppression." A major policy is total opposition to all the institutions of apartheid including

the homelands, whose chiefs, such as Gatsha Buthelezi, are regarded as tools of the Nationalist Party. "We recognise white people as the enemy. For us all white people are united against black solidarity whatever they claim to be," the BPC's spokesman, Saths Cooper, said.

The new party's leaders know that the government will not hesitate to crush them as it did the African National Congress in the 1960s. But the BPC's overtly segregationist stance has placed it in a position of tactical strength, coinciding as it does with the Nationalist Party's credo that "nonwhites" must create their own separate organisations.

"We are aware that they can shove us in gaol at any time," said the party's secretary-general, Drake Koka. "That is why we are not a movement of confrontation but a movement of introspection — our aim is to awaken black consciousness."

The line between political activism and confrontation is a narrow one and it is open to question how long the BPC, whose very existence is a direct challenge to the government, can survive. To succeed it must have time to grow, for only about 100 delegates representing up to 20 branches attended this first national congress. The talk of a membership of one million within three years is at present just talk.

In the end its success — or that of a similar black power party, should it be banned — will depend on just how alienated and discontented urban blacks are with white South Africa. Here one enters a speculative area where few claim to know what is happening with any certainty.

One of the more reliable pieces of evidence is a recent study published by the South African Institute of Race Relations on the attitudes of high school pupils in Soweto, the vast African township just outside of Johannesburg. The survey showed that "black consciousness" is not merely a fever dreamed up by disenchanted black intellectuals. At the head of a list of what they consider to be their five greatest grievances, 73 per cent of the pupils put inadequate political rights, 67 per cent influx control and the pass laws, 65 per cent inadequate income and inadequate educational facilities, and 50 per cent put inadequate opportunity for employment. Complaints about the lack of entertainment and recreational facilities were far down the list, with less than 7 per cent.

The director of black theology, an organisation seeking a united black church, said recently that polarisation as now accepted by black students is "the only positive response to a situation which sought to bend the black man for ever under the white's yoke of oppression and dehumanisation." The new president of the South African Students' Organisation, Jerry Modisane, summed up his new militant attitude after his election this summer. "We do not need the cooperation of the whites on any score and we do not want it. We are fighting to liberate ourselves from the shackles of perpetual servitude."

Ironically, the growth of Black Power has given a new twist to the prophetic remarks spoken by the blacks in Alan Paton's book, Cry The Beloved Country. "When they turn to loving, they will find we have turned to hating."

22.12.72

Banished leaders

Main picture: **Pan-Africanist Congress leader Robert Sobukwe, at the entrance to his quarters in Robben Island. After serving a three-year sentence, he was "released into detention" there for a further six years**

Left: **Nobel Prize winner Chief Albert Luthuli, who was confined to his farm in Natal until his death in 1967**

create a new popular following for the PAC, particularly among young people and in rural communities. The PAC is contesting the elections on the basis of a radical social programme which particularly emphasises the redistribution of land. Polls suggest it will not take many votes from the ANC this time; but many people view the PAC as their second choice and it may emerge as a leading contender in 1999. The Black Consciousness Movement is rhetorically as uncompromising as the PAC, but much smaller and far less active. The movement has two wings, the Black Consciousness Movement of South Africa (external) and the Azanian People's Organisation (internal). The two function independently, but both spring from the cluster of organisations started by black students on segregated campuses in 1969 and the early 1970s.

A key personality within this group was Steve Biko, who was strongly influenced by American black power doctrines. Indeed, much of his work simply transposes to a South African context the writings of such authorities as Eldridge Cleaver, Stokely Carmichael and Charles Hamilton.

Biko and his contemporaries argued that black people had to overcome their internalised sense of social inferiority. To this end, they should build and lead their own organisations, repudiating political connections with white people. During the 1976 rebellion, Black Consciousness had near-hegemonic status, prompting the government to ban all the movement's bodies in 1977.

By then many of the early pioneers of Black Consciousness were in prison and Biko himself was dead from repeated beatings in police custody. Survivors attempted to resurrect the movement in 1978, incorporating into BC doctrines class analysis and "scientific socialism". In the late 1970s, however, the ANC was beginning to reassert a powerful presence in black politics and many of BC's most effective organisers joined the new bodies, which in 1983 came together to form the ANC-aligned United Democratic Front. Despite a strong following among students and within the intellectual professions, the modern Black Consciousness Movement seems unlikely to recapture its past glory.

Tom Lodge lectures at the University of Witwatersrand

'Scornful of patient organisation-building, the PAC believed the people were ready to respond to a call to arms. "Show the light, and the masses will find the way," said its leader Robert Sobukwe'

Strikes by Africans have increased by 500 per cent in South Africa during the past year. In the last month 5,000 Africans have defied police and staged illegal stoppages in Natal. ADAM RAPHAEL reports on the new black industrial militants

Learning their strength

THE MOST dramatic newspaper picture published in South Africa this month showed an army of striking black brick workers marching behind a red flag in Durban.

Just over a year ago, South Africa's Minister of the Interior warned his countrymen that unless the vast gap between African and white wages was narrowed, there was bound to be bloodshed. Disavowed by his colleagues in the Cabinet, Mr Theo Gerdener resigned shortly afterwards in disgrace. But his warning that "murder and violence" were inevitable if African living conditions were not rapidly improved is now coming home to roost.

Strikes by African dock workers, bus drivers, brick workers and building labourers have recently taken place in Johannesburg, Durban, Cape Town, and Pretoria. In response, cries of alarm have gone up from far-sighted white trade unionists who fear that the discontents of South Africa's five million strong urban black labour force have been seriously underestimated.

"There is no doubt that the tempo is accelerating and that instances of industrial unrest and the degree of action being taken is becoming serious," says the General Secretary of the Trades Union Council, Mr Arthur Grobelaar.

Employers are also con-

cerned by the almost complete lack of communication with black workers who, in industries like mining, construction, textiles, clothing, and footwear, account for 90 per cent of the labour force. Ironically, the fact that Africans are barred from legally-recognised trade unions and thus cannot use the collective bargaining procedures for settling disputes is part of the problem.

"We wish to pay these chaps more," bleated one white engineering employer last week, "but we don't know whom to negotiate with." The large Steel and Engineering Federation has now been asked by its Natal members, who have been hit hard by strikes, to examine ways of resolving the current industrial unrest.

That conditions are ripe for trouble is conceded even by the Government. Ministers are now urging that African wages should be raised, and raised quickly. The wage ratio between average white and black earnings in the mining industry is now a staggering 20:1, and in the overall economy the gap is still widening.

While white workers have been cushioned from inflation by fat increases secured by their unions, the effect of soaring prices on the lowest paid, unprotected black worker has been disastrous. A survey of more than 200,000

African workers last year found that four out of five were being paid wages less than the poverty level: a semi-official datum line which denotes the barest minimum to sustain a decent life for a family of five.

African workers are, of course, accustomed to being exploited. Forbidden to strike by the Bantu Labour Settlement of Disputes Act, which lays down severe penalties for illegal stoppages, they have been forced to rely on Government officials to resolve their grievances. The escalating arrest figures reveal, however, a new black industrial militancy.

In the past two years, the number of strikers arrested was more than double the total arrested for the previous eight years and the increase would have been greater if it had not been for the authorities' self-imposed tactical restraint. Between 1957 and 1967, there were 308 strikes involving 23,000 African workers and though there are no current official figures, the numbers have undoubtedly sharply increased.

"Africans have suddenly become aware that they are being underpaid because they are black," said Miss Lucy Mvubela, the General Secretary of the Clothing Workers Union. "They are beginning to realise that they must stand together."

29.1.73

Photograph: MAYIBUYE CENTRE. Facing page: PAUL WEINBERG/MAYIBUYE CENTRE

Mass uprisings in the townships proved pivotal in South Africa's political history. If they have anything in common, it is that they were not politically driven, and the leadership had to come from behind to direct them

Kaizer Nyatsumba

THE UPRISINGS that have helped to shape South Africa's history fall into three distinct phases: the Sharpeville massacre of 1960, the Soweto June 1976 revolt, and the sustained protests which greeted the introduction of the 1984 tricameral parliamentary system which yet again excluded black people from the highest organs of government. If these waves of unrest, as the government preferred to call them, had a common characteristic, it was that they were not directly driven by the political leadership of the day. They were very much mass-based, and the leadership had to come from behind to try to direct them.

Although there were periodic lulls in organised resistance to apartheid, often following repressive measures taken by the government, at no stage did resistance dissipate. With the seeds of black anger always there, it would not need much to spark off a major rising. They forced themselves on to the ruling MP's agenda and contributed in no small way in the democratisation process.

The 1960 uprising grew out of the movement against the Influx Control Act, embodying the "pass laws". More than any other piece of legislation, the pass laws drove home to black people the fact that they were not citizens in white South Africa. But the true level of police brutality was revealed in the Vaal Triangle township of Sharpeville on March 21. Word had gone round that the PAC had called for a work stayaway, and pamphlets had been distributed in the township. Between 3,000 and 5,000 people had gathered in the centre of Sharpeville. Then for a full 30 seconds, a rattle of police gunfire forced the now panic-stricken crowd to turn and flee. Sixty-nine died and 180 were wounded, most of them shot in the back as they fled.

Shock waves went round the world, and Pretoria responded by outlawing the PAC and the ANC, forcing them to turn to the armed struggle. With most political leaders in jail or exile, the lull that followed in black politics was not broken until the emergence of Steve Biko's Black Consciousness movement, which played no small part in the next rupture. If any event was the turning point in South African politics, it was the June 1976 uprising. It marked a new era in which black youths boldly entered the political arena. Afterwards, the country was never to be the same again. The trigger was the government's insistence that,

Comrades burn the car of a suspected informer after the
funeral of four activists killed by booby-trapped grenades.
Duduza Township, 1985

Deaths in political violence

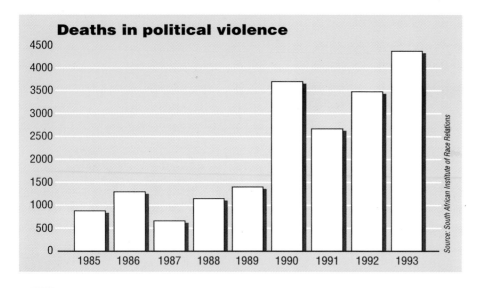

Source: South African Institute of Race Relations

Year	Deaths (approx.)
1985	~900
1986	~1300
1987	~650
1988	~1150
1989	~1400
1990	~3700
1991	~2650
1992	~3450
1993	~4350

Trial of militants ends in uproar

From STANLEY UYS: Cape Town

BLOWS WERE exchanged in the Pretoria Supreme Court today when 13 members of the militant black organisation SASO (South African Students' Organisation) and BPC (Black People's Convention) appeared on charges under the Terrorism Act.

Immediately after Mr Justice Boshoff had postponed the trial until April 21 and adjourned the court, the accused began shouting to relatives and friends in the packed public gallery and leaned over the dock to shake hands and kiss them.

Uniformed and plain-clothes police allowed this to continue for about two minutes and then told the defendants to descend the stairs to the cells. The accused ignored them and in the pushing and shoving that followed, punches were thrown, policemen's caps flew off, and a wrestling group of police and accused bumped their way down the stairs.

The prisoners were still shouting and protesting when they reached the bottom of the stairs and spectators crowded around the dock and joined in the commotion.

The 13 accused had entered the dock singing and giving the clenched fist salute. They turned to face the public gallery and the spectators, mainly young Africans and Indians, stood up and returned the Black Power salute. The defendants and spectators started to sing and when the song ended the accused shouted "power" and "Power to the people." One shouted: "Black people, you are beautiful."

The prisoners were in a militant mood in spite of being in custody since September and October last year. In the 20 minutes before the judge entered the court they taunted the police and jeered at the attempts of a white policeman to pronounce African and Indian names when he called the roll.

They insisted, contrary to court practice, on being called Mister and in one case Doctor, and one of the accused forced a man who was trying to record the remarks in the dock to put away his microphone.

The defendants are charged with conspiring to transform the state by unconstitutional, revolutionary, and/or violent means, conditioning the non-white population groups for violent revolution, fostering race hatred against whites, representing whites as inhuman oppressors of blacks, and persuading blacks to reject the white man and his way of life.

The trial in fact is one of the black consciousness movement in South Africa. An unusual feature is that the accused are charged not only with being members of SASO and the BPC but also the People's Experimental Theatre and the Theatre Council of Natal and with producing and publishing subversive poems and plays.

The trial was postponed at the request of the defence counsel who said they had not had adequate time to prepare their case. They pointed out that the minimum sentence under the Terrorism Act was five years' imprisonment and that the judge could impose the death sentence. They had only received the 100-page indictment a month ago, and had had even less time to study 2,000 pages of supplementary documents and statements by the accused.

13.3.75

Mandela 'may be free'

THE SOUTH African government is considering releasing Nelson Mandela and other black nationalist leaders now serving life sentences in Robben Island Prison, the Justice Minister, James Kruger, said yesterday.

Mr Kruger said he had received requests for the release of certain prisoners from the government of the Transkei, which becomes an independent black "homeland" in October under South Africa's separate development policy. But Winnie Mandela said her husband might refuse the release as it would restrict him to the Transkei. He considered himself a national rather than a tribal leader.

5.4.76

in addition to English, black secondary schools should use Afrikaans as a medium of instruction. This order was met with universal opposition from black students, and Soweto, as usual, was the seedbed of opposition. In addition to being their oppresser's language, the pupils argued that Afrikaans was only a "tribal language". Secret meetings in schools led to the choice of June 16 as the day of a mass march of peaceful protest.

As at Sharpeville, the day began with the protesters in optimistic mood, but it ended in bloodshed, in which the first victim was Hector Petersen, a 12-year-old, whose name has come to be synonymous with the Soweto shootings. Scores of other children were killed, and many more wounded.

The government responded in the manner it knew best — repression. A year later, it banned a host of political, social, church and students' organisations as well as black newspapers. The young activists fled the country to swell the ranks of the ANC's Umkhonto we Sizwe. From then on, South Africa knew neither peace nor internal stability. Now led by youths, mainly high school and university students, the struggle for freedom had entered a new era, and black university campuses became battlefields.

But the whites-only referendum in November 1983 for a tricameral parliamentary system that once again excluded the majority made black anger boil over. In opposition to the new system, a rainbow coalition of non-racial groups formed the United Democratic Front. Implementation of the new constitution was accompanied by violence which threatened to engulf the country. The call had gone out from Lusaka, headquarters of the exiled ANC, to make South Africa ungovernable, and youths in the townships enthusiastically followed the order.

Now championed by the UDF, the struggle widened to include Indian and coloured groups as well as white liberals through the new Congress of South African Trade Unions. People suspected of collaboration with the authorities began to be executed by the barbaric method known as "necklacing", by youths who saw themselves as the foot-soldiers of the revolution and refused to take advice or orders from anyone. These young people had been born bitter and

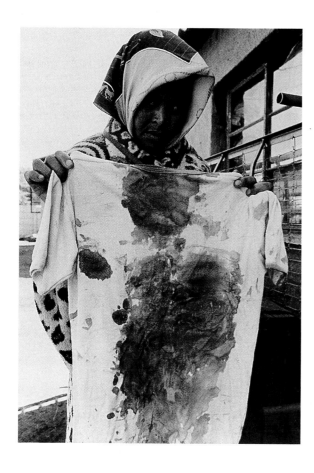

'Young activists fled the country to swell the ranks of the ANC's Umkhonto we Sizwe. Unwittingly, Pretoria had helped reinforce its opponents' guerrilla armies, whose cadres would later return to plant bombs'

S. African riot evokes shades of Sharpeville

Denis Herbstein: Cape Town

IN THE worst racial clashes since the shootings at Sharpeville, 16 years ago, at least eight people died today during riots at the Johannesburg African township of Soweto.

As a result, black leaders have demanded that the Government withdraw the ruling that Afrikaans be used as a language of instruction in Soweto schools.

Though reports are not absolutely clear, the deaths appear to have followed an incident in which policemen threw tear gas at high school pupils protesting against the use of Afrikaans. The eight dead include two white officials of the local Bantu Administration Board, two black adults, three black children and another white man. A further 40 people are in hospital.

The Justice Minister, Mr Kruger, said tonight the police "did everything in their power to bring the students under control and were eventually forced to fire warning shots over their heads." From eye witness reports, it is evident that some blacks were killed in this shooting.

Twenty buildings, mostly belonging to the Government, were on fire, and many cars were overturned and burnt out. A Johannesburg fire brigade appliance was hijacked by the rioters.

Late tonight police were still having difficulty controlling the situation. Mr Kruger said police were trying to move crowds of people into open areas.

The Divisional Inspector of Police in Soweto, Colonel J. J. Gerber, said the police did not "at this stage" think the situation had got so far out of hand that it warranted calling troops, though they had been asked to stand by at two police stations in the township.

Earlier, the police sent their crack anti-urban terrorism unit into Soweto, the first time it has been used. All whites have been evacuated from the township, as well as from the nearby Baragwanath Hospital, the largest in the country.

The riots began when 10,000 high school pupils marched through the huge township (with a population of over one million) to demonstrate against the Government's ruling that Afrikaans be used with English as a medium of instruction in the teaching of subjects like mathematics, history and geography.

Pupils at the Phefeni secondary school in the Orlando West area of Soweto have been on strike since mid-May against the directive.

Striking pupils from other schools joined in, carrying banners with slogans staying "Away with Afrikaans" and "Viva Azania," the name given to South Africa by members of the high school-based South African Students Movement, which figured prominently in the march.

Though the exact sequence of events has not been established, a black newspaper reporter, Miss Sophie Tema, was at the Phefeni school standing behind a group of policemen, mostly blacks, who were facing a taunting crowd of "thousands" of black students.

Then about 10 police vehicles arrived, and some 30 policemen got out. The white policemen, she said, were armed with revolvers. The taunting began again.

A white policeman, without warning, then hurled a tear-gas canister into the crowd, which immediately began throwing rocks and other missiles at the police. Miss Tema then saw a white policeman pull out his revolver and fire it. Other policemen joined in. They were firing into the crowd, she said. She took a child, aged about seven, to a near-by clinic, but he was dead on arrival.

16.6.76

The illusions that lie dead in Soweto

Leader comment

THE CARNAGE in Soweto, tragic though it is, will achieve at least one good result for Southern Africa. Dr B J Vorster will not be able to convince Dr Henry Kissinger in Bavaria next week that South African society is contented, that it is just, or that the government's methods are less than brutal towards black South Africans. No white man can now persuade another that South Africa is anything else but what it is — a police state based on racism. In 1960, the white South African police killed 69 black South African adults at Sharpeville. On Wednesday they started killing children. There can be no place yet for Dr Vorster's regime in the ranks of the civilised and democratic governments.

Wednesday's tragic aftermath in Soweto demonstrated and proclaimed — with the sharpness of a volley of rifle-fire — three reasons why the South African government's claim to partnership with the West is false. The first, and in some ways the most telling, is the nature of the place itself. Soweto is a city about the size of Birmingham, entirely reserved for black South Africans. Its name derives from the initials which describe its usefulness to the whites — South Western Township, the place to the South West of Johannesburg where the whites keep their black labour. Even now only about one third of this large city has electricity. The South African police, so free with their guns and their gas when it comes to a riot, seem to leave it alone at night. Last year Soweto had 701 reported murders, 1,296 cases of rape, and 8,118 of assault. And the International Defence and Aid Fund for Southern Africa has only been able to identify 49 schools in Soweto. It is a kind of half-lit jail house for people who are despised by their jailers because of their colour. Dr Kissinger should remember this when he meets Dr Vorster.

Soweto makes it all the more urgent that the West, through Dr Kissinger, should insist as firmly as diplomacy allows on progress towards democracy and racial reform, not just in Rhodesia, but in South Africa itself. Dr Vorster cannot now appear before the world in the role of a big white genial uncle, ruling a contented and peaceful black majority by methods which are designed solely for the black majority's own good. The majority is neither contented nor — in Soweto anyway — peaceful, and the good it derives from living in South Africa is only relative. Who, in 1976, wants to live in an unlit city with a million others? If anyone needed to prove that Southern Africa is a bomb waiting to explode the South African police proved it on Wednesday with their ill-considered gunfire.

16.6.76

DENIS HERBSTEIN, Cape Town, Wednesday, explains the simmering undertone of yesterday's violent outburst in the African ghetto

Where a pass is not just an exam mark

IF THE revolution ever comes to South Africa, they will tell you here, it will start in Soweto.

Although the rioting and deaths in this sprawling black Johannesburg "township" today can be blamed on an argument about the use of Afrikaans in black schools, the root causes are to be found in the frustrations of the urban blacks.

The same can be said for the 69 blacks shot dead by the police at Sharpeville in 1960 — they were protesting peacefully against having to carry passes, but deeper down they were demanding to be admitted to the good things of their country.

The immediate background to the riots was the Government ruling that African schoolchildren in "white" urban areas must be taught in both English and Afrikaans. Every other group in South Africa — whites, Indians, coloureds, Africans at rural schools, and the Bantu homeland schools — has the right to choose. All homeland governments have in fact dropped Afrikaans in favour of English.

Pupils at schools in Soweto and other black townships are taught in their mother tongue (Zulu, Xhosa, Tswana) until they reach Standard Four, the second last year of primary school, after which subjects must be taught in the two official European languages.

A number of African school boards in Soweto rejected a recent Government order on equal language and told school principals to continue using English exclusively. In February this year two members of the Tswana school board in Meadowlands (Soweto) were sacked by the local (white) Bantu board for refusing to accept Afrikaans. The entire board then resigned in protest. Since then at least five black school board chairmen have been replaced.

But it is the pupils themselves who have become highly militant in the past few years. They consider their parents to be weak-kneed "Uncle Toms." "When we are dead, they will spit on our graves," says Dr Aaron Matlhare, chairman of the Soweto Parents Community Association.

Black secondary school pupils are an elite. Only one in fifty of blacks lucky enough to get some schooling actually enters high school. When he does, he is older than his white counterpart. At 16, his political awareness takes on an acute form when he has to carry the hated pass.

Many of the pupils involved in the rioting belong to the South African Students Movement, a black consciousness grouping allied to SASO, the all-black students association. Since the Portuguese hurried out of Mozambique, the youth has not hidden its admiration for the new black Frelimo Government next door. The promise of black rule in Rhodesia and Namibia (South West Africa) has added to their confidence.

Objections to Afrikaans are both practical and emotional. English is the useful international language. Urban Africans invariably speak English as their main European language, and in cities like Johannesburg, Port Elizabeth, Durban and Cape Town, rarely acquire much Afrikaans. Hence the problems for school children who drop their own vernacular as the medium of instruction and suddenly have to be taught in two foreign languages.

But Afrikaans is also the language of the white masters. In the last 28 years many laws which govern and restrict their daily lives to a minute degree have been issued by the National Party.

Bantu education suffers a remarkable drawback. The most recent figures (1974) show that while well over £300 is spent every year on each white school child, the figures for Africans is £18. Black secondary school pupils still have to pay for their own textbooks, while the other races get them free from the State. And while the Government has pushed up the number of black children at school to nearly four million, three quarters of these never get more than four years in the classroom. The Government has no plans for compulsory education, since the absence of qualified teachers and the insufficiency of classrooms would make it impossible.

17.6.76

The students uprising, Soweto 1976

Above: **Students gather to protest. Hector Petersen (right), the first to be killed on June 16**

Far right: **One of the many children hit by tear-gas canisters during the disturbances**

Mandela's popularity astonishes analysts

From Patrick Laurence

The imprisoned black nationalist leader, Nelson Mandela, has again become the focus of national attention after another campaign to secure his release.

The latest campaign was launched more than a fortnight ago and is backed by all prominent black leaders.

Mandela was sentenced to life imprisonment 16 years ago, but despite being shut away on Robben Island, his name has continued to attract interest.

His nationalist reputation aside, two facts have helped to keep him in the public eye: his wife, Winnie Mandela, has emerged as a leader in her own right and kept his name to the fore, while the passage of time has given Mandela the status of martyr.

There is little evidence of the extent of Mandela's popularity in the community. But one clue was provided by the Bergstaesser Institute of Germany, which published the findings of a survey of black attitudes toward various black leaders and organisations.

Mandela was the preferred leader of 18.6 per cent of a sample of blacks drawn from three urban centres – Durban, Johannesburg (including Soweto), and Pretoria.

He was second only to Chief Gatsha Buthelezi, president of the Inkatha movement, who was preferred by 43.8 per cent.

Mandela's rating was described as "remarkable and astonishing" by political analysts, mainly because he had been out of circulation for so long.

26.3.80

Saboteurs strike at Pretoria's oil installations

From Patrick Laurence

IN A MAJOR strike against South Africa's vital oil plants, African National Congress saboteurs yesterday left firemen to battle against giant fires at Sasolburg in the Free State and smaller fires at Secunda in the Transvaal.

The pillar of smoke and flame which hung over the Sasol I plant and the Natref refinery at Sasolburg bore visible evidence to what specialists in strategic studies yesterday described as a new phase in the guerrilla war against the South African government.

The Minister of Energy, Mr F. W. de Klerk, implicitly acknowledged the skill of the saboteurs when he said: "It is clear that we are faced with a sophisticated attack." He referred to the simultaneous and co-ordinated attacks on the Sasol I and Natref plants at Sasolburg and the Sasol II plant at Secunda, more than 150 miles away.

The attacks were launched late on Sunday night. In both cases the saboteurs appear to have cut holes in the security fences before successfully placing and igniting their explosives. No arrests were reported by police yesterday.

The ANC yesterday claimed responsibility for the attacks. The last major ANC attack was made in April. It, too represented an escalation in the guerrilla war, in that it was the first attack on a police station in a white residential area. No arrests have been announced since the attack.

The Sasol I and II represent what Professor Arnt Spandau, former professor of business economics at the University of the Witwatersrand, in Johannesburg, has described as South Africa's "major defence" against the threat of an oil boycott. Sasol I and II process oil from coal.

3.6.80

Another enemy for apartheid

From Patrick Laurence

THE UNITED Democratic Front was launched at a national level in Cape Town at a rally attended by more than 600 delegates and thousands of observers at the weekend. It was an event reminiscent of the formation of the Congress of the People in the 1950s.

Forged in opposition to the "reformism" of the ruling National Party and riding the tide of the resurgent loyalties to the Freedom Charter, adopted by the Congress of the People more than 28 years ago, the national UDF represents 320 organisations across the country, all united in their hostility to the neo-apartheid of the Prime Minster, PW Botha.

The delegates elected a triad of presidents to head the national UDF: Albertina Sisulu, wife of the gaoled African National Congress leader, Walter Sisulu, and herself a prisoner awaiting trial prisoner; Oscar Mpeta, a veteran anti-apartheid campaigner out on bail pending his appeal against a conviction under the Terrorism Act; and Archie Gumede, another long-time opponent of apartheid.

The immediate origins of the UDF go back to January this year when Dr Allan Boesak, president of the World Alliance of Reformed Churches, appealed to fellow South Africans of all colours to form a united front against Mr Botha's proposals for tri-partite rule by whites, "coloureds" (mixed race) and Indians, with whites cast in the role of senior and controlling partners. Three provincial level UDFs were formed in the succeeding months, one in the Transvaal under Mrs Sisulu, another in Natal under Mr Gumede and a third in the Western Cape under Mr Mpeta.

So far the authorities have adopted a relatively tolerant attitude to the UDF. The arrest of Mrs Sisulu on charges of furthering the aims of the outlawed ANC is an exception to the leeway allowed to organisers.

22.8.83

unafraid of death. Apartheid was under siege, and Pretoria knew it. P W Botha declared a state of emergency which was to be renewed annually for the next four years, and launched a campaign to win the hearts and minds of the black population by relaxing petty apartheid.

But although many activists, including children no older than 10, peopled the jails, there was no let-up in the resistance. The economy went into its worst ever slump and, with the introduction of international sanctions, South Africa became a pariah in the world.

It was this South Africa that F W de Klerk inherited as state president in 1989. It was a South Africa heading for violent confrontation. Deeply aware of the anger and frustration which had accumulated over the years, De Klerk immediately rescinded the state of emergency and allowed an important safety valve by authorising marches and public protests.

In the wave after wave of marches that followed, the demands were the release of Nelson Mandela and all the other political prisoners, the unbanning of political organisations and abolition of apartheid in the provision of health services.

After a decade of harsh repression under Botha's government, people found it difficult to believe they suddenly had the freedom to take to the streets without being tear-gassed, arrested or shot by the police.

The new era reached a climax on February 2 1990, when De Klerk took everybody by surprise by announcing the unbanning of the political organisations and the release of Mandela and others.

With a single stroke of the pen, he had – as many would later say in shebeens – taken the excitement out of being black. He had made life ordinary.

Once Mandela was released, the marches lost their allure and gradually became fewer and smaller. But although they are almost forgotten now, there is reason to believe these huge protest marches will return in the months and years ahead, as an ANC-dominated government of national unity struggles to meet dangerously high expectations among the black majority.

Kaizer Nyatsumba is political correspondent of the Johannesburg Star

20,000 blacks in boycott

NEARLY 20,000 black students throughout South Africa were boycotting, or were shut out of classes, yesterday in a new surge of unrest over inferior black schooling.

The school boycotts, carefully watched because the boycotts of 1976 had erupted into rioting around the country that left nearly 600 dead, spread this week to several more secondary schools in black townships near Johannesburg.

Police confirmed that a 20-year-old youth died from wounds suffered in a clash between boycotting students and police at a technical night school near Pretoria on Tuesday, the second fatality in school unrest this year.

Police used plastic bullets, flexible rubber truncheons, and tear-gas to disperse stone-throwing protesters. Two policemen and three other students were injured.

In Daveyton, a township east of Johannesburg, boycotts spread to four secondary schools, affecting 3,200 students.

17.8.84

Black strike leaders detained after police swoop in Transvaal

From Patrick Laurence

SECURITY POLICE yesterday detained the entire committee which organised the mass stay-away of black workers in South Africa's industrial heartland on the Witwatersrand and in the Vaal triangle.

In consecutive swoops in Johannesburg on Khotso House, where the United Democratic Front has its Transvaal headquarters, and on Freeway House, where the Media and Research Services has its offices, security police detained three Transvaal stayaway committee members.

The remaining fourth committee member had been detained earlier.

Meanwhile, management of the partially state-owned Sasol Corporation dismissed 6,000 workers who took part in the stayaway strike. The powerful Federation of South African Trade Unions, which supported the stayaway, condemned Sasol's action. It said: "Sasol has chosen to provoke an industrial relations confrontation." Sasol workers were paid off in a field in a black township near the white town of Secunda. The field was ringed by armed police.

Black workers protested both at their dismissal and the manner in which it was carried out.

"Paying us in a field like this is another way to humiliate us, to show us that we are nothing," one worker said. Another remarked: "They have sacked us like a bunch of savages. We shall never forget it. We did not cause any damage or resort to violence." Police yesterday turned back white motorists in the Nqethu area near Hillcrest, in greater Durban, after black bus boycotters had earlier burned a ticket office there and stoned police vehicles and buses. A boycott of the local bus service started a fortnight ago after fares were raised.

9.11.84

Mob buries policeman alive in SA

From David Beresford in Johannesburg

A POLICEMAN was buried alive in South Africa at the weekend by a township mob while attending a funeral near the town of Witbank in the East Rand.

The dead officer, Constable SH Mandlazi, had gone to the cemetery as a friend of the man whose funeral was being held, according to a police statement from Pretoria. The original death had no political overtones.

Constable Mandlazi was attacked by a group wielding spades and was buried in a nearby grave. When police arrived on the scene and dug him up, he was found to be dead, in a sitting position. He was wearing civilian clothes.

A series of "necklace" deaths — politically-motivated murders with burning tyres — were reported from around the country at the weekend. From Durban, several victims' bodies in clashes between "vigilantes" and "comrades" (conservative and radical blacks) were found to have been savagely mutilated, with their genitals cut off and eyes and brains gouged out. The parts, it was feared, were being taken for "muti" (magic medicine).

Another facet of the vicious spiral of violence was reflected in a Johannesburg report at the weekend that security forces had shot dead a mother and her six-year-old daughter at a roadblock — and, then shot the father in both legs when he asked them why they had done it. According to the City Press newspaper, the incident took place in Soweto, outside Johannesburg, on Thursday night.

The police account of the incident, in their daily "unrest reports" last week, said: "Shots were fired at a number of vehicles which did not stop at roadblocks in Soweto. A woman and a girl were fatally wounded, while a man and another girl were wounded."

2.6.86

Tutu intervenes to save life of beaten black

From Patrick Laurence

BISHOP DESMOND Tutu, the Anglican Bishop of Johannesburg and winner of the Nobel Peace Prize, yesterday saved the life of a suspected informer at the funeral of four young black activists.

The man was being punched, kicked and *sjambokked* by scores of angry blacks outside the cemetery when Bishop Tutu intervened physically to drag him to safety and rescue from certain death.

Earlier a section of the 10,000-strong crowd at the cemetery intercepted the unidentified man as he drove up a side street near the cemetery. A wall of people blocked the car as the driver was hauled out and accused of being an informer. He was unable to satisfy his impromptu interrogators of his innocence, largely because he was literally paralysed with fear. As he was being quizzed, his car was overturned and set alight. The flames set his assailants into action and they began to beat and kick him mercilessly.

Bishop Simeon Nkoane, Suffragan Bishop of Johannesburg, tried unsuccessfully to stop the assault. Then Bishop Tutu, who had earlier pleaded with blacks not use methods in their 'struggle for freedom' of which they or their leaders would be ashamed, intervened to save him. The man was taken away to hospital by Bishop Nkoane.

11.7.85

SA given black union ultimatum

From Patrick Laurence

THE PRESIDENT of South Africa's newest and most politicised trade union grouping yesterday threatened to launch a campaign of defiance if President PW Botha did not repeal the pass laws within six months. Mr Elijah Barayi's fiery speech, launching the Congress of South African Trade Unions (Cosatu) at a mass rally in Durban, was an unmistakable manifestation of Cosatu's intention to play a militant political role rather than limit itself to industrial relations.

Mr Barayi, a stalwart of the African National Congress before it was outlawed, drew thunderous applause when he delivered his ultimatum.

"Cosatu gives Botha six months to get rid of passes," Mr Barayi said. "If that does not take place we will burn the passes of the black man. I want to give PW Botha a last warning to get rid of the pass laws and to withdraw the troops from the townships before the country burns." Cosatu is, in part, heir to the South African Congress of Trade Unions (Sactu), the trade union wing of the ANC. Sactu was never banned but fell into disarray in South Africa as its office bearers were detained and driven into exile.

2.12.85

School at gunpoint

POLICE AND soldiers forced pupils and teachers to hold classes at gunpoint at an affluent Indian high school yesterday as the Government appeared to be taking a firm step against anti-apartheid classroom boycotts.

For the first time since the latest wave of school boycotts began two years ago, soldiers and policemen with weapons at the ready stood in classroom doorways and marched through the school, literally forcing classes to be held.

The incident took place at a school near Cape Town. Elsewhere, police clashed with black youths hurling stones and setting fire to buildings in 10 areas and arrested 14 people.

17.1.86

ANC's war will be stepped up, says Tambo

From Patrick Laurence, Lusaka

THE ANC leader, Oliver Tambo, yesterday declared that 1986 would be the year of the people's war in South Africa. He promised a stepping up of the armed struggle by guerrillas in the ANC's military wing.

Mr Tambo, who said that South Africans of all races would have to bleed to save their land from apartheid and that black township violence must spread across the country, warned that the weekend land mine blast which killed two whites was only a foretaste of the violence to come.

"We declare 1986 the year of Umkhonto we Sizwe (Spear of the Nation), the people's army," Mr Tambo said in a message to South Africans marking the 74th anniversary of the founding of the ANC.

ANC military operations would focus on "armed enemy personnel" and military installations, but in the course of the "people's war" civilians would be caught in the crossfire, Mr Tambo said. "We do not derive any pleasure from that. We all have to accept it as the inevitable consequence of war."

10.1.86

Soweto chairman defends 'god-given job'

Tension builds in township as blacks threaten to defy ban on mass funeral

From Patrick Laurence in Soweto

THE EXECUTIVE chairman of the Soweto Council, Mr Letsasti Radebe, admitted yesterday that he faced pressure from his family to resign from the government-approved council.

But, he said in his office in South Africa's largest black township, he had little difficulty resisting the pressure. "I tell them it is a job given to me by God and my ancestors," he said.

Soweto councillors were labelled as "collaborators" even before 20 people were killed by police in Soweto last week. After that their position became even more uneasy. The clash between residents and police flared when the council ordered the eviction of rent defaulters.

Some Soweto councillors slept in Johannesburg after the violence. Mr Radebe, aged 54, was not among them, but his house in Naiedi, Soweto, is guarded day and night by members of the hastily recruited Soweto Council police.

A robust, dapper man, Mr Radebe was a leader of the Magotla, a vigilante movement which sought to force Soweto residents to uphold traditional values under threat of lashing. It had its own courts which sentenced people who strayed.

Mr Radebe deplored the "breakdown of discipline" in Soweto, blaming the rent boycott which is threatening to cripple the Soweto Council financially. He said the "Comrades", Soweto's radicalised youth, had frightened residents into joining the boycott by threatening to kill those who did not by placing a burning tyre doused in petrol around their necks.

The Comrades needed discipline, he said. "Their parents have lost control over them. No man will stand up and say they are doing wrong. They are scared of being necklaced. Mr Radebe predicted that the reign of the Comrades would end. "As time goes by, people will give information to the police. Then the rent boycott will die down. The police already have a lot of informers among the Comrades." The rent boycott, launched in June, is supported by about two thirds of Soweto's 75,000 householders. The Soweto Council relies heavily on rent and service charges by residents to pay for water, electricity, sewers and rubbish removal.

Its monthly bill is nine million rand (£2.4 million), of which about five million rand (£1.3 million) comes from rent and service charges. The rent boycott has already reduced the monthly income from house rentals to one million rand (£27,000).

Mr Nico Malan, the council's town clerk, insisted that rent and service charges were reasonable.

The average Soweto householder lived in a small four-roomed house, known as the "matchbox". Rent and service charges amounted to 52 rand (£14) a month, Mr Malan said. Dr Nthato Motlana, the veteran chairman of the Soweto Civic Association, accused the Government of making housing, and rent, a political issue.

He said the authorities had deliberately restricted the number of houses in Soweto to limit the inflow of black people. The official waiting list for houses is more than 20,000 families.

Dr Motlana claimed that money was not spent on Soweto and houses were not built to encourage black people to return to their alloted tribal homelands.

The South African Government was the biggest "landlord outside of Russia", he said. He accused it of raising rents "beyond the means of the average Soweto resident" and then of trying to interpose the Soweto Council between itself and the people.

4.9.86

Show of strength in strike

From David Beresford

BLACK SOUTH Africa flexed its muscles yesterday with what is believed to have been the biggest national strike in the country's history.

More than 70 per cent of the black workforce in the main cities are estimated to have heeded the one-day strike call — to mark May Day — in a chilling show of strength for white South Africa.

Around the country milk and newspaper deliveries failed to turn up at white doors, bread supplies were disrupted, and the usual river of commuters pouring into the cities from black townships slowed to a trickle.

Secretaries and executives had to empty their own bins, black schoolchildren played truant in their tens of thousands – with their teachers – work on construction sites came to a standstill, and production was hit in mines and factories.

The stay-away eclipsed the last such major national strike, called by the African National Congress leader, Mr Nelson Mandela, in 1961 to demand a national convention to resolve the country's racial problems.

The Association of Chambers of Commerce reported that yesterday's stay-away was "massive", varying between 70 per cent and 100 per cent in all the main urban areas with the exception of the Orange Free State where it was "minimal". Yesterday gun and fire-bomb attacks were reported on police vehicles in different areas. Two railway carriages were set on fire in Soweto. A youth was shot dead by police fighting off an attack on a beer-hall on the East Rand, and blacks marching through a white residential area in the Tape were dispersed with teargas.

The President, Mr P W Botha, yesterday offered an effective amnesty to members of the exiled ANC who were "not Communists", renounced violence, and wished to return to the country.

2.5.86

SA marchers capitalise on success

By David Beresford

ORGANISERS of South Africa's defiance campaign were yesterday preparing to challenge the government again as they moved to capitalise on a hugely successful demonstration in Cape Town with plans for another mass protest in Johannesburg tomorrow.

The South African authorities effectively abandoned the streets of the parliamentary capital to the anti-apartheid community as tens of thousands marched through the city, flying flags of the outlawed African National Congress.

Estimates on the size of the march varied wildly, between 25,000 – according to police – and 100,000. But it was unquestionably the most extraordinary demonstration witnessed by the "mother city" since 1960 and the biggest success yet in the defiance campaign being waged by the anti-apartheid movement.

Although chaotic, the march was marked by its peacefulness. Organisers warned that anyone acting violently would be assumed to be "an agent of the system" and would be disciplined on the spot.

Security forces stayed well away and the only police to be seen were a handful of municipal officers on traffic duty. Reserves of riot police were, however, on standby on the city's outskirts.

The demonstration culminated with fiery speeches by leaders of the defiance campaign who ridiculed the last-minute decision by the acting president, Mr F. W de Klerk, to declare the march "legal". The extreme rightwing opposition moved quickly to exploit the march, accusing Mr De Klerk of sanctioning open resistance to the police. "A knife has been thrust into the back of the maintainers of law and order," the Conservative Party's law and order spokesman, Mr Moolman Mentz, said.

Whether leaders of the defiance campaign could sustain the pressure on the government and how Mr De Klerk would attempt to reassert his control on the country were unclear.

The immediate focus of attention will be on Johannesburg, where a "solidarity service" is to be held in the city's Anglican cathedral, St Mary's. Plans were being made last night for the service to develop into a march on Johannesburg's notorious police headquarters at John Vorster Square.

In Cape Town, the crowd, while excited, was comparatively good humoured. The demonstration started with a short service in St George's Anglican cathedral, just a few dozen yards from parliament itself. Thousands packed the cathedral and nearby streets to hear prayers and statements of support from leaders of the city's Jewish and Muslim communities as well as Catholic and Anglican churchmen.

Watched by office workers crowding windows and balconies, the protesters marched through the city behind the two churchmen who have stamped their personalities on the campaign, the Rev Dr Allan Boesak and Archbishop Desmond Tutu, as well as Cape Town's mayor, Mr Gordon Oliver.

A huge banner — declaring Peace in our Country: Stop the Killings — led the procession. Placards bearing the photographs of the ANC leaders Oliver Tambo and Nelson Mandela were brandished and large ANC flags were flown. Archbishop Tutu gave a breathtaking display of crowd control with his inimitable style of sermonising.

14.9.89

SA miners rally to strike banner

From David Beresford

SOUTH AFRICA'S National Union of Mineworkers yesterday scored a stunning early success in its national gold and coal strike when the Chamber of Mines acknowledged that between 220,000 and 230,000 black miners had downed tools, "significantly" hitting 29 mines.

The NUM itself claimed that 340,000 had joined the strike, closing down production in 42 of the 46 mines at which the dispute was formally declared and another two where the union is not officially recognised.

The union, which is the country's largest, has a paid-up membership of only 262,000. Before the strike began, observers said that if it succeeded in calling out 200,000 the strike would pose a serious threat to the mining industry.

A spokesman for the chamber-representative of the country's six big mining houses, which are the strike's targets, said that the strikers represented about 40 per cent of the black workforce and conceded that the figure was disproportionately high since the action was concentrated on a small number of the larger mines. Sixteen gold mines and 13 coal mines had been closed.

The first day of the strike appears to have passed off comparatively quietly, although at least a dozen workers and two security officials are reported to have been hurt in clashes at different mines.

Six of the miners were hurt at the Kinross gold mine at Secunda — scene of one of the country's biggest underground disasters last year, in which 177 people were killed. According to the owners, Gencor, the injuries happened when 200 employees returning from work were attacked by "about 300 strikers."

There were also scattered reports of strikers being arrested.

The NUM's general secretary, Mr Cyril Ramaphosa, claimed that there had been a spate of incidents involving security personnel, including "a number of attacks on miners who have been seeking to attend union meetings" and a two-hour raid overnight by police on union headquarters in Klerksdorp.

At the Vaal Reefs gold mine, he said, workers had been forced underground at gunpoint. This was denied by the Anglo-American Corporation, which counter-charged that "violence has been used to force workers to strike".

11.8.87

Johannesburg bombs hurt 19

From David Beresford

NINETEEN PEOPLE were injured — four of them seriously — in two separate bomb blasts in central Johannesburg yesterday, which are likely to have substantial diplomatic and political repercussions.

At least one of the explosions, in a hamburger bar, was clearly designed to cause civilian casualties.

The blasts coincided with yesterday's ministerial contact with the African National Congress in London and the arrival in South Africa of the shadow foreign secretary, Mr Denis Healey — carrying the message that talks must take place with the outlawed ANC.

Responsibility for the bombs is not yet known, but the South African Government is almost certain to cite them as further evidence that the ANC has adopted a policy of hitting so-called "soft" targets.

It is the latest of a series of explosions in urban areas, one of which killed three women in Durban earlier this month.

25.6.86

Victory goes to sacked railmen

From Patrick Laurence

THE 16,000 black railway workers who were dismissed in April after a two-month strike — during which six workers were shot dead by police — will be re-employed by June, a jubilant Mr Ray Naidoo, secretary-general of the Congress of South African Trade Unions (Cosatu) announced yesterday.

The dismissed workers will resume work without loss of any benefits, and some of their grievances will be redressed, Mr Naidoo said.

He hailed the settlement with white managers of South African transport services as a "major victory".

Changes which the managers agreed to make include extending the right to permanent status to all workers — a right which, according to Mr Naidoo, was previously reserved for white workers — and giving workers the right to elect their own representatives.

6.6.87

Main picture: WENDY SCHWEGMANN/REUTER. Below MAYIBUYE CENTRE

Above: **Striking gold miners hold a noisy demonstration outside the Chamber of Mines, where their leaders were negotiating. Johannesburg, 1987**

Right: **Striking workers outside the Dunlop tyre plant, Benoni, East Rand, 1986**

Even at the height of the struggle, many Christians, both black and white, insisted the church and politics should be kept apart. For a time this became an issue in itself, until events forced black religious leaders like Desmond Tutu and Allan Boesak to use their influence to combat apartheid

The pulpit and politics/Charles Villa-Vicencio

"PEOPLE from outside the churches came and reminded us of the gospel we had forgotten. We could not escape the challenge. Every time we read the gospels we were confronted with the story of Jesus serving the poor and the marginalised society. Once awakened, we felt constrained to fight apartheid."

This reaction by an elderly minister was typical of one strand of Christian thinking in response to the moral dilemma of living under apartheid, but it was by no means the only one possible. Even at the height of the struggle against apartheid, most churches chose not to be politically engaged. "Political" priests were snubbed by conservative Christians and others who had been conditioned to keep church and politics apart.

Nevertheless, the political engagement of such priests gave hope to many black people who had no legal channels other than the church through which to express opposition to apartheid. Clerics were at the forefront of marches. When political detainees were forbidden to sing protest songs in Pollsmoor Prison, they sang hymns. The names of Archbishop Desmond Tutu, Dr Allan Boesak, Dr Beyers Naude, the Rev. Frank Chikane and others became internationally known. Access to the most powerful politicians in the world was theirs for the asking.

Others preferred to avoid confrontation, swelling the membership of conservative evangelical churches, both in black townships and among whites who sought escape from the turmoil of the times. The powerful white Dutch Reformed churches, in turn, provided direct theological support for apartheid.

In addition to these three broad currents, separate courses were charted by numerous African independent and historic black churches. Some were courted by the state and others co-opted by "homeland" governments. Most of these churches made no political headlines. Their members were, nevertheless, part of the political struggles in rural areas, townships and on city streets.

The public confrontation between church and state mainly involved the South African Catholic Bishops' Conference (SACBC), the South African Council of Churches (SACC) and the SACC member churches. The latter include black Dutch Reformed churches, other black churches, the Lutherans and Moravians.

They also include what are commonly referred to as the English-speaking churches, a category that includes Anglicans, Congregationalists (the United Church of Christ), Methodists, Presbyterians and several other mainstream denominations. The majority of members of these churches are black, and "English-speaking churches" is a revealing misnomer, for services are conducted in one of several African languages. Control has until recently been almost exclusively in white hands, and *de facto* racial segregation prevailed in every sector of these churches long before apartheid was officially imposed in 1948.

Conflict between the churches and the state first emerged in 1957. Significantly, the issue which aroused church opposition was one which challenged its accepted sphere of influence, rather than any of the moral questions posed by the imposition of apartheid. In 1957 the architect of apartheid, Hendrik Verwoerd, promulgated the Native Laws Amendment Act, which sought to prevent integration in worship. Refusing to tolerate such state interference in church affairs, the Anglican Archbishop Geoffrey Clayton told the prime minister in a widely publicised letter that he would instruct his priests and people not to obey the measure if it became law. Although several other churches supported the Archbishop, the measure did become law, but it was never enforced.

Next came the Sharpeville Massacre in 1960. The World Council of Churches' (WCC) member churches in South Africa met WCC representatives in the Johannesburg suburb of Cottlesloe to consider an appropriate response. The statement rejected several aspects of apartheid policy as contrary to scripture. It was enough to cause prime minister Verwoerd publicly to reprimand the Nederduitse Gereformeerde Kerk (NGK) delegates, all of whom had supported the statement. He demanded that they recant, insisting that they show support for the "high purpose of apartheid". Beyers Naude, one of the few who refused to submit, formed the Christian Institute as a forum of opposition to apartheid policies, and was forced to resign as a minister and as moderator of the Transvaal synod of the NGK. Together with the Christian Council (later to become the SACC) the Christian Institute was responsible for the Message To The People Of South Africa, which spoke of apartheid as a "pseudo-gospel".

Kerk the champion of apartheid

THE DUTCH Reformed Church (Nederduitse Gereformeerde Kerk), adamant in its adherence to the principles of apartheid, ruthless in their application, and with a highly influential voice in the councils of the ruling Nationalist Party, still has thousands of churches in the African townships throughout the country, and an enormous African following.

The church spends more on its mission work than any other church in South Africa, it claims.

A crippled African who is an Anglican, and who holds a teaching certificate, yet works as a messenger in a big city office, hinted at some of the reasons for the huge support the DRC receives from Africans even though its tenets seem so strongly opposed to their interests. "If I were to desert my church for the Dutch Reformed Church I could be a teacher tomorrow," he said.

"But even though the African schools are desperately short of teachers, and my disability makes me as a messenger extremely uncomfortable, I am not prepared to be 'bribed' into a soft job by a dominee (minister)".

3.2.64

Christians and apartheid – by an archbishop

Bloemfontein
The Roman Catholic Archbishop of Bloemfontein, the Most Reverend William Whelan, a native of South Africa, tonight issued a statement setting out what he said was the Catholic Church's attitude on South Africa's racial policy.

He said there was no teaching of the church "in opposition to the idea of a state composed of a number of national or racial groups, maintained in their separate and distinct identity by the state, of which they form a part."

The church had often declared that, "public authorities have an obligation to assist the cultural and racial groups in a pluralistic state in their distinctive development."

The Archbishop added that, "the church regards as immoral any policy aimed at levelling such ethnic groups into an amorphous cosmopolitan mass."

19.2.64

When Christians should support violence

CANON JOHN Collins, Christian pacifist and a leading opponent of apartheid, said in London yesterday that Christians were bound not to withhold support when, in desperation, victims of apartheid, suffering under the increasing violence of a violent regime, were driven to meet violence with violence.

He said the church had been fenced into a corner over apartheid because of past inaction. Either it did nothing and, by inaction, supported apartheid, or it supported violence.

Collins added: "How do we assume that we have the right to condemn African people when they too – and I think wrongly – decide to resort to violence for the preservation of their own country? We have no right to criticise".

"When men are confronted with desperation and violence of the state, which is responsible for law and order and justice, when they live in dire poverty and deprivation, dare we withhold from them our support because at last they have turned from nonviolence?" The church itself had gained a great deal throughout history by force of arms, he said. Canon Collins, who was preaching in St Paul's Cathedral, said the Archbishop of Canterbury's tour of South Africa had struck a magnificent blow against apartheid. "His visit has killed stone dead South African propaganda, aimed at persuading the Western world and the Christian world that the policies of apartheid are humanely administered, that the bulk of the Africans, Indians, and 'coloureds' are happy, and that any resistance to the racial policies of the regime are simply those of communists.

"As a result of the Archbishop's visit there will be fewer people taken in by South African propaganda".

7.12.70

Church hall gutted

SOUTH AFRICAN right wing terrorists threw a fire bomb into St Thomas's church hall in Rondebosch, Cape Town, last night, destroying it. Only the walls and part of the roof were left standing.

The anti-apartheid Christian Institute of Southern Africa held its annual meeting in the hall yesterday.

A few weeks ago, communist slogans were scrawled on the wall of another church hall used by the institute. Two attempts have been made to burn down the institute's building in Cape Town.

Recently, two petrol bombs were thrown at the home of the Cape director of the institute, Reverend Theo Kotze.

11.9.72

Picture: THE ARGUS, CAPE TOWN

'Divisions among the churches opposed to apartheid reached a new intensity. Black Christians, many of whom had sons and daughters fighting in the liberation armies, pressured the churches to face up to the reality of armed struggle as a last resort'

The Prime Minister warned the nation that there were those "who wish to disrupt the order in South Africa under the cloak of religion". In 1969 the WCC launched the Programme to Combat Racism, and a year later a special fund was announced to support organisations that fought racism, rather than the welfare groups that alleviated its effects. The outcome was that funds were provided for humanitarian aid to the African National Congress (ANC), the Pan-Africanist Congress (PAC) and other organisations.

Divisions among the churches opposed to apartheid reached a new level of intensity. The government threatened to take action against any South African church that supported the WCC financially, and most churches distanced themselves from its programme. Support among black Christians (many of whom had sons and daughters in the liberation armies) was such that the churches were forced to face the reality of armed struggle as a last resort against apartheid.

The Soweto student uprisings of 1976 encouraged fresh resistance in church and state. Large numbers of young people left the country to join the armed struggle. A year later the SACC adopted a resolution on conscientious objection, opposing Christian participation in armed forces used to impose "an unjust and discriminatory society". Black theology became a driving influence in the churches. This deepened the divide between black and white Christians — not least in the non-racial churches. In October 1977, the black consciousness organisations were banned, as was the Christian Institute.

Desmond Tutu was elected general secretary of the SACC in 1978 and Allan Boesak became president of the World Alliance of Reformed Churches (WARC) in 1982. The stage was set for further action by Christians under articulate and able black leadership. The Ottawa conference of the WARC, which elected Boesak as president, declared the theological justification of apartheid a sin — suspending the membership of the NGK as well as the Nederduitse Hervormde Kerk (NHK), which to this day has a clause in its constitution that prevents black people from joining. When the United Democratic Front (UDF) was founded to co-ordinate resistance in South Africa in 1983, it was natural that Christians against apartheid should play a leadership role. Allan Boesak, Frank Chikane and

Beyers Naudé (right) with Rev Theo Kotze in the burned-out church where they had just held a meeting of the Christian Institute. Cape Town, September 1972

Church refuses to segregate

THE ANGLICAN Church has cancelled a performance of Handel's Messiah in St Albans's Cathedral, Pretoria, because the government insisted that whites and blacks must use separate entrances and have separate blocks of seats.

24.6.65

South African ban defied

TWO SOUTH African churchmen yesterday defied government banning orders by attending a religious service in an Anglican church in Johannesburg without official permission. One of them, Father Cosmas Desmond, a Roman Catholic priest and author of an account of conditions in African resettlement camps, had been specifically refused permission last year even to attend mass in his own church.

By attending yesterday's service, which was a thanksgiving mass for "the courage shown and witness given" by Christians who had been banned, the two men ran the risk of arrest and, on conviction, imprisonment. The court could suspend gaol sentences but is not empowered to impose fines.

This is the first time a banning order has been deliberately broken in South Africa. There are clear signs that sections of the church feel the time has come for Christians to take a stand.

In an interview last week, the Anglican Dean of Cape Town, the Very Reverend E L King, said the churches in South Africa might soon have to issue a declaration of beliefs similar to the Barmen Declaration issued by the Lutheran Churches in Nazi Germany. Dean King said he feared the Anglican Church was being forced into a position where it might have to break the law.

African bishop charged

In the Transvaal today, the Right Rev Alphaeus Zulu, Anglican bishop of Johannesburg, was arrested for failing to produce his "pass" — which every African must produce on demand by a policeman.

Bishop Zulu was arrested at the Wilgespruit Fellowship Centre in Roodespoort, where he has been attending a seminar on "Black Theology". Yesterday he had argued with "Black Power" delegates who maintained that Africans should be taught that blackness was more important than humanity.

Bishop Zulu must appear in court or pay a £3 fine.

11.3.71

Living on £2.50 a month

THE REVEREND David Russell, a white South African Anglican who has been living on five rand (£2.50) a month – the average payment to African pensioners in resettlement camps – for the past five months is finding the struggle "long and dreary".

In his latest monthly open letter to the minister of Bantu administration, M C Botha, he said: "It has put me under a strain which I don't believe I could carry for much longer. I feel a great tiredness deep within me. I just do not know how Africans manage."

Mr Russell's parish is in King Williamstown, 30 miles west of East London, and includes the Dimbaza resettlement camp for Africans displaced by the government's policy of creating separate black "homelands" within white South Africa.

He conceded that there had been some recent improvements in Dimbaza and other similar camps, but added: "It is sadly revealing, however, that so many of the "improvements" mentioned are facilities which should have been there five years ago – schools, water supply, cement floors, a new clinic, another rugby field, a telephone."

4.7.72   21.9.72

South African Church leaders to fight on

From Stanley Uys

ANGLICAN CHURCH leaders in South Africa, at a fully representative conference in Durban, have decided to provide legal aid for the political victims of Prime Minister B J Vorster's government and financial aid for their dependants.

This means that the Anglican Church will take over a politically dangerous and legally tricky task performed by the Dean of Johannesburg,

the Very Reverend Gonville ffrench-Beytagh, until his arrest on terrorism act charges. The church has obviously acted under pressure to step into the breach caused by the dean's removal from the scene.

The dean was found guilty of receiving money from the Defence And Aid Fund, London, which is banned in South Africa, and disbursing it to political prisoners and their dependants. He is appealing against his five

year sentence. The Anglican Church, in continuing his work, will raise the necessary funds from its own sources.

The Archbishop of Cape Town, the Most Reverend Robert Selby Taylor, who was asked by the Durban conference to appoint a committee to provide aid for political victims, said today: "We are not seeking a confrontation with the state, nor are we seeking to avoid it. We are standing by our Christian principles."

15.11.71

Pictures: Right: DAVID BARRITT. Main picture: GILL DE VLIEG/MAYIBUYE CENTRE

Right: **Rev. Allan Boesak, president of the World Alliance of Reformed Churches (WARC) at a funeral in Duduza township, Transvaal, 1985**

Far right: **Archbishop Desmond Tutu speaks out against "necklace" killings at a funeral in KwaThema township, Transvaal, July 1986**

Smangaliso Mkhatshwa (secretary of the SACBC) were among the leadership. Another milestone in the church and state confrontation was reached in 1985. Having opposed WCC grants to liberation armies, most churches also officially rejected economic sanctions. And when a group of Christians published A Call To Prayer For An End To Unjust Rule, in which Christians were urged to pray not that the political leaders be given wisdom, but that they be removed from office, this too was opposed by several important church leaders.

The outcry in the media bordered on the hysterical. A leading SACC executive member and head of a member church went on state television to attack the document. Refusing to support the armed struggle and rejecting the call for economic sanctions, he, with several others, would not pray for an end to apartheid. They saw the campaign as "too political". Support for it among black church members, however, ensured that the Call To Prayer was adopted by most church decision-making bodies to which it was presented. As a result, on June 16 (Soweto Day) each year, thousands of people pray for the end to apartheid in special church services and mass rallies across the country.

Later the same year came the Kairos Document. It condemned "state theology" which supported apartheid, as well as "church theology" – which it saw as a statement of liberal opposition to apartheid designed to distance the churches from it while refusing to support the broader struggle of the people. The Kairos Document called for a "prophetic theology" in support of the struggle of the oppressed. Grassroots support for the document was massive.

The Dutch Reformed churches, the NHK and the NGK, have always been more or less content to allow the NGK to define the relationship between the Afrikaner church and state. This relationship was spelled out nowhere more clearly than in the NGK's 1974 statement, Human Relations And The South African Scene In The Light Of Scripture. The statement, written at the height of Afrikaner political power, evoked the scriptures to legitimise apartheid. This remained NGK policy until a revision was published in 1986, under the less presumptuous title of Church And Society. Eschewing the contorted appeal to scripture, Church And Society provided a more pragmatic explanation for

'The stage was set for further action by Christians under articulate and able black leadership. At the Ottowa conference of the WARC, Allan Boesak declared that the theological justification of apartheid was a sin'

Church pay half poverty rate

by Peter Hildrew

WHITE SCHOOLS run by the churches in South Africa are paying their African employees well below poverty line rates, and in some cases no more than £10 a month.

A survey carried out in the Transvaal by Spro-cas, a study project sponsored by the Christian Institute and the South African Council of Churches, has revealed an average wage of only £21.34 a month, compared with the poverty datum line for the area of at least $40.

4.6.73

Church rejects open-school ban

From Stanley Uys

A CLASH between the Catholic Church and the government in South Africa appears to be inevitable now that the minister of Bantu administration has made it clear he will not allow the church to desegregate its schools.

The minister, M C Botha, said last night: "It is not the intention of the government to change the education policy or the application thereof in respect of the different population groups, or to consider such a change."

The minister was reacting to a weekend announcement by the Catholic Church that it had decided in principle to open its 116 primary and 76 secondary schools, with 33,000 white pupils, to children of all races.

Archbishop Denis Hurley, chairman of the Catholic Church's department of schools, said today the church would not abandon its plans.

24.3.76

Church spies 'way of life'

From Stanley Uys

LEADERS OF five South African churches said at the weekend that recruitment of informers by the security police among their clergy and congregations had become part of the South African way of life.

The churches are Anglican, Catholic, Methodist, Presbyterian, and Congregationalist. They have all opposed the country's racial policies in the past.

Canon Robert Jeffrey, chaplain to the Anglican Archbishop of Cape Town, said a "relatively large number" of Anglican clergymen and theological students have been approached during the past three years to act as informers.

16.10.72

Funeral service walk-out

By John Kane-Berman

THE ENTIRE congregation walked out of a church in Germiston yesterday when the minister refused to conduct a funeral service because blacks were present.

The walkout was led by the widow, Robina Smith. She described the behaviour of the minister, Dominee J J du Toit, of the Nederduitse Hervormde Kerk (NHK) in Germiston, near Johannesburg, as "unChristian, insulting, and thoughtless."

More than half of the nearly 200 mourners who arrived for Christian Smith's funeral service were blacks and Indians who had worked with him at a plastics factory in the town, where he was a yard manager.

17.1.80

Coloured church breaks silence on apartheid

From Stanley Uys

FOR THE first time, a member church of the powerful Dutch Reformed Church in South Africa has publicly condemned apartheid. The "revolt" in the Coloured Reformed Church was sparked off by the security police detention of three "coloured" theological students in connection with the present black unrest in the country.

The theological faculty at the "coloured" University of the Western Cape, the only training centre for "coloured" reformed ministers, has come to a halt because of the detentions, according to the Coloured Reformed Church's moderator, the Reverend David Botha.

"All our work has been disrupted," he said. "Staff and students just can't get down to work in these circumstances." At a meeting between faculty staff and students and officials of the church, "students poured out their hearts to us – there were tears."

The three Dutch Reformed churches are the major white church in South Africa. Almost all members of prime minister B J Vorster's government belong to one or other of them. The DR churches support apartheid and have extensive political influence. The Coloured Reformed Church is a "sister" church, with more than 500,000 "coloured" members – about 25 per cent of the total "coloured" population.

Seventeen ministers of the Coloured Reformed Church then issued an unprecedented declaration of solidarity with African aspirations. They said they were "painfully aware that the Coloured Reformed Church has been silent for too long about the situation in South Africa."

18.8.76

---

apartheid. Next came the 1990 statement of the General Synod of the NGK meeting in Bloemfontein noting that, to the extent that apartheid had "begun to function in such a way that the largest part of the population of the country experienced it as an oppressive system", it could not be supported by the church.

Leading voices in the black and "coloured" NGK insisted that this was not enough. They demanded an unqualified confession of guilt from the white church. They also demanded a commitment to unity with the black and "coloured" churches. If the 1974 statement reflected the ideological power of the Verwoerd and Vorster eras of apartheid, the 1986 statement reflected the siege politics of PW Botha. The 1990 statement, in turn, gave expression to the reform policies of De Klerk. No significant commitment was made to anything the government had not already initiated. A leading NGK theologian, Willie Jonker, took matters a step further at the Rustenburg Conference of Churches, held shortly after the 1990 General Synod of the NGK. He confessed his complicity, and that of his church, in apartheid. The next day the moderator, Pieter Potgieter, associated the NGK with the confession to the extent that this could be accommodated within the decision of the Bloemfontein Synod.

The matter has more or less been left there. The next General Synod of the NGK is to meet six months after an election that promises to install South Africa's first non-racial, non-sexist, democratically elected government. Not all Afrikaners within the NGK or the other Dutch Reformed churches are ready to accept this development — nor are they all happy with the 1990 statement of the NGK. The threat of the Afrikaner right wing is yet to be dealt with in the Afrikaner churches, no less than in a democratic South Africa.

South Africa has long been regarded as a deeply religious country. The church enjoyed a high profile in public life. Not all who will constitute the new government are likely to be convinced that this should necessarily continue. It will be up to the churches to convince the new regime that they have something constructive to contribute to nation-building.

Charles Villa-Vicencio is Professor of Religion and Society at the University of Cape Town

Church on the attack

By Baden Hickman
Churches Correspondent

FATHER DESMOND Tutu, whose appointment as first black Dean of Johannesburg was announced yesterday, may be unable to live in his deanery because it is in a white area of his cathedral parish.

Apartheid laws will probably make it impossible for him to solemnise, in the cathedral, white couples' marriages which would be legally acceptable to the Republic.

His appointment by the Bishop of Johannesburg, Dr Timothy Bavin, will be seen as one of the most calculated anti-apartheid moves ever made by the Anglican Church in South Africa. Father Tutu is also on the full-time staff of the World Council of Churches, one of the most suspect of bodies in the mind of the South African Prime Minister, Mr B J Vorster.

Father Tutu, now in London, said: "I am extremely apprehensive. It is a very daunting task to be called to, and I am sure I accept this kind of assignment only because one is assured of the prayers and support of one's friends and a large part of the Church."

12.3.75

Church faced by vital decision on apartheid

From Patrick Laurence

THE POWERFUL Nederduitse Gereformeerde Kerk, largest of the three Dutch Reformed churches serving the white community, has been told by its predominantly "coloured" sister church to repudiate apartheid or face rejection by its sister church.

With 1.7 million white worshippers, the Nederduitse Gereformeerde Kerk, or NGK, is sometimes described as the National Party at prayer and its influence is pivotal to white thinking in South Africa. The ferment in its ranks will thus have a bearing on the political debate in Afrikanerdom.

The NGK synod meets in Pretoria next week to consider its position after its suspension last month from the World Alliance of Reformed Churches and the more recent anti-apartheid declaration by its sister church, the Sending Kerk.

The Sending Kerk labelled apartheid as "an idolatry and a heresy" and called on the NGK to "confess her guilt in providing a moral and theological justification of apartheid and to demonstrate repentance by working out the consequences of such guilt in both church and state."

If the NGK refuses to do so, the Sending Kerk will sever all ties with it. The Sending Kerk assessor, Dr Allan Boesak, was elected president of the 70-million-strong World Alliance of Reformed Churches at the same time as the NGK was suspended from membership of the World Alliance.

Whatever happens, the NGK synod will be of vital importance. If it refuses to "recant" and declares that racial separation is reconcilable with the scriptures, it will strengthen the position of hardline segregationists in the political arena. If it agrees that apartheid is a heresy, the reformists will receive a great stimulus.

As the reformist minister, Dr Nico Smith, has said: "The coming synod is a make-or-break one for the church." Dr Smith resigned as dean of the NGK seminary in Stellenbosch to accept a position as pastor to a black community.

6.10.82

Bishop Tutu's path to peace prize

By Patrick Laurence

BISHOP DESMOND Tutu, the 53-year-old general-secretary of the South African Council of Churches, who yesterday won the Nobel Peace Prize, sees himself as a "simple pastor passionately concerned for justice, peace and reconciliation".

For the past decade he has raised his voice against injustice in South Africa, first as the Anglican Dean of Johannesburg and then, from 1977, as the general-secretary of the South African Council of Churches. Although he had made his mark in church circles before the 1976 rebellion in black townships, it was in the months before the Soweto violence that he first became known to South African whites as a campaigner for reform.

In May 1976, only a month before violence erupted in the sprawling black township of Soweto, he wrote to the then Prime Minister B J Vorster, warning him of the situation. "He dismissed my letter as a political ploy engineered, perhaps, by the official opposition," Bishop Tutu recalled recently. "My letter was dated May 6, 1976. We all know that all hell broke loose on June 16 that year."

Bishop Tutu's earnest pleading for justice and reconciliation in South Africa drew him into the political arena, although he has always insisted that his motivation is religious, not political. For him Christianity is a robust religion concerned about secular matters. It is, as he noted in a submission to the Eloff Commission of inquiry into the SA Council of Churches, "very down to earth."

His attitude was to earn him the wrath of the political establishment, which appointed the Eloff Commission to investigate the council's activities. The commission found that the council had opted for revolutionary rather than evolutionary change and that political considerations weighed more heavily with it than religious values. It concluded that Bishop Tutu had made public statements designed to bolster the outlawed African National Congress and to give it respectability.

Bishop Tutu, however, replied that he wholeheartedly supported the ANC quest for a "truly democratic" and non-racial South Africa and that he would continue to castigate apartheid to his dying day. In his submission to the Eloff Commission, he declared against what he labelled "false or cheap reconciliation", the uttering of "peace, peace when there is no peace".

Bishop Tutu has been attacked by the conservatives for advocating the intensification of all forms of non-violent pressures against South Africa's establishment because, to him, increased pressure is the only alternative to violence. He is not interested in ameliorative steps which "make apartheid bearable rather than dismantle it".

A former teacher who joined the church with the introduction of Bantu education in the 1950s, Bishop Tutu was strongly influenced by many white clergymen in South Africa. They include Bishop Trevor Huddleston, now leader of the anti-apartheid movement in Britain, and Father Timothy Stanton, who went to gaol for six months last year rather than obey a summons to testify for the state in a security trial. Bishop Tutu remembers being amazed as a young boy when the then Father Huddleston doffed his hat to his mother, a domestic servant.

Father Huddleston, said BishopTutu, was the first white man to show that elementary courtesy. It helps account for his warm attitude to whites and his belief that they too, need "liberating" from apartheid.

As he told Mr Justice Eloff: "Oppression dehumanises the oppressor as much as, if not more than, the oppressed . . . whites need to hear and know that their value as persons is intrinsic to who they are by virtue of having been created in God's image."

7.10.84

The theology of liberation

As religious figures in South Africa don the mantle of resistance to apartheid, the Guardian examines the growing climate of confrontation between church and state

David Beresford

Memory brought a whiff of teargas to mind as the strains of We Shall Overcome rang out this week from Cape Town's St George's Cathedral, where some 2,000 people packed the pews to hear Archbishop Desmond Tutu articulate renewed church defiance of the South African authorities: "We refuse to be treated as the doormat for the government to wipe its jackboots on."

The teargas was not there this week, but there were clouds of it – as well as the metaphorical jackboots – some 16 years ago when I first gagged on the noxious fumes, watching police break up a demonstration on the steps of the cathedral.

The protesters, then as now, saw the building as a sanctuary in which the police writ was unlikely to run. It was, as they painfully discovered, a misapprehension. Police disguised as Hell's Angels were sent in to provoke trouble and their uniformed counterparts then charged the demonstrators with batons. The memory was worth bearing in mind this week as the country's main established churches vowed to step in for the restricted anti-apartheid groups to take up the struggle against white oppression.

The importance of the churches to the politics of South Africa is not to be under estimated, because religion – Christianity – is so fundamental to the society. A direct covenant with God is central to the myth of Afrikanerdom as a chosen people; a pastor, D F Malan, led the present government to power in 1948, and on present trends, it will be another clergyman – the leader of the official opposition, Dr Andries Treurnicht – who will lead the country to a disaster born of policies justified, however perversely, in scriptural terms.

Where black South African society is concerned, religion is even more fundamental. As a Catholic priest, at a mission in the Natal foothills, mused recently: "To blacks, the existence of God is never an issue; the question for them is merely how one should worship Him." Statistics bear this out. A 1970 survey showed that only 18 per cent of the black population did not claim membership of a specific church and most churches are dominated, at least in terms of numbers, by black congregations.

Even the Nederduitse Gereformeerde Kerk (NGK) – (Dutch Reformed Church) the largest of the Afrikaner reformed churches – boasts a black majority. And while, in many respects, they have a mixed track record insofar as their own affairs are concerned, the main "traditional" churches have made a considerable contribution to the domestic anti-apartheid struggle.

The comparatively small Anglican church - ranking fourth in size after the NGK, Catholic, and Methodist - has perhaps the longest and most consistent record in fighting racism. As long ago as 1930 its bishops roundly denounced the drift towards apartheid with a ringing declaration that rights of citizenship had nothing to do with race or colour.

It was not until the 1940s and 1950s that the Catholic Church became openly critical of state policies, but it has since taken something of a lead in the struggle, backing conscientious objection, "Africanising" its hierarchy, and encouraging the development of liberation theology. The Methodists, too, with an overwhelming black majority, have taken an outspoken stance. Their contributions to the struggle include one of their ministers, Basil Moore,founding the University Christian Movement in 1967, which played a key role in the development of the Black Consciousness Movement.

But any picture of political activism in South Africa's churches has to be qualified by the apathy of the country's largest single religious grouping. Figures on the so-called "black independent churches" fluctuate wildly, but there are said to be at least 3,000 of them, with a total membership probably exceeding five million. They are primitive in many respects (their ministers frequently differ little from witch doctors), adhering to the traditional values of tribal society - particularly in their authoritarianism.

The churches have already made a significant contribution to the leadership of the liberation struggle. John Dube, the first president of the African National Congress, was a Congregationalist minister. A Methodist minister, Zacheus Mahabane, twice led the organisation.

Albert Luthuli, probably the most famous leader of the ANC, was a Methodist lay preacher and — despite the government's representation of the modern ANC as a force of "Godless Marxism" – both Nelson Mandela and the present president, Oliver Tambo, are devout Christians.

A confrontation has been long in the making, only awaiting a domestic leader – to succeed the exiled ANC and the murdered Biko – to take up the banner.

In some respects that leader has been found, in Archbishop Tutu's co-celebrant at this week's service in St George's Cathedral, the Reverend Allan Boesak. Although Tutu, as a man of great integrity and extraordinarily original character, is likely to go down in history as one of South Africa's most memorable churchmen, it is Boesak who is more obviously cast in the role of a potential liberator – in the mould of Martin Luther King – not least because he has trained himself for the part.

A devout disciple of King's, Boesak has modelled himself on the great man, particularly in his oratorical style. Boesak is a man of great courage, a theologian in his own right, and, above all, has the power to move and excite huge crowds. But while he has all those abilities, seeming to qualify him to take on the leadership of the anti-racist crusade, one cannot help feeling that the role is not there for him in present day South Africa. He has tried to don King's mantle on several occasions, most notably in 1985 when he led a march on Cape Town's Pollsmoor gaol to demand the release of Nelson Mandela.

Instead of securing the ANC leader's liberty, he lost his own, landing in gaol himself for a month. It was a reminder that it is likely to take more than righteousness to bring an end to apartheid.

19.3.88

Police attack youths gathering to join a march on Pollsmoor prison
to demand the release of Nelson Mandela, Cape Town, 1985.
By the mid 1980s, the country had become locked into an ever
increasing spiral of violent opposition and repression

GIDEON MENDEL/MAGNUM

In its 46-year rule, the National Party can lay claim to having created a near-perfect system of state repression. It controlled every aspect of South African life: home, work, schooling, love, religion, politics, culture and reproduction. This thoroughness was the key to its success

State repression/Paula McBride

WHILE ON the campaign trail in Natal on March 3 1994, F W de Klerk roared enthusiastically to a somewhat bemused crowd that "the hands of the National Party are clean". He fluttered his own rather white hands in front of them as if to prove the point. But the audience could be forgiven for wondering what on earth he was talking about — the hands of the National Party may be many things, but clean they are not.

State repression in South Africa did not start in 1948, nor is it likely to end as soon as the world would wish. It has a long and ignoble history spanning many centuries, but the National Party government can lay claim to having created a near-perfect system during its 46 years of rule. It was this that enabled it to maintain one of the most universally despised forms of government ever known to man — apartheid. State repression in South Africa was not the sole responsibility of the security forces, and herein lies its success. The laws devised by the National Party invaded and controlled every aspect of South Africans' lives: home, work, schooling, love, religion, politics, culture and reproduction. Laws were enacted to determine who one could marry, entertain or sleep with; discrimination in public places was legalised through the Reservation of Separate Amenities Act; the Group Areas Act reserved prime urban areas for whites and the Population Registration Act divided the population into neat — and some not so neat — racial categories.

Disobedience in any of these spheres led to the ruthless and speedy intervention of those entrusted with the maintenance of law and order. A highly successful policy of reservation ensured those who worked within the police, the Defence Force, the Prisons Service and the misnamed Department of Justice were predominantly white Afrikaners. Their support for a government that cosseted and preserved them was total and they carried out their duties with vigour.

The job of these civil servants was made easier because those who applied and interpreted the law (the judges and magistrates) did so with great seriousness — regardless of whether or not the laws they applied were just. Learned men in sombre attire accepted the confessions of accused persons whose first appearance in court came after seven months of detention "for interrogation purposes".

Evidence given by state witnesses who were visibly bruised and battered was duly noted and entered into the record. Ludicrous explanations of the accidental deaths of detainees — falling down stairs; slipping on soap in the shower; falling out of windows — were legion, and over and over again these explanations were accepted by the magistracy and the bench. Prison sentences were passed on persons accused of possessing "revolutionary" paraphernalia — an unfortunate young man from the Orange Free State was given a three-year sentence for "mug possession" — the letters ANC were inscribed on the mug in question.

The repressive laws applied by the courts were many, but some of them hold a special place in history: the Terrorism Act, the Suppression of Communism Act, and the all-embracing Internal Security Act. Together, these laws allowed for indefinite detention without trial; solitary confinement; banning of political organisation; house arrest; prohibition of meetings; banishment of individuals to far-flung rural areas and censorship of published materials. Terms such as "free political activity", which today fall from the lips of National Party politicians with righteous ease, formed no part of their political lexicon during this period.

Deaths in detention were an inevitable by-product of the total powers given to police. From 1963 until 1990, more than 80 deaths in detention were recorded by human rights organisations — peaking in 1976-1977 when 26 deaths in detention occurred. The official post-mortem results are interesting: 21 died of natural causes (two of the deceased, James Tyita and Suliman Salojee, had spent less than a day in detention); 33 died as a result of "suicide" (in some instances the magistrate declared "death as a result of suicide by unspecified means"); four died "by accident", seven from "unknown causes" and eight as a result of police killing (seven of them at the hands of "homeland" police). Nor do these figures include deaths in police custody (as opposed to detention without trial); while charged or held under unspecified powers. Monitoring of these deaths began in 1984 and 32 were recorded up to 1990. In addition to the provisions of the Acts described above, the government afforded itself extra powers through the Public Safety Act 1953, which allowed for the declaration of states of emergency. This is not odd in itself — most countries provide for crisis management of sorts. What is odd is that

The end of South African justice

A BILL that, among other things, empowers the police to detain suspects without access to courts, legal advisers, or relatives for recurring periods of three months with its third reading with the support of the United Party Opposition in the South African Parliament yesterday. When the bill becomes law later this week, the state will have total power over the individual. This is the death of the judicial system which has been until now one of the redeeming features of South Africa's public life.

It will no longer be necessary for the government to stage a treason trial and undergo the humiliation of a series of acquittals. It will no longer be necessary to argue in open court whether an arbitrary six months' house arrest was imposed under the strict terms of the law. Guilt and innocence become irrelevant legal niceties and any opponent of the government – or of the local police – can be shut up for good. This might seem the logical end of all the repressive laws which have been introduced in the last few years – and how futile the struggle against them seems now! – but the minister of justice has said he cannot promise that this is the last instalment. He now wields as powerful and evil an instrument as any man anywhere. It is hard to see what more he could possibly want.

But there is a political meaning to the passing of the bill. The Nationalists have pursued their present policy since 1948, maintaining all the time that they were acting for the good of all citizens of all races. The General Law Amendment Bill – the "No Trial Bill" as it has become known – could have been introduced 15 years ago if it had been thought necessary for the swifter achievement of the party's aims. Its introduction now can only mean that the policy has failed and that the party is frightened. The opposition, perhaps haunted by all the liberties it has allowed to go by default, is no doubt frightened too. The civilisation which Dr Verwoerd and his ministers claim to be defending has ceased to exist because personal liberty is the vital part of it. All that is left now is fear and the animal instincts that go with it.

30.4.63

Mr Fischer greets life sentence with a salute

WITH A SMILE and a "thumbs up" sign – the salute of the banned African National Congress – Abram Fischer left the South African Supreme Court here today after being sentenced to life imprisonment for conspiracy to commit sabotage.

Mr Fischer (58), a noted South African lawyer, was found guilty last week on 15 charges. The sabotage charge carried a maximum penalty of death.

In addition to the life sentence, Mr Fischer was sentenced to eight years' imprisonment on each conviction of being an office bearer of the Communist Party, taking part in Communist Party activity before he went underground, and taking part in Communist Party activities after he went underground. All these charges came under the Suppression of Communism Act.

On six charges of using an assumed name in contravention of the Aliens Act, Mr Fischer was fined £10 or one month's imprisonment on each charge. For forging an identity card he was sentenced to two month's imprisonment and for forging a driver's licence one month. All the prison sentences run concurrently with the life sentence.

After the sentencing, Mr Fischer, flanked by several policemen, left the dock and went down the steps into the cells below the court – the same steps used by the men he had brilliantly but unsuccessfully defended in his last case at the Bar – in 1964, the Rivonia trial of Nelson Mandela, Walter Sisulu, and several others.

Mr Fischer is expected to stay in prison for the rest of his life because under South African law there is no remission or parole for political prison sentences.

10.5.66

Many a slip to death

A special correspondent on the mysterious toll in Vorster's prisons

AN UNKNOWN man died on an unknown date from an unknown cause. Not an extract from Kafka, but a South African Minister of Justice accounting to Parliament for one of the 14 people "known" to have died in solitary confinement while being interrogated under his country's no-trial laws.

The inquest on the last of these, Imam Abdullah Haron, which ended in Cape Town earlier this month, has again focused attention on the ugly methods of the Security Police in extracting confessions. The Imam, a respected religious leader and newspaper editor, was arrested last May under the Terrorism Act. Four months later he was dead. Neither his wife nor his lawyer had seen him since his arrest. No charge was brought against the Imam, though the police said after his death that he had engaged in subversive activities.

Doctors found 26 bruises on his back, sides and front, a haematoma (swelling containing blood) on his back, and a broken rib. The injuries, the Security Police explained, came about when the Imam fell down some stairs at the Caledon Square police station in Cape Town.

But further evidence revealed that the fall could not have caused all those injuries and that, from the different colours of the skin, there was a time lag of seven to ten days between one lot of bruises and the other. The magistrate found that death was the result of injuries "caused in part by an accidental fall," but he was unable to establish the cause of the remaining injuries.

The man who was present when the Imam "fell down the stairs" was Sergeant J. F. P. van Wyk, known to special branch colleagues as "Spyker" (Afrikaans for nail).

By the nature of detention in solitary confinement, it is virtually impossible to prove that police brutality is the cause of death. But the brief facts of three deaths of detainees make interesting reading.

Nicodimus Kgoathe, before he died of pneumonia in February 1969, claimed that he had been assaulted during interrogation. The Security Police said he fell while taking a shower. At the inquest the magistrate was unable, on the evidence, to conclude that any person was to blame for the death.

Solomon Modipane died in February 1969, three days after his arrest. There was no inquest. The magistrate endorsed a post-mortem report that death was due to natural causes. Police said he slipped on a piece of soap.

Suliman Salojee died in September 1964 after falling seven floors from Security Police headquarters in Johannesburg. At the inquest the magistrate did not say whether Salojee had committed suicide or was trying to escape, but there was nothing in the evidence, he said, to suggest assault or other irregularities. And so it goes on.

30.3.70

Picture: LAURIE BLOOMFIELD/MAYIBUYE CENTRE

'During the states of emergency of 1985 to 1989, more than 40,000 people were detained and an estimated 30 per cent of them were children; more than 1,000 people were killed by security forces; paramilitary and vigilante groups emerged as surrogate law enforcers'

the drastic powers already at their disposal were not considered sufficient.

The intention, and effect, of the declaration of a state of emergency was in essence "to impose order without law and to grant security forces a licence to operate lawlessly and with impunity". This was a licence to kill for security forces already lacking any form of political accountability to the black communities they policed, and its results were catastrophic. During the states of emergency of 1985 to 1989, more than 40,000 people were detained and an estimated 30 per cent of them were children; more than 1,000 people were killed by security forces; paramilitary and vigilante groups emerged as surrogate law enforcers constructing what Professor Fink Haysom termed "violent stability"; and extensive media restrictions encouraged and fostered unfettered security force actions.

These repressive actions formed part of overt state repression and have, however obscenely, taken place within some framework of law. Covert state repression has been as extensive and ruthless. Covert operations, the "hidden hand" of the state, have filled the extremely small gaps in the battery of security legislation available to those in power. Many prominent anti-apartheid activists have fallen victim to state-sponsored death squads whose activities continue to this day. Matthew Goniwe, Sparrow Mkhonto, David Webster, Anton Lubowski, Eric Mntonhga and Griffiths Mxenge are only a few of those assassinated by persons, many of whom remain faceless and nameless, in the employ of the state. Covert structures have been responsible for massive misinformation campaigns in South Africa and in Namibia before independence. The extensive use of covert operations in South Africa has serious implications — evidence indicates that, once a state or political organisation becomes comfortable in the use of covert and unorthodox tactics of repression, they rely more heavily on them. The extent and nature of covert operations in South Africa is largely undocumented and, unless a Truth Commission with powers of prosecution is established, these structurers and their offspring will remain active well into the future. As well as extra-judicial killings, judicial murder through hanging was well used as a weapon against political opponents as well as criminal offenders. During the 1980s, South Africa consistently occupied a position in the world's top five

Police attack women demonstrators at Cato Manor in Durban, 1959

Left: **Police reload after firing at mourners following a funeral of activists killed in Duduza township in the Transvaal, 1985**

Right: **Training school for black policemen at Hamanskraal, 1978**

Main picture: ABBAS/MAGNUM. Small picture: PAUL WEINBERG/MAYIBUYE CENTRE

Accusers in the dock

Jonathan Steele on the allegations of torture made by Africans now on trial in Pretoria

ALL OF the twenty Africans who went on trial in Pretoria yesterday have been held incommunicado for over a year. Three of the original group arrested in May and June last year have died in detention in mysterious circumstances. One died of "suicide" – information only divulged in Parliament in February this year by the Minister of Police, although the suicide was claimed to have occurred eight months before and no inquest has been published.

Another "fell down a flight of stairs," a third died of "natural causes." Nearly all the other detainees have made allegations of torture. At their first trial in December (the case was dismissed but they were then immediately re-arrested) they filed a series of disturbing affidavits. These are extracts from them.

Mrs Rita Ndzanga, mother of four children: She was taken to a room in the HQ of the security police in the Compol buildings in Pretoria on May 16. Thick heavy planks covered the windows. "I remained standing. It was late at night. One policeman came round the table towards me, and struck me. I fell to the floor. He said, 'Stand up,' and kicked me on the floor."

Later on July 23, in another room: "They closed the windows. I continued screaming. They dragged me to another room, hitting me with their open hands all the time. In the interrogation room they ordered me to take off my shoes and stand on three bricks. I refused to stand on the bricks. One of the white Security police climbed on a chair and pulled me by my hair, and dropped me on the bricks. I fell down and hit a gas pipe.

"The same man pulled me up by my hair again, jerked me, and I again fell on the gas pipe. They threw water on my face. The man who pulled me by the hair had his hands full of my hair... I managed to stand up and then they said, 'On the bricks.' I stood on the bricks and they hit me again while I was on the bricks. I fell. They again poured water on me. I was very tired. I could not stand the assault any longer."

Douglas Mvembe, aged 73: He was unable to balance on the bricks. So they handcuffed him and tied a rope through the handcuffs and to a grating above his head, his feet touching the bricks. Later in the afternoon they undid the handcuffs and tied his hands up outstretched. At night there was a terrible heat above his head; sweat poured down and blocked his ears so that he could not hear what they were saying. "I would thirst and ask for water." Three days and nights later he told them he accepted every word they said. He was taken down and the statement was slowly compiled. "But I didn't sign it," he said.

Joseph Sikalala, a student, 19. He was made to catch and kill with his bare hands cockroaches when they ran over the interrogation room floor. Under the assaults he became groggy and cried. He was not allowed to urinate. He was put for hours on the wobbling bricks: "they had no balance... they would dance." His hands were held up; he was kicked and beaten; a sjambok was used to hit him on his feet, his knees, his genitals.

After hearing these allegations Mr Justice Theron ruled that the matter was "not urgent."

25.8.70

Vorster police 'purge the Church'

From Stanley Uys in Cape Town

IN ONE of the biggest raids they have conducted in South Africa for nearly 10 years, the security police made a dawn swoop on the offices and homes of churchmen and student leaders in Johannesburg, Cape Town, Durban, Port Elizabeth, and Pietermaritzburg. A Church spokesman described the raids as "an obvious purge on the Church."

The raids began at 6.45 am and, in some cases, continued until late into the afternoon. In Cape Town, 10 security policemen searched the premises of the Christian Institute of Southern Africa, and 11 policemen entered the offices of the National Union of South African Students

Stacks of documents were seized in the country-wide raids. The police searched particularly for documents relating to financial aid given to the families of political prisoners.

Dr Bruckner de Villiers, liaison officer of the Christian Institute of Southern Africa, commented: "The raids are an obvious purge of the Church by the Government. Today's swoop is part of the old tactics. They don't raid the top men, but the second echelon churchmen. This tends to intimidate. If this intimidation is meant to demoralise, I can't see it succeeding in the long run."

26.2.71

hanging nations. In 1987, some 164 people went to the gallows and a significant number of these were political offenders. Death Row in Pretoria was a ghastly microcosm of South African society — predominantly white, Afrikaner warders watched over predominantly black prisoners and saw them to their death. While they were living, every aspect of the prisoners lives' was regulated, and defiance of regulations brought various forms of punishment. Twenty-four-hour neon lights and observation ensured that even minimal privacy was denied.

Total silence was enforced. Separate lives and separate worlds co-existed within the concrete walls of the prison in an uneasy bond of total repression. Life and death were regimented and controlled, and those in positions of power abused and tortured those who were not. The character of one such factory of death was summed up by a warder who remarked: "I think we are all prisoners here." The National Party government that gave birth to and nurtured all these forms of state repression will remain in power until April 27 1994. It has a new logo, new colours and calls itself the New National Party — it remains for me the National Party with new strategies and tactics. It was unable, finally, to maintain control through extreme repression and saw that, if it was to have any political future at all, these methods would have to change. Last year, when President de Klerk was awarded the Nobel Peace Prize, the Nobel committee was rewarding a man for discovering that a particular brand of repression was not working. However, we can live in hope that the forces of good are greater than those of evil and that we will move into a society which affords its citizens greater dignity and security. The stories in this chapter are stories of brutality and the stripping of human dignity. We all need to read them and remember. Not for the sake of revenge, but to remind ourselves of where we have been so that we will never go there again. Some of the stories will leave a sense of horror and disbelief, while others are dangerously close to the absurd. Sadly, they are all true. This chapter is, therefore, dedicated not only to those who fell victim to the perpetrators of repression but to all those who have survived and have not allowed this government to conquer their spirit or humanity.

Paula McBride is a member of the Lawyers for Human Rights group

'Separate worlds co-existed within the walls of the prison in an uneasy bond of total repression. Life and death were regimented and controlled, and those in positions of power abused and tortured those who were not'

Hilda Bernstein reports that the banishment of Winnie Mandela to a remote township is the latest move in 15 years of trials and torture

The woman South Africa locks up in the place without a name

I LAST saw Nomzamo Winnie Mandela thirteen years ago as she walked down the steps of the Palace of Justice in Pretoria. Her husband, Nelson Mandela and seven others had just been sentenced to life imprisonment. (The ninth defendant, my own husband, had been found not guilty the previous day.)

The crowd outside the court was waiting, as they had waited for the weeks and months of the Rivonia Trial. Winnie raised her arm in salute and called "Life!" and the people burst out singing and unfurled banners they had been concealing from the police.

We had sat on separate benches in the courtroom for eight months. Our husbands sat together in the dock, but we were divided, blacks on one side, whites on the other. We had passed, looked but never greeted each other although we were old friends, for we were both banned, and banned people are prohibited from communicating with each other. Even a smile, a whispered greeting, has been interpreted by the courts as "communication." We could not risk it under the unremitting gaze of so many police.

Nomzamo Winnie Mandela was born and brought up in rural Pondoland. Her father was Minister of Agriculture and Forestry in Kaiser Matanzima's Transkei Bantustan. "He was a political man," Winnie said. "I was political in another way."

She matriculated, came to Johannesburg, obtained a social science diploma and became a social worker. In 1958, she married Nelson Mandela, one of South Africa's first black lawyers, a leading member of the African National Congress (then still legal); and at the time of their marriage, one of the 156 accused in a four-year-long treason trial that ended with the acquittal of all defendants.

When the African National Congress was declared an illegal organisation in 1961, Nelson Mandela went underground. From that time, the life of Winnie Mandela and her two small daughters, Zenani and Zindziswa, became one of police raids and unceasing Special Branch vigilance and harassment.

Nelson was arrested in 1962 and sentenced to five years in jail, but subsequently sentenced again at the Rivonia Trial to life imprisonment, and has been imprisoned on Robben Island ever since.

When his wife had a permit to visit Robben Island (1,000 miles away from home in Soweto) in 1966, she was required to travel by train. But the train was full and she caught a plane to Cape Town to see her husband before her permit expired. For this, she was charged with breaking the exemption to her banning order: twelve months' imprisonment, all but four days suspended.

In May 1969, she was arrested at 2 am, and thereafter remained in prison for 491 days, most of it in solitary confinement.

Perhaps because world attention centred on the name of Mandela, or perhaps because the police knew she suffered from a heart condition, she was allowed to remain seated during five days and five nights of continuous interrogation (others arrested at the same time were less fortunate; three died in detention, one became mentally unbalanced).

On the third day, when she showed the police her blue and swollen hands and feet, Major Swanepoel said, "For God's sake, leave us some inheritance when you decide to pop it; you cannot go with all that information."

In the early hours of the sixth morning, Swanepoel stopped the interrogation, and then they continued only day by day, with the prison floor to lie on at night. "I used to wake up screaming and found myself talking aloud and suffered from nightmares."

Yet in February 1970, the case collapsed and the accused were found not guilty and discharged. They were immediately re-arrested and put back into solitary confinement. (While on trial they had at least been treated as ordinary prisoners.) Six months later, after a second trial on the same charges, they were again found not guilty.

It was now two years since Winnie had visited Nelson. But she was served with an even more stringent banning order, confining her to a small area of Soweto and keeping her under house arrest every evening and weekend. The application to leave her home to visit Robben Island was refused. Police came to her home three or four times a day to "check up" and harass her.

Another arrest and charge followed in July 1971: contravening her banning orders by receiving one of her sisters. In September of that year she was again arrested and accused of breaking her banning orders.

This time, she had communicated with Peter Magubane, a friend and well-known photographer, in a Johannesburg street. She had spoken to the children, who spoke to Magubane. For this infringement she served six months in prison.

In September, 1975, the bans expired and were not immediately renewed. After 13 years of restrictions, harassment, imprisonment, constant searches of her house, burglary and attempted assault, Nomzamo Winnie Mandela was free for a very short while to move around, to speak openly, to be interviewed.

She now spoke bitterly about the untold hardships of the years that had left scars which nothing could remove. She was bitter that while her daughters grew up she could not properly fulfil her role as a mother.

Yet "I am even more opposed to this violent system now than I was in 1962. I will express my views. I am aware of the risks I will have to face."

She said she could not be a spectator to the cause of her people. "As long as our people are imprisoned and as long as whites continue to do what they are doing, my life will remain unchanged." She dismissed détente as playing for time. "Is it possible that whites are not aware of the agony of the black people? Can they be unaware of how explosive the situation is in South Africa?".

Only eight months later, the explosive situation of which she spoke erupted in Soweto, and Winnie Mandela was one of dozens of leading blacks who were arbitrarily arrested and put into "preventative detention" under the Internal Security Act. She was released six months later and once more banned, restricted to her district in Soweto.

Last month, she was forcibly removed to the place without a name, called officially the "Brandfort Bantu residential area," outside the small Free State town of Brandfort. Local blacks have dubbed it Phatakahle, which means 'handle with care.'

Now like the 725 identical houses in the township, Winnie Mandela's three-roomed house is without electricity, running water, a bath or stove. It has no water-borne sewerage and a door that locks only from the outside. She is house arrested every night and weekend, but allowed to go into Brandfort during the week.

There are no libraries, no cinemas; the location has one primary school, one general store. "The Security Police visit us three or four times a day, they won't leave us alone." Every half hour a police van drives through the location streets, sending up clouds of dust. When mother and daughter went into Brandfort to shop for groceries, they were escorted everywhere by both black and white security police.

Her youngest daughter, 16-year-old Zindzi had visitors at the house where her mother has been dumped. Immediately Winnie Mandela was again arrested and charged, with "receiving guests." "She can leave the country if she wishes," said Vorster. She would then, of course, never see her husband again.

The Minister of Justice, Jimmy Kruger, said she would be paid R100 a month. R15 would go in rent for the house. (She had been earning R350 a month in Soweto.) She would get all the basic amenities she would require, said Mr Kruger. "And we are giving her R100 for free. What more does she want?"

5.7.77

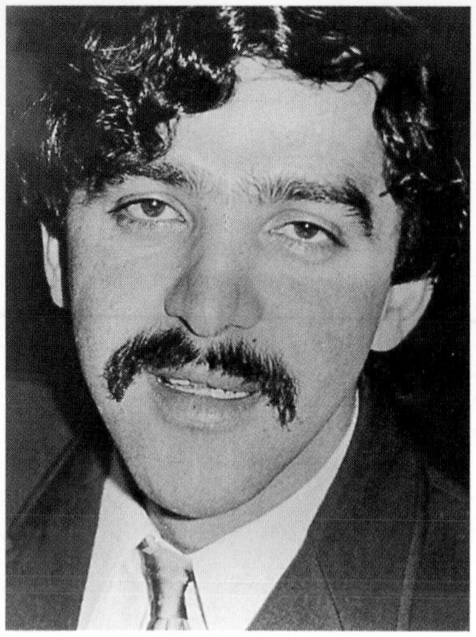

Ahmed Timon

Death jump was 'not fault of police'

From Stanley Uys: Cape Town

WHILE PUBLIC clamour for a judicial inquiry into the death of an Indian political detainee, Ahmed Timol, aged 30, mounted this weekend, two senior police officers have given their version of what happened when Timol allegedly jumped from the tenth floor of police headquarters in Johannesburg while being interrogated last Wednesday.

The officers' version is published in a pro-Government newspaper, "Rapport", today. Last week no comment could be obtained from official sources on Mr Timol's alleged suicide. He is the 17th political detainee to die in detention in the past ten years and the tenth allegedly to commit suicide.

General Stoffel Buys, CID chief, told "Rapport" "Timol was sitting quietly on a chair. Security police were with him. At one stage two of them walked out of the room. Then Timol suddenly jumped up and headed for the door. One security policeman jumped up and ran to the door and stopped him. But the Indian then stormed towards the window and jumped through it. No one frightened or touched him. The post mortem will show this."

Communist hero

Brigadier Piet Kruger, deputy chief of the security police, said Timol was a "hero of the Communists" today. "We who know the Communists know that when they plan to use violence they make their people swear an oath to commit suicide rather than to mention the names of their comrades. They are taught to jump out before they are interrogated."

Brigadier Kruger said there were no bars in front of the windows of the room in which Timol was. The brigadier was replying to newspaper reports that the windows at John Vorster Square are sealed and barred, and that access to the ninth and tenth floors, which are occupied by the security police, is protected by an electrically operated iron grille outside the lift.

Timol's mother, Mrs Howa Timol, said today: "My son was not the type to commit suicide. He would have faced trial like a man if he had done anything wrong."

Mrs Timol said that the day before her son died, the police told her she would not see him again. "I cannot sleep now. I fear for the life of my other son, Mohammed, who was detained in Durban on Monday."

1.1.71

Strong arm

A FORMER South African police station commander was gaoled for six years in Cape Town yesterday for "culpable homicide" of a coloured man under interrogation. The court found he had "no intention" of killing the man and had not appreciated the injuries he was inflicting — a fractured skull, brain haemorrhage, 12 broken ribs and lacerations of the liver. (19.08.73)

19.8.73

Blacks jeer as warders go to gaol

STANLEY UYS; Cape Town

ABOUT 150 black spectators whistled, hissed, and shouted "They should rot in gaol" when three prison warders, two whites and an African were each sentenced to 18 months' imprisonment in the Supreme Court, Johannesburg, today for assaulting a black prisoner who later died, and causing bodily harm to another black prisoner.

Mr Justice Hiemstra described the assaults on the two prisoners as barbaric, cruel, and inhuman. He said there had been evidence of torture, and that such assaults were not rare at the prison.

The Minister of Prisons, Mr Kruger, said today he had called for the trial record. "It looks to me as if there will have to be an investigation," he said.

The judge said they attacked them "mercilessly." The deceased prisoner's heart had failed because of bruising of a heart through blows with a baton and kicks.

The judge said the prisoner must have suffered "unbelievable pain" when they were beaten on the soles of their feet for hours with batons.

I had personally tried a baton blow on his hand and the pain was intense.

9.10.74

ANC man killed by bomb

JOHN DUBE, representative of the African National Congress of South Africa was killed in an explosion on opening a book parcel bomb addressed to him at the Liberation Centre, Lusaka, writes our correspondent. Two other congress men were seriously injured and slight injuries were received by two members of Coremo, a Mozambique liberation movement.

The centre is used as an administrative base by liberation groups and is controlled by the Zambian Ministry of Defence.

13.2.74

South Africa denies bombing

From Stanley Uys

THE SOUTH African Government, in a communication to the United Nations, has denied "categorically" that it was responsible in any way for the parcel bomb which killed a black exile, Mr Abraham Tiro, in Botswana on Friday. Mr Tiro's body was found at a house outside Baborone. The explosion damaged a kitchen stove and part of the ceiling.

Mr Tiro, 27, a BA graduate, was expelled from the black South African university of Turfloop after making a strong attack on black education at the graduation ceremony in 1972. His expulsion led to mass walkouts at other black universities.

The parcel bomb opened by Mr Tiro had a Geneva postmark, but the educational organisation that was alleged to have sent it disclaims any knowledge of it.

15.2.74

Pictures: PETER MAGUBANE/MAYIBUYE CENTRE

'40 arrested' in police raids

From STANLEY UYS

ABOUT FORTY black militants in South Africa have been arrested by the security police and are being held incommunicado under the Terrorism Act, according to sources here.

Most of the detainees are office-bearers and supporters of the south African Students' Organisation and the Black People's Convention. They have been arrested since September 25, when two pro-Frelimo rallies were broken up in Durban and at the African university of Turfloop in the Transvaal.

The police say SASO and the BPC tried to exploit Frelimo's victory in Mozambique to increase their own support in South Africa.

The extent of raids on SASO and BPC leaders and supporters during the past six weeks is becoming apparent only now.

Yesterday in Cape Town security police arrested at least four men in pre-dawn raids. The police are not disclosing how many arrests they have made and are not allowing some of them to see their lawyers yet.

9.11.74

Prison 'suicide' by black

From Denis Herbstein, Johannesburg

ONE OF THE leaders of South Africa's Black Consciousness movement "committed suicide" last night while detained by the security police. Mr Mapetla Mohapi, former full-time official of the South African Students' Organisation (SAS0), was the 23rd black person known to have died while in the hands of the police.

Mr Mohapi, aged about 25, is reported to have hanged himself by his jeans in the Kei Road Prison, near East London, in the Eastern Cape Province.

Mr Mohapi had once before been held under the Terrorism Act after being arrested in October 1974 with 39 other members of the SASO and the Black Peoples' Convention. He was released without being charged after 164 days in solitary confinement.

He was then elected full-time general secretary of the SASO in Durban, but when banned under the Suppression of Communism Act six weeks later, he was forced to give up his job and return to the magisterial district of King William's Town, near East London. At the time of his final arrest, Mr Mohapi was administrator of the Zimele Trust, which helped former political prisoners start a new life.

7.8.76

Banned SA lecturer shot dead in midnight attack

From Patrick Laurence

A BANNED university lecturer, Dr Richard Turner, was shot dead in his home in Durban at the weekend by an unknown assailant. The killing appeared to be part of a pattern of right-wing terrorism. Dr Turner died in the arms of his 13-year-old daughter, Jan, early yesterday morning after a shot was fired through a window.

According to friends of the family, Jan woke up after midnight to see her father looking out of a window and asking who was there. Then a shot was fired and her father collapsed. Police said yesterday that Dr Turner had earlier answered a knock on the front door but found no one there.

Dr Turner, aged 36, a graduate of the Sorbonne, died less than two months before his five-year banning order was due to expire. He was one of eight people banned in February, 1973, after a parliamentary commission was appointed to investigate the activities of the National Union of South African Students.

9.1.78

Detainee 'was hung by ankles'

By Martin Walker

THE INQUEST tomorrow for Lungile Tabalaza, a South African black who is said to have fallen to his death from a fifth-floor window of Security Police headquarters, will be told by his family that the 20-year-old student was murdered by the Security Branch.

According to officials of the African National Congress, photographs taken at the postmortem suggest that he may have been ill-treated before his death, and that he may have been hung by his feet from the window deliberately.

"The injuries on the feet and legs show that he was deliberately suspended by his feet before falling," Mr Francis Meli, a spokesman for the ANC in London, whose organisation smuggled the photographs from South Africa, said in London yesterday.

Mr Tabalaza was arrested on July 10 by riot police in Port Elizabeth. Police officials have said that he was to have been charged with criminal damage for allegedly taking part in petrol bombings of property during a riot. He died before any charges were laid against him.

Within two days of his death, the Ministry of Justice ordered a series of transfers in the local Security Branch. Its local chief, Colonel P. J. Goosen was transferred to another district, and two other Security Branch officers, Major P. de Jongh and Sergeant P. J. Nel, were transferred from the Security Branch back into ordinary police duties.

The Commissioner of Police, General Michael Geldenhuys, who has launched an official inquiry into the affair, the 44th death of a detainee in Security Branch custody, has said that "strict police instructions regarding the safety of detainees have not been strictly adhered to."

Colonel Goosen was the officer in charge of the former leader of the black consciousness movement, Mr Steve Biko.

14.8.78

'Steve Biko, Chris Hani, Ruth First, Hector Peterson, Solomon Mahlangu, David Webster and Matthew Goniwe are just a few of those who died in the fight for liberation'

Those who died/Beathur Baker

UNDER THE sweltering African sun, more than 10,000 members of the Pan-Africanist Congress packed in to the Transkei's Independence Stadium for the funeral of their leader and hero, Sebelo Phama Gqwehta. Mourning his sudden death, crowds paid their final tributes to "a soldier of the people" in song. He was military commander of APLA, the Azanian People's Liberation Army, who on the day of the burial went public for the first time in 30 years. Phama died in a car crash, early in February, while on the way back to South Africa. It was a long overdue homecoming after dedicating most of his life to fighting for the freedom of the "African masses". The patron of APLA unity left the masses with only his memory, and the moving chords of a song dedicated to his brave spirit. Like the scorching heat, it rose to fill the still air. "Sebelo has not fallen down … he is simply kneeling," they sang, and rekindled their hope for the future.

Phama's death, like those of hundreds of other political activists and leaders, brings memories flooding back to the minds of black South Africa. Known and unsung heroes died in the fight for liberation, and the memory of their bravery marks the road to political freedom.

Such people's heroes as Steve Biko, Chris Hani, Sebelo Phama, Hector Peterson, Solomon Mahlangu, David Webster and Matthew Goniwe will not see their goal realised. Posthumously they have inspired, mobilised and spiritually motivated a nation bereft of political and basic human rights and, even as we prepare ourselves to embrace our freedom, we remember the slain heroes. Their contribution to the liberation of the people is immeasurable, and they did so, for the most part, as fugitives, in exile or banned. Freedom to them was a fight, first and foremost, for the mental emancipation of the people, because that is where true freedom begins. The earliest forms of organised and effective mass action occurred after the founding of the African National Congress in 1912, with protests such as the Alexandra bus boycotts.

Leaders such as Robert Sobukwe, who went on to establish the Pan-Africanist Congress in 1959, believed that black people should identify the demands, pinpoint the injustices against them and mobilise themselves. In March 1960, 69 black people were killed in the township of Sharpeville when police opened fire

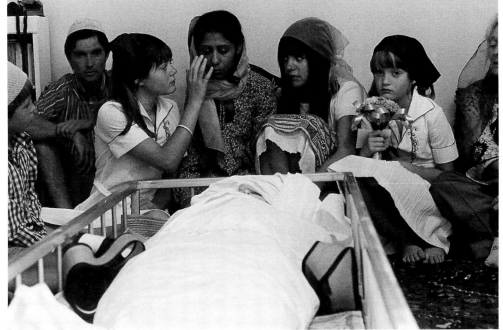

Above: **The funeral of Matthew Goniwe and his companions murdered by a police hit squad. The inquest on their deaths was reopened in 1993**

Right: **Wife and daughters grieve at Rick Turner's wake in Durban, 1978**

BIKO AND SOLIDARITY

BLACK PEOPLE'S CONVENTION
TRIBUTE TO THE LATE
HONORARY PRESIDENT
BANTU STEPHEN BIKO

One Azania: One Nation

Above: **Steve Biko's son at his father's funeral**

on crowds demonstrating against the pass laws. The people were enraged, and the state intensified its crackdown on the leadership of the growing black resistance movement. The Rivonia Treason Trial and the banning of the African National Congress followed in 1960. Political leaders such as Nelson Mandela and Oliver Tambo were banished or imprisoned after being arrested for an alleged plot to overthrow the government. And, after the death of Sobukwe, the fight for freedom was threatened by a leadership vacuum.

Exiled political organisations used underground methods — the ANC launched the armed struggle — while people's anger simmered and the government tightened its security legislation and apartheid laws to maintain white minority rule. Then, in 1976, the damn holding back black anger gave way, and powerful national uprisings in the townships started throughout the country.

Mass detentions and anarchy ensued when the young Hector Petersen was shot dead as police opened fire on crowds of schoolchildren. His death infuriated the nation. People retaliated with hard-hitting protests, and the country came close to going up in flames. Hector Petersen is a symbol of courage in the liberation struggle, and the day of his death, June 16, is commemorated in South Africa as the day of the youth.

After the turbulence of the mid-1970s, and the political disillusionment that ensued, black people were left without a channel through which to voice their anger. It was then that the father of Black Consciousness, Steve Biko, and others stepped in, realising the need to continue the fight for liberation. Biko's movement raised the spirit of black people, encouraging them to be proud of who they were in the face of oppression by the white government.

Then, in 1977 at the age of 30, Biko was hounded by the government, declared a banned person, and arrested for defying the restrictions. Steve Biko died in detention at the hands of the South African security police on September 12 that year. The 46th South African activist to die in police detention since the introduction of detention without trial, Biko is still deeply mourned, especially among the grass roots, where his spirit is remembered and his ideology upheld.

Yet on April 10 1993, South Africans were again shockingly reminded of Biko's

A long night's journey into shame

AS THE damning evidence about Steve Biko's final days is drawn from police witnesses at the inquest two illuminating facts about South Africa are put in evidence also. First, there can be few other countries where the minister responsible, either for Biko's treatment or for the attempt to conceal it, would remain in office after exposure. Secondly, there can be few other countries where those events could happen and the evidence still be brought to light. This poise cannot be maintained for ever. If Mr Vorster dismissed his minister he would give some much needed weight to the right side of the balance. If he fails to do so the balance is almost bound to tilt the other way.

Biko died on the night of September 11-12, and the official recital published on September 13 was most affecting in its solicitude. Since he was a well-known man, but since, like many before him, he had died while in police custody, the Minister of Justice, Police, and Prisons must have felt that a fuller than usual account should be provided of the constant medical attention he had received. Accordingly Mr Kruger put out a statement. It recorded Biko's arrest on August 18 outside the area to which he had been restricted, and it went on:

"Since September 5 Mr Biko refused his meals and threatened to go on hunger strike. He had been regularly supplied with meals and water, but refused to partake thereof.

"On September 7 a district surgeon was called in because Mr Biko appeared unwell. The district surgeon certified that he could find nothing wrong with Mr Biko.

"On September 8 the police again arranged for the district surgeon and the chief district surgeon to examine Mr Biko and because they could diagnose no physical problem, they arranged that he be taken to the prison hospital for intensive examinations. On the same day Mr Biko was examined by a specialist.

"The following morning he was again examined by a doctor and kept at the hospital for observation.

"On Sunday morning, September 11, Mr Biko was removed from the prison hospital to Walmer police station on the recommendation of the district surgeon. He still had not eaten on Sunday afternoon and again appeared unwell. After consultation with the district surgeon it was decided to transfer him to Pretoria. He was taken to Pretoria that same night.

"On September 12 Mr Biko was again examined by a district surgeon in Pretoria and received medical treatment. He died on Sunday night."

The scene depicted by Mr Kruger is of grave consultants gathered at the foot of Mr Biko's bed, unable to make out what could possibly be the matter. What the statement omitted to say, and what has emerged from police witnesses, is that on September 7 (when "Mr Biko appeared unwell") he had a fight with five security policemen. According to Major Harold Snyman he "bumped" his head against the wall and cut his lip. Since this may have been the "bump" which caused the extensive brain injury mentioned in the post-mortem report, and the kidney failure and uraemia which followed, the magistrate asked Major Snyman whether he had seen Mr Biko bump his head, and on being told no, asked: "The possibility therefore exists that he did not bump his head against the wall?" Major Snyman replied: "That is so." Another thing that Mr Kruger overlooked is that at least from September 6-8 (when two surgeons were called and could find no physical problem) Mr Biko had been kept naked, in leg-irons, and in manacles, on the floor of his cell. Why was he kept naked? To humiliate him? No, said Major Snyman; because he might kill himself. "With a pair of underpants?" asked the family's counsel. A third omission from Mr Kruger's statement is that there were signs that Biko had taken his bread and coffee, and a fourth concerns the journey from Port Elizabeth to Pretoria. It was made on the recommendation of a surgeon but it was not made, as the bare statement might suggest, with the patient on a stretcher in an ambulance. Throughout the journey of 750 miles Mr Biko was kept naked in the back of a Land-Rover. No records of his medical condition were sent with him and the medical equipment was confined to a container of water.

That is the balance in South Africa between the savagery of the police cell and the civilisation of the courtroom. It is precarious. "Where do you get your powers from?" counsel asked another policeman, Colonel Goosen. "Show me a piece of paper that gives you the right to keep a man in chains." "We don't work with the law," the colonel replied. "We work with our own powers." Has Mr Vorster anything to add, or is that all that his opponents need to know?

18.11.77

Biko might have led a black South Africa

By Eric Abraham and Richard Norton-Taylor

AN INTELLECTUAL and charismatic leader, Bantu Stephen Biko was the 21st black political detainee to die in detention in South Africa since June 1976. He was, perhaps, the only South African leader who could claim to have the mass support of the young radical urban blacks, a force which is playing an increasingly significant role since the Soweto uprisings last year.

Internationally, Steve Biko has been hailed as one of South Africa's most important and astute politicians. Visiting American congressmen, Western diplomats, academics, and newsmen seldom left South Africa without paying him a call.

Andrew Young, the US Ambassador to the United Nations, yesterday described Biko's death as a major loss to the future of South Africa. "No nation can afford to lose its most dedicated and creative leadership and yet prosper," Mr Young said.

"I know personally how much the United States suffered nationally as a result of the similarly tragic deaths of President John Kennedy, Dr Martin Luther King Jr, and Senator Robert Kennedy. These losses cost us nearly a decade of progress."

Mr Biko began his career as a medical student in the mid-1960s at the University of Durban-Westville, and took part in the activities of the white-led National Union of South African Students. In 1968, he spearheaded and argued for the need to create a separate organisation for black students which would help black people to regain their identity and self-respect, as well as provide political direction.

The South African Students Organisation came into being the following year, with Steve Biko as president. Since then, he has been the moving force behind the creation of numerous other Black Consciousness organisations, including the Black People's Convention and community self-help programmes in King William's Town in the Eastern Cape, where he lived under banning orders.

Detained and arrested several times, and banned in 1973, Mr Biko proved a painful thorn in the side of the South African Government — one which was difficult to remove because of his immense stature and following.

South Africa's account of Mr Biko's death was quickly derided by those in Britain who knew him. Lady Birley, wife of the former headmaster of Eton who lectured in South Africa for many years, said that the idea that Mr Biko committed suicide was absolute nonsense.

Lord Birley, who is in hospital, believed that Biko was a potential prime minister of South Africa. The Rev Paul Oestreicher, chairman of the British Section of Amnesty International, said that people did not die of hunger strikes so quickly. "I would like to see the medical evidence," he said.

Praise for Mr Biko's personality as a leader of Black Consciousness has also come from Christian Concern for Southern Africa, the Black People's Convention, and the Catholic Institute for International Relations.

Mr Donald Woods, the white editor of the Daily Dispatch of East London, a close friend of Mr Biko's, called him "the greatest man I have ever met". Mr Woods once wrote an article in which he speculated that Mr Biko might become the first prime minister of a future South Africa under a black government.

When news of Mr Biko's death was broadcast by Radio South Africa, about 400 blacks and whites gathered for a spontaneous memorial service at the Dikonia Hall, in Braamfontein, near the centre of Johannesburg.

At the close, the crowd sang the anthem of black nationalism, Nkosi Sikelele Afrika (God Bless Africa), and gave the Black Power clenched fist salute.

The British Labour Party last night expressed "extreme disquiet and shock" at Mr Biko's death.

14.9.77

Biko's death leaves police chief 'cold'

From Patrick Laurence in Pretoria

THE BLACK consciousness leader who died in detention, Mr Steve Biko, was a violent revolutionary whose death "leaves me cold," the Minister of Police, Mr Jimmy Kruger, said yesterday.

He told the Transvaal National Party Congress: "I am not glad and I am not sorry about Mr Biko. He leaves me cold. I can say nothing to you. Any person who dies . . . I shall also be sorry if I die (laughter)."

15.9.77

Security Police oversight 'amazing'

PRETORIA: THE chief state pathologist told the court of inquiry into the death of the Black Consciousness leader, Steve Biko, that he was "amazed" that so many witnesses had missed the forehead injury suffered by the prisoner while in detention, writes James MacManus.

Professor Johann Loubser told the court under questioning from the counsel representing the Biko family, Mr Sydney Kentridge, that he found it hard to understand how three doctors and some 10 policemen who questioned Mr Biko had overlooked the wound.

The professor agreed with counsel that Mr Biko would have had to have dashed his head against a wall repeatedly to sustain the extensive brain damage subsequently shown to be the cause of death. He also agreed that had such an incident taken place, bloodstains might have been found on the wall to which Mr Biko was manacled. No bloodstains were found.

26.11.77

Kruger challenged over truth of Biko's death

From Patrick Laurence

MR DONALD WOODS, the outspoken editor of the Daily Dispatch, yesterday challenged the Minister of Police, Mr Jimmy Kruger, to resign if the official version of the death in detention of Mr Steve Biko is proved false. In return Mr Woods offered to resign his editorship if the official version is correct.

In a statement on September 13, Mr Kruger said Mr Biko died as a direct or indirect result of a hunger strike and that the police and prison authorities did all they could to save his life.

Mr Woods, a close friend of Mr Biko, has pledged himself to do all he can to reveal the truth about Mr Biko's death. He issued the challenge during an address to students of the University of the Witwatersrand. He said that he and Mr Biko had discussed the possibility of Mr Biko being detained and dying in detention. Mr Biko had said he would never conduct a hunger strike and added that if he were detained and it was announced that he had died after conducting a hunger strike, Mr Woods should know that the statement was false.

An autopsy on the body has been attended by a private pathologist appointed by Mr Biko's family but its findings are not expected to be made known for about a month, when microscopic examinations have been completed.

Mr Woods accused Mr Kruger of promoting interracial hostility by saying, at the recent Transvaal congress of the National Party, that the death of Mr Biko "left him cold". Mr Woods described the remark as an insult to millions of blacks.

Mr Woods has already put several questions to Mr Kruger about the official version of Mr Biko's death. One related to the succession of anonymous doctors — five are mentioned in the official statement — who examined Mr Biko but could find "nothing wrong with him". If the doctors found nothing wrong with Mr Biko why did they constantly refer him to other doctors?

Another question concerns Mr Biko's transfer from Port Elizabeth to Pretoria. According to the official statement the decision was taken on the advice of the Port Elizabeth district surgeon.

It has been disclosed that Mr Biko was not admitted to the prison hospital in Pretoria but died in a prison cell. Why was Mr Biko not admitted to hospital in Pretoria if he was transferred on the advice of the district surgeon?

17.9.77

Pictures: MAYIBUYE CENTRE

16 blacks gaoled on conspiracy charges

From John Kane-Berman in Johannesburg

MR JUSTICE CURLEWIS yesterday imposed prison sentences totalling 147 years at the end of the long Pan-Africanist Congress trial in Bethal, Transvaal.

The sentences follow the conviction last week of 17 of 18 accused, charged under the Terrorism Act with reviving the outlawed PAC, sending people out of South Africa for insurgency training, and inciting riots in Kagiso township, which is near Soweto, in June 1976.

Mr Zeph Mothopeng, aged 66, was give 15 years on each of two counts, the sentences to run concurrently. Mr Michael Matsobane, of Kagiso was given 15 years, while five of the other accused received 10, 11, or 12 years imprisonment. The remainder were given shorter sentences, though no sentence was less

than the minimum of five years stipulated by the Terrorism Act. One man had his sentence suspended.

Five of the accused are now in their early twenties, indicating that they were teenagers at the time some of the offences were committed. They have been given sentences ranging between five and eight years.

The trial has been in progress since the end of 1977, and has taken up about 170 court days, making it one of the longest political trials in the country's history. The judge said that the older accused had corrupted the younger men and incited them to undergo military training and cause extensive riot damage. They were "wicked men and what they did was wicked," he said.

The judge granted about 60 state witnesses indemnity from prosecution.

27.6.79

Police gaoled

TWO WHITE South African policemen were gaoled yesterday for forcing black children to have sex in front of them at a police station.

Nico Swanepoel and Johan Terblanche, both aged 22, were sentenced to 24 and 32 months in gaol respectively.

16.10.78

South Africa is blamed for First's murder

From Joseph Hanlon in Maputo

TWO POWERFUL bombs were involved in the killing on Tuesday of Ruth First. The other had been intended for Aquino de Braganca, director of the Centre for African Studies in Maputo.

Ruth First was research director of the centre and its driving force. During a meeting in her office on Tuesday afternoon, she was opening her post, as she often did during meetings. She came across two identical letters, one addressed to her and the other to Braganca. When he opened his, it failed to go off.

But when First opened hers, there was a blast powerful enough to kill her instantly and to blow a large hole in the outer cement wall of her office.

First had been research director of the Centre for African Studies since 1978. And she moulded it into a group which did research of high academic standard, but which had practical application to the problems facing Mozambique's transition to socialism.

She remained a militant member of both the African National Congress and the South African Communist Party, and was the wife of the ANC leader, Joe Slovo.

19.8.82

Exiled SA nationalist shot dead in Salisbury

From Jay Ross in Salisbury

THE GOVERNMENT of Zimbabwe has blamed Pretoria for the murder of a veteran South African black nationalist Joe Gqabi, who was shot dead in Salisbury on Friday night. He was leader of the banned African National Congress in Zimbabwe.

Mr Gqabi's murder was the first known violent incident in Zimbabwe involving the Congress, which has been responsible for a series of bombings in South Africa during the past year. The killing will probably increase the tension between Pretoria and the Government in Salisbury.

Mr Gqabi, aged 52, was a veteran of the African National Congress's struggle against South Africa's white minority regime. He was imprisoned for 12 years on Robben Island, off the coast of Cape Town, where Nelson Mandela, the Congress's leader, has been held for two decades.

3.8.81

Storm of anger at South African gaol death

From Patrick Laurence in Johannesburg

Anger and anguish greeted the news yesterday that a detained trade union official, Dr Neil Aggett, was found hanged in his cell at security police headquarters in Johannesburg.

Dr Aggett, aged 28, a medical doctor, was the Transvaal secretary of the African Food and Canning Workers' Union, one of South Africa's oldest black trade unions. He was detained in last November's security police swoop on unionists, students and Church leaders.

Dr Aggett is the first white person and the 46th detainee to die in detention since the introduction of detention without trial in 1963.

6.2.82

'Hani struck a balance between his keen intellect and his revolutionary ideology on freedom. He was despised by white South Africa for his belief in the armed struggle'

brutal death at the hands of the Nationalist government when the charismatic people's leader Chris Hani was gunned down by a "Communist-hating" right-wing assassin. Hani, former chief of staff of the ANC's military wing, Umkhonto we Sizwe, and secretary-general of the South African Communist Party, was referred to as a "super hawk" within the ANC. Months before his bloody assassination, on the doorstep of his Boksbury home, Hani said: "Nobody wants to die. I've lived with death for most of my life." Death had stalked Hani, who had previously survived two other assassination attempts.

Hani struck a balance between his keen intellect and his revolutionary ideology on freedom. He was passionately despised as a militant by white South Africa for his belief in the armed struggle. He consistently advocated that, through armed combat and resistance, "the people have forced the regime to unwillingly recognise the legitimacy of our struggle". Hani's support extended from grass roots to intelligentsia, and after the unbanning of liberation organisations in 1990, when he was refused amnesty by the government, mass protest action followed, forcing the government to reverse its decision.

Hani's assassination came at a time of rampant political violence in the country, and people could not accept the blow dealt to them. The period following Hani's death will be remembered as one of the few in South Africa's history when the country came within inches of a full-scale civil war.

Hani believed that "we are living in a time pregnant with changes", but, like other slain leaders of the people's liberation movement, he did not live to see the birth of the new order. Although a proponent of the ANC's armed struggle, he showed political integrity and called for peace. When the movement was called upon to suspend armed combat, Hani willingly laid to rest the spear of the nation.

His memory and his repeated call for peace, were part of what calmed down thousands of angry youth who had grown impatient with the government's laid-back approach to reform. One of their few remaining heroes, "comrade Chris" was to them a true revolutionary leader and soldier for freedom — something they all wanted for their country. The assassin, arrested within hours of Hani's death, was a Polish immigrant who had a "hit list" of black leaders. The firearm

Above: **Outside the South African Embassy in London are (l to r) T&GWU organiser Ron Todd, Frank Dobson MP, Alf Dubbs MP, Helen Livingstone (Aggett's girlfriend's sister) and Ruth Mompati (London representative of the ANC), 1982.**

Right: **Joe Gqabi and Ruth First, both murdered in exile**

Courts hit hard at tea-mug subversion

From Barry Streek in Cape Town

SUBVERSION AGAINST the State has been widely defined in the law for some time, but a number of court cases this year have illustrated just how wide this definition is in practice.

This week, a Johannesburg factory worker was convicted for engraving African National Congress "propaganda" on his tea mug at work.

Last month, three people were acquitted after three months in detention, having been charged with participating in ANC activities by organising a function for Women's Day, an event held annually in South Africa to commemorate a 1956 march by women in protest against the pass laws.

In June, two Rastafarians were sentenced to four years' gaol after chants they had sung during a musical were held by the court to be furthering the aims of the ANC.

This week, a nun, Sister Mary Bernard Mncube, was sentenced to 12 months in gaol, eight months of which was suspended, for being in possession of ANC leaflets which had been sent to her anonymously through the post from London.

Sister Bernard's room in her convent was searched at 3 am on March 5, and she was stripped naked by a police-woman. The police left five hours later after the offensive literature was found in the sisters' community room.

In June a court rejected the appeal of a 17-year-old youth against a 300 rand (about £166) fine and a six month suspended sentence for being in possession of three stickers with pictures and names of three ANC members on them.

The judge held that they were "arrogant and blatant" propaganda for the ANC.

Other trials have involved tape-recordings, posters and pamphlets.

A former Soweto school teacher was given a four year sentence in March for playing friends a tape-recorded speech by the exiled president of the ANC, Oliver Tambo.

The common thread in all these cases has been the promotion of aims and activities of the ANC.

The conviction this week of Matthews Thabane Ntshiwa, aged 23, for engraving slogans on his tea mug emphasised this trend. He was found guilty of having engraved Amandla nowethu (sic) which means the "power is ours", "release Nelson Mandela", "remember our leader" and "PW we want our land back".

10.12.83

South African air raids kill five in Maputo suburb homes

From Joseph Hanlon in Maputo and John Kane-Berman in Johannesburg

FIVE PEOPLE were killed and more than 20 injured yesterday morning in a South African air-force raid on Maputo. Only one of the dead, and none of the injured, was linked to the African National Congress.

The raid took place during the morning rush hours. About seven South African jets attacked at least seven sites in Maputo's western suburbs. In most cases, planes flew over twice and hit their targets with machine-gun and rocket fire.

At all seven sites there was nothing to indicate targets of military significance. There were no ANC bases or missile batteries, and only one ANC house.

A South African Air Force spokesman said the air strike wiped out guerrilla bases. Intelligence sources said that it inflicted heavy casualties on the ANC. The intelligence sources said there were early indications that "scores of ANC members were killed". But the sources conceded that the estimate was based on early projections on how many used the houses.

A missile site of the Mozambique armed forces was "neutralised" in the attack, which was announced by the Defence Minister, General Magnus Malan.

In a statement from Dar es Salaam the external mission of the ANC admitted that its military wing, Umkhonto we Sizwe, was responsible for Friday's bomb explosion in Pretoria, in which 18 people were killed. The latest victim died in hospital yesterday.

General Malan said: "Although the retaliatory attack could never compensate for the cowardly car bomb attack in a busy central area of Pretoria, it will at least demonstrate to the world and the South Africa's enemies that South Africa is ready to act where and when necessary. South Africa will not allow any part of its population — white, brown, or black – to be destabilised by terrorism.

The Somopel jam factory in Matola was attacked just as workers were arriving. Three workers, including an eight-month pregnant woman, were killed as they washed up to prepare for work. Several others were injured. The crèche was riddled with machine-gun fire just minutes before the first workers' children were due to arrive.

The ANC's Lusaka office yesterday denied that the organisation had military bases in Mozambique.

24.5.83

Children shot dead in ambush of black rioters

From Patrick Laurence

TWO OF the three people killed in a police ambush in the "coloured" township of Athlone, in Cape Town, were children, not adults as stated in first police reports.

Police yesterday strongly defended the use of a government vehicle to lure stone-throwers into the ambush. A lorry carrying armed policemen hidden in wooden boxes drove past a barricade, inviting the stone-throwers to attack it. When they failed to do so, the lorry turned round and drove past again.

As stones shattered the windscreen, police leapt from the boxes and opened fire with shotguns loaded with bird shot.

Captain Jan Calitz, of the Cape Town police, confirmed that two boys, aged 12 and 16, were killed. The third victim was aged 20. Three people were seriously injured, one of them a woman. Twenty-eight people were arrested for stone-throwing. Some were youths who fled into a nearby house. Police kicked the door down when the occupant refused to open up.

People congregated near the scene of the ambush. Barricades burned in the streets and police fired teargas to break up crowds.

17.10.85

---

he used was from a missing South African Air Force consignment.

Still mourning the loss of Hani, South Africans were grief-stricken by the death of Oliver Tambo soon after, on April 24 1993. Tambo was a veteran and internationally famous. In 1956, after being in the struggle from the early 1940s, he and his friend, Nelson Mandela, were among the 56 anti-apartheid leaders charged with high treason. He died as the result of a severe stroke, not surviving to see the fruits of his labour. But he was an inspiration, instrumental in securing the freedom of the people.

It was after the unbanning of political organisations on February 2 1990, that a spate of violence and politically motivated killings swept the country, and assassination attempts on the lives of grass-roots leaders such as Chris Hadebe grew frequent. Hadebe, a colleague of Chris Hani, was the most senior member of Umkhonto we Sizwe to be killed following F W de Klerk's annoucement. Shortly after his release from Robben Island, Hadebe was gunned down in broad daylight in Imbali township, Natal, on August 8 1992.

His death came in the wake of threats on the lives of other prominent figures in the anti-apartheid alliance such as Jay Naidoo of the Congress of South African Trade Unions and Harry Gwala, the ANC leader in the Natal Midlands district.

At the time, activists knew they themselves were not safe but they continued the call for swift political negotiations and a peaceful settlement. Like Hadebe, they knew that change would not come easily and that, on the path to freedom, violence against them was inevitable. The political aim was to ensure that a new constitution in South Africa reflected the requirements of the people, and these grass-roots leaders vocalised the need to address issues affecting people directly, such as fair representation, the right to vote and participate in preparing a new constitution, as well as the right to housing, jobs and education.

On the path of struggle, there have been some leaders who create the impression that theirs is a fight for democracy despite the people, and others who simply fight for democracy on behalf of the people. David Webster was one of the latter. Webster was assassinated outside his home in Toyeville, Johannesburg on May 1 1989, as thousands commemorated Worker's Day. A fierce opponent of

Right: **Some of 800 children arrested in raids on schools being transported back to Diepkloof after their release from custody in Soweto, 1985**

Below: **Vigilantes, unopposed by the police, set fire to squatter homes. The government used the vigilantes to clear the camps and then prevented those who fled from returning to Crossroads, 1986**

SA gaols policeman

A WHITE South African security policeman was gaoled for 10 years yesterday after being found guilty of killing a black political detainee.

Lawyers said that Sergeant Jan Van As, aged 27, appeared to be the first member of the Security Police, to be convicted of killing a detainee in South Africa.

The prosecution, on a charge of culpable homicide, was brought by the state. Van As had denied shooting the black detainee, Mr Paris Malatsi, during interrogation in the black township of Soweto last July, saying that Mr Malatsi had committed suicide after grabbing his gun. (2.2.84)

2.2.84

Cape black leaders are killed

From our Correspondent

THE CHARRED bodies of two black community leaders from the eastern Cape were found at the weekend some distance from the gutted shell of their car on the road between Port Elizabeth and the town of Cradock.

Two men who were travelling with them have disappeared. Both are central figures in the anti-apartheid United Democratic Front (UDF) and its affiliate, the Cradock Residents' Association (Cradora).

The four men left Port Elizabeth for Cradock last Thursday evening after attending a UDF executive meeting. They did not arrive at Cradock.

As the families of the missing men waited for news yesterday, local police were investigating the killing of Mr Sparrow Mkhonto, a member of the Cradora executive, and Mr Silelo Mhlawuli, a teacher from the neighbouring town of Oudshoorn.

The missing men are Mr Matthew Goniwe, a school principal from Cradock much loved by local black scholars, and Mr Fort Calata, chairman of Cradora.

The killings and disappearances follow the bizarre deaths of eight men in East Rand townships last week. Police said all eight were blown up when explosives they were carrying detonated prematurely. But local blacks were sceptical of the police account and the South African Council of Churches declared that it believed the violence which killed the men came from the authorities.

Mr Goniwe was at the centre of an 18-month boycott by school pupils in Cradock, sparked off by an attempt by the department of education and training to transfer him to a neighbouring township.

1.7.85

South Africa – a licence to kill

THE FIRST state of emergency in South Africa for 25 years means that president Botha has decided to answer the massive and sustained escalation of black protest against discrimination with more repression rather than reform. The decision appears to be the result of pressure from the police and the army which have obviously failed so far to gain the upper hand in the seething townships. As such, it is an admission of defeat as well as another disturbing sign of the increasing influence on government of the blue and khaki generals which rises in inverse proportion to their success rate.

They have already felt free to send squads of men coyly attired in balaclavas into the townships, and there is disturbing evidence of the existence of a death squad which chooses as targets for murder people whose continued existence is most likely to embarrass the government. At the same time the violence by and among black residents has become generalised, a fact which the authorities attribute to a conspiracy by the banned African National Congress and the hitherto unbanned United Democratic Front, which wants to replace apartheid with one person, one vote. The new anger seems to have taken ANC and the UDF by surprise so that they, like the authorities, are finding it hard to gain control.

The new disorder is qualitatively different because those involved have found a terrible answer to the network of black officials and police informers who until recently underpinned white domination. By murdering African councillors and police officers, or hounding them out of the townships and butchering suspected informers, the youthful gangs in the forefront of the troubles have changed the balance of power in their areas by making alleged collaborators more afraid of them than of the state. All the emergency powers in the world will not change this fact, but they will enable the authorities to round people up by the thousand, as they did after Sharpeville. It will enable them to impose curfews so that those breaking them can be shot on sight and to arrest and search at will (under the cover of censorship and immunity from prosecution for the state's agents) when their zeal runs away with them. For a police service which was never taught the principles of minimum necessary force and the equality of the citizen before the law, this amounts to a licence to kill without fear of retribution or even publicity. It is already clear that South Africa passed a point of no return when president Botha and Nelson Mandela, the imprisoned ANC leader, failed to come to terms on the latter's release so they could negotiate on justice for the African majority, which still admires Mr Mandela above all others.

The government's promises of reform having been met by widespread revolt, Mr Botha's problem now is to regain the initiative which could have been achieved by the release of Mr Mandela. The repression before and after the state of emergency will however ensure that no offer from the government stands the slightest chance of being taken seriously at home or abroad. This is because the authorities have chosen to see the unrest as a law-and-order problem rather than as a simmering uprising against the legalised discrimination which even the government publicly recognises as unjust. Any African who puts his head above the parapet with a view to leading his people has always faced detention or worse. The present unrest shows that the black majority is hydra-headed, so that when its leaders are swept off the board, new and harder figures take their places. As the lights go out at the Cape and the townships brace themselves for the coming wrath, our duty in the West, to which Pretoria purports to belong, is clear: to call the untrammelled security forces and those who have unleashed them to account before the court of world opinion for everyone who now disappears.

22.7.85

detention without trial, 44-year-old Webster was a lecturer at the University of the Witwatersrand and regarded as part of the growing white Left. But he was known for his work among the grass roots, more especially his commitment to seeing the end of indefinite detention without trail. Webster stirred up international awareness around this inhuman government practice and publicised the fact that during the 1980s the number of detentions had swollen to more than 30,000.

His death, and the investigations which ensued, helped unveil the activities of one of the biggest clandestine spy and state-funded killing networks — the Civil Co-operation Bureau or CCB.

It was during the during the 1980s, in the absence of their exiled, incarcerated and slain leaders, that the youth mobilised themselves along with other organisations in the townships to pursue new methods of waging the political struggle and to intensify the pressure on the Nationalist government. They wanted to voice their demands audibly, so that the government could heed these demands and act on them. But the country remained under P W Botha's militaristic regime, suffering at the hands of his policy of divide and rule, and his strategy of deploying the South African Defence Force in black townships to maintain order.

Dissatisfaction and anger caused by this move spurred the greatly effective defiance campaigns, launched by township civic and youth structures throughout the country under the banner of people's organisations such as the United Democratic Front. The people had the support of their banned, underground organisations such as the ANC and PAC, and forced the government to acknowledge their demands and lead the way to the end of apartheid rule and constitutional negotiations.

Politically, ours is a story of mixed achievement. Over the years, we have confronted our oppression through the example of exiled, slain and imprisoned leaders of the liberation struggle. But the spirit of those who died in this fight continues to be our inspiration, and they are remembered as the true heroes of this country who paved the way for our political freedom.

Beathur Baker is a journalist on the Johannesburg Star

On patrol with South Africa's peace-keepers

A national serviceman's view of duty in the townships

WHEN WE first deployed for the unrest, it was to protect a white suburb for the duration of a large (black) funeral procession. But it was mostly a release from army camp and an opportunity to chat up the girls. Next time we were called out we began doing patrols with the police in the black townships.

As we entered one of the Port Elizabeth townships and began our run, the police express contempt at the rubbish and dirt around. But they keep their litter to dump in the township, throwing it out of the vehicle at pedestrians minding their own business.

The streets are busy: there is a funeral of someone shot by the police, and vehicles overloaded with blacks roar back and forth. The police respond to the chants and clenched fists with shouts of abuse and of "white power". They also keep watch for members of the media, especially cameras.

We come on a pick-up truck loaded with children and youths who show us the clenched fist salute. The cops go into action: the pick-up is overtaken and forced to stop. Black bodies spill off in all directions as the cops tumble out in pursuit. Soon, they return in triumph with their catch, a boy aged about 10 years whom they hit and slap as they drag him into the vehicle, where they continue to slap and punch.

The pneumatic steel doors shut, and the vehicle moves off. They force him to slap himself with both hands, while telling us he won't show a black power sign again in a hurry. This, for me, is the central image of this time: a small black boy with wild frightened eyes (but no tears) slapping himself, and the sudden stream of bright, bright blood appearing from his nose and dropping from his chin on the carpeted floor of the vehicle. Drip, drip, drip. Slap, slap, slap.

A few blocks later we pause and he is dumped. For the first time, I look at the other guys. Only one shows any discomfort. On the faces of the rest I see only a leer. The young men are not afraid or confused. They are either bored or excited. They want action, they are callous, and they are enormously arrogant.

We trundle on. The cops talk about white politicians interfering on behalf of blacks, Helen Suzman and Molly Blackburn are mentioned. There is a loud "dong" as a stone hits the metal and bounces in through the roof opening.

The sergeant reacts immediately, sending off a 37mm gas canister. It lands on a house and the residents pour out coughing, eyes streaming. We go and watch briefly, the cops laugh loudly, pointedly. An old man wags his finger at us, and the cops bawl at him threateningly before we move on.

The funeral is over. The returning crowd starts to break up. Knots of people on street corners sing and shout defiance. The sergeant radios, asking permission to disperse a small crowd. A sudden hail of stones is what they've been waiting for. "Yahoo, let's go" and we launch into a hurtling, lurching circuit, past streams of panicking, running people, pumping out gas and rubber bullets.

It's over in a couple of minutes. The cops prepare for the second round but the crowd has dispersed. There is an atmosphere of sport: "kaffir" baiting, beating and hunting.

Eventually we return to the police station. The police brought in a man (ostensibly a stone-thrower) and derive much sport from beating and poking him with their sjamboks (whips) and truncheons, in front of the station and in the back of a van. After half an hour he was released.

The sjambok – traditionally a rhino hide whip – is perhaps the truest symbol of the police in South Africa: for herding humans, baiting and punishing them – the tool of a base and perverted shepherd. I have seen policeman wielding them on trapped or cowering offenders with all their might. A wrist flick is enough to produce a yelp of pain from my fellow soldiers.

Almost throughout these four months, the army has been mixed with the police, with SADF members in police vehicles. For the black population there has been no opportunity to differentiate between the two forces, and the SADF almost immediately inherited the lack of credibility and bad reputation of the police.

It is not so much the acts of violence that shock as the level of racism that allows them to flourish: so many people who are normally fair and reasonable but who simply "hate kaffirs". They have an attitude of hatred, loathing and contempt for blacks and a complete lack of human feeling and compassion towards them.

Action, especially for the young serviceman, is often a thrill, an ego trip.

There is a sense of power in beating up someone: even if you're the most put-upon, dumb son-of-a-bitch, you are still better than a kaffir and can beat him up to prove it.

My own guilt at my inaction in the face of the brutality, as well as the sheer physical impact of it, created an enormous tension and conflict of behaviour. My response was enough to get me labelled a "kaffir-lover" and a "Communist". The experience undid much of the nine months of training. Yet it is almost impossible to isolate yourself completely – you've been living "fart to fart" with the people for nine months, so you are forced to compromise and, treacherously, you lose the sense of outrage.

One's superiors are not much help. Although they step in when breaches of instructions become obvious, they seem not to want to know what is going on and won't interfere with another security force. Once we reported by radio that the cops were beating up a drunk in full view of the community and the headquarters radioed a reply which amounted to "What must we do about it?" These generalisations are not just drawn from one day's experience, but are based on incidents over a period of months. Other surreal scenes come to mind. A stolen vehicle is spotted – we give chase and, siren going, career through the alleys. We catch up. Others already there, haul the man out and start laying into him. As we leave, they smash his head into the stolen car.

Another night, another fire. We hang around while the fire-tanker does its work, when stones start dropping about us. Suddenly one smashes a police windscreen and two cops with shotguns bound off like dogs let off the leash.

They stalk the lone thrower and corner him. He continues his desperate barrage. They shoot him dead. He is about 16.

As we arrive to take over from another group at one small town, a policeman is whipping a black man. He is surrounded by a small knot of army spectators. The officer in charge must know what was going on, as the man's groans were clearly audible. In another town a couple of army boys take to removing the points from their ammunition and pinching the cartridge closed to make blanks. There is also drinking on duty and, more innocuously, 2 o'clock in the morning barbecues on the township's outskirts. Many incidents stem from a lack of discipline.

This may all seem over-pessimistic. After all, great changes are taking place in our society. But it has hardly touched the reality of township life. The daily assault on the dignity and self-respect of the black man goes on, if anything it is made worse by the economic situation and the unrest.

6.9.85

Beast of Soweto regrets soft line by police

Former South African policemen Swanepoel on suppression of uprising in black township

By Phillip Van Niekerk in Johannesburg

IN THE townships they call him "The Beast". Among the South African police he is known as the Red Russian. Today Brigadier Rooi Rus Swanepoel is to be found in retirement on a farm near Pretoria, with a 9mm Beretta pistol habitually strapped to his waist. "I enjoy war," he says as he sips coffee on the veranda.

If there is one man in South Africa who could be said to represent the philosophy of hard-line policing, it is Brigadier Swanepoel. The chief interrogator of the 1964 Rivonia trial – which put Nelson Mandela and others in gaol for life – and the founder of Koevoet, (crowbar) the notorious Namibian anti-terrorist unit, he is best known as the officer who crushed the Soweto revolt which exploded 10 years ago today.

He remembers June 16, 1976, with a sense of regret, nursing resentment against "certain unnamed police officers" who failed to take adequate action. He blames them for the spread of the insurrection.

"If the police had enough men available on the 16th and used sufficient force — irrespective of the number being killed — we could have stopped them. I'm not going to go into if we had killed 1,000 or 10,000 that day – I'm saying that if we had used enough force we could have stopped the riots in Soweto and it wouldn't have spread throughout the country," he says.

"It's not a question that the police could not deal with the situation. But it is my honest opinion some of our officers were dragging their feet. They were not scared but they were reluctant.

"It's always difficult. It is not easy if you are in command and things get out of hand. You are trying everything to pacify the rioters and you see things are already completely out of control and it's not so easy to psyche yourself up to give the command to fire and say: 'Right, pick off the leaders and shoot them'. Talk was out of the question. You must realise that we were dealing with black people, we are dealing with a very emotional person. Whereas other racial groups would give you an opportunity to talk, with the blacks when they are out of control, they are completely out of control.

"The only way you can get them under control is to use force — more force than they can take," he argues.

"If you have to shoot one person, or wound one person in the leg, you stop him. But if it's necessary to shoot a hundred to get the situation under complete control, do so. There are no half measures when you are dealing with riots."

Swanepoel was a colonel on June 16, stationed in north Johannesburg. He got drafted into Soweto because "at that time it was completely underpoliced.

They could not control the riots so outsiders were called on to send in task forces."

What of the hundreds of dead in Soweto and Alexandra? "A lot were killed by police," he agrees. "You regret it when you have to kill one person, but you are a professional man. You can't allow personal feelings to rule your judgement. force must be used."

Swanepoel does not deny that the demonstrators had legitimate grievances.

"Every community in South Africa has legitimate grievances. I'm not happy because I've got to pay a lot of taxes." But he says the riots were cleverly organised by the South African Communist Party.

16.6.86

Death squad blamed for SA killing

From David Beresford and Patrick Laurence Johannesburg

BLACK organisations reacted with fury yesterday to the killing of the treason trial lawyer, Mrs Nonyamezelo Mxenge.

The United Democratic Front "agents" of apartheid. describing it as a "cold-blooded assassination" which was aimed at "wiping out all leading UDF cadres and supporters violently". The statement, issued by a spokesman for the organisation currently being hunted by the police, added that "a clear pattern is emerging that those who cannot be imprisoned will have to die".

Mrs Mxenge, a prominent figure in the UDF, was shot dead by four men who ambushed her as she arrived at her home in Umlazi, a township near Durban, on Thursday night.

Mrs Mxenge was a solicitor and member of the defence team in the trial of 16 UDF members who are facing treason charges in Natal.

Four years ago, her husband, Mr Griffiths Mxenge, was knifed to death by, in the words of the inquest magistrate, "persons unknown". His throat was slit and he was stabbed 49 times.

Like his wife, Mr Mxenge, a former Robben Island prisoner and ex-member of the ANC, was a lawyer.

3.8.85

South Africa vigilantes 'helped by police'

Witnesses say attackers were supplied with weapons.

EVIDENCE IS growing of South African police involvement in the activities of vigilantes – conservative blacks responsible for much of the death and destruction taking place in the townships.

In the Transvaal a civic association, the East Rand People's Organisation (Erapo), has produced two men who allegedly confessed to taking part in a number of petrol bomb attacks on the homes of anti-apartheid activists, including one which killed a month-old baby.

One of the men, Mr Abraham Zwane, aged 19, claimed that he had been part of a group of five security policemen (two white and three black) and 13 'vigilantes' who had been paid for the attacks.

The police have denied the allegations, saying: "The police do not go about killing people." Even more compelling evidence of police collaboration with vigilantes is detailed in an affidavit released to the Guardian by lawyers in Cape Town.

The 46 sworn statements submitted to the court repeatedly allege that the vigilantes had been supplied with weapons by the police and that security forces provided protection for the vigilantes as they went on their rampage. They also say that the vigilantes destroyed homes with a special incendiary device supplied by security forces and that troops and police themselves took part in attacks on squatters.

At least eight of the affidavits testify to police use of what is described as a gun firing canisters of flammable material which ignited on contact with shacks.

Noting that the Government was refusing to allow more than 30,000 squatters evicted in the fighting to return to the sites of their destroyed homes, the Urban Foundation said this "legitimises violence as a method of achieving community objectives and sets a dangerous precedent". The foundation had been expected to supervise improvements at Crossroads costing R25 million.

18.6.86

South Africa names detainees

From David Beresford in Johannesburg

THE SOUTH African Government yesterday published the names of 8,501 detainees being held without trial under the state of emergency which was declared on June 12.

It was the first time an official figure had been set on the number of detainees, which had been variously estimated at between 8,000 and 12,000.

Monitoring groups, which had been trying to maintain unofficial lists, are likely to take several days comparing the government list with their own, to see if there are discrepancies.

The names were released to the South African parliament yesterday at the beginning of a special session to deal with various pieces of 'reform' legislation.

The names were listed on 171 pages of foolscap paper which did not specify the addresses of detainees or the regions in which they were held.

19.8.86

Pretoria arsonists raze Catholic HQ

By Patrick Laurence in Johannesburg

TWO UNEXPLODED limpet mines were discovered yesterday in the charred debris of the Pretoria headquarters of the Southern African Catholic Bishops' Conference (SACBC), after a fierce fire started by arsonists before dawn had swept through the building.

Dr Rob Lambert, a labour relations lecturer at the University of Natal and one of the quartet of people on the balcony, said: "If it hadn't been for the fast action of the fire department, we would have all been killed."

Petrol cans wired with cordite, and fuses, were found on a stairway and in the corridor outside the bedrooms, he said. Describing the arsonists as "professionals," he added: "They were aiming to destroy the whole building."

13.10.88

Racial contrast in sentencing

By Patrick Laurence in Johannesburg

A WHITE farmer convicted of culpable homicide for killing a black worker after he had accidentally driven over two dogs was given a suspended sentence, South Africa's largest black daily newspaper, the Sowetan, reported yesterday.

Juxtaposed on the same page was a report on another court case, in which a black journalist was jailed for four years for faililng to report the presence of two African National Congress fighters.

The Sowetan ran the reports without somment. But, approached for comment, Professor John Dugard, of the University of the Witwatersrand said: "The facts speak for themselves."

Mr Sambo, aged 35, had been employed as a tractor driver by Vorster's father. One day late last year he was sent to Vorster's farm to plough.

After taking a lunch break, he started the tractor and he accidentally drove over two dogs that had fallen asleep under the tractor.

Mr Sambo was beaten and killed afterwards by Vorster, aged 21.

4.11.88

Detainee found hanged in cell

From Patrick Laurence in Johannesburg

A YOUNG detainee held under the emergency regulations was found dead in his cell shortly after dawn yesterday. He was hanging from his long-sleeved shirt.

Benedict Mashoke, aged 20, is the third detainee to die in custody since the full state of emergency was imposed last June. He was the 64th South African detainee to die since detention without trial was first introduced in 1963.

All except one, Dr Neil Aggett, have been black.

Mr Mashoke was held at police cells in Bugersfort in the eastern Cape.

Policemen are required to check on detainees at hourly intervals, and a police statement said that standing regulations were adhered to, suggesting that Mr Mashoke hanged himself some time after 6am.

A doctor was called immediately after he was found. All he could do was to certify that the detainee was dead. A full investigation has been ordered.

Last December, another detainee, Mr Simon Mrule, aged 20, died in hospital one day after he was admitted. His illness was diagnosed as epilepsy, but his family insisted that he did not have a history of epilepsy.

Before that, a third detainee, Mr Xoliso Jacobs, also aged 20, was found dead in his cell at Uppington in the northern Cape.

A black youth died after being arrested last month, but his death is not recorded as a death in detention because he died before he was goaled.

According to police, he died when he jumped from a moving armoured vehicle in an "attempt to escape from custody". The youth, aged 17, was arrested for throwing stones.

Meanwhile, the inquest into the death in detention of the Northern Transvaal president of the United Democratic Front, Mr Peter Nchabeleng, has been postponed until June 22. Mr Nchabeleng died on the same day he was detained by police in the tribal homeland of Lebowa last April.

A post-mortem report showed that he died after being beaten extensively.

In cross-examination before the inquest, two constables admitted Mr Nchabeleng was whipped as he was forced into the police van. They claimed, however, the whipping was done by a sergeant who has since died.

South Africa said yesterday that a black policeman had been shot dead by gunmen, the 66th to die in over three years of political violence.

27.3.87

Pretoria gives tortured cleric £5,000 damages

By David Beresford in Johannesburg

A LEADING South African cleric has been given nearly £5,000 by the government, as well as his legal costs, in an out-of-court settlement of a damages claim for torture.

The former secretary-general of the South African Catholic Bishops Conference, Father Smangaliso Mkhatswa, had sued the Minister of Law and Order after being tortured and humiliated while in detention in 1986.

He said yesterday that his lawyers had been informed by the Attorney-General that the six soldiers who had taken part in the assault on him had been charged with causing bodily harm, but that the case had never been brought to trial.

While in detention, Father Mkhatswa was stripped and interrogated for 29 hours. His anus and genitals were interfered with and shots fired next to his head. He was released in June last year to be charged with a minor firearms offence, for which he was fined Pounds 125.

Father Mkhatswa called yesterday for criminal proceedings against the officers involved. He said that the assault on him had been "brutal, shameless and degrading" and that the government had settled his civil action to avoid a full investigation.

7.12.88

S African police officers killed by army in ambush bungle

David Beresford in Johannesburg

SOUTH AFRICAN police admitted at the weekend that two of their officers and an alleged informer had been killed by the army in an abortive attempt to ambush a unit of the African National Congress.

The bungled ambush took place in Johannesburg's Soweto township when the army and police apparently received separate tip-offs about an arms cache in a house.

Five soldiers, who arrived at the house first, set up an ambush. A police contingent later arrived, together with a car thief who had told them about the ANC "hide-out." The police burst into the house – in the White City area of the township – kicking down the front door.

The soldiers, assuming they were being attacked by an ANC unit, immediately opened fire. A fierce gun battle ensued, lasting nearly half an hour, during which police reinforcements were called in.

19.12.88

SA accused over blast

David Beresford Cape Town

Leading opponents of apartheid angrily challenged the South African Government yesterday after a huge explosion destroyed a Johannesburg office block housing some of the country's most important anti-apartheid organisations.

The bomb blast, in the early hours of yesterday morning, was a replica of an attack on the headquarters of the country's biggest trade union federation, Cosatu, in May last year.

Twenty-three people were injured, most of them suffering from shock and cuts caused by flying glass. But the bomb, which was planted in an underground garage, caused major structural damage to the building, including the collapse of the foyer into the basement.

The building, Khotso House, housed organisations including the Soth African Council of Churches, the Black Sash, the Lutheran Church, various trade unions and the Detainees Parents Support Committee. Like Cosatu House, it is likely to be condemned.

1.9.88

SA police 'operated hit squads'

By David Beresford in Johannesburg

THE SOUTH African police appear to have been running assassination squads on a regional basis with at least two teams of killers, based in Pretoria and the coastal city of East London, as well as a possible third team in Cape Town.

The full ramifications of the assassination squad scandal began to emerge yesterday as investigators started piecing together evidence after claims by former policemen that they had been part of a murder squad based outside Pretoria.

Sunday newspapers on both sides of the country's political divide were swamped by the latest disclosures about the police "hit squad", made by a former commander, Captain Dirk Coetzee.

The captain, who has fled to Europe since making his allegations, has now been joined in exile by another member of his killer unit, Mr David "Spyker" Tshikalange, believed to be in Zimbabwe. A third member of the hit team, Mr Almond Nofomela is on death row awaiting execution for an unrelated murder.

The apparent existence of regional murder squads was discovered by the Guardian yesterday in the records of a Cape trial in which a state witness claimed to have been recruited to one such team.

The witness, Bongani Jonas, was to have given state evidence against 14 people charged with terrorism, but changed his mind at the last minute. He was sentenced to three years' jail for failing to testify.

In evidence he gave in June — long before either the Nofomela, or the Coetzee allegations surfaced — Mr Jonas told the Cape Town Supreme Court that he had been recruited into a police murder squad.

His description of the squad's operations ties in with the disclosures made by Captain Coetzee. He claimed that the squads included "Askaris" — ANC guerrillas "turned" by the security forces — who were sent to "seek and kill" their former colleagues.

20.11.89

SA police and army fall out over evidence of murder as state policy

DAVID BERESFORD reports on an inquest that shows top-level involvement in assassination

THERE CAN rarely have been such a falling out of thieves or suspected murderers – as in a South African court in recent weeks where the military and police forces have been busily trying to blacken each other's names.

Allegations of premeditated murder by the state – of a routineness which would have shocked even the most prejudiced anti-apartheid activists during the years of "the struggle" – are emerging from a supreme court inquest into the 1985 killings of the "Cradock Four", Matthew Goniwe and three colleagues.

The state president, F W de Klerk, was forced to hold the hearing after the Transkei homeland leader, General Bantu Holomisa, released a copy of an army signal showing that the present head of military intelligence, General van der Westhuizen, had ordered the "elimination" of Goniwe and his colleagues.

In an extraordinary twist, the South African Defence Force (SADF) legal team decided to defend the military at the inquest by turning on the police and accusing them of the killings. The SADF claimed that a senior police officer had masterminded the murder of three colleagues and a police informer to stop them talking about the Goniwe murders.

The three security police officers and the informer died when their car blewup in 1989. Police blamed the ANC at the time for planting the bomb.

But the SADF's lawyers have told the Port Elizabeth inquest that a security police major, Deon Nieuwoudt, was responsible. The major, who appeared as a witness, denied it. He admitted, however, that among other things he had suggested the four men take the car which contained the bomb, had suggested a remote rendezvous where the explosion took place, had been first on the scene and had "found" a small detonator which triggered the bomb.

25.8.93

Picture: MORRIS ZWI

The funeral of trade union organiser Andries Raditsela who died of a brain injury in hospital two days after being detained by police. On the day of his funeral, at the Tsakane township in East Rand, workers downed tools for two hours as a tribute, 1985

'At present we know only that the imagination, like certain wild animals, will not breed in captivity.' George Orwell in *The Prevention of Literature,* January 1946

Censorship/Anton Harber

RWELL WAS WRONG. The imagination can breed in captivity. Or the minds of South Africans were never really caged. Or maybe the imagination, like certain wild animals, can never really be tamed. In South Africa, the history of censorship is long and colourful, and it includes some of the most original and far-reaching attempts to control and manipulate the imagination. But just as lengthy and even more colourful is the history of subversion of censorship, and it is here, in the annals of anti-censorship activity, that we find the richest tales of imaginative and creative, and often successful, endeavour.

The South African Union of Journalists has an annual Thomas Pringle Award and Fairbairn Memorial Lecture, commemorating the two mentors of South African journalism who set the tone for principled resistance to censorship as far back as the 1820s. When Pringle arrived from Scotland and proposed to start an independent journal, inviting his friend Fairbairn to join him, the governor, Lord Charles Somerset, wrote, "I foresee great evil", and described Pringle as "an arrant deserter who has scribbled [for a journal in Scotland]".

When Somerset intervened to control even the mild criticism of his administration in their publication, as well as in the South African Commercial Advertiser, they both ceased publication and fought a five-year battle for the right to publish freely. The case was won in London and when Somerset was replaced in 1829, the new governor removed all press restrictions. The main problem for the editors then became the fierce popular resistance to their liberal ideas, in particular their criticism of the treatment of slaves. But the press flourished. By 1858, Cape Town had eight newspapers. Further north, the diamond rush brought a journalistic rush: during the 1870s there were six papers serving the diggings. Colonial Office records in Cape Town dated 1881 list 125 journals.

That is the pattern of South African censorship history: brave beginnings, followed by crude state interference, a long, legalistic struggle to overcome it and an equally tough fight against popular distaste for dissension, with the press surviving and sometimes even flourishing.

It is more a tale of the fight against censorship than of life under it. The build-up to the Anglo-Boer War brought bitter conflicts between English and Afrikaans newspapers and The Star was banned for three months in 1897 after running a cartoon that showed President Kruger being examined by something then called a phrenologist. The Star set a trend that was to last for many decades when it published a new newspaper the next day, The Comet, identical in everything but name to the banned paper. The publishers also appealed to the courts, and won, and The Comet reverted to being The Star the following day.

Of course, victories over censorship were not always so quick. Often the fight lasted decades, and the finances of a distorted and racially divided society took as big a toll as direct government repression. An independent black-owned press was started in the 1880s and during the 1920s came to provide the first voice for the then moderate demands of the newly formed African National Congress. However, it fell into white hands during the 1930s, largely for economic reasons, and was changed from a vehicle for early African nationalism to a commercial attempt to corner this market. That was the end of any significant, independent black-owned press for many years.

Much later, it was financial failure which closed the Rand Daily Mail and Sunday Express, the two flagships of liberal opposition to apartheid. In a country that is 80 per cent black, the main problem was a short-sighted advertising industry that had little interest in targeting the predominantly black readership of the two titles. But the next wave of direct suppression came with the radicalisation of resistance politics in the 1950s, when the leftwing press, mostly associated with the Communist Party or the ANC-led Congress Alliance, faced repeated closures and banning.

They followed the fine example set by their ideological opponent, The Star, and repeatedly changed mastheads, moving on to a new one as soon as the old one was restricted, until every avenue was blocked. The apartheid era, and the suppression of resistance in the 1950s and early 1960s, brought with it the age of total control over expression, or at least the most formidable and comprehensive attempts to achieve it. It was at this point that censorship, in myriad forms,

Strachan sentenced to 2½ years

HAROLD STRACHAN, aged 40, a former art lecturer, was sentenced to two and a half years' imprisonment today for his account of South African prison conditions, but was released on bail pending an appeal. Bail was set at £1,000 double what it had been during his trial.

Strachan was convicted on charges of perjury and causing publication of false information about prison conditions. In three articles in the Rand Daily Mail he gave his version of conditions in various prisons in which he served a three-year sentence for conspiring to commit sabotage. The newspaper said at the time that Strachan's account made "grim and often sickening reading", but Judge M. E. Goodhead said today: "He skilfully used harmless facts on which to build his edifice of lies."

28.1.66

S. Africa to tighten press laws

THE SOUTH African Prime Minister, Mr Vorster, announced today that his Government was planning legislation to enable it to take legal action against South African newspapers publishing false or distorted reports. He hoped to introduce the legislation during the next session of Parliament.

Mr Vorster told a public meeting at Koffiefontein: "I am sick and tired of newspapers not quoting their sources, but resorting to the time-worn clichés – 'We have been informed or understand that.'" He added: "The proposed legislation will make things very difficult for newspapers making use of these tactics." Heavy fines would be imposed on newspapers whose employees were guilty of offences under the proposed legislation.

The new law would compel newspapers to disclose the names of their informants if and when required. But journalists who obtained their facts from reliable sources had nothing to fear, he said. The existing libel laws were not strict enough, he said, adding "the time has arrived when untruths should be punishable as well".

12.8.67

Judge ends ban on magazine

Durban

A JUDGE of the Supreme Court today lifted a Government ban on the South African magazine, Scope, which published a picture of a black man embracing a white girl.

Mr Justice S. Leon said he regarded as far-fetched in the extreme a submission by the State Publication Control Board that the photograph, apparently taken in a street in Greenwich Village, New York, was contrary to accepted and social standards in South Africa and that it would "encourage young readers to try to follow its example".

The board had argued that the picture would offend and disgust those who were against integration.

13.5.72

A small flap on statue

From Stanley Uys

THE CONTROVERSY that has been rocking the Transvaal town of Middleburg over the appearance of Michelangelo's nude, David, in the window of a women's hairdressing salon has ended in compromise.

The salon's owner, Mr Allan Shelton has given the statuette a tribal G-string and the guardians of Middleburg's morals are satisfied.

28.10.72

A man who no longer exists

Leader comment

EVEN IN the long catalogue of state terrorism in South Africa there are some cases that stand out from the others by their stark cruelty. One such is the plight of the newspaper photographer, Mr Peter Magubane, who has now spent more than 570 days in detention. He was an employee of the Rand Daily Mail and a winner of the South African Best Press Pictures of the Year Award. Now his employers, his friends, and his family do not know where he is, nor even whether he is alive. All that they know is that he was seized by the police on March 7 this year and taken to a secret cell for questioning.

Mr Magubane was one of the Africans who figured in the notorious trial that came to be known as the Winnie Mandela trial. First arrested in June, 1969, and held incommunicado for four months, he was charged with 21 others in October, 1969, under the Suppression of Communism Act. The trial ended with an acquittal in February last year, whereupon he and the other defendants were immediately re-arrested in court. Again held incommunicado, again charged (this time under the Terrorism Act), and again discharged last September when the court dismissed the case, Mr

Magubane was harassed yet again. He and the 17 other discharged defendants were served with banning orders confining them to a small area of the country. Winnie Mandela, the best-known of them, and the wife of Nelson Mandela, the former leader of the African National Congress, was put under house arrest and in March was given a one-year prison sentence for receiving Mr Magubane as a visitor. It is an offence for a person under house arrest to communicate with a banned person.

The following Sunday Mr Magubane was detained. That is the last that is known of him. All appeals to the Security Police have produced no response. The Rand Daily Mail, which has pleaded his case in its columns, is not even allowed under the Prisons Act to publish his photograph. The South African regime claims that, in contrast with other regimes, it tolerates a free press. What use is that freedom if a man becomes an unperson by having his whereabouts and even his photograph suppressed? The South African regime claims that in contrast with other regimes the country's courts are free. What use is that freedom when a man twice acquitted can be detained incommunicado as long as the State sees fit?

2.6.71

'Censorship, in myriad forms, invaded all aspects of South African life. By the 1970s, there were well over 100 laws that controlled the flow of information to every nook and cranny'

invaded all aspects of South African life. By the 1970s, there were well over 100 laws that controlled the flow of information in every nook and cranny: police, the army, the prisons, nuclear research . . . Some of these were comic. The infamous Key Points Act made it a serious offence to photograph "key points". One would assume that newspaper editors would have to be told what these "key points" were so that they could avoid publishing illegal material, but no, it was too dangerous to tell them — if a list fell into the wrong hands, it would identify targets for our enemies. One could only know the "key points" one could not photograph if one photographed them — and was prosecuted.

Secret censorship committees, dominated by conservative white Afrikaners, sat in judgment on films, books, theatre, cabaret, sex aids, key-rings and any other paraphernalia that threatened the South African way of life. These included the 1960s peace sign, the book Black Beauty and key-rings with suggestive remarks on them. The legal findings of these committees make some of the best reading in the annals of officialdom. On a 1978 calendar, the Publications Appeal Board chairman had this to say: "This nudity can be clearly seen from a distance of four metres. According to the view of the board regarding South African community standards, the entire or partial or substantial visible nudity of female breasts is indecent or obscene . . . "

On the film Roots, the chairman said this in 1984: "It appears that if a substantial number of blacks would, judged on the probabilities, substantially experience great or greater hate against the white as a result of seeing this film, the film would be prejudicial to the relations between black and white."

On the film, Playing With Fire, in 1984, he said: "Although certain aspects of the nudity in this film are functional in so far as they illustrate the seduction and the reasons for it, certain medium and close-up shots amount to a blatantly shameless invasion of the privacy of the female body and are regarded as indecent or obscene. In a film such as this, short and long shots of nude breasts are usually found to be not undesirable."

It was not all light-hearted. In 1977, the World newspaper was banned

Police arrest a foreign television crew as vigilantes attack
the KTC squatter camp, Cape Town, 1986

No reprieve for Afrikaans book

From Stanley Uys

A BLEAK future is foreseen for Afrikaans literature in South Africa as a result of dismissal by the Supreme Court in Cape Town of an appeal against the banning of "Kennis van die Avand" (Knowledge of the Night) by the controversial young writer and lecturer, André P. Brink.

The novel will be published in England on October 14 by W. H. Allen under the title "Looking on Darkness". It will be re-submitted to the Publications Control Board in South Africa, which no doubt will ban its English version as well – it deals with sex across the racial barrier.

Afrikaans writers and academics said gloomily today that the Supreme Court's ruling would have a withering effect on Afrikaans literature.

The judge president described Brink's book as indecent, improper, and damaging and offensive to morals. A substantial number of likely readers would find it shocking and disgusting, he said. It handled in an improper manner gruesomeness, murder, drunkenness, lust, sadism, and similar phenomena. It was also offensive to the religious feelings of a section of South Africa's population.

3.10.74

Vorster press code opposed by editors

From Stanley Uys

ALTHOUGH AT least nine editors of major English-language newspapers in South Africa are known to be totally opposed to the revised code of conduct drawn up by the Newspaper Press Union, the NPU Chairman, Mr Leyton Slater, announced today that the code will come into operation within the next few weeks.

Editors will be bound by the code, as their managements are ready to sign a voluntary agreement enforcing it. The code has been sent to the Prime Minister, Mr Vorster, who threatened last year to legislate to close down newspapers that published racially "inciting" reports if the press in South Africa did not "put its house in order".

Editors and journalists who opposed the new code regard it as an unacceptable form of self-censorship. They say the code will make editing a newspaper in accordance with the traditional principles and functions of the press impossible.

They are concerned particularly by a provision which will make it an offence for a newspaper to publish any report "which can have the effect of stirring up feelings of hostility between different racial, ethnic, religious or cultural groups".

This provision, they claim, is so wide-ranging that it covers almost the entire field of reporting of race affairs in South Africa. Stirring up feelings of hostility is an offence under present South African statutory law, but intent has to be proved.

Under the new code, which was published in full today for the first time, an offence is committed if a report merely has the "effect" of creating hostility. A Press Council consisting of a retired judge and two other members will decide whether a newspaper has contravened this provision, and will be authorised to pay a fine of up to £6,000.

7.8.74

TV brings new fears to S. Africa

From Stanley Uys

SOUTH AFRICA Television will make its debut tomorrow with a nightly five-hour programme — earning for South Africa the distinction of being the last developed country to get television.

About 210,000 sets have been sold at prices among the highest in the world — more than £800 for a 26-inch screen. Renting costs £27 a month and licence fees £17 a year.

The Prime Minister, Mr Vorster, who will appear on tomorrow night's programme to launch SATV, opposed television for many years until his Government was forced to yield to public opinion.

One reason why television has been kept out of South Africa for so long is that the Government feared its ability to corrupt. A former Minister of Posts and Telegraphs, Dr Albert Hertzog, held bizarre views about the medium's potential for evil. He once claimed that if an African "houseboy" was on his hands and knees polishing the drawing room floor and he looked up and saw a scantily dressed white woman on the television screen he would "rush upstairs and rape the madam".

The SA Broadcasting Corporation claims to be autonomous like the BBC, but is in fact under strict Government control. South African Radio is a dull propaganda arm of the Government and there is no reason to suppose that SATV will be different — although probably the bias will not be quite so blatant.

SATV will have only one channel at first, offering a mix of English and Afrikaans programmes. Later, "ethnic" channels will be introduced for African tribal groups. Plays showing white and black actors are unlikely to be screened, and to protect the cinema industry, old movies will not be shown on Friday or Saturday nights.

5.1.76

> **'After many years of resistance to the malign and satanic influence of television, it was finally introduced in 1976 and kept rigidly under state control. Similarly, radio broadcasting was a strict state monopoly'**

because it was seen as the voice of the Soweto uprising. Individual journalists were detained without trial, banned and put under house arrest. The tightest hold was maintained over broadcasting. After many years of resistance to its malign and satanic influence, television was introduced in 1976 and kept rigidly under state control. Similarly, radio broadcasting was a strict state monopoly.

The effect was substantial. South Africa was able to invade Angola in 1976 and keep it hidden from its own people for months. Censorship reached its height during the series of states of emergency that began in 1985 and lasted five years.

The state used a highly developed method of enforced self-censorship: rather than scrutinising material before publication, the government would threaten drastic measures against anyone who broke emergency regulations; and the regulations were so vague and so widely cast that the most straightforward reporting became a hazardous task. Inevitably, most of the country's media took the line of most likely survival: self-censorship based on the most cautious interpretation of the rules.

The effect, as is usually the case with censorship, was to distort rather than hide the truth. Nelson Mandela, Oliver Tambo and the ANC became mythical figures because the state went to such lengths to prevent anyone knowing anything substantial about them. They were not simply human beings and they were not plain politicians: they were transformed by censorship into symbols of resistance. To have a picture of Mandela, no matter how dated, was to defy; to have a Tambo speech, no matter how boring, was to refuse to submit. Thus state censorship served to build up the government's enemies.

When the public knew that security force action was being hidden from them, they did the natural thing, which was to imagine the worst. Often what people believed the authorities had done in secret was far worse than what they had actually done. Blank spaces and obliterations — used by the Weekly Mail to signal censorship — were banned. The authorities realised that nothing frightened the public more than white spaces in newspapers: vivid imaginations filled the spaces with reports far worse than those that had been removed.

Peter Se-Puma and Judy Leeuw starred in a South African version of Guess Who's Coming To Dinner. The film, made in the 1960s, was banned in South Africa until recently

How we all rely on the men of The World

FIVE BLACK journalists are becoming legendary for their courage in covering the riots in South Africa's black townships and as prisoners of South African security police.

Nicknamed the Riot Squad, they are Arthur Molefe, Moffat Zunga, Godwin Mohlomi, Willi Bokolo, Duma Ndhlovu. Since the riots erupted in June, they have provided the core of news coverage for The World, South Africa's only black daily newspaper, and one of the continent's most highly rated publications. They have also provided the most

crucial link between black and white in South Africa – and with the outside world.

The paper is owned by the white-run Argus newspaper chain, but enjoys a large degree of editorial autonomy. But it has paid a heavy price for its persistence. All five reporters on the Riot Squad have been detained by police under South Africa's tough new internal Security Act. All were arrested while on duty, according to Percy Qoboza.

A total of 15 African journalists have been arrested since July under various security laws, several being

the token blacks on white newspapers' staffs.

"The authorities are trying to cripple The World and intimidate those who remain," said Percy Qoboza. "I can vouch for every one of those men. They were never involved in anything besides their jobs – they couldn't afford to be doing anything else."

The only explanation, that the Government wants to cut off publication over the past few months, is partially reflected in its soaring circulation from an average of 105,000 to 175,000 daily, with 220,000 on big news days.

26.10.76

Vorster tries to silence black voice

Patrick Laurence
in Johannesburg

IN A MOVE unprecedented in South African political history, the Minister of Justice, Mr J. G. Kruger, yesterday cracked down on the press and the black consciousness movement, banning two newspapers, detaining one editor and banning another, and banning 18 organisations.

The two newspapers were The World and The Weekend World, both of which have predominantly black readers. The detained editor is Mr Percy Qoboza, editor of both publications. The banned editor is Mr Donald Woods, the outspoken editor of the Daily Dispatch.

With one exception all of the banned organisations are part of the black consciousness movement. The excep-

tion is the Christian Institute, which was, however, sympathetic to the movement. The director of the institute, the Reverend Beyers Naude, was served with a five-year banning order. Two of his colleagues in the institute were banned as well. They were the Reverend Theo Kotze and Mr Cedric Mason.

In a front page editorial, The Star, a Johannesburg-based newspaper, said: "Repression in a land that has already experienced democracy and freedom is a bitter admission of failure. Today a dozen or more organisations are banned and many people detained, but the thoughts they expressed and the things they stand for will not go away simply because of a clumsy attempt to stifle them. Instead they will multiply in the dark.

"The Government seems

bent on bringing about chaos. It seems bent on transforming moderate black opinion into extremism. There appears to be a frantic, suicidal element in the Cabinet which, unless checked, will destroy the country and plunge us into confrontation."

Mr René de Villiers, a former newspaper editor, described the banning of the The World and its sister newspaper as a "disastrous move" which marked the beginning of the end of press freedom in South Africa. Mrs Helen Suzman, the veteran MP, labelled the Government action as "stupid" and warned that it would lead to the "gravest possible consequences". Instead of doing what they had been doing legally the "black" organisations would pursue their aims unlawfully.

20.10.77

Sacking strikes hard at SA liberalism

THE SACKING of the editor of the Rand Daily Mail, Mr Allister Sparks, is the latest – but probably the most ominous – in a series of blows struck at vigorous Opposition journalism in South Africa. Mail reporters and liberal opinion in Johannesburg believe it may even spell the beginning of the end of an era in the country's newspaper history. Already there are signs that a purge of other Mail staff may be in the offing.

Some months ago, five black journalists were effectively sacked by government banning orders. Then, two black newspapers were closed down by their management after government threats to ban them if they appeared again. Thirdly, a number of senior Government officials urged the Steyn Commission on the press to recommend curbs on newspapermen, including a "register of journalists".

As the official Opposition spokesman on press matters, Mr David Dalling, put it: "The suspicion has been created that under threat of Government intervention pursuant to the anticipated Steyn Commission report, the management of South African Associated Newspapers – owners of the Mail – have bent their knees to the authorities and offered a sacrificial lamb in the form of Allister Sparks."

3.6.81

Suddenly one could not even be allowed to imagine what might have happened. The fight against censorship became a central part of the fight against apartheid. The "struggle" was foremost a struggle to make the voice of the majority heard, to have Mandela and Tambo noticed, and to make white people aware of the harsh realities of apartheid. Freedom of expression was at the core of the fight for political change. And there was no shortage of people prepared to fight that battle.

Wally Serote, Nadine Gordimer, Andre Brink and their fellow writers challenged the faceless censorship committees at every turn. Drag artist Pieter-Dirk Uys ridiculed them with devastating effect. Cape Times editor Tony Heard defied the law to publish an interview with ANC president Oliver Tambo, and a wave of new newspapers — the Weekly Mail, New Nation, South, New African, Vrye Weekblad — appeared as beacons of hope in the darkest days of emergency repression.

The weapons used in the battle against censorship were the traditional ones: legal challenges to the censorship regulations; crafty ways of getting around the law; mockery and ridicule; and, finally, open defiance. Censorship followed the old patterns: newspapers were closed down, individual editions seized, journalists detained, editors prosecuted. But it was a cat-and-mouse game: every new regulation brought a new challenge to find a way around it; every new prosecution was marked up like notches on a gun barrel.

The Weekly Mail once ran a join-the-dots picture of security force action with the caption: "*Don't* join the dots. If you do, you will get an illegal picture." When was closed down, the Weekly Mail ran its front page. When the Weekly Mail was closed down, its articles appeared regularly in The Star. When police said we could not print the names of detainees unless they were released officially — which they never were — we formally asked police if they informed families when their kin were held. Of course, they said in a protest of innocence, we would never hold people without their family knowing. That, we said, constitutes official confirmation — and we published the names.

All of which is really saying that we bred in captivity — the more they

'Newspapers were closed

down, individual

editions seized, journalists

detained, editors

prosecuted. But it was a

cat-and-mouse game:

every new regulation

brought a new challenge to

find a way around it'

Closure attacked by Afrikaans press

From Patrick Laurence in Johannesburg

SOUTH AFRICA'S pro-Government Afrikaans press yesterday unleashed a salvo of sharply-worded criticism at the Government for forcing the closure of the two Black-oriented newspapers, Post and Sunday Post.

In another critical reaction the Newspaper Press Union, an organisation representing the management of both Afrikaans and English newspapers, expressed its opposition to the existence of laws enabling the Government to ban newspapers without trial.

Perhaps the most cutting criticism came from Beeld, the Johannesburg-based Afrikaans daily which has close links with the Botha administration and which has campaigned strongly in favour of the "reformist" politics of the Prime Minister, Mr P. W. Botha.

Whatever technical points may have led to the closure of the newspapers, the State had effectively banned them, Beeld said in an editorial. It added: "We cannot understand why."

22.1.81

Blank space banned

From David Beresford

THE CONTROVERSY over censorship in South Africa reached new heights of absurdity yesterday with the announcement that white spaces had been declared "subversive".

The disclosure that state security is threatened by such spaces in papers was made yesterday by the Sowetan, the country's main black daily.

"We have been advised that the police interpret the blank spaces we have left in the newspaper over the past few days as being subversive," said a front-page announcement. "We will now fill the spaces with the most innocuous of writings." Inside, in the "comment" column, the newspaper said simply: "No comment."

A government spokesman, challenged at yesterday's daily press conference in Pretoria as to whether this was binding, advised newspapers to consult their lawyers.

Another periodical, the Weekly Mail, was published yesterday with huge white spaces, including most of its front page, and blanked-out sections of text including a list of detainees under the state of emergency.

21.6.86

DAVID BERESFORD in Johannesburg on what the new restrictions mean for newsmen and the reader

All the news that's fit to print in Pretoria

ON THE first floor of a grubby, three-storey building in downtown Johannesburg early yesterday afternoon there was that sense of controlled panic familiar to newsrooms around the world, but to none more than those in South Africa.

Fourteen pages of the 28-page Weekly Mail had already been laid out and they had just received the details of the most far reaching press restrictions yet promulgated in the country. On one side of the room editor Anton Harber was hunched over page-proofs with his lawyer, frantically scanning the Government Gazette and copy in search of possible breaches – a single one of which could be punished by a term of imprisonment for Harber and a fine big enough to wreck the newspaper.

A full-page spread headed "Why are activists murdering activists?" was causing problems. One of the writers anxiously leant over the lawyer, asking: "Isn't that subversive — 'enhance the striking capacity of the liberation forces ... direct their justified anger against the Pretoria regime'?" The lawyer shook his head: it was not specific enough to be subversive. But other paragraphs were spotted which were in breach of the regulations. The problem was how to fill the spaces — the regulations had now prohibited white spaces or "boxes" indicating censorship.

After an hour's debate less than a dozen offending paragraphs had been pulled out and the problem of the empty spaces resolved in principle. They would be filled with the words: "For further information telephone your minister." A reporter began preparing a list of work and home telephone numbers of the Cabinet and senior government officials, including the head of the country's secret service.

The scene in the Weekly Mail said much about the latest clampdown. Importantly, it showed that the South African press has not been silenced . . . yet. Less than half a dozen paragraphs in 14 pages — four of them news pages — is less than all-embracing censorship. And the spirit in which the telephone numbers of officialdom were being slotted into page one made it clear that the flame of journalistic defiance — in the tradition of Thomas Pringle, Anthony Sampson, Laurence Gandar, Donald Woods and Tony Heard — still flickers in South Africa.

It is beyond doubt that the new restrictions will have a major impact on public awareness of what is happening in the country, as a glance through recent stories out of South Africa quickly shows.

The death of an 11-year-old boy and the wounding of five others in Soweto township on November 5 — the "Guy Fawkes day shootings" — will be reportable, but not the allegations that the gunmen were police randomly opening fire from a hijacked bus on a bunch of kids playing in the street.

That horrendous account two weeks ago by the detainees' parents support committee on the plight of children in detention — including related allegations of child abuse and torture by interrogators — will now be unreportable.

The double murder of Robert Sobukwe's sister and her husband, Dr and Florence Ribeiro, last week would be published, but the involvement of a security branch car would not.

And then yesterday there was a story on page 6 of the early editions of the Star — South Africa's biggest daily newspaper — containing allegations by an 11-year-old boy just released from detention who said: "They put a dummy into my mouth, and the dummy had wires connected to it. The wires were connected to a socket in the wall and when . . ." But time has run out, both for the Star and this correspondent. In the final edition of the Star, published after the Government Gazette, the child's story had been replaced by: "Hail, rain and wind lash West Rand."

12.12.86

Picture: E HAMILTON WEST; WEEKLY MAIL

censored, the more imagination was brought to bear to find ways around it. Every new idea brought new regulations, which in turn were seen as a challenge to find new ways of circumventing the rules. Teams of lawyers were employed, not to tell us what we could not publish, but to find ways of publishing it. The result, after the collapse of apartheid, is that South Africans, even the most reactionary whites, cannot say, "We didn't know." The only ones who did not know the full horror of apartheid were those who chose not to.

Since 1990, we've had freedom. Not relative freedom, but almost complete freedom to publish as we see fit. More than 100 laws remain on the statute books, but no one pays any attention to them. The old enemies of freedom of speech have become its most vigorous defenders. Every day, in our newspapers and on our airwaves, we hear a range of views from those of the world's only growing Communist Party to the ravings of the racist far right. Our news-stands are now filled with soft porn, which is getting harder every month. And after April, we will have a Bill of Rights, and a constitutional court, both of which will equip us with more weapons than ever to fight future anti-censorship battles.

Battles there certainly will be. There is no shortage of those who are already arguing that a new government should be "given a chance", that criticism will have to be withheld "in the national interest", that violence will justify extraordinary state methods. And for the first time we are likely to have a government that can lay reasonable claim to represent "the national interest". At the same time, violence threatens media coverage of areas of conflict, with journalists less able to travel safely in key areas. Recently, during a single week, black journalists were thrown out of a rightwing political meeting and white journalists were threatened by gun-wielding Pan-Africanist Congress guerrillas.

All our experience tells us that the combination of political pressure, violence, a history of intolerance and the "national interest" is a deadly Third World mix. Now, like certain wild animals released back into the wild, we have to see whether we can survive in freedom as well as we did in captivity.

Anton Harber is editor of the Weekly Mail

The Weekly Mail front page with blank spaces showing which news was censored

'Blank spaces — used to signal censorship — were banned. The authorities realised nothing frightened the public more than white spaces in newspapers: vivid imaginations filled them with reports far worse than those that had been removed'

THE WEEKLY MAIL

Volume 2, Number 24 FRIDAY JUNE 20 to THURSDAY JUNE 26, 1986

THE PAPER FOR A CHANGING SOUTH AFRICA

BACK ON THE STREETS! The paper that was seized last week will be on sale as usual from today

| The EPG report: An extraordinary document made ordinary by our extraordinary times | 8 | A leaf-munching plan to beat malnutrition | 7 |

FRONT PAGE COMMENT

Our lawyers tell us we can say almost nothing critical about the Emergency

But we'll try:

PIK BOTHA, the Minister of Foreign Affairs, told US television audiences this week that the South African press remained free.

We hope that ▉▉, was listening.

They considered our publication subversive.

● If it is subversive to speak out against ▉▉▉▉▉▉▉, we plead guilty.

● If it is subversive to express concern about ▉▉▉▉▉▉▉, we plead guilty.

● If it is subversive to believe that there are better routes to peace than the ▉▉▉▉▉▉▉, we plead guilty.

● To PAGE 2

RESTRICTED Reports on these pages came been compiled in terms with Emergency regulations

'Vicious' foreign coverage provoked news ban, says SA

Patrick Laurence

THE SOUTH African Government's prohibition of all but officially approved television coverage of conflict was justified at the weekend by Foreign Minister Pik Botha as a bid to end "vicious and venomous" coverage by foreign TV crews.

The ban, which has been expected since a CBS team filmed a police ambush of young stone-throwers in Cape Town last month, was condemned by the Foreign Correspondents Association as a step down the "slippery slide toward a totally controlled press".

The opposition Progressive Federal Party accused the Government of drawing an "Iron Curtain" around the troubled areas.

The measure, imposed under the emergency regulations, prohibits the televising, photographing, recording, or even drawing of conflict situations in the 38 magisterial districts covered by the state of emergency, except with the permission of the Commissioner of Police.

Penalties for contravention of the new rules are severe. They include confiscation of equipment, a fine of up to R20,000 (£5,400) or imprisonment for 10 years without the option of a fine.

4.11.85

Newspapers seized as Botha meets Tutu in 'frank' exchange

S. Africa tightens grip on media

From David Beresford

THE SOUTH African Government yesterday demonstrated a new ruthlessness in implementing the national state of emergency. Issues of two newspapers were seized, one television journalist was issued with a deportation order, film crews filming in central Johannesburg were stopped, and no details of detentions — now thought to number thousands — were released.

A government spokesman went so far as to threaten the expulsion of foreign correspondents who persisted in describing the Government as "a white minority regime". An abbreviated "unrest report" — issued by the Information Ministry instead of the police as before — disclosed that seven people had been killed in violence after the emergency was declared.

The two newspapers impounded yesterday were the Sowetan, the country's main black daily, and the Weekly Mail, a liberal tabloid which has established a formidable reputation as a critic of the government and the security forces.

Newsagents around the country reported that police were visiting them to seize copies of the two newspapers. The action against the Sowetan may have been in retaliation for a front-page editorial written by the editor, Joe Latakgomo, demanding that the government resign.

Confirming that the seizures were on the instructions of the Law and Order Minister, a spokesman for the information department, Mr David Steward, said: "So I want to tell you this: We're not kidding. We're serious about this." Mr Steward said that the Government objected to the term "white minority regime" because it was inaccurate — it was a government and it included members of other racial groups. "Journalists who continue to use this factually incorrect approach will place their position in South Africa in jeopardy," he said.

14.6.86

Death beyond the silence

THE SOUTH AFRICAN authorities, having imposed sweeping censorship on the media, at first claimed that the tenth anniversary of the Soweto rising on Monday had passed off with only minor incidents. The main justification for the latest state of emergency and the gag on journalists was an alleged plot to create anarchy, if not worse, on the anniversary, even though anti-apartheid organisations had done nothing more than call for a strike. When the strike was massively supported but unaccompanied by the forecast anarchy, it was asserted that the state of emergency had been vindicated. But at a press conference yesterday it was disclosed that 11 Africans had been killed, four by the police.

If 11 violent deaths in 24 hours (assuming that is the whole story, which it almost certainly isn't) constitute a quiet day in contemporary South Africa, one dreads to think what level of killing now makes a busy one. Journalists were absolutely right to ask at the conference why anyone should believe the Government, which was given a particularly hard time over the amazing technical coincidence which cut off thousands of telephones in townships all over the country on Monday. But moral victories will not bring out the facts we are being prevented from publishing. The silencing of the media, unprecedented in South African history, has destroyed one of the few remaining arguments Pretoria had to support its dubious claim to Western values.

18.6.86

Pretoria turns on its press

Leader comment

IF THERE was ever an open and shut legal case it is surely the one brought yesterday by the South African authorities against Mr Anthony Heard, the editor of the Cape Times. The single charge on the sheet accused him of quoting a banned person, contrary to section 56 of the iniquitous Internal Security Act of 1982. The evidence was spread all over the paper's main feature page last Monday in the form of an exhaustive, question-and-answer interview with Mr Oliver Tambo, president of the banned African National Congress, the leading anti-apartheid organisation. Mr Heard took the unprecedented decision to publish the interview "as a contribution to peaceful solutions in South Africa in a matter of overwhelming public importance" — because the ban on the ANC has denied South Africans the chance to know its view in the raging debate over their country's future.

Thus, just as Pretoria extended the widespread internal censorship to the foreign media (especially broadcasting), in the hope that a world starved of pictures would forget apartheid, a South African editor decided to flout the law of the land in what he clearly saw as the true public interest. The official reaction was muted: the charge could have been graver and Mr Heard was released on his own recognisance pending another court appearance on December 9. But there should be no misunderstanding of the seriousness of his position or underestimation of the moral courage which put him there.

The statute used against Mr Heard is evil because it puts the executive above the law, notably in detaining people without trial and "banning" them and their organisations. But defying any law, whether on grounds of conscience or for any other reason, is dangerous because it entails direct defiance of the state. The interview, as shown by the extracts we published on Tuesday, was mostly innocuous by British standards, but that is neither defence nor mitigation in South Africa, any more than one editor's conception of the public interest.

5.11.85

Editor acquitted on appeal

Patrick Laurence

A SENIOR South African editor, Mr Donald Woods of the Daily Dispatch, was acquitted on appeal today of a charge under Section 83 of the Criminal Procedure Act. Had the appeal not been upheld, Mr Woods would have been the first editor — but not the first journalist — to be sent to gaol under the relevant section of the Act.

Section 83 empowers a magistrate to ask journalists to name their informants and to sentence them to up to 12 months' imprisonment if they refuse to do so without "just excuse" in law. Nine South African journalists have chosen to go to gaol rather than reveal the identity of their informants without their permission.

Mr Woods refused to disclose the name of an informant and was sentenced to six months' imprisonment by a magistrate last December. His appeal was heard on October 29, but judgement was withheld until today. His acquittal was largely on a technicality.

9.12.87

S. Africa expels British TV men

By David Beresford

SOUTH AFRICA has thrown out the BBC and ITN correspondents amid widespread reports that a new government crackdown on dissent is imminent.

Michael Buerk of the BBC and Peter Sharpe of ITN have been given 10 and eight days respectively to get out of the country after the Government's refusal to renew their work permits. It brings to nine the number of foreign correspondents expelled since the current state of emergency was imposed last June.

The expulsion of the two TV correspondents coincides with reports quoting "government sources" in local newspapers, predicting "a sweeping security clampdown on trade unions, universities, organisations using foreign funds for domestic political purposes and alternative media publications".

15.5.87

Freed black editor faces fresh bans

By David Beresford in Johannesburg

THE SOUTH African editor, Mr Zwelakhe Sisulu, was released from detention yesterday after being held for nearly two years without charge or trial. Tight restrictions were immediately placed on his movements.

Mr Sisulu, editor of the Catholic weekly newspaper, New Nation, was released with six other detainees, including Mr Eric Molobi, the national co-ordinator of the National Education Crisis Committee — a key affiliate of the banned United Democratic Front (UDF).

Mr Molobi had been held for nearly a year without charge. Despite previous protestations from the South African government that Mr Sisulu's detention had nothing to do with his activities as a journalist, he has been prohibited from working for any newspaper under a new banning order imposed on him.

The leader also prohibits him from leaving his home in the Johannesburg township of Soweto between dusk and dawn; leaving his local magisterial district at any time. He has to report to his local police station daily.

He is also banned from attending any meeting of more than 10 people, or any meeting at which the government is criticised, contributing to "any manner" to any publication, or participating in any interview; taking part "in any matter whatsoever" in the activities of a series of organisations including the United Democratic Front and the South African Council of Churches.

It was the second lengthy period of detention which Mr Sisulu, aged 37, has undergone. In 1981 and 1982 he was held in solitary confinement for 251 days without charge.

He is the son of Mr Walter Sisulu, the former secretary general of the African National Congress, who was gaoled for life with Mr Nelson Mandela and others in 1964.

"Thank God. I had heard the rumour, but I had not dared to believe it," said Albertine Sisulu, told of her son's release yesterday. "I am hoping that this will lead to the release of other political prisoners."

3.12.88

S. Africa newspapers attack censorship

CONFRONTATION between the media and the South African government over continued censorship under the state of emergency is steadily growing.

The country's biggest daily newspaper, The Star, and the major black daily, The Sowetan, yesterday carried white spaces on their front pages in imitation of the famous protest by the Rhodesia Herald against censorship under UDI. The leading financial newspaper, Business Day, published a front page warning: "This newspaper has been produced under conditions amounting to censorship."

The use of blank spaces by The Star yesterday was particularly striking. Among four stories affected was one dealing with a speech delivered by a homeland leader, Mr Enos Mabuza. Headlined "Mabuza speaks on emergency detentions," the story said the Chief Minister of Kangwane had commented on detentions under the emergency. "Addressing the South African German Chamber of Commerce and Industry, he said . . ." A blank space followed.

The report went on to say: "Mr Mabuza also spoke of the detention of someone known to him. He said: " . . ." Another blank space followed.

Earlier yesterday, The Sowetan carried a white space which it said had been reserved for a photograph of people in Soweto "playing, praying or whatever" which they had been unable to take because of the restrictions.

19.6.86

Above: **Supporters at a mass rally demand press freedom, 1989**

Right: **Zwelakhe Sisulu, editor of the Catholic weekly New Nation, was detained for nearly two years without charge**

Comrades carry the coffins of two victims
of violence in the Pietermaritzburg area.
The war which began in Natal in 1985 was
one of the most tragic consequences of
the apartheid regime's efforts to set
disadvantaged groups against each other

CEDRIC NUNN/AFRAPIX

Calls for the diplomatic isolation of the apartheid regime tended to focus on economic and sporting sanctions. But it was possibly the ban on the sale of arms — the only mandatory UN sanction ever imposed — which proved the most effective

Sanctions/Joseph Hanlon

ON FEBRUARY 7 1994, President F W de Klerk admitted for the first time that international sanctions had been a key factor in crippling South Africa's economy. It was an early salvo in an election campaign aimed at blaming the African National Congress (ANC) rather than De Klerk's own National Party for South Africa's ills. The National Party, he said, "is not responsible for poverty in South Africa. One of the main problems was the effect on our economy of the international sanctions campaign spearheaded by the ANC."

This statement has the same level of bluster and hyperbole as National Party claims a decade earlier that sanctions were having no effect. "The sooner sanctions come, the better," declared then Foreign Minister Pik Botha in 1986. The truth of the matter is that sanctions did have a significant economic and military impact, although hardly a devastating one. Their real effect was political and psychological. The Commonwealth Independent Expert Study on Sanctions in 1989 concluded: "Sanctions will help to convince white South Africans that it is in their own interests to dismantle apartheid and enter negotiations to establish a non-racial and representative government . . . The minority must see that apartheid is no longer a viable option because the economic and political cost is too high. By reducing the power and will of the apartheid state and its beneficiaries to resist change, sanctions will support and shorten the struggle." In the end, this proved accurate.

Sanctions were imposed on South Africa over a period of nearly 50 years. India imposed a trade ban in 1946 and by 1964 had cut all links. The Nobel Peace Prize winner Chief Albert Luthuli tried to put sanctions on the international agenda in 1960 by presenting their implementation as a means of achieving a peaceful transition to a non-racial South Africa. "The alternative," he said, "[is that] violence, rioting and counter-rioting will become the order of the day. It can only deteriorate into disorder and ultimate disaster."

Chief Luthuli went on to counter the arguments so frequently used later — that sanctions would hurt the very people they were supposed to help: "The economic boycott of South Africa will entail undoubted hardship for Africans.

We do not doubt that. But if it is a method which shortens the day of bloodshed, the suffering to us will be a price we are willing to pay." It was a prophetic statement, but it was largely ignored. Initial efforts to isolate the apartheid state were dramatic, but fitful. It was forced to leave the Commonwealth in 1961, it was suspended from the Olympic movement in 1964, and took no further part in the United Nations General Assembly after 1974. In 1973, most oil exporters agreed to impose sanctions on South Africa. But it was only the massacre of schoolchildren in Soweto in 1976 that put the issue of full-scale sanctions on the international agenda.

In 1977, the UN Security Council agreed on the only mandatory sanction ever imposed on South Africa — a ban on the sale of "arms and related materials of all types". In the same year, the Commonwealth's Gleneagles Declaration banned sporting contacts. Some European and US companies withdrew. Sweden banned new investment in 1979, while many banks limited new lending. Needless to say, South Africa did not meekly submit to such impositions. It became skilled at breaking the arms embargo, importing via third countries and building close links with other pariah states, particularly Israel and Chile. It built up a major arms industry of its own and even became a significant weapons exporter.

Nevertheless, the arms embargo was the only sanction enforced tightly enough and for long enough to have a direct and identifiable impact. Indeed, it was responsible for one of the most important events which finally pushed the regime into negotiations. From 1977, South Africa was unable to buy modern weapons systems and, in many cases, even spares for existing equipment. The air force was particularly badly hit. In July 1987, South Africa invaded southern Angola in an effort to shore up the rebel Unita guerrillas and to capture the strategic town of Cuito Cuanavale. In previous invasions South Africa had depended on air superiority to limit casualties on the ground. This time the Soviet-supplied Angolan air force and anti-aircraft defences were so superior that Pretoria lost several planes, which it was unable to replace.

As a result, the South Africans put more emphasis on ground forces. Without air cover, their artillery was pushed back out of range of Cuito Cuanavale, while

"BOYCOTT S. AFRICAN GOODS"
Call by students' union

BY 101 VOTES to 17, with 72 abstentions, the council of the National Union of Students, meeting at Margate, decided early today to call on all members for an "individual boycott" of South African goods. The boycott is in protest against the Union government's policy of racially separate universities.

The motion, tabled as an "emergency" one, offers support to South African students' own boycott of South African goods and calls on the NUS executive, subject to legal advice, to prepare and publish a list of goods which should be banned.

16.11.59

Call for sanctions against S. Africa
From RICHARD SCOTT
United Nations (NY)

GHANA TODAY called for sanctions against South Africa in order to compel her to change her racial policies. The demand for action, which would completely isolate South Africa from the rest of the world, was made in the General Assembly's Trusteeship Committee.

The committee was continuing its debate on race conflicts in South Africa. In the same committee the Libyan delegate suggested that South Africa might be expelled from the United Nations.

28.3.61

Ban on South African goods
Council's move

LIVERPOOL CITY COUNCIL has yesterday decided by 77 votes to 39 to instruct all corporation committees and departments to boycott South African goods until further notice.

The boycott was recommended by the Finance Committee after it had considered a motion from Councillor William Sefton (Ind. Lab.), who asked for the ban in support of the "coloured" people of South Africa and as a protest against the segregation policy of the South African government.

Protesting against the boycott, councillor H McDonald Steward, MP for Stockport South, said he thought it was utterly wrong to introduce this subject on the day of the prime minister's departure and "so poison the atmosphere in which he is hoping to do his best for both countries."

7.1.60

Relief and sadness
Leader comment

THE OPERATION is over and the unhealthy limb has been removed. It is an occasion for relief rather than for rejoicing. With South Africa as a member, the life of the Commonwealth, and still more its further growth, were in serious doubt. Now the Commonwealth can be expected to live and grow with vigour as an association believing in the equal worth of all races. It is the only body in the world which regularly provides a meeting place for intimate and unhurried discussion among leaders of countries with different problems and greatly different outlooks. As it grows in numbers its value is in meeting this need increases. It was worth preserving. It could not have been preserved in its present form if one member continued to be out of sympathy with a principle which the others held dear.

But to rejoice that the necessity has been accomplished would be to insult the many good people in South Africa whose feelings today will be of bitterness and shame. The severance of their link with the Commonwealth cuts them off from the civilisation from which they have drawn much of their strength. They will wonder, along with many in this country, whether it was necessary to push South Africa to the point of withdrawing her application for re-admission. They will wonder whether a few more years of influence and persuasion would not have shown the South African government the need for a change in her racial policies. They themselves will go on working for a change and they may feel that their work has been discounted and themselves snubbed.

South Africa — not her present government but the representatives of her people — will be missed at future conferences, and the older members in particular are bound to feel the gap in their numbers. They will remember the wisdom which Field-Marshal Smuts brought to so many of their meetings and the encouragement he gave to the Commonwealth when it faced its last great test during the war. They will hope — and here the younger members will join them — for the day when South Africa is able to resume her place. The shock which yesterday's decision must give to South African political life could be a salutary one. It could be the catalyst to bring about the change which is bound to come one day and which the other Commonwealth members want to see soon. It could start people thinking who have never thought before about the nature of the system which they take for granted and which the rest of the world abhors. When that happens South Africa will not need to apply to join the Commonwealth as a republic. She will be invited.

16.3.61

British arms for S. Africa confirmed
By PATRICK KEATLEY, Diplomatic Correspondent

THE CONSERVATIVE Government will reverse Mr Harold Wilson's policy and resume the sale of arms to South Africa.

This has been agreed between the Prime Minister, Mr Edward Heath, and his Foreign Secretary, Sir Alec Douglas-Home, and is the first major policy decision of the new Heath administration in foreign affairs.

The decision is certain to be attacked from Labour and Liberal benches when Parliament resumes in 10 days. But the Tory Front Bench will retort that these contracts are worth a potential £75 millions a year to British factories.

23.6.70

vintage Centurion tanks proved vulnerable to air attack. White casualties began to rise and ultimately the South Africans were forced to withdraw. It was to be their last major invasion of a neighbouring state and finally put paid to the military's claim that the ANC could be beaten by fighting the war beyond South Africa's borders. Negotiations over Namibian independence and a settlement in Angola were a direct result of South Africa's defeat at Cuito Cuanavale. In less than three years, Nelson Mandela was out of prison and negotiations had begun in South Africa itself.

The oil, sporting and cultural embargoes were also effective, but in very different ways. Initially, South Africa was easily able to circumvent the oil sanctions because all of its needs were supplied by Iran. But after the fall of the Shah in 1979, the new government cut off supplies. President P W Botha admitted that at one point South Africa only had enough oil reserves for a week. Strict enforcement of the embargo at that time would have brought South Africa to its knees, but sanctions-busting by western oil companies ensured that the regime survived. Nevertheless, in 1986 P W Botha acknowledged that breaking the embargo had cost the country $25 billion (then about £15 billion).

Despite this shock to the apartheid system, external circumstances conspired to relax the pressure at a critical juncture. The outcry following the Soweto massacre, the 1977 round of sanctions, and President Carter's application of his strong human-rights policy to South Africa had combined to cause a tempering of the repression. But 1981 saw a major reversal, following the election of right-wing governments in Britain and the United States. Added to this, the gold price briefly doubled to more than $800 an ounce in 1980, after the 1979 oil crisis, making the South African government feel wealthy. The result was a new hard line under P W Botha, involving attacks on the neighbouring states and crackdowns at home.

Throughout much of the 1980s, Ronald Reagan and Margaret Thatcher led a vociferous campaign against sanctions. "There is no case in history that I know of where punitive, general economic sanctions have been effective to bring about internal change," Mrs Thatcher said in 1986, although four years earlier she had

Top: **Tennyson Makiwane, director of the boycott movement, speaking in London, 1960**

Middle: **Demonstrators picket Westland Helicopter's offices in Westminster to protest against the sale of helicopters to South Africa, 1971**

Bottom: **An anti-apartheid demonstration crosses Chelsea Bridge, 1986**

The Anti-Apartheid Movement

SIR–Nelson Mandela faces trial in Johannesburg as leader of South Africa's underground resistance to apartheid. It seems a good time for us all to ask ourselves whether we do not share the blame. We in Britain have just agreed to sell Verwoerd Buccaneer Mark II aircraft worth some £20 millions, and have in the past provided the tanks, guns, and ammunition without which apartheid could not survive; and we tremble to make the modest economic sacrifice that embargo against South African goods – for which African leaders like Mandela and Chief Luthuli are asking – might involve.

The Anti-Apartheid movement is embarking on a campaign this winter to organise support for the oppressed people of South Africa in their struggle against apartheid. This support can take several forms: a personal boycott of South African goods by the British public; the refusal by sportsmen and entertainers to participate in events which reflect the policy of segregation; a demand by the British public for an immediate embargo on the export of arms to South Africa. We also want our Government to vote in the United Nations for collective economic sanctions against South Africa. The UN will soon be debating a new Afro-Asian demand for action: if the British delegation is once again seen as an opponent of effective measures, and an indirect bastion of the Verwoerd regime, we may find ourselves, rather than Mandela, arraigned before the court of world opinion.

The Anti-Apartheid Movement has been forwarding messages of support to Mandela from British sympathisers and we have been asked by him to express his deep appreciation of these messages, which he has been permitted to see in gaol. We shall be glad to continue to forward further letters, postcards, or telegrams during the course of the trial.

Yours sincerely, Barbara Castle,
Hon. President Anti-Apartheid Movement,
House of Commons.

17.10.62

SANCTIONS AGAINST SOUTH AFRICA

UN recommends economic and diplomatic boycott

BRITISH OPPOSITION

From HELLA PICK

THE GENERAL ASSEMBLY today recommended sanctions against South Africa, and asked the Security Council to consider its expulsion from the United Nations. This is the first time in its 17 years of existence that the Assembly has taken such action.

A resolution requesting member governments to take collective measures against South Africa in a further effort to persuade its government to abandon apartheid was carried by 67 votes to 16 with 23 abstentions and four absentees.

Britain and the United States were among those voting against and most of the abstentions were from Latin America. Immediately after the vote a British spokesman made it clear that, although Britain abhorred apartheid like other member countries, it could not comply with the request to take sanctions against South Africa.

The African delegations were elated by the vote, and though nobody has any great illusion over the prospects of putting the resolution into operation on a world-wide scale, they do believe that today's vote will result in a more concerted attack on apartheid.

Earlier in the day the South African Foreign Minister, Mr Eric Louw, had defended his government's policy by claiming that the African population of the republic was provided with education, health services, ample opportunities, and deeply appreciated the separate Bantu States that were being created. Only a minority complained, encouraged in their complaints by outsiders whose own governments had nothing to boast about.

Domestic Issue

South Africa considered apartheid to be a purely domestic issue, of no concern to the UN, since the UN Charter did not permit interference with the domestic affairs of member states. By way of explanation he added that apartheid was part of the white south African population's bid to survive in the country which had now become its irrevocable home.

7.11.62

Authors' sanctions on South Africa

BY OUR PARLIAMENTARY STAFF

FORTY-EIGHT prominent playwrights have agreed to ban performances of their plays in South Africa in any theatre where discrimination is made among audiences on grounds of colour.

The list includes Mr Graham Greene, Mr Arthur Miller, Mr John Osborne, and Mr J B Priestley. The demonstration has been organised by the Anti Apartheid Movement.

The playwrights explain that they do not want to impose political censorship; colour discrimination transcends the purely political.

Mr Arthur Miller wrote in his letter to the movement: "It must be made clear that the production of a play or the distribution of any art work is not a privilege but a right for all people. It is because the African is now denied his right to see my plays in conditions no different than the white man that I join this protest."

26.6.63

imposed sanctions against Argentina over the Falklands and was to do the same against Iraq in 1990. Britain refused to join in Commonwealth sanctions and successfully pressed for the watering down of Commonwealth and European Community measures. The US turned a blind eye to sanctions busting, and the CIA was even involved in breaking the oil embargo as part of a complex deal to obtain support from Saudi Arabia for the Contras in Nicaragua.

This high-level opposition did reduce the strength of the embargo, but it was not sufficient to stop a growing wave of sanctions. Botha's repression of the township uprisings, which escalated from 1984, led the UN Security Council to approve packages of voluntary measures in 1984 and 1985. The European Community, the Commonwealth and even the US imposed further measures in 1985 and again in 1986. These confirmed the oil embargo, further limited military and nuclear co-operation, restricted investment, imposed certain diplomatic sanctions, and banned the imports of gold coins, arms and iron and steel.

Each ban drew on precedents set by others. Sweden banned the import of fruit, a measure previously claimed to violate the General Agreement on Tariffs and Trade (GATT). Ireland followed suit, dispelling the myth that no EC country could act alone. Then Denmark imposed a total trade ban, which was soon adopted by the other Scandinavian countries. These governmental initiatives were reinforced by thousands of local and consumer actions.

One of the most important moves of all was the decision of US and then European banks in 1986 to refuse new loans to South Africa and even to stop rolling over old ones. This was a direct response to state and city councils in the US withdrawing their large accounts from banks which dealt with South Africa. The refusal to roll over loans forced South Africa to freeze payments on short-term debt and the government never again gained access to international finance. There was a rush to quit by US and European companies. The UN Economic and Social Council estimated that 500 transnational corporations withdrew from South Africa, among them such big names as IBM, General Motors, General Electric and Coca-Cola. After the arms embargo, this was probably the most successful "instrumental" sanction. In general, however, such sanctions took a

500 academics make pledge to S. Africa

A TOTAL of 509 British academics, including A J Ayer, Isaiah Berlin, and the novelists Angus Wilson and Iris Murdoch, have sworn never to accept posts in South African universities.

Mr Angus Wilson argued that the boycott would have a practical effect if the "technical professors" ceased to bring new learning to South African universities.

17.11.65

Olympics ultimatum for South Africa

SOUTH AFRICA has been given another 50 days to renounce racial discrimination in sport, or she will not be allowed to take part in the 1964 Olympic Games in Tokyo. The decision was taken by the executive board of the International Olympic Committee in Lausanne today.

The move was described as "one last chance" by Otto Mayer, a member of the Committee. "We want to help them as much as possible," he said. "Naturally, we want them there as much as they want to come."

He explained that South Africa had until August 16, the date by which all teams for the 1964 Olympic Games must be submitted, to fulfil the Committee's condition that the South African Olympic Committee publicly renounce racial discrimination in sport over the radio and in the press.

Denial of policy

South African sport sources in Lausanne said that it was most unlikely that the South African Olympic Committee would be able to fulfil this condition,since it meant denial of the government's policy of apartheid.

27.6.64

Sports move for white S. Africans

THE SOLE member of parliament of the multi-racial Progressive Party, Helen Suzman, said in Johannesburg today that the "slight concessions" in the sport colour bar announced by the prime minister, John Vorster, yesterday had been made for the benefit of white South Africans who were worried because they were threatened with no longer seeing international teams.

"They have not been made for the benefit of non-whites and certainly not for overseas sportsmen," she told parliament. The concessions were anyway conditional, one condition being that the subject should not be dragged into politics."What nonsense!" she said. "Why is the matter being discussed in the first place if it is not an acute political matter?"

13.4.67

SA athlete refuses to run

By Rafiq Mughal

A TOP white South African runner, Johnny Halberstadt, has declined to accept Springbok colours in a personal protest against alleged racism. Halberstadt's stand was backed yesterday by another top white runner, Kevin Shaw.

Halberstadt cited the case of Loop-En-Val Motshwarateu as the reason for his decision.

Motshwarateu, one of the finest black athletes South Africa has produced has won a scholarship to the United States but has been unable to get a South African passport, Halberstadt said.

8.9.79

Stars run into trouble in SA

ADAM FAITH and Dusty Springfield are on the Foreign Office agenda today. Mr.Walter Padley, Secretary of State, is meeting representatives of Equity to discuss the misfortunes of the two singers, and the whole troubled business of British entertainers in South Africa.

The problem has dragged on for years, but recently it came to a head. In December the Searchers, Eden Cane and the Zombies cancelled their tours. Miss Springfield was deported at 24 hours' notice because she sang before mixed audiences, and is now being sued for £5,000 for breach of contract. Only last week Mr Faith cut short his tour, was arrested at Johannesburg airport and had to put down a bond for £20,000 before he was released. In spite of this history of irritation, cancellation, and loss, the three main entertainment unions in Britain are far from agreeing between themselves on what to do about it

Firm Policy

Only the Musicians Union – which with 35,000 members and much the biggest of the three organisations – has a firm policy clearly stated. Since 1957, it has forbidden all engagements in South Africa. This is, says the union, a protest against apartheid: you can't go to South Africa, take the profits and then salve your conscience by playing to the occasional coloured audience.

The Variety Artistes' Federation (3,000 members, mainly "principal artistes") has no policy at all, says R W Swinson, its general secretary. It has no political views, and its members may perform where they please and to any audience. But perhaps it may soon arrive at a view. "We are wondering at the moment."

The third organisation is Equity, whose 11,000 members include straight actors, comedians, ballet dancers, and opera singers. Today the union meets Mr Padley, and at next Tuesday's meeting of the council of Equity the main discussion will be about South Africa.

Concession

In 1961 Equity managed to wring from African Consolidated Theatres the concession that all shows, to white or coloured audiences, should be substantially the same and in the same theatre. But still the proportion of performances for coloureds was low. In 1962, when My Fair Lady made a 20-week tour only eight performances out of 160 were open to non whites.

14.1.65

Coloured footnote

THE BRITISH Medical Journal has finally decided not to accept any more job advertisements from South Africa unless it is quite clear that black and white applicants will be offered the same salary.

28.9.73

Equity row over S. Africa sale

A FRESH dispute broke out in the faction-ridden actors' union, Equity, yesterday with the news that two Thames Television series, The New Avengers and The Sweeney, have been sold to the South African Broadcasting Company.

The 22,000 union members are currently involved in a ballot on whether to ban the sale to South Africa of all recorded television, film and taped material.

Although reports in the South African press claimed that the deal had been done in a "cloak and dagger" fashion to avoid the existing agreement banning the sale of in-house produced programmes, it became clear yesterday that both series had been sold under a different contract.

16.10.76

Just a sporting chance

IT ISN'T hard to find South Africans delighted by the demonstrations against the Springboks. Go into Soweto, or any other township, and just talk to people, writes Jonathan Steele.

When they hear an English accent, and if you are not accompanied by a white South African, the masks fall. Eagerly, they want the news confirmed. "Is it true that they're having to use a thousand police to hold back the demonstrators today? Is there really so much feeling against South Africa?"

I had happened to be in Soweto the afternoon of the Springboks' match in Gosforth. Although I had no more up-to-date information than they, I was bombarded with questions.

In the house where I finished up there were four Africans, intelligent, articulate, and, like most in Soweto, detribalised. Three had clerical jobs. Two were graduates. Their views on the tour were straightforward. They were against it. And so were their neighbours, and anyone else you talked to.

They admitted perhaps three-quarters of the African population in South Africa were not fully aware of the tour or the British backlash against it. If you have to rely on the government-controlled African language radio, that is hardly surprising. But those that knew of it were totally opposed. Which again is hardly surprising.

Africans who are allowed into white South African sporting fixtures have traditionally cheered for the Springboks' opponents.

Some are upset at Basil D'Oliveira's statement that the cricket tour should go on. One man explained: "He is a 'coloured', and they have never taken the African's side. They feel closer to the whites." Others welcome the statements about multi-racialism which a few white sportsmen have started making, though they are cynical about them.

Gary Player's plea that the great Indian golfer, Papwa Sewgolum, be allowed to re-enter the whites-only South African championships came soon after the first talk started of an international boycott of all South African golfers, whites included. Some years earlier when Sewgolum had had to go through the farce of receiving a trophy outside a clubhouse in the rain, because the clubhouse was reserved for whites, Player had said nothing.

But then that is what international pressure is all about. South Africans have a fierce pride in sport and take it very seriously. It gets acres of space in the papers, often on the front page. Every whisper of any suggested new boycott of South Africa in sport is reported in detail. Sport is their weak point, and the demonstrations have shown they are vulnerable.

5.3.70

Barclays answers the protestors

By Rafiq Mughal, Financial Staff

BARCLAYS BANK chairman Mr Anthony Tuke yesterday launched a strong defence of the group's involvement in South Africa, but also announced that the bank's stake in its subsidiary there was likely to be reduced from 60 per cent to below 50 per cent.

Mr Tuke told 350 shareholders at the group's annual meeting in London that he regretted the Nigerian government's decision announced last month to withdraw funds from Barclays because of its connections in South Africa. He said the Nigerians had misunderstood the bank's policy on South Africa.

The oil-rich Nigerian government ordered its public agencies to withdraw immediately their funds from Barclays because of the bank's "continued collaboration" with the South African government. Nigeria is Barclay's second most important African operation after South Africa, and last year contributed £12 millions to profit. Mr Tuke was unable to put a value on the withdrawal.

6.4.78

Fonteyn's plan for coloured-only Swan Lake condemned

From Stanley Uys, Cape Town

ONE OF THE most prominent figures in the 2,000,000 Coloured community in South Africa, the poet, lecturer, and philosoher, Adam Small, said today that plans for Dame Margot Fonteyn to give a special Coloureds-only performance of Swan Lake were "disgusting in the extreme".

He said: "Here it is all over again — the sickening phenomenon of the patronising white man and woman graciously condescending to 'do something for us non-whites'. The business is doubly sickening because it is all happening in the name of art. This must be said even if Dame Margot Fonteyn is the greatest ballerina in Christendom."

Mr Small said the issue at stake for the Coloured people was "the rescue of our pride and our self-respect from the trampling of it underfoot by white 'sympathy'".

Dame Margot first ran into controversy when it was announced that she would give three performances of Swan Lake at the whites-only Nico Milan Theatre in Cape Town which has been boycotted by many Cape Town white people since it opened last year because of its race bar.

The government granted a permit for Dame Margot's Coloureds-only performance to be presented at another whites-only theatre, The Three Arts. It refuses though to grant the permit for the Nico Milan Theatre because it wants to preserve this theatre as a symbol of white exclusiveness.

17.3.72

Poet's Boycott

A GROUP of leading South African poets said today they would boycott one of the country's biggest poetry contests because entry was restricted to white authors.

In a statement published here, the writers said the whites-only stipulation for the Roy Campbell poetry prize was "objectionable and unacceptable".

8.9.73

Blind Eye

POLICE turned a blind eye in Capetown when white women donned black make-up to get into a blacks only performance of Swan Lake, starring Margot Fonteyn.

29.4.72

Blacks allowed

JOHANNESBURG City Council reversed a decision to exclude black swimmers from training at an Olympic size-pool. Ellis Park pool will be closed to the public for two evening hours for integrated training.

6.12.79

British firms pay Africans starvation rate

By ADAM RAPHAEL

THE MAJORITY of British companies in South Africa are paying substantial numbers of their African workers below officially recognised subsistence levels.

An investigation of 100 British companies found only three — Shell, ICI, and Unilever — who were paying all employees above the minimum sum needed for an African family to avoid malnutrition. Some prominent British companies earning large profits in South Africa are paying between a third and a half of this minimum subsistence standard.

"If your income is below the poverty datum line (£10-£11 a week for a family of five) your health must suffer. In a real sense this is starvation," said the research office for Johannesburg's Non-European

Granada award

GUARDIAN reporter Adam Raphael was yesterday named Investigative Reporter of the Year in 1973 in Granada's What The Papers Say awards for his detailed exposure of the low wages paid to black South Africans by British firms.

Mr Denis Forman, Granada Television joint managing director, said that the award had gone to a reporter who "went to South Africa and examined in detail the wage rates paid to black Africans by 100 British firms, and found that, with three honourable exceptions, they were below the poverty line. His work was so effective that by the end of the year wages being paid in South Africa to black workers had risen dramatically."

Affairs Department. This comment proved to be no exaggeration. On two wattle farms owned by Slater Walker SA, I saw several children suffering from open sores, distended stomachs, and weakened limbs. A Zulu interpreter and a University of Natal lecturer accompanying me said they had kwashiorkor, a deficiency disease.

The farm manager of Newlands Estate near Pietermaritzburg, controlled by Slater Walker's subsidiary, Natal Tanning Extract, acknowledged that malnutrition was rife. "What can I do about it?" he asked.

A distraught Zulu father on Natal Tanning's Boscombe Estate, earning only 24p a day, said: "My child is dying but I cannot buy milk, I must earn more money." The farm manager dismissed the malnutrition sores as "flea bites" and said that he himself received plenty of milk. Any left over after he had fed the dogs was "given to the Bantu."

This was perhaps an extreme case. Other British companies, however, whose subsidiaries are paying substantial numbers well below the poverty datum line include: Associated Portland Cement, Tate and Lyle, Metal Box, Courtaulds, General Electric, Reed, Rowntree Mackintosh, Chloride Electrical, Associated British Foods and British Leyland.

Mr W E Luke, chairman of the United Kingdom South Africa Trade Association, acknowledged that there were real grounds for concern. "All I can say is there are some British firms whom I am not

proud of. But we can't tell our members what their morals should be. I would very much like to see wages increased," he said.

British companies paying low wages to their African employees are, of course, following closely the practice of much of South African industry. But in some cases, British companies were found to be paying wages low even by South African standards.

Natal Tanning Extract pays many of its workers less than £2.50 a week. Single and married employees are fed and housed free but on the two NTE farms I visited conditions were bad.

In one compound on Newlands Estate, seven women had to live, sleep, and eat in a bare room measuring 10ft by 15ft. The only washing facility was a cold tap 30 yards away. Many of the timber workers were in rags and said they could not afford to buy clothes. No sick leave or holidays are given to the lowest paid — the vast majority of the work force. If unable to work because of bad weather, which is frequent, they get paid nothing.

One man, aged 50, who hurt his foot while loading a lorry, said he had not been paid for nearly three months. "My children are getting very sick," he said. "They are sleeping on the floor and dying. I can't do anything except pray to God." The University of Natal's wages commission's conclusion that they are living at "sub-human level" is hard to dispute.

Slater Walker SA, which is quoted on the Johannesburg Stock Exchange, had profits of

A woman with her sick baby at the Boscombe Estate wattle farm. The sores on the baby's back are caused by malnutrition. OPPOSITE: a woman on the same farm complaining about bad mealie meal, her staple diet

more than £1.5 million in the first six months of last year, an increase of 71 per cent After last month's strikes, which crippled Durban's industry,

the city's Chamber of Commerce urged every employer to "examine his conscience". For many British companies this process has yet to begin.

'Starvation wage' blow for PM

THE LIST of UK companies paying "starvation wages" to black South African workers includes a subsidiary of Burmah Oil where the Primer Minister's husband, Dennis Thatcher, is a director, and British Petroleum, which is 46 per cent owned by the Government.

The Burmah offshoot Quinton Hazell — Mr Thatcher has been a director for several years — was paying 134 blacks less that the widely recognised minimum living level (MLL). BP, through its 50 per cent stake in the Eikeboom Colliery project, has been paying 125 black workers below MLL.

Details are contained in the reports submitted by 202 British firms under the EEC Code of Conduct for UK companies with interests in South Africa.The Secretary for Trade has repeatedly refused to publish names of underpaying companies.

Dockers block 'illegal' S. Africa cargo

SOUTHAMPTON dockers yesterday stopped sophisticated production equipment being shipped to South Africa in breach of the United Nations mandatory arms embargo. The equipment, a numerically controlled milling machine, has been sold by a British firm, Berox Machine Tool Company, to the Atlas Aircraft Corporation via a third party, Johannesburg-based Fritz Wallaberger Machines. The planned export was first revealed in the Guardian on Saturday.

Atlas Aircraft is a wholly-owned subsidiary of the South African Armaments Corporation, Armscor, and is responsible for the production and maintenance of all military aircraft in the country.

18.1.74　　　　12.3.80　　　　5.6.80　　　　31.7.85

World ban for South Africa soccer visitors

CLUB FOOTBALLERS who take part in the two-week tour of South Africa due to start this week will be suspended from international matches, Dr Joao Havelange, the Brazilian president of FIFA, the world governing body for soccer, said in Madrid yesterday.

But the FIFA threat is unlikely to affect the British players, who are said to have been contracted to the 18-man squad due to make the tour. The Football Association chairman, Bert Millichip, said they could face disciplinary action, but most of the players named in the South African press are past their international best or stand little chance of being selected for a national team.

If the Johannesburg reports are true, the most notable success will be the recruitment of the Argentinian who left Spurs during the Falklands crisis, Oswaldo Ardiles. He has been named as the possible captain and may be joined by his Argentinian team-mate Mario Kempes.

12.7.82

The high price of breaking a boycott

THE RELATIVE quality and youth of many of the West Indian cricketers now converging on South Africa make their agreement to play the Springboks look like the biggest breach so far in the international sporting boycott and a great embarrassment to their home governments.

But the nature of the coup pulled off by the promoters and their big-business backers tends to obscure the facts that the rules of the boycott game, if not its underlying goals, have changed. The very fact that something like £2 million seems to have been sunk in the forthcoming tour does show that the South Africans still have money to burn after recent disasters in this field. It also shows how effective the boycott has been and remains.

The principal component of this success for them is undoubtedly the cheque book they were able to wave in front of the players who earn very little from the game in which they are generally held to be the champions. The same cannot be said of Gooch and Boycott and the other English players who took part in the hole-and-corner tour of South Africa last March.

Those players were either on the verge of retirement from the game or unlikely to be disturbed in the future by an urgent call for their services from the MCC. The five-figure sums they got thus amounted to little more than a useful nest egg, an adjunct to a pension or the last drink from a dying stream.

But some, if not all, of the West Indians are expected to collect a six-figure sum for their services, enough to set them up for life back home, even if they have to blush all the way to the bank and their hitherto unprofitable domestic cricket careers are ended forever.

Unlike the English blockade-runners, any West Indians who might be persuaded to stay on in South Africa for a while will notice no improvement in climate or quality of life. Material conditions in some of the "coloured" districts in which the Group Areas Act would force them to live might surpass Port of Spain or Kingston, but South Africa would set stifling limits on their gregariousness and make second-class citizens of them. If they stay it is hardly to be for long.

In fact only an outstanding success is likely to prevent this most expensive piece of boycott-busting from being the last of its kind. The Sri Lankan "tour" was a flop in spectator terms and was firmly boycotted by South Africa's Asians. The English one that preceded it was little better. Last year's soccer tour, financed like most of these things by South African Breweries, was abandoned in the middle when the spectators stayed at home and the top (by definition African) teams refused to play.

13.1.83

Politics at scrum centre

Leader comment

SALOON BAR sportsmen and South African segregationists have greeted with predictable delight the decision to proceed with the British Lions tour this summer. Peter Hain and his followers have been told where to get off. At least the rugby unions have the courage to keep sport out of politics — whatever the cost. Meanwhile, back at the laager, Omar Henry, the only non-white cricketer with a regular place in a provincial side, attempted to get a New Year's Day meal with his white team-mates after a game. The restaurant owner refused to serve him under South Africa's Liquor Act.

Mr Hain's Stop All Racist Tours Organisation quotes a similar case from rugby itself in its notably restrained and well-researched submission to the Jeeps' commission (which arrives in South Africa on Sunday to investigate segregation in sport).

A white former Springbok trialist "Cheeky" Watson, joined the non-racial South African Rugby Union and wants to play for a multi-racial team in the SARU local league. He has been arrested several times for entering the black township of New Brighton to reach the ground. It is an offence to enter the "wrong" racial area without a permit.

By its very nature, politics in sport, has been eroded in recent years. But it has been a calculated and partial erosion, limited almost entirely to international and high visibility occasions. The Hain memorandum suggests that the sporting boycott be maintained until the South African parliament specifically exempts all sports from apartheid legislation, bans racially exclusive sports clubs and removes the pro-white bias from state aid to sport. Until such changes are made South African sport will remain politicised — by order of the authorities. And teams which elect to tour South Africa are taking a political decision to endorse politicised sport. It is the protesters who are attempting to take the politics out of South African sport.

11.1.80

By its very nature, politics, South African style, constantly intrudes on sport. And South African politicians have no hesitation about exploiting sporting events for political ends. Thus the 1977 World XV tour was used by the then Sports Minister, Dr Piet Koornhof, to boost white self-confidence by claiming (as he did in a long speech before the Pretoria match) that the visit proved that the Republic was not isolated. South Africa had many friends. Similarly the four home unions' decision to go ahead with their tour — in spite of appeals from a conservative minister of sports, Hector Munroe — is being sold in South Africa in political terms.

South Africa — despite some advances — remains a segregated society and it is apartheid and not Mr Hain which has forced politics on to the playing field just as it has forced politics on to the restaurant, the residential area and even the bedroom. The British Lions will be allowed to play with hand-picked black men this summer. They will find it rather more difficult to eat with them publicly or to visit their homes – far less date their daughters.

Apartheid, particularly in sport, has been

> '**For most white men, the sports boycott rankled more than any other. The reality of apartheid was brought home to them more starkly by this sanction than by anything they might have seen in a black township**'

long time to have a serious impact on government policy; the post-1984 wave had little direct practical effect. New foreign investment and foreign loans had dried up after 1977. South Africa countered the cancellation of loans by freezing repayments, so there was no financial loss. Many of the firms withdrawing left their infrastructure in place, delaying the consequences of their departure. But the psychological impact was devastating, in part because sanctions took on a life of their own.

The first consumer boycott had been the Boycott Barclays campaign, begun in Britain in 1969. Barclays' subsidiary was the largest bank in South Africa. Seventeen years later, Barclays sold it because, as its chairman Basil Hersov admitted: "Political pressures on Barclays plc to withdraw from South Africa finally became irresistible."

In October 1986, under heavy public pressure, the US Congress overrode the veto of President Reagan to approve the Comprehensive Anti-Apartheid Act. The realisation in South Africa that support from world leaders such as Reagan and Thatcher was not enough and that further isolation was inevitable, was a sharp blow to the morale of white South African business people. It demonstrated that business could not remain above politics and shifted many business leaders into the reform camp.

Perhaps even more damaging psychologically was the sports boycott. For sports-mad white South Africans, it was a constant reminder of their isolation and of the price of maintaining apartheid. For most white men, the sports boycott rankled more than any other. The reality of apartheid was brought home to them more starkly by this sanction than by anything they might have seen in a black township. By the late 1980s, South Africa was banned from 90 per cent of world sport. Widely publicised attempts to break the boycott only underlined the level of isolation. South African athletes could not compete abroad unless, like the runner Zola Budd, they were able to obtain the passport of another country. Any visiting team, no matter how weak, made front-page news.

The cultural boycott ended visits by nearly all big-name performers. Few British television programmes were shown and white South Africans began to

Top: **Sport-mad South Africa's ban from international competition was, for many, more painful then economic sanctions. A Springbok rugby player savours victory at Lyons, 1992**

Right: **Nationalistic fervour, which had little chance to express itself during the country's sporting isolation**

Far right: **Springbok rugby tours were particular targets of the demonstrators, like this match in Leicester during a British tour, 1969**

Investment ban is blow to Pretoria

By Roger Omond

MASSACHUSETTS has become the first US state to stop all state pension funds investing in companies doing business in South Africa.

The move was announced in London yesterday by the exiled South African journalist, Mr Donald Woods, who is director of the Lincoln Trust, a British-American organisation he founded to work for increased Western economic and diplomatic pressures against apartheid.

"Connecticut and Michigan are now enacting similar legislation and it is hoped that up to 25 other states under Democratic Party control

will follow suit by the end of the year to effect the withdrawal of billions of dollars from apartheid supportive investment," he said, predicting that Wisconsin and Minnesota would also legislate against state investment in companies dealing with South Africa.

He said that the new Massachusetts law involved the withdrawal of $105 million of investment. It was the culmination of a three-year campaign led by Representative Melvin King, who led a delegation with Mr Woods to the Massachusetts Governor last month, after reports that the bill might be vetoed.

10.1.83

Into the breach

By Richard Boston

IN 1980 THE United Nations General Assembly resolution 35/206 requested all member states "to take steps to prevent all cultural, academic, sporting and other exchanges with South Africa", appealed to "writers artists and musicians to boycott South Africa" and urged all academic and cultural institutions to terminate links with South Africa.

The call is for a banning of all links, all exchanges. That is to say that, as with sport, trade, investment, diplomatic and military contacts, the cultural boycott works both ways. It is not only against our artists visiting and performing in South Africa but also against visits abroad by South African artists.

This fact doesn't seem to be widely realised. It certainly came as news to some of the black actors I talked to at the Riverside Theatre where they opened the musical Poppie Nongena on April 4. In fact it required a copy of an Anti-Apartheid Movement statement to convince them.

The Movement is faced with an awkward problem by such visiting productions as Poppie Nongena, Woza Albert!, Master Harold and the Boys and Saturday Night at the Palace which has just opened at the Old Vic.

These plays are part of the flourishing multi-racial theatrical activity in South Africa which is as remarkable an assertion of cultural identity as that of the cinema in Australia in recent years.

Hillary Belcher, the director of Poppie Nongena, describes the multi-racial theatre of South Africa today as a crucible of creativity, consciousness-raising, and cross fertilisation. It is mostly centred on the Johannesburg Market Theatre Company, which was founded in 1974, operates without any subsidy, and produces plays which are openly anti-apartheid.

The company is multi-racial and plays to desegregated audiences. As with sport, supporters of the boycott can claim some credit for this having become possible. In the cinema, where there is no boycott, films are heavily censored and all audiences are still strictly segregated (except at film festivals).

Visits by such groups as the Market Theatre Company put the Anti-Apartheid Movement in a bit of a quandary. They say that in the interests of consistency they have to be opposed to them, "whatever the content of the play, or however committed to struggle against apartheid". This doesn't mean that they think that such groups visiting Britain are collaborating with the regime but they do think they are ill advised. They can't promote these visits, but they are not going to protest against them or picket theatres as they have (successfully) against visiting government-backed groups.

In South Africa, although Market Theatre audiences are not now segregated as they were 30 years ago, it is

argued that the changes are cosmetic. For the government, such a theatre is a useful safety valve. And, after having been to a show, if a black member of the audience and a white member of the audience were found in bed together they could each get ten years in gaol.

But many playwrights who are in theory totally in support of the boycott are in practice selective.

Mary Benson, who edited Athol Fugard's recently published Notebooks, used to be in favour of a total cultural boycott but now agrees that art can change people. In her own case her attitudes, as a white South African, were changed by Alan Paton's Cry The Beloved Country. Fugard himself wrote in 1962 that he thought that art cannot change people ("That is what life does"), but by 1968 came around to the view that it was time to lift the ban by overseas playwrights. He wrote: "Anything that will get people to think and feel for themselves, that will stop them delegating these functions to the politicians, is important to our survival. Theatre can help do this.

"There is nothing John Balthazar Vorster and his cabinet would like more than to keep us isolated from the ideas and values which are current in the free Western world. These ideas and values find an expression in the plays of contemporary writers. I would like South Africa to see these plays."

13.5.84

SA visits keep stars off air

From Jan Tystad in Oslo

A TELEVISION programme in which Cliff Richard and Shirley Bassey were due to appear was stopped by the Norwegian broadcasting corporation, NRK, at the weekend just a few hours before it was due to be sent out live.

The decision was taken after trade unions involved in the show threatened to black the concerts if the two appeared.

The two British artists were censored because neither of them was willing to

promise that they would stop singing in South Africa in the future.

Shirley Bassey and Cliff Richard are both on the UN blacklist of artists who are not boycotting South Africa. Anti-apartheid demonstrators protested when they arrived at their hotel in Oslo, last Friday.

Shirley Bassey was furious when met by demonstrators and said: "You whites started the hell in South Africa. I could not care less about politics. All I want to do is entertain."

26.8.85

Main picture: **When powerful anti-apartheid dramas like Woza Albert from the Market Theatre in Johannesburg came to Britain they posed a problem for those advocating a total cultural boycott. Starring Attie Kubyane and Ewen Cummings at the Young Vic, London, 1984**

Right: **Billboard at the Market Theatre in Johannesburg, 1988**

talk openly of being "starved" of culture. Of course sanctions never threatened white South Africans with anything like real starvation. Nor did they ever run out of oil or anything else important to their living standards. The true economic impact can perhaps be gauged from the Commonwealth Independent Expert Study, which estimated that the wave of sanctions in the mid-1980s cut the value of South African exports by about one-eighth. South Africa also had to pay extra to import arms, oil and computers.

Sanctions did impose an extra strain on the economy, a luxury which white South Africa was increasingly less able to afford. The failure of South Africans to invest in their economy after 1975 was more damaging — but this was itself a result of the lack of confidence caused by the effects of apartheid, including sanctions.

Despite all the bravado about returning to the laager and surviving in isolation, whatever the cost, the pressure of being an international outcast increasingly took its toll. South Africans continued to travel abroad, but with more difficulty and to an increasingly hostile reception. White South Africans, who saw themselves as part of Europe, were hurt by their rejection there.

A visitor to South Africa in the early 1990s could not ignore the impact of more than a decade of isolation. Fashions and standards were those of another era. From wine to sport, what was of international standard in the 1970s no longer came up to scratch after two decades of rapid advances in the outside world. Attempts to keep up the spirits of white South Africans through the 1980s failed to obscure the reality that lack of contact with the industrialised world meant they were falling behind.

Sanctions were only one of many interlinked factors in bringing about change. They were surely less important than the growing ungovernability of the townships. But sanctions were central to the demise of apartheid in one respect. They made clear to white South Africans that a failure to accept majority rule could only mean growing isolation — and in the end that was simply untenable.

Joseph Hanlon has written, among other works, The Sanctions Handbook

'The cultural boycott ended visits by nearly all big-name performers. Few British television programmes were shown and white South Africans began to talk openly of being "starved" of culture'

Thatcher claims sanctions victory

From Hella Pick and James Naughtie

THE LEADERS of the Commonwealth set to work in Nassau last night on choosing the "eminent persons" who will hold talks with Pretoria aimed at ending apartheid, after agreeing on a twin-track strategy combining dialogue and external economic pressure on the South African regime.

Mrs Thatcher welcomed the dialogue effort with enthusiasm, claimed that the agreement was a victory for her stand against economic sanctions, and said that, in concluding a deal with the other Commonwealth leaders, she had moved only "a tiny little bit". But the Prime Minister is now deeply involved in a united Commonwealth effort to bring an end to apartheid by talking to the South African government and to the black leaders – including the banned African National Congress. Britain is now in line with the Commonwealth in asking for the ban on the ANC to be lifted.

The British Government will be represented in the group of "eminent persons", which is expected to begin work in a month. It will consist of senior political figures who can devote their energies to the formidable tasks mapped out in the Commonwealth accord.

The agreement reached late on Sunday after difficult negotiations and see-sawing prospects, came about only after Mrs Thatcher had been confronted with an ultimatum by all of her Commonwealth colleagues. They warned her that they would, if necessary, go ahead without her, and issue their declaration, leaving her isolated.

Mrs Thatcher had proclaimed all week that she would resist all moves to impose new sanctions. In the end she signed a document committing Britain to a couple of new minor sanctions – she calls them "signals" – consisting of a ban on the import of Krugerrands and an end to Government help for trade delegations and trade exhibitions in South Africa. The document also formalises the policy of no Government loans to Pretoria.

British sources yesterday expressed considerable satisfaction at the outcome – as did the other principals in Nassau – and argued that Mrs Thatcher had successfully resisted full-scale economic sanctions and had gained specifically the inclusion of a reference to a cessation of violence as part of the dialogue process. This was the decisive turning point in the argument after which Mrs Thatcher agreed concessions on economic measures.

22.10.85

Summit abandons Britain

By Hella Pick, Diplomatic Correspondent

BRITAIN has refused to join the rest of the Commonwealth in imposing hard-hitting sanctions against South Africa. The worst split in the organisation's history will see Britain's 48 former colonies and dominions, including Canada, Australia, and India, pressing ahead with tough measures based on those agreed at the Nassau summit, while Britain imposes only a limited package of "gestures indicating disapproval".

As the London mini-summit ended last night, the seven heads of government withdrew while their foreign ministers went line by line through the draft joint communiqué. Canada, Australia, India, Zambia, Zimbabwe and the Bahamas agreed that they could not wait for Mrs Thatcher to adopt a more radical approach on sanctions. The communique, completed just before midnight, expressed concern and regret "that the UK does not join in our agreement".

Going beyond the list of sanctions drawn up at Nassau, the six countries also decided to ban new bank loans to South Africa and to withdraw consular facilities. They will also ban uranium imports from South Africa and will go ahead immediately with a ban on imports of coal, iron and steel, without waiting for an EEC decision in September.

The conference communique emphasised Britain's isolation, saying: "We must do more to look beyond the Commonwealth to the wider international community."

5.9.86

Kodak to shut down operations in South Africa

From David Beresford

ANOTHER American multinational – Eastman-Kodak – yesterday announced complete disinvestment from South Africa. It is selling its assets and barring the export of any of its products to the country.

Following the lead of more than 60 American companies, Kodak announced the shutdown of its operations with effect from April 30 next year. The corporation appears to be taking a far tougher line than its counterparts in the snowballing disinvestment drive: its decision to halt the supply of products contrasts sharply with IBM and General Motors, which have sold out to South African businessmen in deals designed to protect continued sales in the country.

20.11.86

Apartheid group

A GROUP of entertainers and athletes, headed by the singer, Harry Belafonte, and the tennis star, Arthur Ashe, yesterday launched a cultural boycott against South Africa because of its policy of apartheid. The new organisation called Artists and Athletes Against Apartheid, was launched at a news conference at UN headquarters in New York sponsored by the Organisation of African Unity.

13.9.83

Elton John shuns apartheid

ELTON JOHN agreed yesterday never to return to South Africa while apartheid exists. As a result his concert in Sheffield tonight is expected to go ahead without incident.

Mass demonstrations had been planned for the arrival of the rock star in protest at his South African connections. He is on the United Nations blacklist for appearing in South Africa.

26.11.85

US Senate votes for SA sanctions

From Michael White in Washington

THE REPUBLICAN-LED Senate yesterday approved 84 to 14 a package of wide-ranging economic and political sanctions against South Africa because of its apartheid policies of racial discrimination. The overwhelming vote was a strong rebuke to President Reagan, who has long opposed punitive sanctions against the Pretoria government.

The House of Representatives already has approved a much stronger bill, and yesterday's Senate action makes final passage by Congress of a complete sanctions package next month a virtual certainty.

The Senate bill would bar all new US invest-ments in South Africa and loans to the private sector, ban imports of uranium, coal, steel, iron, textiles and agricultural products, and freeze deposits in US banks held by Pretoria or state-owned firms. It also would end landing rights for South African Airways, ban imports from companies owned or controlled by the South African government and withdraw consular facilities for South Africans.

The Senate, in an earlier vote, rejected a stronger bill, already passed by the House of Representatives which calls for a near-total trade embargo and complete withdrawal of all US companies from South Africa.

16.8.86

Pretoria suspends its repayment of debts

From Patrick Laurence

SOUTH AFRICA last night unilaterally announced a four-month suspension on repayments of its foreign debt of more than $17 billion (£12.1billion), to protect the rand from further depreciation.

The decision, announced at a special news conference by the Minister of Finance, Mr Barend du Plessis, came at the end of a four-day suspension of the foreign exchange markets and stock exchange trading.

Describing the suspension of repayments as a temporary measure, Mr du Plessis said: "All repayments of foreign debt by South African residents shall be postponed until after December 31, 1985, to enable the South African authorities to negotiate a satisfactory system for repayment of foreign debts with all the parties concerned."

Mr du Plessis repudiated reports that the governor of the South African Reserve Bank, Dr Gerhardus de Kock, had gone overseas "cap in hand begging for money".

Dr de Kock left South Africa for Britain and the United States last Wednesday. His purpose, Mr du Plessis said, was to inform banks in Britain and the US of the steps the South African authorities plan to take to protect the rand.

Mr du Plessis emphasised that the moratorium on repayment of foreign debt would not affect payments for current imports, or dividends on foreign investments in South Africa, or interest owed on foreign loans.

The crisis had not been caused by disinvestment through stock exchange transactions, but by the "withdrawal of short-term credit lines by foreign banking institutions". About 12 billion rand (£8.5 billion) of South Africa's foreign debts consists of short-term loans.

Mr Malcolm Rifkind, the Foreign Office minister, described the suspension of debt repayments as a short-term response to a problem whose eventual solution would involve substantial political reform.

"South Africa is clearly experiencing a major financial crisis, partly for economic reasons and partly because of civil disturbances," he said.

2.9.85

S. Africa fears more may follow Barclays Bank

From David Beresford in Johannesburg

SOUTH AFRICA yesterday was putting a brave face on the most sensational anti-apartheid disinvestment move to date – Barclays Bank's sale of its stake in the country after six weeks of secret negotiations.

The Governor of the South African Reserve Bank, Dr Gerhardus de Kock, said the move "is not expected to exert any adverse effect nationally or internationally on the South African banking system." Barclays management in South Africa insisted that it would have little more effect on local operations than a change of name.

But the decision by Barclays, long a "friend" of South Africa, immediately prompted fears here of a domino effect among European companies – especially in Britain, as the country's biggest single foreign investor – with attention focused on Standard Chartered and the oil companies, Shell and BP. Shell in particular is seen as crucial, because of suspicions in the anti-apartheid lobby that it has played a key role in propping up South Africa's vital oil supplies.

The anti-apartheid movement reacted jubilantly to the news, describing it as "an historic victory".

25.11.86

Right: **'When it is his, we will still be here,'** reads a Barclays billboard outside Johannesburg, 1986

Far Right: **Barclays became the chief target of anti-apartheid protests in Britain, 1978**

Below: **Barclays Soweto branch, 1976**

Wanneer dit syne is, sal ons steeds hier wees.

The shadowy 'Third Force' may not even exist, but is used as a generic term to describe the contribution to township violence by an unholy alliance determined to spoil progress made by the government and the ANC. These mismatched malcontents include army generals, policemen acting on their own initiative, security force units out of control, rightwing extremists and Inkatha

Township violence and the 'Third Force'/David Beresford

THE YEARS of transition in South Africa — from the unbanning of the ANC in 1990 to the 1994 "liberation" election — have been dominated, bizarrely, by an organisation the very existence of which has been heatedly debated. The "Third Force" made its mysterious appearance in mid-1990 when a series of massacres started speculation that there was a conspiracy afoot to derail the negotiating process set in train by President F W de Klerk. In the absence of proof as to the existence of the conspiracy — at least until recently — the term became a useful one to describe a loose alliance between killers identifying with those bitterly opposed to a political settlement between the ANC and government; essentially the white right and conservative homeland leaders of whom KwaZulu's Chief Mangosuthu Buthelezi is the outstanding figure.

There was a time when it was something of a principle in South Africa that the right would inherit the earth on the southern tip of the African continent. In 1913 Barry Hertzog walked out of the South Africa Party of General Louis Botha and in 1924 his National Party took power.

In 1934 the "purified" National Party broke from the United Party and in 1948 D F Malan came to power. So, when Dr Andries Treurnicht broke from the National Party in 1982 to form the Conservative Party, there were many who believed that he, in turn, would eventually lead the country.

But, as it transpired, time had run out for right-wing Afrikanerdom. In the face of the realities of international isolation and fast-developing domestic dissent it became apparent that Dr Treurnicht — "Dr No" as he was known during his years as a cabinet minister, for his adamant opposition to any kind of reform — had led the "constitutional" right into a political dead end. Frustration led at least the more extreme elements of the right into flirtations with extra-parliamentary politics.

A plethora of extremist groupings sprang up — more than 60 at the last count — within which fantastic schemes were hatched ranging from arcane projects to create white homelands in the wilderness to more murderous plans to sabotage the national peace process. At the centre of these groups was the Afrikaner Weerstandsbeweging (AWB), the "Afrikaner Resistance Movement". Cursed by the buffoon-like leadership of Eugene TerreBlanche, the AWB was reduced by scandal and incompetence to a shell, an umbrella group in the shade of which various small groupings formed, hatched further conspiracies and either ended up in jail or melted away with the realisation of futility.

A characteristic, if extreme example of these groups was the "Order of Death", an AWB off-shoot which plotted the assassination of President F W de Klerk in 1989. When police raided the group — after lengthy surveillance — they found in one member's home an arsenal ranging from mortars and sniper's weapons to a blow-pipe with poison darts.

The would-be assassins are reported to have trained as divers in preparation for an under-water attack on President De Klerk's holiday home. They also plotted the assassination of a collection of budgies owned by another rightwing leader in the constitutional mould, Jaap Marais, in an attempt to intimidate him into joining a move for right-wing unity.

It is a world of bizarre fantasy, but one which holds out a form of vicious romanticism for a certain type of personality.

One of the romances of South African history into which the white right inevitably locked was that of the so-called "warrior tribe", the Zulus.

The story of the Zulus past and present is essentially the story of two men who lived more than a century apart; Shaka, the founder of the Zulu nation, and his direct descendent, Chief Mangosuthu Buthelezi.

There are several disconcerting similarities between the two men, one of which is the circumstances in which they were named. Shaka was named after *iShaka* — an intestinal beetle customarily blamed for menstrual irregularities.

The great warrior chief was lumped with the name through the sly humour characteristic of the Zulus, because he was the product of an illicit liaison between a Zulu maiden and a neighbouring chief. When her pregnancy was discovered the elders of the culpable tribe attempted to dismiss it as the work of *iShaka*. Mangosuthu means "lie of the royal household" and it also seems

Black power takes sterner turn
From STANLEY UYS: Cape Town

THE South African Students' Organisation (SASO), a black power group, has instructed its executive to have nothing to do with black Bantustan leaders, such as chief Gatsha Buthelezi and paramount chief Kaiser Matanzima. It dismisses them as "the so-called leadership of the white racist institutions".

This instruction follows the expulsion of Temba Sono, SASO's chairman, because he urged the organisation to cooperate with the Bantustan leaders.

When Mr Sono made his plea for cooperation at a congress of the group in the Transvaal last weekend, the entire executive walked off the platform and joined delegates in the hall, and the congress as a body then forced Mr Sono to resign and to leave the gathering immediately.

SASO, which claims 6,000 black, "coloured" and Indian members, has come out openly for the first time in opposition to the Bantustans and similar apartheid institutions.

It thus rejects totally the view that the Bantustans can be turned into black power bases, and that black Bantustan leaders can be seen as potential black power leaders. It brands the Bantustans and the National "coloured" and Indian Councils as "extensions of the oppressive system".

6.7.72

Blacks accept a Vorster reality

TWO black leaders in South Africa have said the Vorster government's policy of "separate development" is irreversible and that all political parties should accept its basic outline.

Addressing the South African Institute of Race Relations in Cape Town last night, the Zulu leader chief Gatsha Buthelezi said: "I am convinced that the homelands (Bantustans) concept could easily be the formula for a basis of a future South Africa depending on certain conditions."

Today, the conference heard chief Lucas Mangope, the Tswana leader, say: "The homelands are a reality and a reality with which we have to live."

Each black leader took a bold line, rejecting violence as a solution of South Africa's racial problem, and stressing the interdependence of black and white.

Chief Buthelezi suggested whites and blacks should get together to discuss how powers could be conferred on white and black areas so that they could build themselves from the bottom up.

The stumbling block, he said, was whether the federal parliament should be under white or black control, but this "hardy annual" could be shelved for "several generations".

18.1.74

SA may try to 'silence' defiant Buthelezi

THE Zulu leader, chief Buthelezi, has thrown down the gauntlet to the South African Government in the most outspoken speech of his career in which he has referred to the country's "approaching hour of crisis".

His speech is the first major public declaration by a black leader in South Africa to reflect the new self-confidence and impatience that is gripping blacks all over Southern Africa. Chief Buthelezi's speech, which is seen here as a watershed occasion, is certain to provoke a strong reaction from official quarters. The government has always regarded chief Buthelezi as being the most troublesome of the Bantustan leaders.

Chief Buthelezi also rejected the government's homelands policy which proposes to fragment South Africa into independent African states based on the old tribal lands.

"South Africa is one country," the chief said. "It has one destiny. Those who are attempting to divide the land of our birth are attempting to stem the tide of history. Most black people do not want to abandon their birthright. They have toiled for generations to create the wealth of South Africa. They intend to participate in the wealth of the land."

16.3.76

BOSS funds 'given to new Zulu party'

Johannesburg

CHIEF Gatsha Buthelezi, leader of the Kwa Zulu African tribal homeland, has claimed that the South African secret police are covertly financing his political opponents.

If the allegations are substantiated, they would lay the police open to charges of illegal and unethical behaviour, contradicting the government's apartheid policies under which South Africa's nine black homelands are due to get eventual political autonomy.

At the centre of the development is a newly formed Zulu political party called Shaka's Spear. Named after the great Zulu chief, it is expected to oppose chief Buthelezi when the homeland in Northern Natal Province holds its first general election soon.

Chief Buthelezi claims that the secret police — the Bureau of State Security (Boss) — founded Shaka's Spear and provided the party with an initial fund of 12,000 rand (£8,000).

There has been no comment so far by the security police, but the leader of Shaka's Spear, chief Charles Hengwa, has denied the allegation.

Chief Buthelezi, nominated by a council of chiefs to lead the Zulu nation in 1970, has emerged as the most outspoken and charismatic black politician at liberty in South Africa today.

28.5.74

Chief Buthelezi warns young black radicals of African backlash
From STANLEY UYS: Cape Town

THE Zulu leader, chief Gatsha Buthelezi, has warned young black radicals in South Africa against a backlash from the "silent majority" of Africans who, he says, are "appalled" by the destruction of African schools and equipment in the recent riots.

Chief Buthelezi, an outspoken opponent of apartheid, deplored the "arrogance of young people who think they know what is best for the people". He reminded them that their parents had saved and suffered humiliation so that they could be educated for real and meaningful leadership.

Chief Buthelezi's remarks are a further indication of the resistance the militant youth movement among Africans is encountering in some black quarters. The Zulu leader himself has been mocked by young blacks as a "stooge" for "playing the system" in the KwaZulu Bantustan.

The chief called this weekend for the establishment of vigilante groups to protect black property against political action. He said he did not associate himself with a move by police last week to allow "law abiding" African workers to arm themselves with clubs, but he felt vigilante groups should be set up by people representing the "silent majority" of blacks who totally rejected the methods of the radicals.

16.8.76

Picture: IAN BERRY/MAGNUM

'The ANC became concerned that they were losing control of Buthelezi, and their attempts to rein him in led to a breach which became ever more bitter. Suffering a steady erosion of support, the chief turned to those who shared his hostility towards the liberation movement'

to stem from the circumstances of his birth. He was the product of a marriage of convenience in the 1920s between Princess Magogo Constance Zulu, sister of the then King Solomon, and the then head of the Buthelezi tribe. When Buthelezi's father was informed he had a son, he reputedly reacted by crying out, cryptically: "It is a lie of the royal house."

Both Shaka and Mangosuthu appear to have grown up without benefit of a close relationship with their fathers, developing instead an almost obsessive devotion to their mothers. A shared childhood insecurity seems to have stoked the drive in Shaka which led to the creation of a tribal empire and fuelled the ambition in Buthelezi to try and bring about a Zulu renaissance.

Accepting the mantle of chieftainship in the 1950s, Chief Buthelezi founded Inkatha as a "national liberation movement" in 1975. He took both steps with the support and encouragement of the ANC, openly flaunting his support of the banned organisation when he hoisted its black, green and gold colours at the opening of the KwaZulu homeland's Legislative Assembly in 1979.

By this time he was ranked in the opinion polls among black South Africans as possibly their most popular leader — ahead of even Nelson Mandela.

But also at about this time the ANC, concerned that it was losing control of the chief, tried to rein him in. The result was a breach between the two sides which became ever more embittered and violent as the years went by. Increasingly paranoid about ANC threats to his life (some of which may have been justified) and suffering a steady erosion of his support base in Natal, the chief turned for help to those who shared his hostility towards the liberation movement.

In 1991, what was left of his reputation for principled independence was shattered by the Guardian's "Inkathagate" disclosures — showing that the chief was being secretly funded by the South African government through the agency of the security police. In 1993, Inkatha openly confirmed the

Chief Mangosuthu Buthelezi joins his supporters in a rally at the Kwazulu capital, Ulundi, 1991. Through Inkatha, Buthelezi resurrected the romantic image of a Zulu warrior tribe – an image which suited the ideology of apartheid

Zulus defy call to end reprisals

From STANLEY UYS: Cape Town

The black township of Soweto, outside Johannesburg, was a bloody battlefield last night and today as Africans clashed with Africans in an alleged backlash against the stay-at-home movement and police fired on warring factions and young demonstrators.

At least 21 Africans have died and hundreds have possibly been injured. Though Africans were shot dead this afternoon, the unrest is continuing, and the minister of justice and police, Mr Kruger, has cancelled a visit to Namibia. Senior police officers went to Soweto today to investigate.

Five thousand Zulu and other inmates of the Mzimphlophe hostel, in Soweto, which was set on fire yesterday, rejected an appeal by a Zulu leader tonight to stop their violent retaliation.

The Zulus, who ignored this week's stay-at-home call, said they wanted "only 10 minutes"

to deal with the young Africans who were intimidating Soweto people from going to work. Police are patrolling the township regularly. The Johannesburg Rand Daily Mail reports that one of its black reporters hid in a coalbox in the hostel and overheard a policeman tell the inmates not to continue damaging houses (which all belong to the government). The policeman allegedly said: "You were asked to attack people only."

Another policeman speaking through an interpreter allegedly said: "You have been ordered to kill troublemakers only, not to damage Bantu Administration Board property."

At one stage more than 1,000 Zulus were storming through the streets, attacking men, women and children indiscriminately, and bursting into houses. An eyewitness said he saw at least 50 houses being smashed.

26.8.76

S. Africa's cautious attitude to revolutionary talks in London

THE South African government is taking a cautiously low-key attitude towards the talks in London last week between chief Gatsha Buthelezi's Inkatha movement and the exiled African National Congress which is committed to the armed overthrow of the Pretoria administration. Brigadier Coetzee predicted that chief Buthelezi's dialogue with the ANC would soon run into difficulties because he was a convinced

Christian while the ANC was a "Communist-dominated movement". Brigadier Coetzee said: "Chief Buthelezi won't go along with the Communist cause." Manifestations of their different philosophies included their contrasting stand on disinvestment of foreign capital from South Africa and the use of violence, Brigadier Coetzee said. Unlike the ANC, chief Buthelezi is opposed to both.

7.11.79

Black leader's challenge to Pretoria

From Patrick Laurence in Johannesburg

The black leader, chief Gatsha Buthelezi, yesterday threw down the gauntlet to the South African Government by quoting from the banned writings of the imprisoned African National Congress leader, Nelson Mandela. He was cheered by more than 1,500 blacks.

Chief Buthelezi, president of the Inkatha movement and chief minister of the black "homelands" of KwaZulu, was speaking at a rally in Soweto, near Johannesburg.

Among the people in the crowd was the chief of security police of Soweto, Major Schalk Visser. Chief Buthelezi quoted from No Easy Walk To Freedom, a collection of the speeches and writings of Nelson Mandela, who is serving a life sentence on Robben Island.

The gist of the quotation was an argument for collective participation in government-created political institutions if it was calculated to thwart fulfilment of apartheid objectives.

22.10.79

Mandela snub for chief over meeting

THE gaoled black leader, Nelson Mandela, has snubbed South Africa's most powerful tribal chief, Mangosuthu Buthelezi, over attempts to set up a meeting between the two men at Cape Town's Pollsmoor prison.

Mr Mandela's rejection of the meeting was conveyed to the Zulu leader in a telegram. The text was released by Buthelezi. Mr Mandela, while expressing appreciation of the chief's efforts to secure his release, believed "very strongly that the best time for such a meeting would be after he and his colleagues have been released from prison" and "ideally when his other colleagues presently outside South Africa would have returned to the country."

4.6.86

Buthelezi sneers at "safe" blacks

From Patrick Laurence in Johannesburg

Internecine warfare between South African blacks flared at the weekend when at least four people were killed in fierce fighting between supporters of the Zulu Inkatha movement and the supra-tribal United Democratic Front in the black township of Lamontville, near Durban.

Shortly before the fighting, the Inkatha leader, chief Gatsha Buthelezi, launched a blistering attack on the outlawed African National Congress, its president, Oliver Tambo, and the UDF, at a rally in honour of the founder of the Zulu nation, Shaka, in the neighbouring township of Umlazi. Chief

Buthelezi scoffed both at the exiled ANC leadership as men who "drank whisky in safe places", while plotting how to provoke black school pupils into attacking fellow blacks, and at ANC guerrillas for failing to engage the South African security forces. Chief Buthelezi, who has previously accused the UDF of acting as a "slimy stepping stone" for the ANC, again charged the UDF with responsibility for intra-black violence.

At the same rally the Zulu monarch, King Goodwill Zwelithini, referred to the UDF as a hyena and attacked Indian, "coloured" and white activists for urging blacks to destroy their schools while preserving their own.

30.9.85

Above: **Buthelezi and prime minister Vorster in talks at Cape Town, 1973**
Right: **KwaZulu police with Inkatha vigilantes, Durban, 1985**

partnership which had developed between itself and white racists, by going into the "Freedom Alliance".

There is a third element to the so-called Third Force, in the contribution which has been made to the political violence by the security forces. It has long been a wise rule of thumb in South Africa to assume the guilt of the authorities where murderous conspiracy is concerned, at least until they get around to proving themselves innocent.

During the apartheid years, for example, there were a number of mysterious disappearances, attacks on, and deaths of anti-apartheid activists. But, although there was widespread suspicion that there might have been some security force involvement, it was only in 1990 that it was discovered the police and army had their own, formal assassination units.

Their murderous activities were so refined that the military hit squad — the "Civil Co-operation Bureau" — was run on corporate lines, headed by a "managing director".

Although the Inkathagate disclosures showed that the "great reformer", F W de Klerk, was not above secret conspiracy, most commentators would absolve him of responsibility or involvement in Third Force activities. But a contribution to the political violence by the security forces at some level is inescapable, if only in the manner demonstrated by the case of the Black Cats of Wesselton.

The township of Wesselton is situated outside the Transvaal town of Ermelo, about 200 miles east of Johannesburg. It is home to a gang known as the "Black Cats" who were named after the black whips they used on their victims.

The gang was formed early in 1990 and worked in close collaboration with Ermelo police in carrying out a series of attacks on ANC sympathisers.

In August 1990 there was an assault on an ANC funeral by a team of professional hitmen sent to help the Black Cats from Ulundi — Chief Buthelezi's capital in KwaZulu. The eight-man squad ambushed the funeral procession with weapons including AK-47s, pump-action

Anti-sanction black union launched in South Africa

From Patrick Laurence in Durban

IN A huge display of support for the black leader, chief Gatsha Buthelezi, 60,000 black people packed into a rugby stadium here yesterday to applaud his decision to launch a new trade union, the United Workers Union of South Africa.

Thousands of blacks of all ages, many wearing red T-shirts emblazoned with the message "Jobs — not hunger", roared their approval for his campaign against sanctions and disinvestment and his belief that they damage the economy without toppling the government.

The acronym for the new trade union, Uwusa, echoed around the stadium as it was formally launched, largely in response to, and in competition with, the giant Congress of South African Trade Unions (Cosatu) founded last year.

Unlike Uwusa, the congress, which is closely aligned to the militantly anti-apartheid United Democratic Front opposition grouping, firmly favours disinvestment. One phalanx of stick-wielding Zulus carried a black coffin with the words "Cosatu is dead" on it. Another exultant group displayed a banner proclaiming their anger with the Nobel peace prize winner, Bishop Desmond Tutu, for advocating sanctions. "Tutu deserves to be executed," it said.

Cosatu general secretary, Jay Naidoo, called the formation of Uwusa "tragic and reactionary" and calculated to destroy the "unity we have built up".

2.5.86

Buthelezi claim of black civil war

From David Beresford in Johannesburg

THE South African Zulu leader, chief Mangosuthu Buthelezi, yesterday claimed that the killing of the wife of one of his MPs last week showed that black civil war in South Africa had now started.

The Kwazulu chief minister, in a statement from his capital of Ulundi, said that he could not see how the "spiral" of black-on-black violence could now be stopped.

27.8.86

Zulu group blamed for township massacre

ANTI-apartheid activists were yesterday reported to be fleeing from the Natal township of KwaMakhuta in the belief that an overnight massacre of 12 people — including seven children — was the work of the Zulu organisation, Inkatha.

There were conflicting reports of who was responsible for the massacre, in which gunmen armed with assault rifles opened fire on the inhabitants of a house in the township at 2am yesterday.

The government said that Russian-made AK-47 rifles had been used — weapons usually identified with the African National Congress — and that "terrorist" involvement had not been ruled out.

But residents believe that the gunmen were seeking a young anti-apartheid activist, Victor Ntuli, whose father, killed in the shooting, owned the house.

Unconfirmed reports from the townships said that the killers arrived in a minibus and opened fire through the windows of the house before bursting in and continuing to shoot.

More than 10 gunmen were alleged to have taken part in the attack. The scene in the house was described as resembling a butchery, with blood splashed over the walls and bullet holes all over the place.

22.1.87

Black deaths, white lies

Leader comment

THE prolonged violence in the townships of South Africa has spawned a few phrases which are a linguistic match for the ugliness of the events they describe. One such is black-on-black violence, much used lately in the context of the fratricidal strife in the province of Natal over the past few months, in which more than 250 Africans are officially reported to have died. The expression is full of unconscious irony, distinguishing as it does between attacks by blacks on blacks and those by whites on blacks (or occasionally vice versa). For the victims the distinction, which is overtly racialist, is probably academic as the pain is the same. But the evidence from Natal is that the distinction is far from academic in the eyes of the rulers of the apartheid state.

The defenders of the status quo exploit this internecine unrest among Africans in several ways. They use it to buttress their claim that the blacks are not ready for a responsible role in government and also as a stick with which to beat liberal and foreign critics who make such a fuss when the security forces shoot a black person but allegedly keep silent when one black murders or maims another. Yet there is no reason for apartheid's enemies not to address the fact that Africans are killing each other as well as being killed for resisting the tyranny of a racial minority — on the contrary. Nor is it glib to blame apartheid for this problem along with everything else for which the system is rightly castigated.

The purpose of apartheid is to divide and rule. Deaths attributed to "faction-fighting" — another ugly usage for inter-tribal violence — are commonplace, regardless of political unrest, and have been endemic since long before the creation of the South African state. Apartheid's hypocritical fostering of the "separate identity" of South Africa's peoples in "a land of minorities" hardly encourages Xhosa and Zulu to bury the hatchet (except, in extreme circumstances, in each other). More recently it almost led to war between the two Xhosa "independent national states" of Transkei and Ciskei.

But the trouble in Natal is essentially political, reflecting the rivalry between chief Buthelezi's conservative, Zulu-based Inkatha movement and the nationwide United Democratic Front, which upholds the more radical aims of the banned African National Congress. These two organisations oppose apartheid in their different ways but are engaged in a fierce struggle for influence in the Natal townships. Appeals for a truce from such leaders as chief Buthelezi and Archbishop Tutu fall on deaf ears as feuding Africans, denied institutional channels for redressing their grievances, take it out on each other and play into the hands of their oppressors.

Meanwhile the police who use everything from whips to armoured cars on blacks protesting against the state are usually to be elsewhere when blacks turn on blacks. If the Zulus who attacked each other had diverted their energies to the nearest police station the response of the security forces would have been decidedly different. The social contract in this way has no moral claim on the loyalty of its people.

31.12.87

Picture: KEVIN CATTER

Right: **Black Cat vigilantes in Wesselton, Transvaal, 1990**

shotguns and pistols. "When the funeral procession came past they started shooting," said a 21-year-old Black Cat who witnessed the ambush.

"The one carrying the flag fell near the coffin . . . The one who fell was not dead. The one (hitman) ran forward and shot him in the head. (Then) he opened the coffin and shot the dead body many times."

About 30 people, including the eight members of the assassination squad who all turned out to be KwaZulu policemen, were subsequently arrested by troops and their weapons confiscated. But the suspects were all released shortly afterwards. It appears that the police did not take statements, while the confiscated guns were believed to have been returned to Ulundi.

In October 1990 — apparently after suffering reverses at the hands of young ANC militants in Wesselton — a contingent of about 22 Black Cats was taken to what was known as the "Ghost Mountain" training camp near Mkuze in northern Natal.

The camp was financed by two front organisations for South African military intelligence, Creed Consultants and Adult Education Consultants. There is evidence that intelligence channelled at least £1.5 million to the Mkuze camp through these fronts (as well as indications that it may have pumped substantial additional sums into Inkatha itself).

Creed and Adult Education Consultants were just part of a countrywide network of "consultancy" firms set up by military intelligence in the 1980s — firms with names like Go High in Cape Town, Good News Marketing Service in Pretoria, Go-Set in Kimberley and Eduguide in Port Elizabeth.

The network was headed by a retired government official, Louis Pasques, who ran an association called the South African Christian Cultural Organisation, based in Pretoria. In 1987, Dr Pasques was awarded the Star of Africa medal by P W Botha, then South Africa's president, for "services to state security".

Part of the work of the "consultancies" forming the Pasques network was to encourage and support groupings opposed to the ANC and associated

'The South African Police conducted a "deplorable" investigation into a gun attack at the funeral of an ANC member murdered by the Black Cats in which several people died. Despite "clear" evidence of public violence, no such charge was investigated by the SAP'

Slaughter of 26 commuters threatens to spark vengeful conflagration

Massacre on Soweto train bewilders South Africans

David Beresford in Johannesburg

SOUTH Africans were yesterday trying to make sense of the latest and most appalling of the attacks on black people to date: the indiscriminate massacre of commuters on a train in which at least 26 people were chopped and shot to death and 100 injured.

The massacre took place on the 5.15pm train to Soweto from Johannesburg's Jeppe station the same station where unidentified gunmen killed seven commuters in another massacre last week. The train loops through Johannesburg's suburbs, from east to west. On board some of the passengers were praying, taking part in one of the impromptu church services which are a feature of train journeys to South Africa's black townships.

It had just pulled out of George Goch station, on a five-mile leg to Denver station, when the nightmare started. A gang of men, who are believed to have boarded with weapons hidden, began moving methodically through the crowded carriages, hacking and shooting at the passengers.

"I saw about five people with shotguns, pistols and *pangas* (machetes)," said a survivor, Patrick Makhado. "They just started killing everyone. Then two or three people came from the back, also with guns and *pangas*. They had trapped us all. I jumped off the train." Another commuter, Thomas Ndimande, said: "Everyone opened their eyes from praying and started screaming and running. Some jumped out of the train and others hung on outside the doors and windows."

"A man standing next to me was hacked to death and I was (to be) next," recounted Dinah Mosie, who is six months' pregnant. "I threw myself off the moving train and lost consciousness. Praise God that me and my baby are still alive." Some of the survivors said the killers shouted "*Viva*", suggesting they were ANC supporters. Some insisted they went about their murderous work in complete silence. Others said they were shouting "*Bulala Zonke Izinja*", Zulu for "Kill the dogs". "They were Zulus, they had Zulu fighting sticks," said a woman who had been stabbed in the arm.

After about five minutes of mayhem in the carriage behind him, the train driver realised there was something wrong and made an unscheduled stop at Benrose station. The injured staggered on to the platform while other passengers and the killers fled.

The attack came just 24 hours after a man came running into the Guardian's Johannesburg office, as gunfire started outside, shouting: "The police are shooting at the taxi queues." Sure enough, a few hundred yards down the road there were two corpses lying in pools of blood, surrounded by abandoned shopping left behind by fleeing commuters, a wounded man groaning in a gutter. But the police were there, giving first aid to the injured.

An old man who had seen it described how a mini-bus of blacks pulled up and started firing indiscriminately at the long queue of commuters waiting for taxis to take them home to the townships. "One of them got out and ran to the wall there and wrote 'Fuck the Taxi Men'." Sure enough, there was the graffiti on the wall, testimony to another of the vendettas between rival taxi operators that from time to time develop into street shooting wars here. But the writing was too small and cramped to have been the work of a gunman in a murderous frenzy.

A security guard came running down the road, holstered pistol flapping at his side. He had returned fire and hit one of the killers, the guard panted to police. But then a second gunman had opened up with an AK-47 rifle and he had to dive for cover. Were they blacks? Yes. "One of them was wearing a red bandage around his head." *Rooidoeke* (redcloths), the Zulu killers of Inkatha.

Later that evening a local radio station quoted eye-witnesses as saying a group of whites in a mini-bus had opened fire indiscriminately on black commuters at a taxi rank in downtown Johannesburg.

The taxi rank shootings, which took place on Wednesday night leaving three dead and 17 injured, were one of a series of attacks over the last week which are threatening to plunge South Africa into political chaos. But, as the "eye-witness" accounts of Wednesday's events suggest, it is the chaos which is breeding chaos; the very uncertainty as to who is responsible, and why they are doing it, is creating a national mood of vengeful suspicion which is threatening to start an even greater conflagration.

15.9.90

organisations. One such hostile grouping was the Black Cats. According to a teenager who went to the Mkuze camp, they received training in the use of AK-47 assault rifles, 9mm handguns and shotguns. "Peter Msame taught us in English about leadership. We once watched a video of Shaka Zulu. Msame also taught us practical skills like how to hijack people by covering their mouths and dragging them into cars."

Msame, like other trainers at Mkuze, was a graduate from another mysterious training centre called "Hippo" which was situated in Namibia's Caprivi strip. In 1986, 200 members of Inkatha were flown to the Hippo camp, for what the authorities were subsequently to claim was training as guards to protect installations and VIPs in KwaZulu.

But affidavits subsequently made by men who attended the camp indicate emphasis in the training was heavily on offensive rather than defensive duties. Several of the graduates of the camp have been identified as key Inkatha hitmen in Natal who have contributed to the violence, as well as instructors at Mkuze.

On their return to Wesselton from Mkuze the trainees passed on the skills they had learnt from the Caprivi graduates to other Black Cats. "We met at the home of Chris Ngwenya (leader of the Black Cats) and we practised how to shoot with a .45 pistol and a 9mm parabellum (pistol).

"I liked the parabellum, because it is very powerful," one youth in the gang recounted. "They had one AK-47, two 9mm, a .38 (pistol) and four *xhwashas* (home-made guns)," another of the gang said of the returning trainees.

"They gave us the weapons without bullets and showed us how to shoot. About 45 youngsters immediately joined them and we became a group of about 80 . . ."

The story of the training camps at Caprivi and Mkuze and the activities of the Black Cats was originally reported by the Guardian and its sister newspaper in South Africa, the Weekly Mail.

It was subsequently investigated by a judicial inquiry into the causes of political violence, the Goldstone Commission, which confirmed most of the

'The police and army's murderous activities were so refined that the military hit squad — the "Civil Co-operation Bureau"— was run on corporate lines, headed by a managing director'

Township rally brings Inkatha violence to Transvaal

South African clash leaves 24 dead

David Beresford in Johannesburg

THE Natal civil war appeared to be spreading to the Transvaal yesterday, with at least 24 people reported killed in Sebokeng township, south of Johannesburg, in clashes between followers of the ANC and those of chief Mangosuthu Buthelezi's Inkatha movement.

Nineteen bodies were found in Sebokeng after fighting which followed an Inkatha rally in a local stadium on Sunday. One of the dead was a policeman, killed by a spear hurled from the crowd.

There were allegations that police allowed Inkatha supporters to attend the rally heavily armed, and that they went on a rampage after the meeting.

Both the Congress Alliance and chief Buthelezi blamed each other for the fighting. The Congress of South African Trade Unions (Cosatu) said the violence reflected an attempt by Inkatha "to widen its killing fields . . . to bargain for a stake in the political future of this country".

Chief Buthelezi retorted that ANC supporters in Sebokeng were seen stoning Inkatha buses and carrying petrol bombs, and his supporters felt "the need to defend themselves and carry arms".

24.7.90

Law and order minister may resign over police cash scandal uncovered by Guardian investigation

Inkatha crisis deepens

Patrick Laurence in Johannesburg

SOUTH AFRICA'S minister of law and order, Adriaan Vlok, last night told television viewers that he was considering resigning from the government.

"If I am an obstacle to negotiations and the future of this country, then I will reconsider my position . . . I am reconsidering it at the moment and I will discuss it with the president (F W de Klerk)," Mr Vlok said.

The startling admission came after the disclosure in the Guardian and the South African Weekly Mail that police had made two secret payments to the Inkatha Freedom Party in late 1989 and early 1990.

Mr Vlok conceded during a televised debate with the editor of the Weekly Mail, Anton Harber, that the amount of money channelled to Inkatha and allied organisations was far in excess of the 250,000 Rand (about £50,000) officially admitted on Friday.

As much as R1.5 million could have been secretly funnelled into Inkatha's trade union arm, the United Workers Union (UWUSA) over six years.

The money started flowing even before UWUSA was founded in 1986 as a counter to the pro-African National Congress trade union federation, the Congress of South African Trade Unions.

It was launched in mid-1986 at Kings Park Stadium in Durban, the venue for the two Inkatha rallies that were later financed by the police in November 1989 and March 1990.

Mr Vlok said Inkatha gave receipts for all the money it received, and it was impossible that senior Inkatha officials did not know of the payments.

On the same television programme the president of Inkatha, chief Mangosuthu Buthelezi, was challenged by an Afrikaans journalist, Max Du Preez, to say whether he would resign if it could be proved that Inkatha was funded by the intelligence services or the police.

Chief Buthelezi evaded the challenge, saying: "That is hypothetical. Let it happen, then we shall see."

At Inkatha's annual conference at the weekend, chief Mangosuthu Buthelezi was unanimously re-elected as president of the Zulu-based organisation. An election was not due, but chief Buthelezi, angered by calls for his resignation in the wake of the disclosure, asked for a vote.

Delegates who opposed chief Buthelezi were invited to stand. Nobody did.

Chief Buthelezi had earlier denied all knowledge of the payments, saying: "I swear before the Lord God that I am not aware of the police ever depositing money into Inkatha's account."

Earlier in the weekend Dr Gerrit Viljoen, minister of constitutional development and President De Klerk's chief negotiator, dismissed the sums of money paid to Inkatha as "insignificant" compared to the "vast sums of money paid to the ANC and its alliance partners by foreign organisations and foreign governments".

The money paid to Inkatha had the "limited purpose" of boosting the anti-sanctions campaign, added Dr Viljoen, who led a high-ranking National Party delegation at the Inkatha conference.

Foreign minister Pik Botha defended himself by saying that the transfer of money was "strictly within the mandate to combat sanctions".

22.7.91

SA defence force 'trained Inkatha men'

FURTHER evidence is emerging in the wake of South Africa's Inkathagate scandal that the De Klerk administration is continuing to cover up collusion between the security forces and Inkatha and their role in fomenting township violence.

Details of secret training facilities provided for Inkatha by the South African Defence Force appear to contradict assurances made last week by president, F W De Klerk, that they were limited to instruction in VIP protection.

In fact the Inkatha recruits were trained in guerrilla warfare and were subsequently used by chief Buthelezi's organisation in attacks on political opponents — notably ANC supporters.

In at least one instance a member of chief Buthelezi's homeland cabinet in KwaZulu appears to have used Zulu graduates of the SADF training camp for political assassinations.

9.8.91

details. But the commission found the violence was "criminal" and there was no evidence of security force involvement.

The Goldstone Commission has, at least until recently, shown itself sceptical of the existence of a Third Force as such, insisting at one stage that the political conflict was the product of rivalry between the ANC and Inkatha.

But the commission — and South Africa — got a rude shock a month before the election when a senior police officer, code-named "Q", contacted Judge Goldstone and disclosed evidence that a formal conspiracy did exist at the very heart of the security forces, among the general staff of the South African police.

The mystery informant claimed that three of the country's top police officers — the deputy commissioner of police, Lt-Gen Basie Smit; the head of counter intelligence, Major-General Krappies Engelbrecht; and the commander of the CID, Lt-Gen Johan Le Roux — had been financing and organising the destabilisation of the country.

He repeated claims that assassination squads, trained and funded by the police, have been targeting members of the ANC since the unbanning of the liberation movement.

He also claimed that large quantities of weapons brought into South Africa both from Namibia and Mozambique have been widely distributed among members of Inkatha and that the security forces were continuing to give combat training to Inkatha supporters.

At the time of writing the allegations remained unproven although, for those who have followed the Third Force controversy, persuasive.

The three generals were sent on "compulsory" leave and further investigations were promised. Whether or not its existence is proven, history is likely to judge that the Third Force has had a major and tragic impact on South Africa's historic transition to majority rule.

David Beresford is the Guardian's South Africa correspondent

Inkatha blamed for Boipatong township massacre

Zulu group linked to slaughter of 39

David Beresford
in Johannesburg

FRESH evidence of involvement by the Zulu-led Inkatha movement and police in township violence emerged yesterday from one of the worst massacres seen in South Africa this year, in which up to 39 people were shot, speared and hacked to death in their homes overnight.

There were horrific scenes in the township of Boipatong, south of Johannesburg, during the day as police and mortuary attendants carted away corpses of men, women and children killed in a rampage by some 200 suspected Inkatha men.

Elizabeth Kolatswewu said her sister-in-law, Elisa Mbatha, banged on her door. "I could hear her chil-dren crying next door. I opened my door and she fell on the floor. She had been stabbed and chopped on her neck. She died there on the floor." Her baby was strapped to the dead woman's back.

In another street a mother was lying with her nine-month-old infant clasped to her breasts; both had been stabbed to death. On the next block a year-old child lay dead.

The inevitable war of words began between the ANC and the authorities. The ANC secretary-general, Cyril Ramaphosa, said: "We charge [President] F.W. de Klerk and his government with complicity in this slaughter." An Inkatha spokesman indignantly denied his organisation was involved.

There were also allegations yesterday of police complicity in the massacre. A church minister acting as a "peace monitor" for a local civil rights organisation, Peace Action, described how he had received a series of telephone calls from frantic residents of Boipatong, describing the build-up to the attack and reporting the progress of the massacre.

The minister said he reported the calls to police at 7.44pm on Wednesday night. At 10.19pm he received calls that gunfire had started.

At 7.02am yesterday morning he had a call from police to say they were having difficulty entering the township. At 10am he had a call saying police in armoured vehicles were driving around the township, shooting residents. Police later confirmed this, saying that residents had opened fire on them first.

19.6.92

Mandela calls a halt to talks

DAVID BERESFORD
in Johannesburg

THE CRISIS in South Africa over the latest security force and Inkatha massacres worsened last night when Nelson Mandela — declaring the police were not fit to be regarded as human — announced the ANC was calling off talks with the government.

"I can no longer explain to our people why we continue to talk to a government which is murdering our people," the ANC leader told a rally.

The ANC decision came after an extraordinary succession of events in the Transvaal township of Boipatong, beginning with last Wednesday's massacre of 42 people by Inkatha and culminating on Saturday with police killing three more residents in front of the world's press after president F W de Klerk had been forced to flee.

After being forced out of the township by furious residents — beating on his car, shouting "go away you dog" and brandishing placards saying "To Hell with de Klerk and his Inkatha murders" — the president reportedly made a cryptic reference to the need for regrettable security measures to protect lives.

22.6.92

Inquiry head says urgent proposals to curb violence are being ignored

SA judge chastises state

David Beresford in Johannesburg

THE judge investigating South Africa's political violence protested yesterday at the failure of the authorities to implement recommendations aimed at halting the carnage.

Judge Richard Goldstone's complaint came as police reported another 27 people killed in political violence over the weekend.

In his first direct criticism of the government over the township violence, Mr Justice Goldstone expressed "regret" that a series of "considered and urgent recommendations" had been ignored by the state.

One set of recommendations was that steps should be taken to try to control the single men's hostels — regarded as the focus of the violence in the townships — with perimeter fencing and weapons searches at entrances.

"The only response to date has been a statement on behalf of the government that 294 million rand (£57 million) has been allocated for the upgrading of hostels," said the judge. "No action had been taken to date." Mr Justice Goldstone also protested at the government's failure to withdraw from township duties the controversial 32 Battalion — a unit drawn from the Namibian bush war and recently found responsible for rape and other assaults during "peacekeeping" operations.

He also complained about the failure of the police to act on his referral of a case in December last year in which there was prima facie evidence of the involvement of police officers in an unsuccessful conspiracy to murder an ANC leader in the town of Schweizer-Reneke. He said the police investigation had taken an "unacceptably long time".

Judge Goldstone said he did not expect his commission's recommendations necessarily to be respected or acted upon, but he did not expect them to be ignored.

The judge softened the criticism a little by also announcing in a statement that his commission had not discovered, to date, any justification for allegations that the president, members of the cabinet, or high-ranking security force officers were involved in the township violence.

He said that in the absence of such evidence, allegations to that effect were "unwise, unfair and dangerous" and would only give rise to violence.

7.7.92

Buthelezi lines up with white extremists

David Beresford

CHIEF Mangosuthu Buthelezi moved closer to the cause of white extremists when he made a hardline speech expressing sympathy with the recent neo-Nazi attack on the national negotiating forum at the World Trade Centre in Johannesburg.

The South African Press Association reported yesterday that Chief Buthelezi received five standing ovations from a mixed crowd of about 500 attending an Inkatha meeting in the Conservative Party stronghold of Algoa Park, Eastern Cape.

The chief vowed not to return to the multi-party talks until he had received guarantees that the new constitution would provide for federal government.

Chief Buthelezi said Inkatha's walk-out from the talks and the Afrikaans Weerstandsbeweging (AWB) invasion of the trade centre were linked by their "rejection of the connivance of the African National Congress and their new-found allies, the South African government, in bulldozing through agreements which are totally rejected by the majority of decent and peace-loving South Africans".

14.7.93

King of Zulus threatens to declare UDI

Chris McGreal
in Johannesburg

THE King of the Zulus, Goodwill Zwelithini, warned yesterday that he intends to declare his kingdom independent of South Africa for the first time since it was conquered by the British.

At a meeting in Durban with President FW de Klerk, the king presented a memorandum saying that the collapse of Afrikaner rule, and before that of the British Empire, effectively reinstated the sovereignty of the KwaZulu kingdom.

"Those who conquered us, namely the white nations of Afrikaner and British, are now relinquishing their sovereignty over the land of South Africa," he said.

"The nation which was exercising sovereignty over the land is abdicating its power to open the door for new nations to exercise their sovereignty over the land.

"Under this set of circumstances, I take the position that the sovereignty of the Zulu nation is revived and I am advised that this position is also supported by the international law of decolonisation."

The king warned that the Zulu nation would not be bound by South Africa's new constitution, under which the first multi-racial elections will be held in April. Because the ANC had not defeated the Zulus in war, they had no right to rule over them.

The meeting came on the heels of the decision by the king's uncle, chief Buthelezi, not to register his Inkatha Freedom Party for the elections. Rejecting participation, chief Buthelezi made what amounted to new threats of violence, portraying the struggle as a nationalist one that would lead to more killing, even though large numbers of Zulus back the ANC.

But Mr De Klerk said there was no reson why Zulus should feel excluded by the interim constitution, and argued Inkatha should participate in the elections.

At least one person was killed and one wounded when the king's supporters grew impatient as the talks dragged on and let loose a volley of shots outside the meeting hall.

15.2.94

Buthelezi dampens hope of election compromise

David Beresford
in Johannesburg

CHIEF Mangosuthu Buthelezi yesterday dampened hopes of a peace deal when he again made an uncompromising demand for Zulu "self-determination".

South African newspapers yesterday trumpeted a breakthrough in Tuesday's talks between the chief and the African National Congress leader, Nelson Mandela. But the Inkatha leader appeared unaware of it on his return to the KwaZulu capital of Ulundi.

Addressing a caucus meeting, Chief Buthelezi told members of the KwaZulu legislative assembly that they had to separate the "kingdom" of KwaZulu from the rest of South Africa.

Without referring to the meeting in Durban with Mr Mandela, he said: "The position of our government regarding the failure of the South African government and the ANC to accommodate our reasonable demands remains exactly the same as before. To deny citizens of KwaZulu the right to self-determination is a savage attempt to strip us of our cultural heritage, to belittle the traditional importance of His Majesty the King of the Zulus and to eradicate all evidence of our Zulu existence."

Returning to the familiar rhetoric of civil war, the chief added that if South Africa went ahead with the April 27 election without reaching agreement with King Goodwill Zwelithini on self-determination, "the KwaZulu government cannot be held responsible for the anger of the Zulu nation".

● A magistrate denied bail yesterday for three Inkatha officials, arrested over the killing of 14 ANC election workers sleeping in an abandoned house in Mahehle, Natal, last month.

19.3.94

Right: **The King of the Zulus, Goodwill Zwelithini, left, with his advisor Chief Mangosuthu Buthelezi in Ulundi, 1994**

Below: **Inkatha impis (warriors) prepare themselves for war as the King of the Zulus proclaims the sovereignty of KwaZulu, 1994**

What was it that finally led to the demise of apartheid? Many believe it was the foreclosure of the American banks on loans in 1985, but the rot had set in many years before with the assassination of Hendrik Verwoerd, the architect of apartheid, in 1966

The end of apartheid/Stanley Uys

IT IS DIFFICULT to find the moment when the system's back was broken. Some would place it in 1960, the Sharpeville year. More probably, it was 1966, when the architect of apartheid, Dr Hendrik Verwoerd, was assassinated. Certainly, it was not broken by international sanctions, nor, as recent wisdom has it, by the foreclosure of American banks on loans in 1985 and Pretoria's resultant declaration of bankruptcy. That was simply the *coup de grâce*.

It is necessary to understand what was meant by apartheid. Before 1948, General JC Smuts practised race discrimination and imposed white hegemony, but he was already reading the writing on the wall. The 1946-48 Native Laws Commission repudiated the 1922 Stallard Commission's commandment that permanent residence in the towns was the exclusive right of whites.

The Fagan report stated that "the idea of total segregation is utterly impracticable; secondly, that the movement from country to town has a background of economic necessity — that it may, so one hopes, be guided and regulated, and may perhaps also be limited, but that it cannot be stopped or turned in the opposite direction; and thirdly, that in our urban areas there are not only native migrant labourers, but there is also a settled, permanent native population."

This is the core of race politics. The National Party, on gaining office in 1948, sounded the retreat: back to Stallard. Smuts's policy was seen at best as *laissez-faire*, at worst suicidal. The 1948 general election was a contest between whites — Afrikaner nationalists versus the rest — over how to govern black people.

Apartheid was a closed system. "Petty apartheid" — segregation at post office counters, in lifts and parks, on beaches and benches — was as important as "grand apartheid". Unless everyone understood who was white and who was not, and were reminded daily, in the smallest detail, that white survival depended on separation, the system could not be hermetically sealed, and could not work.

If black people were allowed to settle in towns as permanent residents, not "temporary sojourners", they would inexorably invade the white institutions, and in the end numbers would count — the black majority would take over. So every black man and woman had to be siphoned out of the "white" system, constitutionally if not physically. When this failed, apartheid failed.

It must be understood that apartheid is separable from white supremacy, which continued long after the ideological decline had begun, although with its confidence increasingly sapped. What obscured this descent was that no one told the security police, whose torture chambers remained open for business.

Verwoerd controlled the ascent of apartheid. He had a steely intellect and ideological self-discipline untypical of Afrikaners, who are generally much more pragmatic and, yes, *slapgat* (loosely, slapdash). When Verwoerd was assassinated (in his parliamentary bench by a schizophrenic half-Greek half-Mozambican, wielding a massive knife bought at Cape Town's poshest cutlery store), it was as if a tyranny had been lifted from his Afrikaner cabinet. They certainly wanted hegemony, but not at the price of an ascetic self-denial. With his death, the "gigantic Verwoerdian dream of social engineering" rapidly lost momentum. Thereafter, the half-hearted amateurs took over, blundering towards an ever-receding goal of an ethnically cleansed South Africa.

The prime minister who took over from Verwoerd was John Vorster, more a policeman than a thinker, who let apartheid's moral pretensions decay while he turned to the torture chambers ("If you get them by the balls," was his motto, "their hearts and minds will follow"). Almost immediately after Vorster's accession, the rot of "reformism" spread in the National Party, and by 1969 the first rightwing breakaway had taken place, with four Members of Parliament being expelled to form the Herstigte Nasionale Party, which still survives as a kind of tiny political Jurassic Park.

The MPs charged Vorster with diluting Afrikaner nationalism by seeking the support of English-speaking whites, admitting black diplomats (a solitary representative from Malawi), and by opening the doors to racially mixed sports teams from abroad. Early in his premiership Vorster began the critical fudge — hinting that 1978 would not remain the deadline, set by Verwoerd, for reversal of the flow of black people from the impoverished homelands to the urban centres.

It is when believers feel betrayed that the signs of change should be read — when the insight into pending failure comes from within the laager. This was

Horror in Cape Town

Dr Verwoerd killed in Parliament

MPs in violent struggle with white assailant Cape Town.

DR HENDRIK VERWOERD, the South African Prime Minister and architect of apartheid, was assassinated in Parliament today by a white messenger, Dimitrio Tsafendas, who stabbed him repeatedly in the neck and chest.

Tsafendas is reported often to have expressed his concern about the cost of living for poor whites in South Africa. He had told other parliamentary messengers that the Government was doing too much for coloured people and not spending enough on whites. But Dr Donges, the Finance Minister, in a statement after the assassination, emphasised that the motives were still not known.

7.9.66

John Grigg

Messenger of doom?

THE DEATH of Dr Verwoerd is rich in symbolism – the murderer disguised as a messenger, the bloodstained floor of Parliament – and the sheer drama of the event recalls Shakespeare's "Julius Caesar". But what are the practical implications?

Was the assassin a messenger of doom for the whole wretched system of apartheid, or only for one misguided individual? And perhaps we shall never be sure of his motives. He may be a fanatical idealist, a self-conscious agent of destiny like Charlotte Corday, whose original intention was to stab Marat in the hall of the Convention, as Brutus stabbed Caesar. Or he may be a sad little psychopath with a personal grudge. Or he may, as is rumoured, be a champion of poor whites – the irony of ironies. His motive is less important than the likely results of his desperate act.

Deadly heresy

ASSASSINATION can be effective only when the evil of the regime depends largely on the life of one man. Dr Verwoerd was certainly the ablest theoretical and practical exponent of apartheid, but the system was not his creation nor will it die with him. Indeed, his supposed martyrdom may give it additional strength.

When a man is butchered, the normal civilised reaction is one of horror and pity – above all, of pity for his wife and children. And when he is a prominent man, those emotions are mixed with the awe we instinctively feel when the mighty are overthrown.

We must not, however, be blind to the wickedness of Dr Verwoerd's political creed or to the huge legacy of wrong he and others have bequeathed. Apartheid is the most deadly of all heresies, since it denies Christianity in the name of Christ and betrays Western culture while purporting to defend it.

Instead of sharing the treasures of European knowledge and liberty with their African compatriots, the white racialists of South Africa are determined to hoard those treasures for themselves and keep everyone born with a dark skin in a state of permanent subjection.

During his premiership Dr Verwoerd contrived to frustrate the last efforts at non-violent opposition to white, oligarchic rule. He leaves behind him a system established by force, and which only force can destroy. An extremely clever man, he combined fanaticism with the touch of a master politician. His work may endure for several generations – the power of the modern State is so hard to shake – but in the long run it must surely be doomed.

8.9.66

Lecturer tarred on stage

PROFESSOR Floors van Jaarsveld was tarred and feathered on Wednesday night in Pretoria while advocating that other racial groups should not be forced to treat the Afrikaners' Day of the Covenant as a religious holiday.

As he spoke in the University of Pretoria lecture hall, about 40 men, claiming to be members of the Afrikaner Resistance Movement, jumped on to the stage.

The Day of the Covenant is regarded as the holiest day in the history of the Afrikaners. The day commemorates the 19th century Battle of Blood River, when an outnumbered group of Afrikaners defeated a Zulu army.

30.3.79

Unacceptable face of apartheid?

Hundreds of university students, most of them white, disrupted a speech by a South African Cabinet Minister yesterday shouting "Fascist" and "Sieg Heil," and singing the anthem of the banned African National Congress (ANC).

Dr Piet Koornhof, Minister of Cooperation and Development, was shouted down at Johannesburg's University of the Witwatersrand by the students, who also pelted him with paper missiles and hurled a stinkbomb.

21.3.81

Left: **Hendrik Verwoerd, architect of apartheid, was assassinated before his edifice was completed**

Right: **'Reasonable South Africans will not accept the principle of one man, one vote . . . it would lead to chaos.' PW Botha speaking to the Natal Congress of the National Party, 1985**

always the ANC's shortcoming: it was so preoccupied with portraying the National Party as an unchanging and unchangeable tyranny that it could never exploit the obvious internal tensions and contradictions.

The alarm that gripped the Afrikaner establishment at the time of Sharpeville — business, professions, academics, the church, the declaration by a senior cabinet minister that the "old book" of apartheid had been closed — should have warned even Verwoerd that the state had over-reached itself. Employers of two-thirds of South Africa's black male labour force went in an Afrikaner-English deputation to persuade him to see reason. Instead, he defiantly took South Africa out of the Commonwealth.

A blow of a different kind was struck in March 1973 when 50,000 Durban workers walked out of their factories, beginning an upsurge of strikes. In 1977, Vorster appointed the Wiehahn Labour Commission, whose report in 1979 recommended statutory recognition of collective bargaining by black unions. This was a major admission that apartheid was on the skids.

To Chief Mangosuthu Buthelezi, too, must go some of the credit for destroying apartheid. His relations with Vorster (1966-78) were brittle and with PW Botha (1978-89) even worse. He accepted "self-government" for KwaZulu (to turn apartheid against itself, he explained), but refused to accept independence.

This refusal, in the opinion of Professor David Welsh, "tore the heart out of separate development". Had KwaZulu become independent along with Transkei, Bophuthatswana, Venda and Ciskei, "the demographic chicanery of apartheid's enthusiasts would have enabled them to say that a 'majority' of blacks had opted for independence". The failure of homelands consolidation in 1983 — assembling homeland fragments into wholes — pulled the rug from under the 1959 Act.

The 1980s saw the formal collapse of apartheid. It is often forgotten that it was PW Botha who changed the labour laws; co-opted "coloured" and Indian representatives into the all-white parliament (thereby weakening white hegemony, although this was not his intention); restored a common South

'The alarm that had
gripped the Afrikaner
establishment at the time
of Sharpeville,
the declaration then that
the old book of apartheid
had been closed, should
have warned even
Dr Hendrik Verwoerd that
the apartheid state had
over-reached itself'

Botha's New Trek

Total strategy – trick or retreat?

John Kane-Berman, in Johannesburg, assesses the reality behind Mr Botha's loosening of apartheid

.PRIME MINSTER P. W. Botha's speeches are sometimes like a breath of fresh air in the fetid atmosphere of South African politics. When he declares that the time for treating "coloured" people as lepers is over, or that it is now more urgent that ever for Afrikanerdom to practise Christianity towards others, even some of his opponents must applaud. And when he adds that he will extend friendship to blacks even if his own people reject him, his courage must be acknowledged. But what does it mean? Are these real winds of change at last?

One thing is certain. Mr Botha's speeches are not just cosmetic. He knows they fool only those who wish to be fooled. Even the budget, that most telling of yardsticks, has begun to reflect a shift in national priorities.

Defence spending will rise by 46 per cent this year, but black secondary and advanced technical education in the white areas will get about 55 per cent more than last year. Black adult education spending will get 180 per cent more – at a time when the increase in total government spending will be held at 14 per cent. In addition, black housing in the white areas will get 29 per cent of the housing loan finance for all races, against 14 per cent last year.

Given the size of the backlogs, these increases may seem small beer – and their psychological impact was lost because the Finance Minister also chose to put the price of bread up by 20 per cent. Yet paradoxically, those least likely to applaud the extra money for housing and education are the white radicals who have been loudest in condemning the government for neglecting these areas for so long. They see the increases as self-serving, just one more part of Mr Botha's "total strategy". In their eyes this involves an unholy alliance between government and business to create an urban black middle class and labour aristocracy and then to co-opt it to the defence of capitalism against the unemployed and the dispossessed in the rural areas. They see it as a sophisticated plan to enlist selected black allies to help perpetuate white hegemony.

"Adapt or Die" – Mr Botha's phrase – is thus the new slogan of hitherto undiluted white supremacist politics. But to the Treurnichts and other white reactionaries it means "Adapt and Die." They fear that even minor concessions to black demands will be the thin end of a wedge leading to black majority rule. This is why the differences between Mr Botha and his right-wing are not superficial, but fundamental – not in intention, but in ultimate consequence.

The problem is that apartheid is not merely a policy which can be repealed, an ugly aspect of a otherwise normal society, it is a total way of life, written into the South African constitution, enshrined in law, education, and religion. It has an unstoppable momentum of its own. Mr Botha and his generals may now see some of the folly, but apartheid is greater than they are.

Along with Indians, coloured leaders are to be given seats on Mr Botha's new "president's council" but recent lengthy discussions I have had with "moderate" coloured leaders have convinced me that even they dare not take them. It is had to know what weighs more : deep suspicion of Mr Botha's motives, fear of the dreaded stamp of "Judas", or anguish at the possible consequences of ganging up with whites against blacks when three of South Africa's neighbours have seen the end of white rule in less than a decade.

9.4.80

Defiant Botha holds back reform pledge

Patrick Laurence in Durban

THE SOUTH African president, PW Botha, yesterday told a world which had been waiting and hoping for at least some gesture in the way of concrete reform that his government would not be pushed or panicked into hasty or dangerous concessions.

The president's much heralded "reformist" speech to the Natal Congress of his National Party was a defiant restatement of existing neo-apartheid policy, a castigation of critics at home and abroad, and a questioning of the role of the media in the reporting of violence in the country's rebellious black townships. None of the reforms or concessions which have surfaced in the rumours or counter rumours about the speech was more than touched on. In particular, Mr Botha took the hardest of lines on the possible release of the ANC leader, Nelson Mandela, and indicated that there was no question of re-integrating the homelands politically with the republic.

Mr Botha ended by describing his speech as a manifesto and the principles contained in it as a watershed. "I believe that we are today crossing the Rubicon. We now have a manifesto for the future of our country and we must embark on a programme of positive action." Chief Gatsha Buthelezi, the head of South Africa's largest black tribe in KwaZulu, voiced disappointment yesterday with president Botha's failure to ease apartheid policies. He said the speech promised too little to stem a tide of black violence in his country.

The Nobel Peace Prize winner, Bishop Desmond Tutu, commenting on the speech, said: "It was almost a parody. I have to laugh or else I would weep."

16.8.85

African citizenship (1985); and abolished the Mixed Marriages and Immorality Acts, Job Reservation and, above all, Influx Control (1986).

Once that went, and rural black people streamed into the urban areas, mostly to squatter camps, nothing could save apartheid. By the time De Klerk made his speech in February 1990, the game was up. Botha had left him a bankrupt apartheid estate. All he could hope for was to salvage "power-sharing" from the wreckage.

The foreclosure by US banks on loans in 1985, and the momentum of sanctions, were only the last blows. The back of apartheid had been broken not only by the black struggle, like the 1976 Soweto uprising and the turmoil that started in black areas in 1984, but by the inherent incapacity of five million white people to impose a lasting hegemony on a 34 million African, "coloured" and Asian population. The Fagan Commission foresaw it all.

Afrikaner leaders have bowed to the inevitable, but not all are following De Klerk. The referendum in March 1992 may have delivered a 69 per cent vote in favour of his reforms, but Afrikanerdom since has split, with the majority leaning towards the Conservative Party, which broke away from the National Party in 1982 to return to Verwoerdism.

But not even the Conservative Party aspires to white supremacy over the whole of South Africa. It will settle for a homeland (*volkstaat*). General Constand Viljoen, former chief of the SA Defence Force and a founder of the Afrikaner Volksfront, plans a homeland that will encompass 15 per cent of South Africa and 12 per cent of its GDP. No one has drawn a final map, because there is not a single magisterial district which does not have a black majority. Wherever the homeland boundaries are drawn, the majority of Afrikaners will live outside it.

Two impossible options now present themselves to the ANC. One is to accept an Afrikaner homeland, and risk tearing itself apart; the other is to deny it, and risk tearing the country apart. This is a cruel choice, but there is a possible compromise. By contorted map drawing, Afrikaners possibly can be offered fragments in the Transvaal and Free State, grouped around town

Leader from the fringe

From David Beresford
in Johannesburg

Eugene Terre'Blanche – catapulted to the forefront of South African politics by fighting at a rally in Pietersburg on Thursday night – is considered by many to be an embryonic Hitler.

A former police officer – he was at one time bodyguard to the South African Prime Minister, Mr John Vorster – Mr Terre'Blanche founded the Afrikaner Weerstandsbeweging (Afrikaner Resistance Movement) with six others in 1973, in a garage in the Transvaal town of Heidelberg.

The organisation first attracted public attention in 1979, when members tarred and feathered a prominent 'verligte (enlightened) historian, Professor Floors van Jaarsveld, for publicly arguing that the Day of the Covenant – the anniversary of the Afrikaner victory over the Zulus – should be de-sanctified.

In 1982, in a swoop on the AWB, police seized arms caches and, as a result, in 1983, Mr Terre'Blanche himself was sentenced to two years in gaol, suspended for five years, for terrorism.

A trial the same year of two other members of the AWB gave an insight into the sort of thuggish elements who numbered among Mr Terre'Blanche's followers. It was disclosed that they had hatched a plan to infect Sun City – the luxurious casino complex in the homeland of Bophuthatswana – with syphilis by infecting white rats with the disease and letting them loose.

The two men got 15 years for terrorism. One had a previous conviction for beating a black man to death with a bamboo pole.

The AWB was dismissed as a lunatic fringe until reports began to emerge of its rampant growth – particularly in the northern Transvaal – in a reaction to the Government's reform campaign. It began to edge towards centre stage in white politics with a series of incidents in which members disrupted meetings addressed by senior Nationalist Party figures – culminating in Thursday's fracas in the meeting in Pietersburg which was to have been addressed by the Foreign Minister, Mr Pik Botha.

Mr Terre'Blanche – the name, which he changed to the Afrikaans "Terre'Blanche" by deed poll, means White Earth – is a man of personal charm. An amateur poet and playwright, he is a mesmerising speaker. But he is considered anti-semitic as well as an arch-racist.

He has, in the past, said that under his rule the Jews would be disenfranchised and makes references to international Jewish conspiracies.

The AWB's emblem resembles the swastika, being made up of three inter-locking sevens. 'It is intended to represent numbers in the Bible which counter the so-called Mark of the Beast: 666. The organisation is committed to the re-establishment of the old Boer republics of the Transvaal and Orange Free State as a white state.'

Founded as a secret organisation recruits reputedly have to undergo an initiation ceremony during which they are prepared to "take up arms against the liberal government." They are believed to have been pursuing a strategy for some time, of infiltrating the security services.

24.5.86

A symbol in crisis

Leader comment

The words are from the Guardian. 'A real-life heroine of immortal stature.' In the awful perspective of the wider drama of the South African black people, the judgement of our reviewer on a recent book about Winnie Mandela surely stands. Heroic people may be flawed by their own weaknesses or by the accumulated pressure of intolerable events. They may even come crashing down. In Mrs Mandela's case, it was apparently the relief of pressure – the lifting of restrictions in 1986 on the 'mother of the nation' – which led her to tragically lose touch with a movement that she had inspired for a quarter of a century. Whatever the truth about Mrs Mandela's 'football team' and their treatment of the four youths whom they allegedly abducted in December, she was already slipping fast from the pedestal.

The first version of events of December 29 at the Orlando Methodist Church in Soweto and, later that night, in Mrs Mandela's home, was reported by the highly respected 'Weekly Mail'. This was no knocking campaign. The newspaper's anti-apartheid credentials are underlined by its recent two-month suspension from publication. The fact of the abduction has not been denied: Mrs Mandela claims that the youths were removed after allegations that they had been sexually molested. But the news that the four were then apparently beaten, and that one of them is missing and may be dead, alarmed many in a community already deeply disturbed by the behaviour of Mrs Mandela's bodyguards. A crisis committee had been set up several months previously after a separate row when she negotiated with a conservative black American businessman to copyright her family name. The committee included senior anti-apartheid figures such as the church leader Reverend Frank Chikane and the mineworkers' leader Mr Cyril Ramaphosa. Last week

the South African police began investigations, and the crisis committee – after a meeting when Mrs Mandela failed to appear – said it could not longer pursue its own inquiry. At the weekend more damaging allegations were published alleging Mrs Mandela's personal involvement in the beatings. These may become the subject of legal action.

Winnie Mandela suffered 25 years of harassment, solitary confinement, silencing and legal restrictions while the husband whom she loved was in jail, seen occasionally through wire mesh or glass. In her autobiography 'Part of my Soul' she has described how the iron entered her heart. Once a social worker with the instinct to preserve human life, now she would fire the gun if she thought it right. 'That is the bitterness they create in us . . . And if need be, you will use their own methods, because that is the language they understand.' There was no reason why the girl from a kraal in the Pondoland Hills should have been beatified by her suffering.

Her South African biographer, Nancy Harrison, writing before her release from restriction, notes that Mrs Mandela can be both 'autocratic' and 'too trusting.' Two years ago her apparent endorsement of 'necklacing' showed, at the least, lack of political judgement. This was followed by the controversy over a palatial new home built with the proceeds of foreign royalties and awards. (Bowing to pressure, she resolved not to move into it until her husband was freed.)

'I have wondered,' Nelson Mandela wrote to his wife in 1985, 'whether any kind of commitment can ever be sufficient excuse for abandoning a young and inexperienced woman in a pitiless desert.' Tragically, the price for the sacrifice which they both made may have been paid by 'Stompie' Moeketsi, the youth who has disappeared. It will be extremely grindable grist to the mill of those who compelled the Mandelas to separate for what may still be a lifetime – the South African government. Yet the issues raised by decades of struggle do not depend on one man or one woman, nor only on the ANC.

The UDF, church and union leaders were unable to resolve the crisis of Winnie Mandela, but they continue to wrestle with the larger crisis which is still the dominating shadow over South Africa.

14.2.89

Troops on guard at SA beaches

From Patrick Laurence
in Johannesburg

ARMED POLICE and soldiers were on guard at the weekend near beaches reserved for whites in the coastal city of Port Elizabeth after the American General Motors company pledged financial and legal help to any of its 30,000 black employees who are prosecuted for using beaches designated for whites.

24.2.86

South Africa business chiefs demand release of Mandela

From Patrick Laurence and AP in
Johannesburg

THIS REPORT was compiled subject to the emergency regulations imposed on the press by the South African Government.

Leading South African businessmen and industrialists yesterday called on the Pretoria Government to release Mr Nelson Mandela, leader of the outlawed African National Congress.

In a statement published in Johannesburg's Sunday Star newspaper, Mr Gavin Relly, chairman of the giant Anglo American Mining Corporation, said: 'Whether one likes the ANC or not – and I personally do not like its policy of violence nor its Marxist economic thinking – it constitutes an important factor in the South African political set up.'

7.7.86

South African whites stage mass protest against conscription

Anthony Barker
in Johannesburg

Scores of young white South Africans publicly refused yesterday to report for compulsory military service in a gesture of mass defiance that could earn them up to six years in gaol.

At secretive press conferences in four cities, 143 men, mainly professionals and students, simultaneously announced that they would not serve because they saw the army as an instrument of unjust race policies.

Mr Marais, describing his experiences in the army operating on both sides of the border between Angola and South African-ruled Namibia, told reporters: 'What I am angry about is that I was conscripted into waging war against a people that I had no quarrel with ... that I was part of a crazy and brutal occupation.'

7.8.88

Blacks buy control of white firm

JOHANNESBURG: In one of the largest purchases ever by black South African businessmen, a taxi owners' association has bought control of the country's biggest white-owned bus company.

After weeks of negotiations, the South African Black Taxi Association, Sabba, has agreed to buy a 52 per cent share of the Putco bus company, the Rand Merchant Bank, which is handling the deal, said.

Sabba said it was working with black South African business leaders to finance the deal, estimated at 150 million rand (about £47.5 million).

8.8.87

ANC leader is freed from goal after 23 years

From David Beresford in Port Elizabeth

GOVAN MBEKI, the former national chairman of the outlawed African National Congress, was last night released under a pre-Christmas amnesty, after more than 23 years in gaol.

'They told me that I was being released without conditions,' said Mr Mbeki, declaring that he would continue to live in South Africa and would be retaining his membership of the outlawed South African Communist Party.

Mr Mbeki was taken off Robben Island, where he has served most of his sentence, to Cape Town's Pollsmoor prison, where he had an hour's meeting with the former president of the ANC, Nelson Mandela, before being formally released and flown to this coastal city.

6.11.87

Afrikaans paper demands Botha's resignation

David Beresford
in Johannesburg

The Afrikaans newspaper, Beeld, yesterday sounded what could prove to be the death knell of the political career of the State President, Mr PW Botha, with a direct appeal to him to retire.

'There is a time to come and there is a time to go,' the Transvaal daily declared, quoting a remark once made by South Africa's first National Party Prime Minister, Dr DF Malan.

Urging Mr Botha to reread his one-time mentor's words, Beeld said that Dr Malan's 'voice from the far past still has much to say to us all'.

It warned of the tragedy for Mr Botha if he were to become a divisive factor after many years of service to his country.

The rebellion against Mr Botha's continued leadership developing in the government-supporting press indicates that a startling momentum has built up among Nationalists for the so-called 'great crocodile' to stand down in favour of the new party leader, Mr FW de Klerk.

The odds against Mr Botha's being able to hang on to office in the wake of his stroke now appear to be considerable.

7.3.89

ANC unbanned; Mandela release 'imminent'; Townships rejoice; Death penalty halted; State of emergency continues

De Klerk heralds a new era

By David Beresford in Cape Town

SOUTH Africa's President, Mr FW de Klerk, took his country into a new political era yesterday with a package of sweeping reforms that earned plaudits from around the world.

The President, addressing the opening of parliament, announced the immediate unbanning of the African National Congress and said the government would release unconditionally Mr Nelson Mandela, the jailed ANC leader. He is expected to be freed within days, opening the way for negotiations.

'The time for talking has arrived,' said Mr De Klerk.

Spontaneous celebrations broke out in townships around the country as well as in the parliamentary capital itself, as blacks sang, danced and chanted in their excitement.

Some of the most outspoken critics of the government in the domestic anti-apartheid community reacted with incredulity to the sweep of Mr De Klerk's announcements. 'He has taken my breath away,' said Archbishop Desmond Tutu, the Nobel Prize winner.

'I'm surprised and encouraged,' said another anti-apartheid leader, Dr Allan Boesak.

The main initiative announced by Mr De Klerk aimed at facilitating negotiations is the unbanning of the ANC, the South African Communist Party, and the Pan Africanist Congress (PAC) and the lifting of restrictions on the activities of various domestic organisations.

Mr De Klerk did not announce an amnesty for political crimes, stressing instead that the lifting of the ban 'does not signify in the least the approval or condoning of terrorism or crimes of violence committed under their banner'.

But ministers insisted that the implication of the unbanning was that the exiled leaders of the organisations were free to return home immediately, including the ailing ANC president, Mr Oliver Tambo whom Mr De Klerk's predecessor, Mr PW Botha, once vowed to bring back 'in a cage' and put on trial.

Opponents of the government were yesterday critical of Mr De Klerk's failure to lift the state of emergency, although the authorities explained this as precautionary until the consequences of the reform moves have been assessed.

Mr De Klerk did announce the lifting of the emergency restrictions on the press, but this was seen as nominal. He is to reimpose the ban on television and photographic coverage of unrest, regarded as the main handicap to the media posed by the emergency regulations.

Newspapers have been using loopholes to circumvent the emergency restrictions and are anyway subject to control under other legislation.

The President also announced a moratorium on hangings, bringing new hope to 279 people on death row, including the Upington 14 condemned for a controversial 'necklace' burning and Barend Strydom, the rightwing extremist sentenced to death for gunning down eight blacks at random in Pretoria.

The ANC reacted to the news by announcing an urgent review of 'the new situation that has emerged'. The United Democratic Front, which has led the liberation struggle in South Africa, welcomed the 'boldness' of Mr De Klerk's moves, while cautioning that apartheid remains in place. Enthusiasm in the main liberation movement for the speech was qualified by fears it would result in the lifting of international pressure, robbing them of crucial leverage on Pretoria.

The smaller PAC reacted with complete hostility, however. In a statement issued in Dar es Salaam, it said: 'The reforms announced by De Klerk today are irrelevant and meaningless because apartheid cannot be reformed. We can only eliminate it.' Mr Mandela's wife, Winnie, was also strongly critical, saying: 'We are not going to accept a bone without any meat . . . The unbanning of the ANC, the South African Communist Party and the Pan-Africanist Congress in the prevailing South African climate is simply a recipe for further problems.'

Mr De Klerk's speech is expected to turn attention from the anti-apartheid struggle to the extreme right. The leader of the official opposition, Dr Andries Treurnicht, reacted strongly, demanding a general election.

However, the more immediate threat is likely to come from the lunatic fringe on the right, notably the neo-Nazi Afrikaner Weerstandsbeweging (AWB) whose leader, Mr Eugene TerreBlanche, reacted with fury yesterday to the De Klerk speech.

He said Mr De Klerk was 'handing over the government to the ANC and the communists', and that legalising the ANC would not lead to peace, but only to more conflict and eventually to revolution.

3.2.90

Mandela free after 27 years ● Appeal to black and white

'The struggle must go on'

By Roger Omond in Johannesburg

MR NELSON MANDELA walked out of prison a free man yesterday, and within hours told an ecstatic crowd of supporters in Cape Town that the armed struggle against apartheid would continue.

In his first public speech since he was jailed 27 years ago, the African National Congress leader said the guerrilla war launched in 1960 was 'a purely defensive action against the violence of apartheid. We have no option but to continue.' He added: 'Now is the time to intensify the struggle on all fronts. To relax our efforts now would be a mistake which generations to come will not be able to forgive.'

The 'immediate ending of the state of emergency and the freeing of all political prisoners' was necessary before negotiations with the government could start.

Addressing the international community, he said: 'To lift sanctions now would be to run the risk of aborting the process towards the complete eradication of apartheid.'

The rally in Cape Town came at the end of a dramatic day which earlier saw Mr Mandela walk to freedom through the gates of Victor Verster jail near Cape Town hand in hand with his wife, Winnie, to meet a waiting crowd of supporters and the ranks of the world's media.

He greeted the crowd with a clenched fist salute, then walked back to his car before leaving at the head of a long cavalcade for Cape Town along a route lined with emotional well-wishers.

Celebrations erupted throughout the country at the news of Mr Mandela's release. But in Cape Town police fired birdshot and rubber bullets to disperse parts of the crowd awaiting him after youths allegedly smashed windows and looted shops on the square.

Doctors worked by torchlight only 100 yards from where Mr Mandela spoke to treat scores of people with gunshot wounds and a South African Council of Churches spokesman said at least two were killed.

Elsewhere, residents said they had unconfirmed reports that police travelling in a car through Mdantsane township in the independent homeland of Ciskei shot dead three people among a crowd celebrating the release.

Police fired shotguns and teargas at a crowd of rejoicing blacks in the Duncan Village township outside East London, an Indian Ocean port bordering Ciskei, residents said.

Mr Mandela's speech was finely balanced between the demands of his largely black constituency and magnanimity towards whites and repeated hope for peace.

Mandela's first words to the cheering crowd contained a message of peace. 'I greet you all in the name of peace, democracy and freedom for all,' he said.

'I stand here before you not as a prophet, but as a humble servant of you, the people.' Thanking South African anti-apartheid groups and the world community for campaigning for his release, he urged that the struggle against apartheid had to be intensified on all fronts.

But almost immediately he expressed the hope than a climate could be created for negotiations so that the armed struggle would no longer be necessary.

And he made a special point of pleading with whites to join the struggle against apartheid. He paid tribute, too, to the President, Mr F. W. de Klerk, who had gone further than any other National Party president towards reaching settlement. But blacks were still suffering under the Nationalist government, he said.

Mr Mandela also denied that in his meetings with members of government he had begun negotiations.

There could be no negotiations above the head or behind the backs of the people.

Before Mr Mandela spoke, trouble began in central Cape Town when members of the crowd, estimated at up to 60,000, that had gathered to listen to him smashed the windows of a clothing store.

Reporters said that many looters appeared drunk.

Last night the United Democratic Front and other organisations concerned with Mr Mandela's release appealed for calm throughout the country.

Marshals tried to stop the looters who were on the edge of the crowd as the windows of the shop were broken and later tried to maintain order after the incident.

Mr Mandela's release from prison, due at 3pm, was delayed for 75 minutes.

By the time he should have left the gates of Victor Verster prison the Grand Parade was jammed with up to 60,000 people, said to be the largest crowd there since the second world war.

Similar crowds gathered at towns and cities throughout the country. The centre of Johannesburg, normally deserted on Sundays, was thronged with celebrating people. Traffic police patrol cars cleared the way for them.

In Soweto, the sprawling black township outside Johannesburg where Mr Mandela has his home, crowds of supporters danced and sang in celebration, many under umbrellas because of steady rain.

The Grand Parade, a traditional site for political protest meetings in the late 1950s and early 1960s, was decorated with a flag of the ANC. A huge banner with portraits of Mr Mandela hung from a balcony.

But Mr Mandela's first arrival at what should have been a historic rally turned into chaos when his motorcade ended up amid the crowd in front of the City Hall that faces on to the Parade. At times his car could not be seen behind a wall of people.

Half an hour later, after frantic appeals for people to move had failed, officials managed to get it free and it went towards what was then said to be a new rally site in District 6, an international by-word for apartheid in the 1960s when it was declared reserved for whites and thousands of its Coloured inhabitants moved out.

However, Mr Mandela later returned to the Grand Parade and the rally went ahead.

Mr Mandela's release was shown live on dozens of television channels around the world but South African viewers had to wait for some minutes before his appearance was broadcast.

Mrs Thatcher abruptly called off a press briefing she was due to give on the steps of Downing Street last night to hail Mr Mandela's freedom.

Downing Street denied the cancellation was because of Mr Mandela's call for the armed struggle and international sanctions to continue. It was said that she felt her earlier comments were sufficient.

12.2.90

Leaving Victor Verster prison,
Cape Town, February 11 1990

Flag falls on colonialism in Africa as Swapo leader sworn in as president

Joy and happy chaos as Namibia becomes free

**David Beresford
in Windhoek**

The flag was finally lowered on colonialism in Africa last night 18 minutes late, but with undiluted rejoicing from thousands of Namibians who packed a Windhoek sports stadium to celebrate the independence of their country from South Africa.

The delay in the formal hand-over of sovereignty was characteristic of the long-awaited independence celebrations, which were marked by amiable CHAOS coupled with high emotions.

There were ecstatic scenes as the South African flag was lowered to the sound of the Last Post, watched by Pretoria's President, F. W. De Klerk, hand over his heart and seemingly close to tears standing next to a beaming Sam Nujoma, the Swapo leader.

'(This is) the moment our people have been awaiting for more than a century . . . a day for which tens of thousands of Namibian patriots laid down their lives,' said Mr Nujoma after being sworn in as President exactly 24 years after he was arrested and deported from the country by the South African authorities, to begin his long war of liberation.

21.3.90

Swimming over the shoals of desegregation

Eyewitness
....

Phillip van Niekerk
in Johannesburg

THE first black tourist to visit the small town of Ermelo, 175 miles east of Johannesburg, sauntered into the town council offices this week looking for information. He was sent to the wrong office, but by the time he got back everyone had settled down.

'Welcome to Ermelo,' said the smiling publicity manager, taking it in his stride, handing the visitor a few brochures on drives and places of historic interest. 'I hope you enjoy your stay.' The tourist was Phil Molefe, a black reporter who was to play many roles as we tested the racism level in a randomly selected rural South African town.

Our first stop was the swimming baths. The Separate Amenities Act had just been scrapped and for the first time in decades, racially segregated public facilities were outlawed.

When we got there a small white boy in a swimming costume tried to bar our entrance. 'There is no swimming bath today,' he said. We brushed past and walked straight in. Unlike other public swimming baths in the Eastern Transvaal, no entrance charge had been introduced for 'non-residents' as a way of keeping blacks out.

The lifesaver, a burly man in his 20s, was in an extremely foul mood. While Phil splashed around on the edge of the pool he screamed angrily: 'Swim. De Klerk said you can swim.' Then, with sarcasm: 'I'll give you some soap to wash with.' We waved genially to the lifesaver on the way out. 'Thanks for leaving,' he said. In the car park a white-haired man with a walkie-talkie was writing down our number plate.

At the butcher's, three pot plants serve as a divider. Whites buy their meat on the left, blacks on the right. Phil bought a steak on the left side. An old woman buying her meat on the right side stifled a giggle and was warned by the woman behind the counter, in Afrikaans: 'You mustn't listen to those Mandelas.' When we left she came out to write down the registration number of the car, which belonged to the Weekly Mail. The next day the Weekly Mail managing director, Clive Cope, received a mysterious phone call threatening to kill him.

That night we visited the local pub. The room fell silent for a moment — Phil was the only black man in the bar — before the regulars went back to their pool game.

The waiter explained in Zulu that blacks sometimes got beaten up in this bar, so now they stay away. The white guys wait until you go to the toilet and then pummel you like putty, he said.

19.10.90

Apartheid dies as S Africa kills race classification

David Beresford

THE record books can now show that the race classification system which made South Africa the pariah of the world in the post-war era bit the dust at 2.55pm on Monday, June 17, 1991, when the parliament in Cape Town repealed the Population Registration Act.

But on a preliminary estimate the line-up was 89 votes in favour of repeal, with 38 against and 11 abstaining who probably did not. Which is not to forget the Coloureds who backed the majority with apparent unanimity, or the Indians, who did likewise – the blacks, needless to say, being allowed no say in the matter at all.

Nevertheless, it was enough for the State President, FW de Klerk, to declare that the votes had 'finally brought an end to an era in which the lives of every South African were affected in the minutest detail by racially-based legislation'.

Apartheid 'now belongs to history', he told the country's tricameral Parliament. 'And everybody is liberated from the moral dilemma caused by this legislation, which was born and nurtured under different circumstances in a departed era.' There may be cynics who argue that the declaration is premature – pointing, for instance, to the small print of the 'Repeal Bill' which stipulates that 'the population register as compiled' remains in force until the constitution as a whole is repealed. For the time being, it appears, apartheid is only dead for babes and sucklings.

18.6.91

councils controlled by the Conservative Party, where they can govern themselves, provided they do not appropriate the whole white tax base, leaving dormitory black townships to rot in their poverty, or reintroduce apartheid practices and white hegemony.

Within that framework, they can govern themselves, that is, until economic realities force them back into mainstream South Africa. Two events in March altered the balance of force in South Africa. Early on Friday, March 11, a convoy of vehicles packed with members of Eugene TerreBlanche's Afrikaner Resistance Movement (AWB), drove into Mmabatho, capital of the Bophuthatswana homeland, to rescue President Lucas Mangope from striking civil servants, who had not only brought the territory almost to a standstill, but also had drawn in the support of ANC followers and defectors from the police force and army.

No better than a mob, ignorant and racially arrogant, TerreBlanche's ridiculous army thought they were the US cavalry. But what they had not expected was that the Bophuthatswana police and soldiery would turn against them and unceremoniously kick them out of town. They left, with the newly arrived South African Defence Force to escort them.

However, when shots appeared to be fired from the last car in their convoy, a red Mercedes, Bophuthatswana soldiers fired back, killing one occupant instantly and wounding two others. The wounded men crawled out of the car, one begging for medical aid for his wounded friend. Then a Bophuthatswana soldier pushed through the crowd and pumped six shots into the three bodies — a formal, almost ritualistic, execution. He has since been arrested on a charge of murder.

The executions seared through the white rightwing. Safely across the Transvaal border, TerreBlanche's brandy-and-coke brigade swore terrible vengeance, but the trauma could not be concealed. Afrikanerdom was in shock. The rout had immediate consequences.

Mangope was deposed by Pretoria (an act of *force majeure* without any pretence at constitutionality) and, following the Ciskei's earlier default, the

Ramaphosa devastates opposition to win key job of secretary-general

Union leader emerges as man to watch in ANC

David Beresford
in Durban

SOUTH AFRICA'S mineworkers' leader, Cyril Ramaphosa, yesterday emerged as a leading candidate for the future leadership of South Africa when he was elected secretary-general of the African National Congress.

His appointment was seen as the most significant outcome of leadership elections at the ANC's national conference, in which Nelson Mandela was confirmed as president and his Rivonia co-accused, Albert Sisulu, deputy president. The outgoing president, Oliver Tambo, was made chairman.

Mr Ramaphosa's triumph at the ANC conference in Durban was overwhelming. He defeated the organisation's head of intelligence, Jacob Zuma, by 1,156 votes to 450. The former secretary-general, Alfred Nzo, trailed in third with 371 votes.

The election of the 39-year-old trade unionist and lawyer reflects impatience among more than 2,000 delegates attending the conference at the 'Old Guard' which led the ANC while in exile. It could well prove a turning point in South African politics.

At the same time, Mr Ramaphosa's election may fuel a simmering controversy over the alliance between the ANC and the South African Communist Party. Mr Ramaphosa, general secretary of the National Union of Mineworkers – the largest single union on the African continent – is widely believed to be an undeclared communist. His victory in yesterday's election is likely to be seen in some quarters as the outcome of a communist strategy aimed at placing one of their number within striking distance of national leadership.

6.7.91

Pretoria frees criminals in amnesty deal

Patrick Laurence
in Johannesburg

THE South American government is releasing thousands of criminals to avoid a dispute over the definition of a political prisoner, the Human Rights Commission alleged yesterday.

Max Coleman of the HRC calculated yesterday that 50,000 prisoners had been released since December last year, each release being timed to coincide with critical stages on the political agenda.

Viewing the releases as a whole the HRC said: 'There can be no doubt that a substantial number of unidentified political prisoners have walked free, perhaps as many as 2,000. But at the same time so have a huge number of criminal prisoners. Perhaps as many as 50,000 (will be freed) by the time the process has run its course.' The freed criminals included two policemen, Jack la Grange and Robert van der Merwe, who were each given a double death sentence in 1988 for killing two drug dealers.

Included in the latest releases were 15 ANC guerrillas, all of whom were convicted of murder for their actions as combatants in the ANC's armed struggle.

12.7.91

Sweeping SA vote for reform

Even Afrikaners support De Klerk

David Beresford
in Johannesburg

SOUTH Africans on both sides of the racial and political divides were stunned last night by the size of the 'yes' victory in the country's referendum, which seemed set to propel it into an early power-sharing administration.

As congratulations poured in from around the world, South Africans themselves were trying to make sense of the result which went beyond the wildest dreams of anti-apartheid activists.

European leaders expressed unrestrained delight. Ruud Lubbers, prime minister of the Netherlands, ancestral home of Afrikaners, said simply that the result was 'beautiful'. The Foreign Secretary, Douglas Hurd, echoed many when he said: 'I think a 'No' vote would have thrown South Africa right back into deep trouble in the world and at home.' The man who presided over the triumph, President F. W. de Klerk, said he had been confident of victory, but one 'nowhere near' the margin which had emerged.

Mr De Klerk, who celebrated his 56th birthday yesterday, confirmed that he saw the poll as the last whites-only vote in South Africa, although he added: 'If we have obstacles (with negotiations), then obviously I will somehow or another go back to the electorate.' Final figures showed there had been a 68.6 per cent 'yes' – 1,924,186 votes against 875,619 – in an 85.08 per cent turnout of the white electorate.

Analysts estimated that 62 per cent of Afrikaners participating voted 'yes', and 79 per cent of English-speakers.

There was some apparent concern in other quarters at the enhanced standing which his referendum victory might give to the president. The general secretary of the South African Council of Churches, the Rev. Dr Frank Chikane, called on the international community 'to remain vigilant against giving an advantage to De Klerk and his National Party against the victims of apartheid'.

The ANC leader, Nelson Mandela, said it was a mandate for the negotiators to expedite an interim government that would make way for a constituent assembly. 'Ending apartheid is not just announcing the result of a referendum. It means there should be enough houses, more medical facilities and better pensions for blacks. We are still far from this point. Above all, I still cannot vote in my own country. But the 'yes' vote means that whites are now prepared to address these problems,' he said.

19.3.92

Massacre wrecks hopes of peace

David Beresford in Johannesburg and Agencies

THE South African peace process was torpedoed by a massacre again yesterday, when soldiers in the Ciskei homeland opened fire on tens of thousands of African National Congress demonstrators marching on the capital to oust the Ciskei ruler, Brigadier Joshua 'Oupa' Gqozo. When the dust cleared at least 28 were dead and 190 injured.

Hopes of a resumption of the stalled peace negotiations between the ANC and the government of President F. W. de Klerk appeared in tatters last night as each side blamed the other for the massacre.

'It's impossible to negotiate with these people because they don't stick to agreements . . . We must study if we can continue negotiations with the ANC-Communist Party alliance,' South Africa's foreign minister, Pik Botha, said.

The ANC accused the South African government of complicity in the killings.

'We are blaming the De Klerk regime... We do not intend to respond meekly to this atrocity,' an angry ANC secretary-general, Cyril Ramaphosa told a news conference.

Mr De Klerk announced that South African security forces had been sent to the Ciskei capital, Bisho, to maintain order.

Ciskei troops poured two bursts of automatic fire into a crowd of about 70,000 ANC supporters who had marched on Bisho. The first fusillade lasted for six minutes, then there was a pause followed by another five-minute burst of shooting, it was reported. Bodies lay scattered in pools of blood along the line of razor wire erected to contain the march.

No ambulances came to help the injured, some frighteningly still and others writhing in pain. Instead, private cars came and went with wounded people bundled into open boots and bleeding limbs drooping from open doors.

8.9.92

Ramaphosa warns summit failure would be disastrous

ANC risks talks with De Klerk

David Beresford in Johannesburg

THE stalemate between the South African government and the African National Congress appeared to have been broken last night with the unexpected announcement by the ANC that it was accepting President F. W. de Klerk's invitation to talks about the current level of violence in the country.

The decision represents a volte face on the part of the ANC, which had adopted a hitherto resolute policy of no talks with the government following the Boipatong massacre on June 17. But this week's Ciskei massacre, in which the known death toll rose yesterday by one to 29, appears to have prompted a high risk strategy.

At the same time the ANC warned that the talks about violence would have to be carefully prepared and produce results, otherwise the country would be hurled irretrievably backwards.

The ANC secretary-general, Cyril Ramaphosa, told a Johannesburg press conference that 'the ANC is prepared to participate in a summit,' but he added that 'it would be a disaster for the country as a whole if it failed to produce concrete results'.

He also said that the ANC leadership remained convinced that 'the complicity of the South African government and the South African Defence Force' in the 'premeditated' massacre in the Ciskei 'will come out'.

That view was echoed by the United Nations Security Council which said in a statement that it deplored the Ciskei killings carried out by what it described as 'security elements in South Africa'.

11.9.92

Winnie Mandela quits ANC leadership posts

David Beresford
in Johannesburg

WINNIE MANDELA has finally bowed out of the South African political arena, resigning all her leadership positions in the ANC with a characteristically emotional outburst at her 'enemies' inside and outside the organisation.

Her capitulation follows publication in the South African press earlier this week of a passionate letter to a young lover, which appeared to indicate maladministration of funds in the ANC's social welfare department which she headed.

In a statement issued overnight the one-time 'mother of the nation' said she was giving up her seat on the ANC's national executive and the national and regional executive committees of the Women's League. In what appears to be a bitter gesture towards female members of the ANC for their part in her downfall, she also withdrew her membership of the Women's League, while declaring she remained a 'loyal' member of the ANC.

11.9.92

De Klerk says sorry for sins of apartheid

David Beresford in Johannesburg

SOUTH AFRICA'S president, F. W. de Klerk, teetered yesterday on the edge of an historic apology for apartheid, but in a manner which is likely to have critics chorusing that 'a miss is as good as a mile'.

In the small Orange Free State town of Winburg, the National Party leader declared: 'For too long we clung to a dream of separated nation states, when it was already clear that it could not succeed sufficiently. For that we are sorry.' He conceded: 'Yes, we have made mistakes. Yes, we have often sinned and we do not deny this. But that we were evil, malignant and mean — to that we say no.' The issue of whether he should follow the lead of Afrikaans church leaders in denouncing apartheid as a sin and a 'heresy' has become something of an ordeal for President De Klerk, whose father, as a cabinet minister, introduced some of the uglier apartheid laws.

10.10.92

Businesslike communist puts socialism on hold

Chris Hani, the former guerrilla and Pretoria's worst nightmare, talks to **Victoria Brittain**

AS THE most popular figure in South Africa after Nelson Mandela, and as leader of the country's second most popular party, Chris Hani, secretary-general of the South African Communist Party, holds many of the keys to the shape of transition there.

In the see-sawing negotiations, the SACP has been the source of some of the most important concessions offered by the ANC, and of the government's worst nightmares. Mr Hani embodies the nightmare. He is a scholar of Latin and English literature, was once a lawyer and, as a boy, thought of becoming a Catholic priest.

His long-term goal of a socialist South Africa has not changed in 30 years.

'Our ideal is a socialist society – that is the apex of our struggle. But for the moment we are struggling for the Freedom Charter. It is the first step towards empowerment of our people,' he says.

High among Mr Hani's priorities is a pact involving big business and the unions in plans to provide housing, a revamped free education system, clean water and a huge public works programme to mop up unemployment.

Redistribution must go alongside economic growth, he believes. 'I'm not just an idealist. Socialism is the best and most cohesive system for South Africa – we are a third world country,' he says.

Although the ANC's public image has moved far from socialism since its leaders were released from jail or returned from exile to begin negotiations with the government, Mr Hani believes there are still many socialists in the ANC. He also thinks the alliance between the ANC, SACP and Confederation of South African Trade Unions has a long life ahead of it.

Mr Hani credits Joe Slovo, his predecessor as SACP leader, with having opened 'the debate on the nature and form of compromise'. Debate and democracy within the SACP are part of Mr Slovo's contribution to the party, which has influ-ence far beyond its 50,000 members.

As a veteran of the guerrilla war, as Mr Slovo was, Mr Hani knows what would happen if negotiations failed. 'It is crucial that the process is not allowed to slow down. We're facing a regime which, for all its deep crises, has not been defeated. The powers of the security forces are intact and their strategy is destabilising us by low-intensity warfare. The state orchestration of violence is indisputable.' The failed election in Angola and the evidence of 'elements of the South African army lurking there' as the war took hold late last year, have increased the need for the army effectively to be controlled during the transition, he says.

No one, however, is going to have the chance similarly to disrupt South Africa's elections, he believes. 'We have the advantage of sophisticated communications and we can therefore use our only weapon – our people – and paralyse the economy.' Mr Hani, the ANC's top military commander before being elected as SACP secretary-general in December 1991, was a guerrilla leader in Umkhonto we Sizwe's Angolan camps for three years in the 1980s.

Some of the heroic stature accorded to him in the townships stems from his reputation then as an officer who lived in the tough conditions of remote camps, and faced death in Unita ambushes. And in Umkhonto we Sizwe's greatest crisis, in 1984, when mutineers killed their officers and took over the camp at Vianna, it was Mr Hani who went in unarmed and persuaded the dissidents to accept his authority.

Although the ringleaders were arrested by the Angolan army, Mr Hani is generally credited with the reconciliation which followed, and which gave a foretaste of the ANC approach to the present talks. 'We're not planning any Nuremberg trials, although they locked up our leaders, tried to eliminate so many of us in the cross-border operations. Look at Comrade Slovo; he sits there talking to the men who killed his wife.' He is matter of fact about the two assassination attempts he survived, and places the ANC's detentions and torture in the camps – which an ANC report has confirmed – in the context of 'fighting a neo-fascist enemy prepared to use anybody and any methods'. He says the ANC has admitted wrongs were done 'but we could have been destroyed if we hadn't taken certain measures'.

15.2.93

ANC struggles to control Hani Backlash

**By David Beresford
in Johannesburg**

THE African National Congress yesterday battled to contain a township backlash against the assassination of Chris Hani, but the violence seemed in danger of escalating as the Easter holiday came to an end.

A huge march was expected today to the town of Boksburg, east of Johannesburg, to mark the appearance in court of Janusz Jakub Walus, the Polish immigrant, aged 40, accused of murdering the ANC and Communist Party (SACP) leader.

The neo-Nazi leader, Eugene Terreblanche, yesterday confirmed that Mr Walus was a member of the Afrikaner Weerstandsbeweging (AWB), which he joined in 1986.

But Mr Terreblanche said the killer had acted alone. 'We (the AWB) did not give any instructions to do such a deed. I condemned the deed the day that it happened,' he told the BBC.

A third white man died of his injuries after a racial attack in the Cape on Sunday. Two whites were burned to death in the township of Lwandle, near Cape Town. The third, who had part of his tongue cut out as well as being burned, died in hospital yesterday. Police described the attack as a reaction to the Hani killing.

Suspicions that the assassination was part of a rightwing conspiracy were fuelled by the disclosure that the murder weapon was part of a haul stolen by extremists in a raid on a South African air force arsenal in 1990. It also emerged that Mr Walus had police licences for four other guns.

13.4.93

Left: **Chris Hani, former commander of the ANC's military wing and secretary-general of the South African Communist Party, shortly before his assassination in 1993**

Right: **Legal at last! Whites learn to share desegregated beaches in Durban, 1989**

umbrella Freedom Alliance found itself with two of its three black homeland props knocked from under it. General Viljoen resigned from the AVF and the Freedom Alliance, confirmed the registration of his new Freedom Front as a participant in the elections, and took with him at least seven Conservative Party MPs, including the powerful presidents of the Transvaal and Free State agricultural unions, and most of the CP's Natal executive.

Already reduced to less than half a *volk*, Afrikanerdom had split even further. But the real blow that was struck in Mmabatho was at the rightwing's self-confidence — its inner conviction that the Afrikaner dream could survive in some bizarre shape or other. Stricken though it is, the white right in South Africa should not be underestimated.

As Professor Welsh warns: "A thwarted, frustrated right, who are prepared to take up arms, can do untold damage. When you think that the IRA and the Provisional IRA between them probably have no more than about 500 activists, and you look at what they have been able to do, it's very frightening indeed."

Particularly since last year, the right have been preparing seriously for war. The police estimate that the AWB can muster 15,000 armed men; then there are some 200 para-military groups, most of them small and unimportant but about six classified by the police as "dangerous"; the commando arm of the SA Defence Force (largely a rural militia) numbers some 130,000 men, of whom about 100,000 (according to the AVF) are rightwing sympathisers and even activists; an estimated 80 to 95 per cent of policemen and 70 to 80 per cent of soldiers are right-inclined.

Eighty-seven town councils in three of South Africa's four provinces want to retain racially segregated local government structures; plans exist for 98 forms of resistance to be put into practice, ranging from non-payment of taxes and other forms of civil disobedience to industrial sabotage and the establishment of a *volkstaat* through violent secession.

Not all of this falls away just because of the Mmabatho fiasco. Much of the rightwing's success will depend on the prevailing mood in Afrikanerdom. Mmabatho helped to dampen that mood, and when Judge Richard Goldstone

'Unless everyone understood who was white and who was not, and was reminded daily, in the smallest detail, that white survival depended on separation, the system could not be hermetically sealed, and could not work'

De Klerk implicated in cover-up of army intelligence death squad

The South African leader allegedly promised not to allow a witch-hunt over 'good faith' murders, writes **David Beresford** in Johannesburg

SOUTH Africa's state president, F. W. de Klerk, was personally drawn into the country's military intelligence scandal at the weekend following the disclosure that he gave assurances to the defence force there would be 'no witch-hunt' into the activities of a murder squad they ran.

The state president's office issued a defensive statement on the issue yesterday, saying that Mr de Klerk was concerned that all 'wrongdoing' should be exposed. But it notably failed to answer the charge.

The suggestion that President de Klerk was party to a cover-up emerged from evidence given in camera at hearings last week into the 1989 assassination of the anti-apartheid activist and academic, Dr David Webster. Testimony heard behind closed doors from Joe Verster – the former head of the notorious murder unit, the Civil Co-operation Bureau – was released to the local press at the weekend.

His evidence painted a bizarre picture of relations between staff of military intelligence. At one stage, he claimed, the then head of MI, General Rudolph 'Witkop' Badenhorst, beat him up for failing to 'play along' in a cover-up of Dr Webster's murder. At another stage he reported to the minister of defence, General Magnus Malan, his belief that a former member of the CCB, Ferdi Barnard, killed Dr Webster. But Gen Malan allegedly took no action.

Mr Verster, who is busy preparing a multi-million rand legal case against the government for failing to give him and his fellow assassins an adequate redundancy settlement, said President de Klerk's assurances had been given to the then chief of the South African defence force, General Jannie Geldenhuys, in January 1990. Mr Verster said the general had quoted the president to him as saying that 'he accepted that everything we (the CCB) did was in good faith and – those were his words – he was not planning a witch-hunt …

23.11.92

Transition deal agreed

By David Beresford in Johannesburg

THE South African government said yesterday it had reached final agreement with the ANC that the country will be run by an entrenched government of national unity for five years after a final constitutional settlement.

But Nelson Mandela said last night there were 'still major problems' arising from government demands for minority vetoes in the power-sharing administration and the dilution of the sovereignty of a future parliament.

'It's not a proposal, it's a fact,' the deputy minister of constitutional development, Fanus Schoeman, said of the deal after three days of secret talks between the two sides.

'We see it as a five-year period, the ANC sees it as a five-year period. It will continue to be a government of national unity for the full five years.' Proposals for a five-year deal on an extended government of national unity were thrashed out as a substitute for permanent power-sharing, which the government had been seeking.

Representation in the executive would be based on the proportion of votes received by the major political parties in a general election for a constituent assembly — which is to draw up the final constitution as well as acting as parliament. But in a television interview yesterday, Mr Mandela said the government was demanding a form of interim power-sharing 'which we cannot accept'.

He said the government was insisting that all political parties be given the same say, no matter what their size.

The ANC president said: 'Our idea of an interim government of national unity is that it should be based on the principle that a party which emerges as the strongest in a general election should form the government.

'But we believe that the problems of our country can only be properly addressed if the majority party invites other parties to join the government of its free will, not because it is forced by the constitution.' The ANC was also demanding 'an elected and sovereign' constituent assembly.

23.2.93

S African Generals form group to fight black rule

David Beresford in Johannesburg

FORMER commanders of the South African military and police have secretly set up a self-styled 'Committee of Generals' to lead resistance to Pretoria's handover to majority rule.

The committee includes some of the most notorious rightwing figures in the security forces during the apartheid era. Their inaugural meeting was also attended by politicians, including at least two MPs from the rightwing Conservative Party.

Among the former security force commanders on the five-man committee are General Lothar Neethling, who has been accused of supplying hit squads with poison for use against anti-apartheid activists; Lieutenant-General Tienie Groe-newald, a controversial former chief of staff of military intelligence, and General Constand Viljoen, former commander-in-chief of South Africa's armed forces.

The committee was established at a meeting at Silverton, near Johannesburg, on April 21 - the day after the assassination of the general secretary of the South African Communist Party, Chris Hani. A Conservative Party MP, Clive Derby-Lewis, is among those being held in connection with the murder, which police are blaming on a rightwing conspiracy.

There are fears that the formation of the committee heralds a move towards rightwing extra-parliamentary action and unity behind the generals. The death last week of the leader of the Conservative Party, Andries Treurnicht, has left a leadership vacuum.

30.4.93

issued his 100-page report on March 18 naming three top policemen as supplying arms to Inkatha to disrupt the elections and destabilise the ANC, it seemed that a further dampener might be placed on Afrikaner passions.

But at the time of writing, the omens were not auspicious. The policemen, supported by their Commissioner, General Johan van der Merwe, are toughing it out. In Natal, Chief Buthelezi blithely disclaims all knowledge of arms supplies to Inkatha, and war preparations are proceeding among both Inkatha and ANC supporters. A meeting of Inkatha's central committee on the day after publication of the Goldstone commission's report rejected a peace offer by De Klerk — that Inkatha should contest the elections under the banner of De Klerk's National Party.

If Buthelezi's Zulu warriors had been chastened by the knowledge that their connections with the police had been flushed out, 1,500 of them, many armed with AK47 assault rifles, would not have taken occupation of a stadium near Durban on March 20 which had been booked by the ANC for a rally. Buthelezi describes the existing situation in Natal as "low intensity warfare", and various experts on the ground confirm either that the war has started or that it can no longer be avoided.

If Buthelezi remains intransigent and Inkatha continues to try to wreck the elections in Natal, the white right in the Transvaal and Free State could take heart again and swing back into action. This in turn could lift the flagging spirits of white conservatives, and the whole mood of Afrikanerdom could change.

Peace, therefore, is not balanced on a knife edge in South Africa, as some would claim. Parts of Natal and the southern Transvaal have been killing fields for a long time now. Since 1984, when political violence began in earnest, more than 18,000 people, mostly black, have died. South Africa still waits to see whether the scale of violence will increase. Can it be contained, or is Natal plunging into a civil war?

Stanley Uys was formerly the Guardian's South Africa correspondent

Gunmen slay 10 on eve of crucial South African political meeting

Massacre in the church

David Beresford in Johannesburg

SOUTH AFRICA'S president, FW de Klerk, was facing his most serious crisis to date in his efforts to negotiate a political settlement following the massacre of 10 worshippers during an Anglican church service in Cape Town last night.

Gunmen threw hand-grenades and sprayed automatic rifle fire during a service in Kenilworth, an affluent and picturesque suburb inhabited mainly by whites. At least 53 church-goers were reported to have been injured, 11 of them seriously.

The attack came the night before black and white political parties planned to unveil a preliminary draft of a new, post-apartheid constitution in Johannesburg.

A Briton attending the service at the St James Church, Martin Wortley, told the Guardian last night that he saw one of the attacke rs, masked with a balaclava, rush in through a side door and hurl two objects into the congregation before running out again.

"I ducked down behind the pew and my wife followed me. Then we heard bangs and then gunshots as well," he said. "It was so quick – five seconds, maximum."

There were about 1,000 people inside the church when the attack took place – the majority whites, but including several hundred "coloureds".

The minister of law and order, Hernus Kriel, denounced the massacre as one of the most shocking and callous crimes South Africa had yet seen.

Responsibility for the killings was not clear last night. The modus operandi would make the militant Pan Africanist Congress – which has carried out random attacks on whites in the area before – the prime suspect. Others with the demonstrable ruthlessness and a possible motive for such an attack are rightwing extremists and possibly dissident elements of the security forces. The attack is likely to provoke a particularly strong backlash among whites.

Mr De Klerk can be expected to push ahead with today's crucial negotiations, but the massacre will compound serious tensions already existing within the ruling National Party.

26.7.93

Mandela kills off sanctions:

Nations rush to aid stricken economy

**Mark Tran in New York and
David Beresford in Johannesburg**

THE international community rushed to lift sanctions against South Africa yesterday as Nelson Mandela told the world: "Our common victory against the only system to be declared a crime against humanity since the defeat of Nazism is in sight."

Speaking in the United Nations General Assembly, at an extraordinary meeting of the special committee against apartheid, the leader of the African National Congress said it was time to end the economic sanctions "which have brought us to the point where the transition to democracy has now been enshrined in the law of our country".

President Bill Clinton responded yesterday that the United States would take "steps necessary to permit lending to South Africa from the International Monetary Fund". In a written statement, he said: "We must now respect the judgement of the leaders of South Africa and move to lift our remaining sanctions."

Mr Mandela is to hold talks with IMF and World Bank officials today, after president FW de Klerk's visits yesterday.

While many sanctions imposed by the US congress in the teeth of the Reagan administration were lifted by president George Bush, the US has blocked South African access to multilateral lending bodies.

Yesterday, the US immediately approved legislation lifting remaining government economic sanctions. Mr Clinton also urged state and local governments to end their boycotts.

The Commonwealth announced it would begin lifting its remaining economic sanctions. Its secretary-general, Chief Emeka Anyaoku, said in a statement: "The lifting of these sanctions confirms the beginning of a new relationship between the Commonwealth and South Africa, a country that is now irreversibly committed to joining the community of democratic nations."

25.9.93

S African deal clears way for majority

David Beresford in Johannesburg

SOUTH AFRICA'S political leaders last night approved a new constitution, clearing the way for a handover to majority rule after a non-racial election scheduled for April 27.

Endorsement of the interim constitution was made possible by last-minute deals between the African National Congress and the government, including the De Klerk administration's abandoning demands for minority vetoes in cabinet.

'Let us join hands and march into the future,' the ANC leader, Nelson Mandela, told a late-night plenary session of the multi-party constitutional talks. 'We have reached the end of an era. We are at the beginning of a new era.' Switching to Afrikaans, Mr Mandela made a special appeal to rightwing Afrikanerdom to join in the democratic process. 'You have the fullest right to your own language, religion and culture. These rights will never be taken away from you,' he said.

President F. W. de Klerk said the document was 'the product of compromise'.

But he added: 'It satisfies all of us sufficiently to meet our most pressing concerns and hopes.' The plenary finally began shortly before midnight, hours later than scheduled.

18.11.93

Killings highlight SA police inertia

**David Beresford
in Johannesburg**

THE inability of the South African police to deal with political crime was underlined at the weekend as ridicule was heaped on them for their inept handling of Friday's invasion of Johannesburg's World Trade Centre, where the multi-party negotiations were taking place.

By yesterday no apparent action had been taken against rightwingers for crimes including assault on delegates and public violence. This was despite the fact that the attack – in which an armoured van was used to smash through a glass facade — was witnessed and filmed by police.

Police spokesmen forlornly explained they were having difficulty tracing the perpetrators because they had given false names and addresses and used false registration plates.

26.8.93

Shock return to politics for Mrs Mandela

David Beresford in Cape Town

WINNIE MANDELA made a surprise return to South African politics yesterday when she was elected president of the ANC Women's League, re-establishing her power base in the liberation movement.

The election of Nelson Mandela's estranged wife should gain her a seat in next year's parliament and put her in line for the cabinet.

Mrs Mandela was elected president by 392 votes out of 560.

9.12.93

Mandela is first among equals

THERE can hardly be a more fitting recipient of yesterday's honour than the African National Congress leader. His efforts have stopped the peace process from being derailed, as in the aftermath of the murder of Chris Hani. But on the other side of the scale stands a man whose commitment to principle has been of strikingly shorter duration, writes David Beresford

One of the most notable aspects of yesterday's award of the Nobel peace prize to Nelson Mandela and president FW de Klerk is that they are among four South Africans who have received the accolade since the war. Mr Mandela is the second leader of the African National Congress to take it, following Albert Luthuli in 1960. Add to that the 1984 award to Archbishop Desmond Tutu, who identified with the ANC, and the liberation movement can be said to have enjoyed unparalleled honour at the hands of the Norwegians.

More difficult to swallow, perhaps, is the fact that a man with Mr De Klerk's background, as at least a satrap of the apartheid state, should now be given equal status with the leader of the fellow countrymen whom he and his ilk disenfranchised and oppressed.

On precedent there are no grounds for quarrelling with the award to Mr De Klerk; the obvious precedents of course being Henry Kissinger in 1973 and Menachem Begin in 1978. But the coupling of the state president with the man who has every chance of succeeding him in little more than six months time poses an obvious question about their respective contributions to the peace process in South Africa.

Where Mr Mandela is concerned the only grounds for complaint against the Norwegians is that it has taken them so long to make the award, because it was in 1986 that the South African peace process got under way, with the initial, exploratory, meetings between top government officials and Mr Mandela in prison.

The flavour of those early negotiations, particularly Mr Mandela's role, is conveyed by a crucial letter which the ANC leader wrote to the new president, Mr De Klerk, in 1989. A document which deserves a place in South African history alongside his famous speech from the dock at the Rivonia trial, it opens with the statement that the time had come, in the face of the growing crisis of legitimacy, for the ANC and the government "to negotiate an effective political settlement".

Mr Mandela went on — with an observation which underlines the political courage he was showing in pursuing the initiative — by pointing out that, in the circumstances of imprisonment, he could not consult the ANC. "I am acting on my own initiative, in the hope that the organisation will endorse my action," he said.

There followed a typically uncompromising statement of political principle, in the course of which he flatly rejected government demands that the ANC abandon its alliance with the South African Communist Party. "No self-respecting freedom fighter will take orders from the government…

"on who his allies in the freedom struggle should be," he said.

But, underneath the declarations of principles, ran a conciliatory message.

The introduction of a non-racial society was "the only way in which our rich and beautiful country will be saved," Mr Mandela told Mr De Klerk. But it could only be done on the basis of reconciliation - a reconciliation between "the demand for majority rule in a unitary state" and "the insistence of whites on structural guarantees that majority rule will not mean domination of the white majority by blacks".

"Such reconciliation will be achieved only if both parties are willing to compromise," he added. "I must point out that the move I have taken provides you with the opportunity to overcome the current deadlock and to normalise the country's political situation. I hope you will seize it without delay. I believe the overwhelming majority of South Africans, black and white, hope to see the ANC and the government working closely together to lay the foundations for a new era in our country, in which racial discrimination and prejudice, coercion and confrontation, death and destruction will be forgotten."

It was an offer Mr De Klerk seized, and to which Mr Mandela has remained faithful. Mr Mandela has had an extraordinary career, and still has a pivotal role to play in the country's future. Taking into account the unbending stand on principle that led to his incarceration for more than a quarter of a century, his personal role in brokering negotiations between the state and the black majority and his courageous defence of compromise since his release from prison, there can hardly be a more fitting recipient of yesterday's honour.

On the other side of the scale stands a man whose commitment to principle has been of strikingly shorter duration – dating back only to his succession to the presidency.

Mr De Klerk's role in the negotiating process has been vital; in dealing with potentially recalcitrant Afrikanerdom he has walked a tight-rope with a level-headedness and courage for which the country owes him gratitude. He presided over the army's withdrawal from Namibia as well as a substantial winding down of the most powerful military force on the continent.

But at the same time he has the appearance of a man who has been swept up — if gloriously — by a tide of history. Which is why one feels at least some regret at yesterday's joint award. Should the world's greatest honour go to those who, thanks to the quirks of time and diplomacy, find themselves cast in a role as saviours? Or should it be designed to foster individual courage and principle of a kind testifying to a quality in humanity which gives hope to mankind?

16.10.93

Militant youths rebel in the streets against deals struck at the table

The prospect of free elections fails to impress young blacks **Bill Keller** in Guguletu writes

"I CAN leave you here and go away,' Victor Mdekazi told a white guest in this black township of Cape Town. 'When I come back I will find you so-o-o-o much in blood.' He sat around the corner from the petrol station where Amy Biehl, an American Fulbright scholar, was knifed to death in August by a mob of young men for being a white in the wrong place.

Mr Mdekazi, aged 18, an organiser for a black nationalist student body, intended no threat. He was offering instruction on an unpredictable factor of South African politics: the mood of marginalised young blacks.

They are spirits hardened by apartheid and resistance. They scorn deals made in their name, and anticipate the country's first free elections with cynicism or inflated expectations. Even their leaders wonder if they can be led.

'We've got to be realistic and honest here,' said Tsietsi Telite, the chairman of the Pan-Africanist Student Organisation. 'That hatred, you grow up, it develops within you. It needs much political education to give it direction.' For township militants, the trial of seven local youngsters for the killing of Ms Biehl — two of whom were freed after a witness said he was too terrified to testify — offers an opportunity to demonstrate rejection of white authority.

At the courthouse in central Cape Town, they toyi-toyi outside the police hedge of razor wire, chanting 'One settler, one bullet,' and hissing 'Settler!' at passing white journalists. The consensus is that Ms Biehl was at fault for coming where she was not wanted, and that the white courts have no right to judge the accused.

The death has become part of community lore. 'It's the whole country, it's not only the few children,' said Wowo Nofemela, whose son Mzikhona, aged 22, is one of those on trial. 'The environment is not right.' Impoverished rural workseekers have exhausted Guguletu's meagre resources.

Blocks of tiny homes have been swamped by squatter shacks, muddy warrens of smoke-stained sheds.

While Mr Nofemela defers to whites, his children do not. 'Our parents, they are cowards for the boer,' said Linda Mayekiso, aged 21, Mzikhona's girlfriend and, like him, a Pan-Africanist. 'The youth are not scared, and they have power.' Besides, she added, the adults had jobs to safeguard, however poorly paid, whereas the young had nothing to lose.

Militant youth leaders say they discourage racial hatred by avoiding the word 'white', and describing the enemy as 'settlers' or 'oppressors'. But such distinctions are often lost on the streets.

'You see a car of white people,' said Simphewe Mfengu, aged 19. 'You can't define, is it an American or what, is it an oppressor or what?' Mr Mdekazi added: 'There are people living in squatter camps; even if Joe Slovo (the chairman of the Communist Party) goes to that squatter camp, they will kill him.' As the apartheid barriers erode, familiarity breeds more resentment. Vusumzi Noge, who transferred this year to a newly integrated school in the white suburb of Mowbray, described his anger at seeing libraries and laboratories unimaginable in Guguletu.

He responded to the snubs of white students with defiance. 'I don't care, because it's not their land, it's our land.' The prospect of free elections has not diminished the bitterness of the young. 'It's going to get worse, because each and everybody, they have got visions,' said Martha Holobo, aged 23, who runs a fruit stall near a squatter camp. 'People think freedom means they will all move to the rich houses in Mowbray, and the whites in Mowbray will move here.' The African National Congress president, Nelson Mandela, has sought to dampen such dreams. The Pan-Africanists encourage them as a birthright.

Whatever support young blacks offer a new president will be conditional. 'As long as it's an African, we are going to respect him,' Ms Mayekiso said. 'As long as he delivers the goods.' - New York Times.

11.12.93

Inkatha and white extremists vow to boycott poll

Chris McGreal
in Johannesburg

CHIEF Mangosuthu Buthelezi's Inkatha and the extreme white right have rejected participation in April's first non-racial election in favour of what they described as 'resistance politics', widely interpreted as meaning violence, unless there are sudden and unexpected concessions by the government and ANC at talks today.

Chief Buthelezi won backing at a special Inkatha conference yesterday for his call for a boycott of the vote, although a final decision will be reserved until after today's meeting.

White extremists on Saturday rowdily rejected compromise and participation in the election, pushing their demand for a white homeland by forming a symbolic alternative government.

Although the Inkatha leader said he was not preaching revolution or violence he warned delegates that unless power was devolved to the Zulu nation resistance politics would lead to a 'violent clash between the people and an African National Congress government'.

'This is a region where we dominate. No foreign forces shall come into it to rule over us . . . No government has ever won the kind of war against opposition which an ANC-Communist Party government will have to wage against us if we resist the present interim constitution,' Chief Buthelezi said.

Walter Felgate, an influential hardline official, said that while it was still technically possible for the ANC and the government to come to their senses and meet demands for a double ballot, greater autonomy and other constitutional reforms, he thought it unlikely.

Mr Felgate said Inkatha was setting a deadline of tonight for agreement.

While Inkatha kept the door to elections open a crack, white extremists slammed it shut. The Afrikaner People's Front (AVF) elected a rival government and chose the Conservative Party leader, Ferdie Hartzenberg, as 'president' until 'a free election of the Afrikaner nation can be held'. The AVF is a key member of the conservative Freedom Alliance, which also includes Inkatha.

Although the Alliance will attend today's talks, white rightwingers all but rejected a settlement that falls short of the right to govern themselves.

General Constand Viljoen, a former defence force head and hero of the white right, sullied his reputation with them by telling the rally that Afrikaners faced two choices — violence or the strategic option of participating in elections to prove the AVF has support. He was angrily shouted down.

'You are selling us out,' cried hecklers from the neo-Nazi Afrikaner Resistance Movement (AWB) which belongs to the AVF. The AWB leader, Eugene Terre-Blanche, denounced the call.

'We are not prepared to go into an election where the ANC counts Boere (Afrikaner) heads. We asked for an election but not the ANC's ballot box,' he said.

As Nelson Mandela pressed on with his election campaign after the ANC launched its manifesto on Saturday, the government of the nominally independent Bophuthatswana homeland used troops to block roads into South Africa to prevent people attending a rally in nearby Rustenburg yesterday.

The Bophuthatswana leader, Lucas Mangope, has banned ANC activity and joined the Freedom Alliance to demand autonomy for his homeland.

31.1.94

Humiliating flight from black homeland fulfils worst fears of white right

Armed Afrikaners routed

Chris McGreal
in Mmabatho

THE SPECTACLE of white rightwingers fleeing in fear and humiliation from a black South African homeland yesterday crystallised the worst trepidations of hardline Afrikanerdom — that its days are numbered.

In the climax to days of skirmishes in Bophuthatswana, armed whites who tried to intervene in support of the homeland's separatist president, Lucas Mangope, were cleared from the streets of Mmabatho and Mafikeng in a confrontation whose outcome will reverberate far beyond the small empire of a minor dictator.

One incident in particular — in which a black Bophuthatswana policeman shot dead white gunmen as they pleaded for mercy — encapsulated the nightmare of those attempting to defy the plan for universal free elections next month.

South African troops moved into Bophuthatswana last night, defeating a short-lived attempt by thousands of white rightwingers taking advantage of turbulence to try to turn it into an Afrikaner volkstaat.

The whites, including members of the neo-Nazi Afrikaner Resistance Movement, the AWB, fled as the South African Defence Force arrived, and President Mangope agreed to join South Africa's forthcoming national elections.

Violence continued into the night as some rightwingers returned to the area to fight with the Bophuthatswana army. At least three blacks were killed by whites bent on vengeance. The deaths bring to nearly 50 the toll of two days of violence, according to sources at the main hospital.

The gun-toting rightwingers were escorted in convoy from Mmabatho air force base shortly after the first South African soldiers moved in to the capital.

Earlier, the Bophuthatswana army had cleared them from the streets of Mmabatho and Mafikeng and driven them from the homeland in a humiliating spectacle.

A rightwing boycott of South Africa's all-race elections crumbled when the Freedom Front of Constand Viljoen confirmed its participation, minutes before a midnight deadline, Reuter reports from Johannesburg.

12.3.94

Ciskei leader steps down after mutiny

David Beresford
in Johannesburg

SOUTH AFRICA descended into political chaos yesterday with the collapse of another homeland administration while controversy raged around allegations and counter-allegations about destabilisation plots by Inkatha, the security services and the ANC.

The South African Defence Force moved to the Ciskei border yesterday in answer to an appeal for help from the homeland government of Brigadier Oupa Gqozo after police mutinied.

But last night Brig Gqozo stood down and the transitional executive council (TEC) announced it was sending in administrators to govern the territory until next month's election. During the mutiny, police took senior officers hostage and grabbed weapons from a local arsenal.

The collapse of the Ciskei, which follows the recent coup in Bophuthatswana, coincided with claims by Inkatha that it has obtained a blueprint of an ANC plan to topple the Kwa-Zulu administration of Chief Mangosuthu Buthelezi.

The political dramas were being played out against the background of spiralling political violence in Natal and a bomb attack on offices of the ruling National Party in the town of Ventersdorp, which hosts the headquarters of the neo-Nazi Afrikaner Weerstandsbeweging (AWB).

23.3.94

'The Bophuthatswana executions seared through the white rightwing. Safely across the Transvaal border, TerreBlanche's brandy-and-coke brigade swore terrible vengeance, but the trauma could not be concealed'

Boer nemesis. Bophuthatswana policeman shoots AWB gunmen dead Mmabatho, 1994

MANDELA FO

Above and right : **Mandela addresses election rally at the Independence Stadium in Mmambatho after the fall of Mangope, 1994**

Pictures: DON McPHEE

Right: **De Klerk hoping to attract the 'coloured' vote at an election meeting in Cape Town, 1994**

Section 3

Picture: FRANK MARTIN

Endpiece: **Desmond Tutu**

IT HAS happened at last. Apartheid has bitten the dust as comprehensively and as ignominiously as we had always been telling our people it would. How do you describe the almost ineffable feeling of exhilaration and deep gratitude?

In 1990, when it was announced that Nelson Mandela would be released on February 11, I broke out into a dance, I did the *toyi-toyi.* Only so could I give vent to all that I felt, all that I knew our people felt. It *has* happened! How often we had had to help keep up the spirits of our people by declaring that God was not deaf, not blind. He heard our cries, He saw our anguish, He knew what we were undergoing. And He would come down to deliver us, just as He had done when He led the Israelites out of bondage in the glorious deliverance of the Exodus. It had sometimes seemed

like a whistling in the dark, in apartheid's most awful repressive days.

And now it has happened. Evil has been vanquished.

Is it a coincidence or is it providential that our first democratic election marking the demise of apartheid will be taking place at Eastertide, when Christians commemorate the death and resurrection of Jesus Christ, who thereby set His seal on the victory of life over death, of light over darkness, of good over evil, of love over hate?

I have waited all of my 62 years to take part in my first election. Others too have waited a lifetime for this intoxicating occasion: Nelson Mandela and Mangosothu Buthelezi have never voted in an election in the land of their birth.

We thank God that this has come to pass and we thank you, our friends in the international

community, for helping it to come to pass, with support of sanctions and in other ways. You have helped to bring to birth this new South Africa, non-racial, non-sexist and democratic. Our victory is your victory too.

Apartheid has left a ghastly legacy. There is a horrendous housing shortage and high unemployment; health care is inaccessible and not easily affordable by the majority; Bantu education has left us with a massive educational crisis; there is gross maldistribution of wealth and an inequitable sharing of the resources with which South Africa is so richly endowed. Some 20 per cent of the population owns 87 per cent of the land. Then there is the hurt and anguish of those who have been victims of this vicious system, those who were forcibly removed from their homes, nearly 4 million people. Those whose loved ones were detained without trial or banned, or who died mysteriously in detention, such as Steve Biko, or at the hands of death squads.

There is need of healing, of rehabilitation, of confession, of forgiveness, of restitution and reconciliation. Our beautiful land yearns for healing.

And black people have a wonderful capacity to forgive. We believe in our interdependence, for we say a person is a person through other persons and our humanity is bound up with one another. God has made us for friendship, for fellowship, for family, for togetherness.

When we get it right in South Africa, we will provide a paradigm for the rest of the world on how to solve similar problems, and how to cope with the pluralism of culture and ethnicity, with disparities in affluence where the sophisticated and industrialised exist cheek by jowl with the developing. That is why God intends us to succeed, for the sake of the world. When we get it right we will be the launching pad to propel the entire African continent into the 21st century.

Dear friends, do not abandon us as you turn your attention to Eastern Europe. The hard slog of turning freedom into reality has started in earnest, of trying to meet the justified but unrealistically high expectations of those who for so long have been deliberately deprived and systematically oppressed. If we fail, it will be a sad day for democracy everywhere. But we won't fail.

We used to say, in the bad old days of apartheid: "Freedom is coming for all of us, black and white together." It has happened at last.

'The hard slog of turning freedom into reality has started in earnest, of trying to meet the justified but unrealistically high expectations of those who for so long have been deliberately deprived and systematically oppressed'

Chronology

For at least a thousand years before contact with Europeans, Bantu-speaking people lived in what is today Natal, the Transvaal and the Eastern Cape. Khoi herders spread from the Cape to the Orange River and San hunter-gatherers were dispersed over an area from the Cape to the Limpopo River

1488 Bartholomew Diaz lands on the shores of southern Africa.

1552 Portuguese sailors shipwrecked on SE coast meet Xhosa peoples.

1652 Jan van Riebeeck of the Dutch East India Company arrives at Cape of Good Hope and establishes supply station at Table Bay, intending to trade with Khoi herders for meat.

1657 First colonial farmers established on Khoi land. Slaves are imported from Angola, Madagascar, Ceylon and Malaya.

1659 War with the Khoi (First Hottentot War), who are beaten by superior Dutch firepower and then decimated by European diseases.

1688 French Huguenots settle. Dutch farmers search for grazing: northwards they meet San hunters (bushmen), who resist but are almost exterminated, surviving only in Kalahari Desert. Trekboers going east encroach on Xhosa land and meet with resistance.

1779 First of a series of frontier wars between the Trekboers and the Xhosa, which carry on intermittently until the mid-19th century.

1795 After French invasion of Netherlands, the British annex Cape Town. In 1814, at the end of Napoleonic Wars, the Cape is ceded to Britain.

1819 Zulu leader Shaka wins a decisive battle which marks the emergence of Zulu power in eastern Natal. Shaka is murdered in 1828.

1820 British settle in eastern Cape: not allowed to import slaves.

1824 Traders and hunters settle at Port Natal (now Durban).

1833 Slavery abolished from British empire. Afrikaner farmers lose labour force with little compensation: labourers free to work for settlers.

1837 The Great Trek. 6,000 Afrikaners leave Cape Colony, trek north and east to escape British rule, defeating the Ndebele, who retreat over Limpopo River.

1838 Piet Retief leads a trek group over Drakensberg Mountains into Natal, attempts to obtain land from Zulu leader, Dingaan, successor of Shaka. Dingaan has Retief murdered. On 16 December, Boer firepower defeats Zulus at Battle of Blood River: 3,000 Zulus die. This becomes a sacred day for the Boers — the Day of the Covenant.

1842 Xhosa unrest around Port Natal as Boer farmers take their lands. The British intervene, fight the Boers, and then annex Natal. The Boers trek back into the Transvaal.

1852 Britain recognises the independent Boer republic of the Transvaal.

1853 The Cape Colony gains its own elected government. The franchise is based on a property qualification.

1854 Britain recognises independent Boer republic of Orange Free State.

1857 Diamonds are discovered at Kimberley in Griqualand West, an independent area between the Cape Colony and the Orange Free State.

1860 Labourers are imported from India to work in Natal sugar fields.

1871 Britain annexes Griqualand West. Kimberley has 50,000 inhabitants. The diamond mines are short of black labour. Africans buy guns with wages and return home to their farms.

1877 Britain annexes Transvaal after the Pedi defeat Transvaal troops. British and Boer unite to defeat the Pedi. The British order Zulu King Cetshwayo to disband his army.

1879 Anglo-Zulu War. King Cetshwayo's army defeats British forces at Isandhlwana, but the reinforced British army defeats Zulus at Ulundi. The British gain control of Zululand, which becomes a Crown colony in 1887 and is subsequently annexed to Natal.

1881 Transvaal forces win the battle of Majuba Hill against the British and regain their independence. The leader of the Boer rebellion, Paul Kruger, is elected president of the Transvaal the following year.

1884 Germany takes over South West Africa (now Namibia). Offering military protection in exchange for sovereignty, British establish protectorates of Basutoland (Lesotho) and Bechuanaland (Botswana).

1885 After 20 years of war with the British, Xhosa resistance is extinguished, largely as a result of a self-created famine. Xhosa land on both sides of the Kei River – Ciskei and Transkei – is annexed by Britain.

1886 Large gold deposits found in the Transvaal. In the gold-rush, Transvaalers are outnumbered by prospectors, mostly British immigrants.

1890 Cecil Rhodes elected prime minister of Cape Colony and British South Africa Company army invades Mashonaland, territory north of the Limpopo, which becomes Rhodesia (Zambia and Zimbabwe).

1893 Lawyer Mahatma Gandhi arrives in South Africa and establishes the Natal Indian Congress to resist discrimination against Indians.

1896 Friction between Kruger and British miners. Rhodes resigns over the Jameson Raid — an attempt to engineer a miners' uprising. Pass laws introduced to control movement of black miners.

1897 Sir Alfred Milner is appointed governor of the Cape.

1899 Relations between Boers and British deteriorate as Kruger denies the franchise to miners. British troopships sail south. Kruger declares war. British burn Boer farms, herd women and children into concentration camps where 26,000 die. 500,000 British troops are needed to defeat fewer than 35,000 Boers.

1902 The Transvaal and Orange Free State annexed. British money flows into the former Boer colonies for economic reconstruction. British negotiate with Boer War leaders Smuts and Botha to unite colonies.

1904 60,000 Chinese imported to work in goldmines, then repatriated.

1908 Gandhi leads Indian passive resistance to pass laws for Indians and other discriminatory legislation in the Transvaal.

1910 Act of Union. The four colonies are united as a self-governing colony within the British Commonwealth. The franchise is restricted to white people, except in the Cape where existing property and educational qualifications exclude all but a few non-whites.

1911 The first election returns an alliance of pro-British Boers led by Louis Botha, who becomes prime minister, and the more nationalist Afrikaners led by Hertzog. Jan Smuts becomes Botha's deputy. Labour legislation prohibits strikes by African contract labour and reserves certain categories of work for whites.

1912 Formation of South African Native National Congress (renamed African National Congress in 1923).

1913 Native Land Act restricts African land ownership to reserves, only 7.3 per cent of the land, to encourage Africans to work in the mines which are short of labour.

1914 Hertzog splits with Botha and forms the National Party. The government offers to support Britain in the war. Afrikaner nationalist forces revolt but are suppressed. At Britain's request, South African troops occupy German South West Africa.

1918 The Broederbond — a secret group of influential Afrikaners — is formed to promote cultural and economic welfare of Afrikaners. First major African strike, of sanitation workers, in Johannesburg.

1919 A black union, the Industrial and Commercial, is founded. Many strikes, especially by miners. The administration of South West Africa is transferred to South Africa under a League of Nations mandate. Louis Botha dies and is succeeded by Smuts.

1921 At Bulhoek, near Queenstown, a religious sect squats on common land, refuses to leave: police shoot 190 dead. Communist Party of South Africa is founded, calls for a campaign against the pass laws.

1922 Army crushes strike by white miners wanting job reservation. 200 killed, 18 sentenced to death, four hung. Hertzog supports miners.

1923 Hertzog, champion of poor whites, workers and Afrikaner nationalism, combines with the South African Labour Party to defeat Smuts in parliament. In 1924, Hertzog becomes prime minister. Natives (Urban Areas) Act restricts the rights of Africans to enter towns.

1925 Afrikaans replaces Dutch as the second official language.

1927 ANC president Archie Gumede visits Moscow. European Communists begin to organise among black workers. Gumede is later expelled from the ANC for his Communist sympathies. Sexual relations between black and white are made illegal. Native Administration Act makes the governor-general supreme over all Africans.

1930 Native Service Contract Act increases farmers' control of workforce and includes a "whipping clause". ANC launches a pass-burning campaign in Durban, which is ruthlessly suppressed.

1933 Economic problems force Hertzog's National Party to combine with Smuts' South Africa Party to form the United Party. Right-winger Dr Daniel Malan and other separatists leave National Party to form the Purified National Party, which becomes the new National Party.

1936 Native Trust and Land Act transfers black people from Cape voters' roll to a separate list which can elect three white representatives. The Act also increases land allocated to native reserves to 13 per cent. Hertzog hopes this will attract African support for the Act.

1938 Hertzog-Smuts' United Party wins 111 seats against the Purified National Party's 27 in a general election. Re-enactment of Great Trek and centenary celebrations for the Battle of Blood River mark revival of Afrikaner culture: first stone laid for Voortrekker monument.

1939 Hertzog and Smuts split over war with Germany. Smuts narrowly wins parliamentary vote in favour of war. Hertzog resigns and Smuts becomes prime minister. Extreme Afrikaner Nationalists form Ossewa-Brandwag and support Nazi policies. Members include future prime minister, John Vorster, who is interned. Hertzog dies.

1943 In the general election, Malan's National Party wins 43 seats to Smuts' 89. ANC Women's League is formed. First boycott of buses succeeds in reversing an increase in fares.

1944 ANC Youth League formed. Leading figures include Robert Sobukwe, Nelson Mandela, Walter Sisulu and Oliver Tambo.

1946 India wins a United Nations vote censuring South Africa for discrimination against Indians in Natal.

1948 Accusing Smuts of being soft on race, warning of a black threat, the National Party defeats United Party. Malan becomes prime minister.

1949 Prohibition of Mixed Marriages Act — first major apartheid legislation — bans marriages between whites and non-whites, and nullifies mixed marriages by South Africans abroad. On Day of the Covenant, Malan opens massive Voortrekker Monument near Pretoria.

1950 Immorality Act extended to criminalise sexual relations between whites and Cape Coloureds. Population Registration Act classifies adult population as: White, Coloured and Native. Coloured sub-groups include Cape Malay, Indian, Chinese. Group Areas Act permits segregating the country by assigning separate areas to different races. Police shoot 18 dead during a May Day general strike against discriminatory laws. Suppression of Communism Act enables government to define as Communist, and ban, practically any person or organisation hostile to government policy. The South African Communist Party dissolves and many members join ANC.

1951 Government legislation introduced to remove Cape Coloureds from voters' roll. Bantu Authorities Act establishes tribal and territorial authorities, first step in policy of retribalising the African population under government-appointed chiefs.

1952 Natives (Co-ordination of Documents) Act requires all black males over 16 to carry a passbook at all times. Native Laws Amendment Act extends influx control to all urban areas and to black women.

On Freedom Day, June 26, ANC and South African Indian Congress launch a defiance campaign against apartheid laws. Repressive legislation increases protest, transforms the ANC into a mass organisation. Thousands arrested, several killed. Chief Albert Luthuli is elected national president, Nelson Mandela deputy-president.

1953 Public Safety Act empowers the governor-general to declare a state of emergency and rule by decree. Criminal Law Amendment Act makes passive resistance illegal, with penalties of fines, imprisonment and whippings. Separate Amenities Act segregates public amenities and transportation; Bantu Education Act sets out a compulsory inferior curriculum for black education; Native Labour (Settlement of Disputes) Act makes strikes by black workers illegal.

1954 Native Resettlement Act provides for forced removal of black residents from Sophiatown, Johannesburg: this take five years. Malan retires, aged 80, and is replaced by Johannes Strydom.

1955 South African Congress of Trade Unions, first non-racial trade union, formed. 3,000 multi-racial Congress Alliance delegates meet at Kliptown and draw up the Freedom Charter.

1956 South Africa Amendment Act removes 45,000 Cape Coloured voters from electoral roll. Industrial Coalition Act reserves certain skilled jobs for whites and bans mixed trade unions. 156 Congress leaders charged with high treason — the Treason Trial.

1957 Ghana is first African colony to become independent. The Union Jack is removed as the dual official flag of South Africa.

1958 In first all-white election, the National Party wins 103 of 163 seats. Prime minister Strydom dies and Hendrik Verwoerd replaces him.

Nearly 2,000 women are arrested in major demonstrations against the extension of passbook regulations to black women.

1959 Verwoerd plans independent black homelands. Extension of University Education Bill excludes non-white students from white universities and establishes black, Indian and "coloured" universities.

Robert Sobukwe and 300 others split from ANC to form the Pan-Africanist Congress, rejecting ANC policy of alliances with liberal white and Indian organisations. Albert Luthuli banned and banished. Progressive Party formed by 12 liberal United Party MPs. 1,000 black leaders meet in Durban to plan a passive resistance campaign. Natal rural women rise up against apartheid laws.

1960 Harold Macmillan makes "winds of change" speech to the South African parliament. Police fire on a PAC-inspired anti-pass demonstration in Sharpeville, kill 69, wound 178. UN Security Council calls on South Africa to abandon apartheid. The government declares a state of emergency and bans the ANC and PAC. Sobukwe is jailed. State of emergency declared in Pondoland, as people rebel against unpopular chiefs. In a referendum, 52 per cent of the (white) electorate votes "Yes" to South Africa becoming a republic.

1961 Commonwealth Conference criticises South Africa and Verwoerd announces that South Africa will not apply to rejoin as a republic. UN General Assembly proclaims South West Africa's right to independence. South Africa is proclaimed a republic on May 31: 10,000 are detained to prevent disturbances.

Albert Luthuli receives the Nobel Peace Prize. Launch of Umkhonto we Sizwe (Spear of the Nation), military wing of the ANC. Radical whites form the African Resistance Movement and commit sabotage. Treason Trial ends after four years: all are found not guilty.

1962 Mandela addresses Pan-African conference in Addis Ababa: sentenced to five years in prison for inciting a strike and travelling abroad. Sabotage Act provides death penalty for anyone convicted of sabotage, which is widely defined and gives power to ban people and place them under house arrest. There is no right of appeal.

1963 General Law (Amendment) Act permits police to arrest and detain suspects for 90 days without trial or access to legal advice and allows for indefinite detention of Sobukwe on Robben Island. Police capture ANC's underground leadership at Rivonia, and eight, including Mandela, Govan Mbeki, Sisulu and Ahmed Kathrada, are charged with sabotage and planning the violent overthrow of the state.

UN calls for voluntary embargo on arms sales to South Africa. Transkei Self-Government Bill makes Transkei semi-autonomous.

1964 Luthuli banned for five more years. In Rivonia trial, eight are sentenced to life. UN recommends complete economic sanctions as only feasible way of ending apartheid. South Africa is excluded from the Tokyo Olympics after refusing to allow mixed-race teams.

1965 Bantu Laws Amendment Act strips seven million black people of rights inside South Africa, making them "temporary dwellers", and establishes proscribed areas where black workers only are allowed.

Rhodesia declares UDI, but South Africa refuses to embargo it.

1966 National Party wins 126 of 166 seats in general election. Progressive Party retains one MP, Helen Suzman. Verwoerd stabbed to death. John Vorster succeeds him as prime minister.

Bechuanaland becomes independent as Botswana, Basutoland becomes Lesotho. UN terminates South Africa's mandate over South West Africa, placing it under UN responsibility, but Vorster ignores UN. Armed struggle begins in Rhodesia, South West Africa.

1967 Defence Amendment Act makes military service compulsory for white males. Terrorism Act widely defines terrorism as anything likely to threaten law and order, confers unlimited powers of arrest, indefinite detention, trials without jury, tranfers burden of proof to the accused and equates terrorism with treason, therefore incurring the death penalty. Luthuli dies. Oliver Tambo, in exile, becomes ANC president.

1968 Prohibition of Political Interference Bill prohibits one racial group from involvement in political affairs of another. The Liberal Party disbands; the Progressive Party becomes open to whites only. Separate Representation of Voters Amendment Act transfers indirect representation of "coloured" voters to a Representative Council.

South African Students Organisation (Saso) is formed by black students who embrace the ideas of the Black Consciousness Movement. Steve Biko is first president. Swaziland becomes independent.

1969 Bureau of State Security established with wide investigative powers. Newspapers prohibited from reporting its activities. Sobukwe freed but restricted to Kimberley: dies in 1978. Winnie Mandela and 21 others are detained under Terrorism Act. She is held for 491 days.

Vorster calls early election because of split with the right of his party, which is led by Albert Hertzog and opposes a mixed New Zealand rugby team visiting South Africa and the admission of black diplomats. Hertzog forms Herstigte National Party: it wins no seats.

1970 Bantu Homelands Citizenship Act makes all black people citizens of a tribal homeland, irrespective of whether they have ever lived there. 19 acquitted in trial of 20 activists, including Winnie Mandela, who is banned for five years and placed under house arrest.

1971 After a picket of Polaroid HQ in Boston, US, the corporation improves wages and conditions for black employees in South Africa. International Court of Justice rules South Africa's administration of Namibia illegal. Helen Joseph is released from nine years' house arrest.

Anglican Dean of Johannesburg, Gonville Aubrey ffrench-Beytagh, is tried under the Terrorism Act. Found guilty and sentenced to five years' imprisonment, he wins on appeal and leaves the country.

1972 Boputhatswana, Ciskei and Lebowa become self-governing. Zululand becomes KwaZulu, a semi-autonomous homeland with Mangosuthu Buthelezi as chief minister. The Black People's Convention is formed as a forum for black consciousness groups.

1973 Illegal strikes in Durban bring the city to a standstill, as black workers demand higher wages. Bantu Labour Relations Regulation Bill allows limited right to strike, though not in all industries, after strikes in Natal and Johannesburg. In response to rising student agitation, leaders of the National Union of South African Students are banned.

Homeland chief ministers dispute the government's plans which allocate only 14 per cent of the country to the homelands and leave them fragmented. Venda and Gazankulu become self-governing.

1974 Fresh strikes in Durban and the mines. Labour shortage throughout industry forces South Africa to depend upon workers from neighbouring countries. Job reservation relaxed; black nurses allowed in white hospitals, black people allowed to work as motor mechanics, "coloureds" permitted to take office jobs and black recruits join the army. Some dismantling of petty apartheid by city councils.

Riotous Assemblies Act bans any gathering which might threaten law and order. Any journalist quoting a banned person can be jailed.

Affected Organisations Act bans any organisation engaging in politics and obtaining funds from abroad. Coup in Portugal brings independence to Angola and Mozambique. BPC/Saso leaders are arrested after pro-Frelimo (liberation organisation for Mozambique) rally. Eight out of nine homeland leaders reject South Africa's timetable for independence, demand land consolidation and economic infrastructure. Transkei, most viable homeland, wants full independence. South African Defence Force takes over from police in Namibia.

South Africa is expelled from the UN General Assembly.

1975 Government reinstates the right of black residents to buy leases on homes in segregated townships, forbidden by Verwoerd in 1967. Chief Buthelezi re-activates Inkatha, a Zulu cultural movement, and becomes its president. Vorster meets Zambian president Kenneth Kaunda in effort to expedite a Rhodesian settlement. Mozambique becomes independent. Portugal transfers Angolan sovereignty to the "Angolan people" after fighting breaks out between rival liberation movements. South Africa opposes the MPLA because it is Marxist: MPLA supports the Namibian liberation movement, the South West Africa People's Organisation (Swapo). South African forces and United States money aid Unita and another anti-MPLA movement, the FNLA. Cuban forces assist the MPLA.

1976 TV begins in South Africa, previously resisted as morally corrupting. Soweto Students' Representatives Council calls a demonstration for June 16 to protest against use of Afrikaans language in black schools. Police open fire: months of protest follow, often led by the young. Trial of BPC/Saso leaders ends with nine found guilty. Transkei declared independent but recognised only by South Africa.

1977 Commonwealth opposes sporting links with South Africa. UN imposes mandatory ban on arms sales. Rev. Leon Sullivan sets out guidelines for US corporations in South Africa to promote racial equality. Polaroid is the first US company to withdraw.

Steve Biko is detained under the Terrorism Act and dies of brain injuries. 18 anti-apartheid and black consciousness organisations plus two black newspapers are banned.

1978 SADF forces in Angola kill hundreds of Namibian refugees. In negotiations with UN, South Africa agrees in principle to hold independence elections in Namibia, but disputes drag on. The guerrilla war with Swapo intensifies. Azanian People's Organisation founded: Azania is name given to South Africa by black nationalist groups.

Disclosures about the use of secret funds in the Department of Information force Vorster and Connie Mulder, the information minister, to resign. PW Botha becomes prime minister.

1979 Wiehahn Commission recommends changes in labour laws, including recognition of black trade unions. Government accepts most recommendations, lifts most restrictions on black employment.

A peace treaty ends guerrilla war in Rhodesia.

1980 Robert Mugabe's Patriotic Front wins Zimbabwe election with 57 of 80 black seats. Bishop Abel Muzorewa, head of transitional govern-

ment, wins three seats. Joshua Nkomo's Zapu takes remaining 20. SADF involvement in Angolan war and northern Namibia escalates. Umkhonto we Sizwe attacks the Sasol oil complex.

1981 SADF commandos raid Maputo in Mozambique to attack the ANC. Botha's new President's Council, comprising government-appointed white, "coloured" and Indian politicians, meets to advise on constitutional reforms. Botha rejects its advice.

1982 National Party splits over Botha's proposal for limited power-sharing for "coloured" and Indian population groups. Ministers Andries Treurnicht and Ferdinand Hartzenberg are expelled for refusing to support the reforms. Treurnicht founds the Conservative Party. Gold plummets from $800 to $300 an ounce, causing economic downturn, industrial unrest and an approach for IMF loans.

Buthelezi rejects plans to make KwaZulu independent and proposes a single administration for Natal with multi-racial power-sharing. National Forum created by black consciousness organisation to resist constitutional reforms. SADF hits Maseru, capital of Lesotho, to attack the ANC: 42 people are killed.

1983 ANC car bomb outside Pretoria air-force HQ kills 19, injures 200. United Democratic Front (UDF) is formed to co-ordinate resistance to the new power-sharing constitution which excludes black people.

In a white referendum, 75 per cent vote for Botha's power-sharing, with parliament having separate "coloured", Indian and white chambers, each chamber elected by its own group and responsible for legislation for that group. Joint concerns will be considered by all three, but whites will have the largest chamber. The post of prime minister is replaced by a strong executive president controlling the cabinet and President's Council, which include "coloured" and Indian members appointed by the president.

1984 South Africa and Mozambique sign the Nkomati Accord, a non-aggression pact: Mozambique will expel the ANC and South Africa will stop supporting Mozambique rebels, the MNR.

Efforts are made to move squatters from Cape Town camps to the new settlement of Khayelitsha. Exclusion of the black population from the new constitution causes township uprisings. UDF urges "coloured" and Indian groups to boycott elections: fewer than 20 per cent of the electorate vote. Tricameral parliament opens and PW Botha is elected president unopposed. He appoints one "coloured" and one Indian politician to his cabinet. UDF calls for a boycott of elections for local councils in the townships to protest against exclusion from parliament. Those who become councillors are regarded as collaborators and many are killed. Rent boycotts — protesting against lack of services — have been operative for some time. SADF moves into townships.

Bishop Desmond Tutu, Anglican head of the South African Council of Churches, is awarded the Nobel Peace Prize.

1985 Nelson Mandela rejects an offer to release him from prison in return for his renunciation of the armed struggle. At Lange, on the 25th anniversary of Sharpeville, police fire upon a funeral procession for black activists, killing 21. Townships erupt and are in a virtual state of war as Tambo calls on them to "make the townships ungovernable". 35,000 troops are deployed. Funerals become the focus for political demonstrations as more than 1,000 are killed. Indefinite state of emergency is declared around Port Elizabeth, Johannesburg and Cape Town. Police have wide powers of arrest and detention. Congress of South African Students banned after organising school boycotts. Cosatu, the Congress of South African Trade Unions, launched, representing 36 member unions, including mineworkers.

Chase Manhattan Bank announces that it will offer no new loans to South Africa, the rand plunges and South Africa freezes debt repayments. Foreign banks, worried about the stability of the government, refuse to extend credit or reschedule loans. South African business leaders defy Botha and travel to Zambia to talk to the ANC.

Botha's much-awaited "crossing the Rubicon" reform speech offers nothing new, only defiance. Government blames press for inciting township violence and imposes restrictions on the reporting of unrest. Immorality Act and Mixed Marriages Act are abolished.

1986 Lesotho is blockaded by South Africa until the pro-ANC prime minister, Chief Jonathan, is overthrown. Botha ends state of emergency and repeals now unenforceable pass laws.

Commonwealth Eminent Persons Group visits South Africa to seek a peaceful resolution but the SADF attacks the capitals of Botswana, Zambia and Zimbabwe, supposedly aiming at the ANC, but probably intending to sabotage the visit. EPG report calls for sanctions, which are opposed by the Thatcher government. Government-sponsored vigilantes burn large sections of the Cape squatter camps. Squatters flee and security forces prevent them returning. Nationwide state of emergency is declared and strict censorship is imposed. Security forces can do whatever they feel necessary to restore order. More than 8,000, mainly UDF members, are detained.

US Senate overrides President Reagan's veto and imposes strong sanctions on trade and investment. US corporations are encouraged to withdraw from South Africa and more than 500 foreign firms pull out. Barclays Bank withdraws from South Africa.

President Samora Machel of Mozambique is killed in a plane crash inside South African airspace.

1987 White railway workers' strike lasts three months and becomes violent. Trains are burnt, 11 workers are killed. Strikers are sacked but finally rehired. Mineworkers' Union strikes for higher wages.

In the white general election, the Conservative Party emerges as the main opposition, with more than a quarter of the vote. Accused of corruption, Transkei leader General Matanzima is ousted by the military and succeeded by Major General Bantu Holomisa. 60 Afrikaner dissidents, led by former opposition leader Frederick van Zyl Slabbert, meet the ANC for talks in Senegal. Former ANC chairman Govan Mbeki is released, but placed under restrictions.

Fighting between Inkatha and UDF supporters in Natal which had started in 1985 intensifies: more than 230 are killed.

1988 South African troops restore President Mangope in Bophuthatswana after he is deposed in a coup.

18 anti-apartheid organisations are banned. Cosatu is banned from political activity. Church leaders take over as spokesmen for

the resistance movement. 143 conscripts refuse to serve in the SADF. The End Conscription Campaign is placed under restriction.

Delmas Trial of UDF leaders ends with four convicted of treason, seven of terrorist offences and eight acquitted. Responding to world outrage, Botha reprieves the "Sharpeville Six", condemned to die for being in a crowd that killed a black councillor. Mandela is moved to a house in Victor Verster Prison. PAC leader Zeph Mothopeng and ANC leader Harry Gwala both freed on "humanitarian" grounds.

SADF suffers heavy losses and a major defeat in Angola. A year of negotiations results in an agreement on Angola and Namibia. SADF and Cuban forces agree to withdraw from Angola. UN-supervised elections will be held in Namibia, which will become independent.

1989 Botha suffers stroke, resigns as National Party leader: later resigns presidency. FW De Klerk becomes NP leader, then president. In interim, Botha meets Mandela. Mass democratic movement begins defiance campaign against segregation. National Party's majority is reduced in general election, but De Klerk claims a mandate for his reforms and begins talks with black leaders, including Mandela.

Transkei leader Holomisa appears with ANC leaders: denounces Transkei's independence. Sisulu and remaining Rivonia trial prisoners released, address a rally in Soweto and are not restricted. Hunger strike by 600 detainees forces a release. Swapo wins Namibian election with less than two-thirds majority.

1990 Opening parliament, De Klerk unbans political organisations including ANC, South African Communist Party and PAC, announces release of Mandela, end of news censorship and suspension of executions. Mandela released nine days later. Separate Amenities Act is repealed. State of emergency lifted. Talks in Cape Town between ANC and government on removal of obstacles to negotiation.

Violence between Inkatha and ANC worsens, despite peace talks between leaders. In July, the violence spreads to Transvaal townships. There is evidence of provocative security force involvement. "Pretoria Minute" is signed in August: ANC agrees to suspend the armed struggle in return for the release of political prisoners, end of political trials and executions. Massacres on commuter trains spread fear through the townships in the autumn. On December 13 ANC leader Oliver Tambo returns from more than 30 years' exile.

1991 Government and ANC agree on return of political exiles and release of prisoners. ANC will halt military training. In March, 300 prisoners released, in May 10,000 more. UDF disbands to concentrate on building ANC as mass political party. Government scraps pillars of apartheid: Population Registration Act, Land and Group Areas Acts.

Winnie Mandela found guilty of kidnapping, gets six years' imprisonment, sentence lifted on appeal. ANC holds leadership elections and mineworkers' leader Cyril Ramaphosa wins key post.

Fighting in Soweto, Tembisa and Alexandra between Inkatha and ANC supporters. Inkathagate — evidence shows that the government secretly funds Inkatha and that the security force supplies them with weapons and trains hit squads. Defence and law and order ministers demoted for their involvement. Three neo-Nazi AWB members killed by police during protest at Ventersdorp meeting addressed by De Klerk. National Peace Accord signed September 14

between government, ANC, Inkatha (now Inkatha Freedom Party) and 30 other organisations. Violence continues — there is increasing evidence of a "Third Force" from within security forces. Goldstone commission of inquiry appointed to examine allegations. Convention for Democratic South Africa (Codesa) talks: Government and ANC sign declaration of intent towards non-racial, democratic South Africa. Inkatha will not sign, PAC opposes Codesa.

1992 National Party defeated by the Conservative Party in a by-election, De Klerk calls a referendum for whites to vote on his proposals to abolish apartheid. In an 85 per cent turnout, 68 per cent vote "Yes".

ANC breaks off Codesa and bilateral talks with the government after 39 are killed by Inkatha at Boipatong on June 17. ANC accuses security forces of complicity. Most black workers heed an ANC call to strike in support of political reform. Ciskei soldiers fire on an ANC demonstration on September 8 in Bisho, killing 28. Mandela demands the removal of the Ciskei leader. Concerned by violence, the ANC and the government resume bilateral talks. ANC offers "sunset" clauses, including guarantees on civil service jobs and pensions, plus a coalition government until 2000. This becomes basis for a transitional agreement. Azanian People's Liberation Army, military wing of PAC, attacks whites, in support of its slogan "One settler, one bullet". South Africa competes in Barcelona Olympics and Springboks return to international rugby.

1993 Successor to Codesa, Multi-Party Negotiating Forum, convenes with 26 delegations. Riots erupt after Communist Party leader Chris Hani is assassinated by white extremists on April 10. General Constand Viljoen, former commander of the armed forces, becomes leader of white resistance to majority rule. 11 worshippers are killed in gun attack on Cape Town church service. Political violence in Natal and East Rand townships kills 4,000, highest yearly total.

Government relinquishes control over state broadcasting, allowing the appointment of a non-partisan board to run SA Broadcasting Corporation. Addressing the UN General Assembly in September, Mandela calls for an end to the remaining sanctions against South Africa. He and De Klerk are jointly awarded the Nobel Peace Prize "for their work for the peaceful termination of the apartheid regime, and for laying the foundations for a new democratic South Africa". ANC and government agree final terms for new constitution. Buthelezi rejects interim constitution, announces Inkatha will not participate in 1994 election. New interim constitution is approved by parliament but opposed by Conservative Party.

1994 PAC president Clarence Makwetu announces suspension of armed struggle to contest the election. Talks between ANC and right-wing Freedom Alliance to establish an Afrikaner homeland break down. The constitution is altered to encourage the white right and Inkatha to register for the election. In March, Freedom Alliance member President Mangope of Bophuthatswana is overthrown. After an abortive AWB armed intervention in Bophuthatswana, the right-wing alliance splits as Constand Viljoen announces Freedom Front will participate in the election.

Goldstone commission of inquiry finds evidence that senior police officers supplied arms to Inkatha and fomented violence.